The
Edwardian Garden

The Edwardian Garden

DAVID OTTEWILL

Yale University Press
New Haven and London   1989

Designed by Gillian Malpass
Set in Linotron Bembo by Best-set Typesetter Ltd, Hong Kong
Printed in Hong Kong by
Kwong Fat Offset Printing Co., Ltd

Library of Congress Catalog Card Number: 88-50427
ISBN 0-300-04338-4

Frontispiece: Hestercombe, Taunton, Somerset (1904–9).
[Iris Hardwick 1978]

For Patricia

Garsington Manor, near Oxford (Lady Ottoline Morrell, from 1915): formal flower garden. [Author 1985]

Contents

Abbreviations

The following abbreviations have been used in the plate captions and the endnotes for sources referred to frequently:

AR	*Architectural Review*
AWG	Art Workers Guild
BAL	British Architectural Library
BALMC	British Architectural Library Manuscripts Collection
BALDC	British Architectural Library Drawings Collection
CL	*Country Life*
DNB	*Dictionary of National Biography*
G	*The Garden*
GC	*The Gardeners' Chronicle*
GH	*Garden History*, Journal of the Garden History Society
JRHS	*Journal of the Royal Horticultural Society*
JRIBA	*Journal of the Royal Institute of British Architects*
RCHME	Royal Commission on Historical Monuments (England)
RCAHMS	Royal Commission on the Ancient and Historical Monuments of Scotland
RCAHMW	Royal Commission on the Ancient and Historical Monuments in Wales
RHS	Royal Horticultural Society
RIBA	Royal Institute of British Architects
RPG	Reef Point Gardens Collection of Gertrude Jekyll drawings. Microfilm copies are housed at the RCHME.

Preface

The initial idea for this book grew out of my research into the Arts and Crafts Movement and the period at the turn of the century when the Movement was at its zenith. I became fascinated by the universal attention given to gardens at that time and by the combination of formal and informal elements that gave them a distinct Edwardian character. On further investigation I was encouraged by the number of examples that had survived, at least in their basic form. As an architectural historian I hesitated at first to venture into the unfamiliar ground of garden history, yet, since so many of these gardens had been conceived as extensions of the buildings they adjoined, it seemed that a transition had to be made between the two disciplines if a broad picture of the subject was to be attempted. Such a task would have been impossible without the help and guidance of garden historians and I should like first to record my debt to Laurie Fricker who introduced me to the Blomfield–Robinson argument that sets the scene for this book, and to all those, especially Brent Elliott, Charles Nelson and Mavis Batey, who helped me to negotiate some of the thornier horticultural thickets, and read and commented on certain chapters for me. If there are errors, the responsibility is entirely mine. I can only hope that those more qualified in horticultural matters will make allowances in the cause of bridging the gap between architectural and garden history. Some chapters were developed from a lecture given in 1981 at the University of Warwick for a symposium entitled 'The Art of the Garden, c.1870–1914'. Although this represents my principal theme, I hope that the book will not be without interest also to those who are concerned more with plant collections than with design and layout.

Acknowledgements

I should like to record my gratitude to all the owners and administrators who allowed me to visit their gardens. Among those who generously provided information I would name Hon. H.W. Astor, R.J. Berkeley, Mrs Anthony Biddulph, Robert Boutwood, E.G. Broadbent, Ruth Brown, Hon. James Bruce, Captain G.H.L. Campbell, Elizabeth Cartwright-Hignett, Robin Compton, the late Sir Robert Cooke, Euan Cooper-Willis, S. Cross, Revd Fr Seamus Cummins, s.d.b., Michael Edwards, Commandant G.S. Elliott, Lucy Ferry, J. Donald Freeze, s.j., John Grimwade, Peter Herbert, Sir Reginald Hibbert, Martin Lloyd-Morris, Jane Loudon, J. Loyd, Mrs John Makepeace, Mme Mary Mallet, W.H. Mitchell, the late Marchesa Iris Origo, Nicholas Phillips, Stephen Pilkington, Lady Anne Rasch, the late James Silver, Sir Reresby Sitwell, Felice Spurrier, Mrs F. Turnbull, Margaretta Ward and Grace Woodbridge.

I am particularly grateful to those descendants of garden designers of the period who generously provided information including Mrs John Ryan, Giles Blomfield (Blomfield); Christine Loeb (Guthrie); Professor Wilfred Mallows (Mallows); David Mawson (Mawson); Lady Matheson (Peto); Patricia Keith, whose collection is now housed at the BALDC and RCHME (Schultz); Dr John Scott (Geoffrey Scott); Major Reginald Freeman-Thomas, Angus Macnaghten (Inigo Thomas); H.G. Singleton (Tipping); Margaret G. Triggs (Triggs); and Freda Levson (Troup).

My thanks are due to all those who gave permission to include quotations from published or unpublished sources. Among copyright holders I am especially grateful to Felicity Ashbee for extracts from her father's journals, Claire Joyes for her writings on Monet, Mary Lutyens for her memoir of her father, Macmillan Ltd for Blomfield's writings, Frank Magro for writings by Sir George Sitwell and Sir Osbert Sitwell, and Jane Ridley for letters from her great-grandfather to Lady Emily Lutyens.

I am grateful also to all those who kindly provided illustrations. These are acknowledged in the captions but I should particularly like to mention The National Trust, The National Trust for Scotland, Fondation Claude Monet, Ian Leith of the RCHME, Kitty Cruft of the RCAHMS, Jill Lever of the BALDC, Viscount Leverhulme, Sir Geoffrey Jellicoe, Harvard University, Mrs R.L. Goffe, Alan Wyndham Green, Mike Hill, R.W.M. and L.M. Monks, Graham Thomas, Jean-Marie Toulgouat, and Desmond Mandeville of the AWG for allowing me to reproduce photographs from the Guild album.

Some of the subject matter of this book has been covered more fully in the works listed in the bibliography under Modern Books and Articles. Of these, Brent Elliott's *Victorian Gardens* provides an authoritative account of developments preceding the Edwardian period, while, for a general background to many of the gardens included in this book, Clive Aslet's *The Last Country Houses* can be consulted. Among those engaged in biographical studies who generously gave me the benefit of their specialist knowledge I should like to thank Harriet Jordan (for Mawson), Hilary Grainger, Graeme Moore (for Peto) and Gordon Singleton (for Tipping). Others who provided information in specific areas are The National Trust (for Bateman's, Blickling, Bodnant, Buscot Park, Mount Stewart, Polesden Lacey and Snowshill); Hilary Sherrington, RCAHMW; Angela Mace, RIBA archivist and curator of the BALMC (letters of Lutyens); Diana Balmori (Arts and Crafts Movement in the United States); James Bettley (Tilden); Richard Fellows (Blomfield); Keith Morgan (Platt); Stefan Muthesius (Germany and Austria); Margaret Richardson (Arts and Crafts architects); Michael Shippobottom (Lord Leverhulme); the Revd Anthony Symondson (Comper); Lynne Walker (Prior); the late Alwyn Waters (Schultz, including permission to reproduce photographs in his collection); and the Winterthur Museum. I am especially indebted to John Brandon-Jones for inspiration and help over many years in all aspects of the Arts and Crafts Movement.

For help with gardens in Ireland I am grateful to Professor Alistair Rowan and Ann Simmons, Irish Architectural Archive; Elizabeth Cavanagh, Ulster Architectural Heritage Society; Charles Nelson, National Botanic Gardens, Dublin; Anne Grady, Office of Public Works; Patrick Bowe; Cormac Foley; and Jeremy Williams; for gardens in Australia, to Peter Watts and Michael Beasley; and for Spain to Teresa Briales and the late Roma Gelder.

Of the many people who have helped in a variety of other ways I should like to thank Bonita Billman, Eric Byford, Barry Clayton, Alan Crawford, Alastair Forsyth, W.H. Gordon-Smith, Mike Hill, Penelope Hobhouse, Peter Howell, John Dixon Hunt, Neil Jackson, Nancy Jewson, Charles Puddle, Sybil Purser, Mrs John Redvers, Pamela Robertson, John Sales, Kay Sanecki, Rita Skinner, Michael Talbot, Michael Tooley, Tom Turner, Kim Wilkie and Bronwyn Williams-Ellis.

I owe a special debt to many librarians including staff at the British Architectural Library (RIBA) and The National Library of Wales. I should particularly like to thank Brent Elliott and Barbara Collecott of the Lindley Library (RHS); Ian Mayfield and Janet Wilmott of the Frewen Library, Portsmouth Polytechnic; Sheila Harvey, Landscape Institute; and Jill Lever, curator of the BALDC. Without the invaluable help of Ray Desmond's *Bibliography of British Gardens* my task would have been far greater. Among the many archivists who have responded to my enquiries I am especially grateful to Christopher Whittick, East Sussex Record Office.

For copy photography I acknowledge the help of Manchester Reference Library, City Lab Johannesburg, Nolan Hughes, Christine Ottewill and Eileen Tweedy; and for assistance with colour photography, Neil Crighton, Alan Kemp and Ian Meredith.

My thanks are due to Grace Precious for the initial typescripts and subsequently to Barbara Newell who so patiently and conscientiously typed the whole manuscript; also to my daughter Miranda who sensitively drew many of the plans most of which had to be reconstructed from old maps and photographs. Andrew Saint read the whole text for me and I am greatly indebted to him for his comments. At Yale University Press I wish to record my gratitude to John Nicoll for his continual support, and to Gillian Malpass for her editorial skills and for the care and enthusiasm that she has given to the design of the book. Finally, my thanks go to my wife, who accompanied me on all the visits to gardens, was an indispensable guide in plant identification, and for whose constant support and encouragement I am profoundly grateful: this book is dedicated to her.

David Ottewill
December 1988

Introduction

'Under certain circumstances there are few hours in life more agreeable than the hour dedicated to the ceremony known as afternoon tea' wrote Henry James, and few settings more admirable, he added, than 'the lawn of an old English country house.'[1] Images such as this give rise to the romantic nostalgia for an age that, in the minds of some writers and television producers, appears as one long garden party, 'a kind of perpetual fête' as James Laver put it,[2] a seemingly endless succession of halcyon days brought to an abrupt end by the cataclysm of 1914. We are given a tantalizing glimpse into the idyllic gardens of this period, in their heyday before the First World War, from old photographs such as those that appeared regularly in the pages of *Country Life*. Thanks to the care bestowed upon them by their owners a few of these gardens have survived remarkably intact, but most are mere shadows of their former glory or have disappeared, along with the labour-intensive methods of gardening that made them possible.

What is the justification for a book devoted to these relics of a bygone age? One answer lies in their historical value, for upon close inspection these gardens begin to reveal as much about the preoccupations of the times as the houses they adjoined. Most were added to existing houses and, though they took time to mature, were often an immediate response to changes in fashion. And the Edwardians were nothing if not fashion-conscious. Whether or not it felt the end was in sight, High Society let itself go in a continuous and exhausting round of social events. The purchasing power of the pound rose steadily from 1890, reaching a peak in 1896, then declining until it fell dramatically at the outbreak of the First World War.[3] There was an accompanying rise in consumption. Owing to the introduction of the mass market this was no longer confined to the wealthy, but the working mass of the population was a little worse off during the Edwardian period compared with the 1890s. In general, the situation allowed a small élite to amass, more quickly than ever before, immense personal fortunes, a substantial part of which was spent on palatial country houses which came into their own as the setting for weekend houseparties. Some members of the aristocracy added formal gardens to their grounds, often making up for ones that had been swept away in the eighteenth century; while many businessmen acquired at least a semblance of landed status by building a new house or enlarging an old one. The combination of surplus resources and a plentiful supply of labour enabled both groups to indulge in the luxury of gardens on a scale never to be seen again.[4]

This of course presents only the grand view of the period. It also makes it appear merely a prolongation of or sequel to the Victorian age, the final stage of a continuing development, whereas, although its roots are in the nineteenth century, the Edwardian era has distinct characteristics of its own. Furthermore, such a view ignores what was going on outside the conventional garden-party world, which Harold Nicolson dismissed with: 'it never dawned upon them that intelligence was of any value'.[5] There was a more serious side to country-house life, exemplified by the political and artistic circle that the Wyndhams attracted to Clouds; and lower down the social scale was another strand of society—high-minded, individualistic and practical—whose interest in country life lay in a romantic affection for its traditional arts and crafts rather than opportunities for lavish entertaining. The period was not all 'pomp and circumstance', silk hats and splendour. Many of the changes associated with the 1920s and 1930s were already beginning in the second half of Edward's reign, social reforms that laid the foundations of the Welfare State, and important political issues such as industrial relations and women's suffrage. It was also a time of deep questioning among writers and artists from whom sprang many of the creative ideas that were to help shape the twentieth century. The popular image of a 'Last Golden Age'[6] overlooks all this and obscures the underlying tensions and the desire to break away from the complacency of Victorian values.

The historical division into eponymous eras is one source of confusion, for the cultures and styles evoked by the terms 'Victorian' and 'Edwardian' do not correspond to the reigns of these monarchs. The Edwardian period ends with the First World War but its beginning is less clearly defined. In literature and the arts, the four decades from 1880 to 1920 represent a gradual transition from Victorian values to those of modern times, and need to be seen as a whole when reviewing the development of its gardens. They witnessed a rich profusion of types and styles, spectacular changes in flora due to the introduction of trees, shrubs and plants from abroad, and an intensification of the perennial 'art-versus-nature' debate.

The country house, with its flower and vegetable gardens, its orchards and wild and woodland areas, was the principal scene of this activity, together with increasing numbers of 'houses in the country', often built for a 'progressive' section of society who wanted the simple life without the responsibility of large estates. In addition was the burgeoning of suburban villas which followed when the railways made the countryside more accessible especially for commuters after about 1875. A love of nature had always been a strong national characteristic, and, in reaction to Victorian industrialization, many of the urban middle classes now began to be inspired by an Arcadian dream of rural life based on traditional country crafts and furthered by such potent images as the idealized cottage garden.[7] The 1880s brought 'sweetness and light'; they brought also a longing for sunshine and open air which became a cult by the end of the century. 'Everyone who can, now lives in the country, where he is bound to have a garden', wrote J.D. Sedding in 1890;[8] but unlike the Victorian parterre this was not just a garden to look at but one to do things in. Moreover, being British, it was also practical, a garden to walk in at all seasons. As Nikolaus Pevsner observed of his adopted England, it is usually 'too warm not to want to be outdoors, too cool to be idle outdoors',[9] and the 1890s saw a burst of outdoor activities. Owners became active gardeners themselves; garden parties and garden fêtes increased in popularity; and the British propensity for sport was displayed by the bowling green and by tennis, which took the place of croquet on the lawn. The house overflowed into the garden: tea was taken on the terrace; the loggia replaced the conservatory; rose-clad pergolas formed long corridors of shade leading to arbour or summerhouse. The garden was conceived less as a spectacle to be viewed from the house than as a succession of outdoor rooms, each one affording fresh delights for the visitor. This enabled resources to be concentrated in one area if necessary, but, like a Chelsea Flower Show, it had the added advantage of allowing a wide variety of themes and styles: botanical, geographical, historical, literary, sentimental, or even representational, like the garden made at Sedgwick Park, Horsham, by Emma Henderson, whose children invented nautical names for its main features.[10] And beyond these formal enclosures, where the grounds began to give way to the surrounding landscape, one might come across rock and water gardens leading to woodland glades and semi-wild areas.

All these elements could be contained within the grounds of a single country house, their character reflecting the tastes of their owner and the particular approach of their designer, be it garden architect, landscape gardener or head gardener, some interested mainly in the total picture, others focusing on the beauty of the individual plants. Gardens also took account of regional variations in climate, soil and materials, for what suited Surrey or Somerset would be out of place in the Cotswolds or the Lake District. This wide range of factors produced an immense variety in the appearance of gardens, and this is not to include those other types of garden—town, suburban, municipal—all of which are subjects for study on their own. It was country-house gardens, however, that provided most of the resources and opportunities for innovation in design, and it is with them that this book is principally concerned. Written from the viewpoint of garden and architectural history rather than horticulture, it attempts to trace the development of garden design in Britain during this period by reference to the most

significant examples and the attitudes and theories that influenced them.

What then are the distinguishing characteristics of the Edwardian garden? An important feature was the renewal of formality which was partly a reaction to the Victorian practice whereby designers of house and garden worked independently of one another. As Avray Tipping wrote in 1909, 'The house emanated from the office with little regard to its site. The garden wound its gravel paths, extended its mixed shrubberies, dotted its specimen plants, set its lobelia and calceolaria circles, stars and crescents about the lawn without worrying itself where the house stood and what pictures it was going to make in connection with it.'[11] A revival of the architectural layout provided one remedy, but this provoked a bitter argument about the relative merits of the formal and the natural garden. The opening chapter of this book analyses the events that led up to this argument, introducing William Robinson, the High Priest of 'natural' gardening, and his opponents, the architects Reginald Blomfield and Francis Inigo Thomas who looked back to seventeenth-century England when house and garden were designed as a unity. The strongly architectural nature of their work is compared with the views of John D. Sedding, also an architect but one who favoured opening up the garden to the surrounding landscape and who was closer to the idealism of Ruskin, Morris and the 'old-fashioned' garden. In Scotland there was a corresponding revival of the pleasaunce, the old enclosed pleasure garden, highlighted by the work of Robert Lorimer. These developments and the writings that accompanied them helped to arouse interest in garden design amongst architects at the turn of the century.

Yet what gave the Edwardian garden its unique quality was a combination of formal layout with exuberant informal planting. The impetus for this more naturalistic approach came from professional gardeners, also from their publicists led by Robinson, and from amateur artist-gardeners of whom the central figure was Gertrude Jekyll. It was her partnership with the architect Edwin Lutyens that produced some of the finest examples of this fusion of pictorial planting and architectural framework. Many designers followed their example creating gardens that can broadly be labelled Arts and Crafts, a movement concerned more with ideology than style, whose influence spread to the Continent and the United States. Until recently this movement has tended to eclipse the parallel classical stream which was seen as historicist and regressive. Throughout the Edwardian period garden designers continued to glance over their shoulders to past styles, but although there was a strong resurgence of classicism in architecture, gardens were rarely rigidly classical They often included classical features such as loggias, pergolas, ornamental pools and statuary, but more evident was a classical discipline in overall planning by means of axes and vistas. The Italian Renaissance remained for many the one true fount of inspiration. This Italian-villa revival began in the United States in the 1890s, its gardens, and those influenced by the Beaux-Arts, often capturing more closely the mood of the Edwardian era. A chapter is devoted to this school, many of whose designers have for too long been neglected, and the book concludes with some late survivals of its grand manner before the Modern Movement brought a return to naturalism in the 1930s.

Little Bognor, near Petworth, Sussex (Clough Williams-Ellis, 1920): the valley garden. [A. Kemp 1987]

1. Athelhampton, near Dorchester, Dorset (F. Inigo Thomas, 1891–3): vista from the raised terrace. [Author 1983]

1

The Formal-Garden Revival

I think, as a nation, we are beginning once more to realise the charm of a formal garden.
F. Inigo Thomas, 1896[1]

In 1892 a battle raged that was to have a profound effect on the Edwardian garden. It was about whether a garden should be 'natural' or 'formal' and who should be primarily responsible for its design, the gardener or the architect. The chief protagonists were the gardener William Robinson and the architect Reginald Blomfield. Robinson insisted that only the gardener with his knowledge of horticulture could decide on the layout of a garden, whereas Blomfield maintained that it must be the architect's province since only he knew anything about design.

Reginald Blomfield

At thirty-six, eighteen years younger than Robinson, Reginald Blomfield (1856–1942) (Plate 2) was on the threshold of a successful career as an architect.[2] It is, however, more as a scholar and writer that his name has endured. An early member of the Art Workers Guild (founded 1884) and its Honorary Secretary from 1892 to 1895, Blomfield was the first to insist that formality in design was not incompatible with the ideals of the Arts and Crafts Movement.[3] He became one of the leading advocates of a return to the sober classicism of Wren, his influence being mainly through his books. The first of these, *The Formal Garden in England*, appeared in January 1892.[4] In Blomfield's view, the landscape style of gardening was depriving buildings of their proper settings, and he aimed to reform the situation, presenting a lucid and sustained argument in favour of the 'refinement and reserve' of the seventeenth-century garden. He attacked Robinson's view that the garden should be a 'reflex of nature in her fairest moods' and was scornful of a recent book by H. E. Milner, *The Art and Practice of Landscape Gardening* (1890). Although Milner had also recommended formality (a fact conveniently overlooked by Blomfield), he had written in his introduction, 'If we endeavour to define the art of landscape gardening, it may be stated as the taking true cognizance of Nature's means for the expression of beauty, and so disposing those means artistically as to co-operate for our delight in given conditions.'[5] To Blomfield this seemed to suggest that an attempt should be made to reproduce the effects of nature. Furthermore, Milner's advice that 'the lawn of our garden' should present the appearance of a 'growing glade in a wood'[6] was proof to Blomfield of the land-scape gardener's aim 'not to show things as they are, but as they are not'.[7] He thus attempted to expose the fallacy of the 'natural' argument:

In the first place, it is said to be unnatural to lay out a garden in straight lines and regular banks and to clip your hedges. The landscape gardener appears to suppose that he has a monopoly of nature. Now, what is 'nature' and what is 'natural' in relation to gardens?...it is no more unnatural to clip a yew-tree than to cut grass...'Nature' has nothing to do with either straight lines or curved; it is simply begging the question to lay it down as an axiom that curved lines are more 'natural' than straight. As a matter of fact, whatever 'naturalness' there may be about it applies quite as well to a straight path and a plain expanse of grass; and it is open to us to say that the natural man would probably prefer a straight path to a zig-zag, and that when his eye seeks wearily for the rest of some quiet breadth of lawn and the welcome finality of a wall or hedgerow, he is 'naturally' bored by the landscapist with his curves and his clumps...In fact, this vaunted naturalness of landscape gardening is a sham; instead of leaving nature alone, the landscapist is always struggling to make nature lend itself to his deceptions....To suppose that love of nature is shown by trying to produce the effects of wild nature on a small scale in a garden is clearly absurd; any one who loves natural scenery will want the real thing; he will hardly be content to sit in his rockery and suppose himself to be among the mountains.[8]

In his concluding chapter Blomfield wrote:

An attempt has been made in this book to show the essential reasonableness of the principles of Formal Gardening, and the sanity of its method when properly handled. The long yew-hedge is clipped and shorn because we want its firm boundary lines and the plain mass of its colour; the grass bank is formed into a definite slope to attain the beauty of close-shaven turf at varied angles with the light. The broad grass walk, with its paved footpath in the centre, is cool to walk upon in summer and dry on the pavement in winter.[9]

This was the viewpoint of the architect, whose position of overall

2. Reginald Blomfield, c.1919. [Courtesy of R. Fellows]

the question of design, of the treatment of the grounds as a whole as well as in detail, is an entirely distinctive one, which has been confused with that of horticulture, and finally superseded by it. Horticulture stands to garden design much as building does to architecture; the two are connected but very far from being identical. . . . The designer whether professional or amateur, should lay down the main lines and deal with the garden as a whole, but the execution, such as the best method of forming beds, laying turf, planting trees, and pruning hedges, should be left to the gardener, whose proper business it is.[11]

William Robinson

A better-matched pair of combatants could hardly have been found than the truculent, opinionated Blomfield and the belligerent, cantankerous Robinson. William Robinson's independent career started out of acrimony, so it is said: one night, in the bitter winter of 1861, after a quarrel, he put out all the fires and opened the ventilators at his employer's hot-house collection of tropical plants at Ballykilcavan before making off to Dublin and London.[12] Not one to let the grass grow under his feet, through a steam of publications, notably *The Wild Garden* (1870) and *The English Flower Garden* (1883), he established a reputation as the leader of a crusade aimed at replacing both the Victorian parterre and the 'architectural garden' by more natural forms of gardening.

When Blomfield's *The Formal Garden* appeared Robinson had already been incensed by a book published posthumously the previous year, J.D. Sedding's *Garden-Craft Old and New*. Sedding had rather tactlessly asserted,

As one must needs have a system in planning grounds, there is none that will more certainly bring honour and effect to them than the regular geometrical treatment. This is what the architect naturally prefers. The house is his child, and he knows what is good for it. Unlike the imported gardener, who comes upon the scene as a foreign agent, the architect works from the house outwards, taking the house as his centre; the other works from the outside inwards, if he thinks of the 'inwards' at all.[13]

This had been bad enough, but with Blomfield's words Robinson exploded. As Geoffrey Taylor has observed, he must have seen in these books 'an attack on all the ground he had regained from the formalists in twenty years of toil'.[14] Within a few months he launched a counter-attack with *Garden Design and Architects' Gardens*, a vitriolic review lashing out mercilessly against architects who meddled with gardens. In his view the books were

not worth notice for their own sake, as they contribute nothing to our knowledge of the beautiful art of gardening or garden design. . .the authors. . .see no design at all in landscape gardening, and admit their ignorance of it. That men should write on things of which they have thought little, is unhappily of frequent occurrence, but to find them openly avowing their ignorance of the art they presume to criticise is new.[15]

He countered Blomfield's monopoly of design: 'in garden design there are lessons innumerable both in wild and cultivated Nature

control Blomfield was attempting to restore. He maintained that almost up to the middle of the eighteenth century the garden had been conceived by the architect, or architect-builder, as a whole, along with the design of the house; but that since then the architect had been ousted by the landscape gardener:

The question at issue is a very simple one. Is the garden to be considered in relation to the house, and as an integral part of a design which depends for its success on the combined effect of house and garden; or is the house to be ignored in dealing with the garden?. . .The formal treatment of gardens ought, perhaps, to be called the architectural treatment of gardens, for it consists in the extension of the principles of design which govern the house to the grounds which surround it.[10]

Blomfield was also clear about the relative roles of architect and gardener:

which will guide us well if we seek to understand them simply',[16] a theme he constantly reiterated, as in a later edition of *The English Flower Garden*: 'I find it stated by writers on this subject that 'design' can only concern formality—an error, as the artistic grouping and giving picturesque effect to groups and groves of Oak, Cedar, or Fir are far higher design than putting trees in lines.'[17]

The Victorian Parterre

Robinson despised the 'hothouse' mentality of the grand country houses and turned instead to the unsophisticated English cottage gardens (see Plate 79). He described one in Kent that he had happened to pass: 'No pretentious plan to consider, only the yellow sunflowers of the season massed in their own way'.[18] The desire to replace formalism with nature unadorned had a familiar ring, although there was a world of difference between the old gardens supplanted by the landscape movement, and the Victorian parterre. The latter was Robinson's *bête noire*, and he cited amongst others, Mentmore, Drayton, Crewe Hall and Alton Towers. Such gardens were characterized by pools, fountains, statuary, vases, urns, pavilions, specimen evergreens, clipped conifers and parterres filled with intricate geometric beds of exotic flowers. The emphasis was on floral display and the formal bedding-out of half-hardy plants raised in greenhouses. In *How to Lay Out a Garden* (1850), Edward Kemp had recommended that a formal garden should include 'a ribbon-like style of bed' containing 'two or three rows of flowers of a strong colour, such as scarlet Geraniums along the centre, with a marginal row of Calceolarias, or blue Lobelias, or flowers of any similarly contrasting colour'. The garden at Brasted Place, Kent, where H.A. Tipping was brought up, was a typical example:

> There were shrubberies to be dug once a year in such a manner that made the growth of perennials among them difficult and out of place. There were numbers of many-shaped beds cut out of the lawn, showing bare earth for seven months of the year, and only gay during three. Even then they were not interesting. You walked rapidly round, and said it was well done. Then you had finished with them, and said that the lawn was well weeded and the gravel paths well rolled. After that another subject of conversation had to be found.[19]

Geometric flower-bedding of this kind was an off-shoot of early Victorian historicism, particularly the attempt to re-create the spirit of Tudor knot gardens. It spread to the public parks and developed into the more manageable and longer-lasting system known as carpet-bedding, using subtropical foliage plants of uniform height.[20] Well-established by 1870, it has continued in popularity to the present day, but in about 1880 was an embarrassment to William Morris: 'Another thing also much too commonly seen is an aberration of the human mind, which otherwise I should have been afraid to warn you of. It is technically called carpet-gardening. Need I explain it further? I had rather not, for when I think of it even when I am quite alone I blush with shame at the thought.'[21] Shirley Hibberd (1825–90), editor of *Floral World* from 1858 to 1872, considered the bedding method unsuitable for the smaller garden and advocated the hardy herbaceous border.[22] Robinson followed suit, although this did not prevent his including a chapter on 'Summer-Bedding'—written 'by one who carries it out with great success'—in every edition of *The English Flower Garden* up to the First World War.[23]

The Italianate Garden

As well as the bedding system, Robinson inveighed against the increasing dominance of gardens in the so-called 'Italian' manner, a term used at the time to cover a multiplicity of formal styles, including French, Dutch and English. His principal target was the grounds at Sydenham, laid out in 1852–6 when the Crystal Palace was re-erected there by Joseph Paxton.[24] In 1883 Robinson wrote, 'There are, from Versailles to Caserta, a great many ugly gardens in Europe, but it is at Sydenham that the greatest modern example of the waste of enormous means in making hideous a fine piece of garden is to be found.'[25] Almost as bad were the Royal Horticul-

3. The Royal Horticultural Society's Garden, South Kensington, London (W.A. Nesfield, 1861): general view. [RHS 1863]

tural Society's gardens at South Kensington (Plate 3), laid out in 1861 by William Andrews Nesfield (1793–1881),[26] the leading exponent of the High Victorian geometric garden. To Robinson they were 'stiff and ugly', with their canals and emblematic designs in coloured gravels. In his view such gardens were giving the art of landscape gardening a bad name: 'Everywhere—unhappily, even in England, the home of landscape gardening—the too frequent presence of stupid work...offers some excuse for the two reactionary books which have lately appeared.'[27] One of his chief objections was to the excessive use of stonework, at, for instance, Nesfield's Witley Court, Worcestershire, laid out at great expense in the 1850s for the 1st Earl of Dudley, where 'the "architectural" gardening is pushed so far into the park as to curtail and injure the view. If the cost of the stone and stucco ornament lavished on the garden were spent on its legitimate object—the house—how much better it would be for architecture, as well as for gardening!'[28]

4. Shrubland Park, Suffolk (Charles Barry, 1848–52): view west towards the lower parterre. [Author 1985]

Nesfield, who had been a landscape painter before he took up landscape gardening professionally in the 1840s, was at least sympathetic towards English garden traditions, as well as towards horticulture. That was more than could be said of the architect Sir Charles Barry, in Robinson's eyes the arch-culprit, to whom gardening was 'only a handmaid to architecture'.[29] One of Barry's earliest examples of 'architectural gardening' (in which he may have been assisted by Nesfield) was at Trentham Hall, Staffordshire (1840–42). It included two broad terraces stepping down to the lake, punctuated by fountains, urns and statuary, with the object of providing a dignified base to the house.[30] His showpiece was the West Garden at Shrubland Park, Suffolk, where in 1848–52, for Sir William Middleton, he had added a monumental stairway. Flanked by wild planting, it consisted of a hundred steps connecting an archway temple with a parterre and loggia seventy feet below (Plate 4), from which stretched a main terrace almost a mile long. According to Robinson, 'there were strict orders that the walls were not to have a flower or a creeper of any kind upon them',[31] and the beds were laid out rigidly and filled with yellow, white, red and blue flowers edged with box. This was the antithesis of everything Robinson stood for, and in 1883 James Saumarez entrusted him with the remodelling of the garden. He replanted the upper terrace garden on the west front with roses, carnations, lavender and other hardy plants, and created a Bamboo Walk in the lower, wilder garden. Because of the steep fall in the site, Robinson did not object to the architectural terracing at Shrubland, writing in the first edition of *The English Flower Garden*, 'Here it is used with a very pleasing effect to lead from the house down a steep bank to the pleasure grounds below.'[32]

Formality in Gardens

Blomfield shared Robinson's disdain for the Victorian parterre and he did not defend Barry. In his opinion such work had debased the formal garden. Many believed the Italianate style to be a revival of early English Renaissance gardens but, as Blomfield pointed out,

> Those who attack the old English formal garden do not take the trouble to master its very considerable difference from the continental gardens of the same period. They seem to consider the English Renaissance as identical with the Italian, and the public, seeing such dismal fiascoes in the Italian style as the Crystal Palace Gardens and the basin at the head of the Serpentine, confuse these with the old English garden in one wholesale condemnation of the formal style.[33]

The kind of formality he wished to see revived was of a very different order, consisting of a series of spaces divided by walls or clipped hedges, simply planned and proportioned in relation to the house, with raised terraces, gazebos, broad walks, alleys, lawns, flower beds and a symmetrically arranged entrance forecourt. As an example of the latter he included in *The Formal Garden* a plate of Ambrosden, near Bicester, Oxfordshire, from Kennet's *Antiquities* (Plate 5),[34] the kind of sober and dignified setting evoked in Trollope's description of the Tudor Great House in *The Small House at Allington*, surrounded by trim gardens and standing 'much too near the road for purposes of grandeur'. Robinson stubbornly refused to acknowledge that it was this older garden that his opponents wished to revive, not the rigid and elaborate Victorian type. In 1903 he was still maintaining that the old gardens of England, far from being destroyed by the landscapists, had, in fact, disappeared in Victorian times when formal gardens of the 'worst and most deplorable type' had been made, and that 'there was hardly a country seat laid out that was not marred...it is ludicrous to see a young architect weeping over their loss'.[35] In his missionary zeal for the natural garden he could not bother to distinguish between these two sorts of formality. In fact, Robinson did not condemn formalism as a whole; his particular abominatioin was formal *planting*. Gardens laid out with different coloured gravels or sand may be called formal, 'yet one might plant every one of them beautifully without in the least altering their outline', he wrote, probably with

5. Ambrosden, Oxfordshire. [From Kennet's *Antiquities*, 1695]

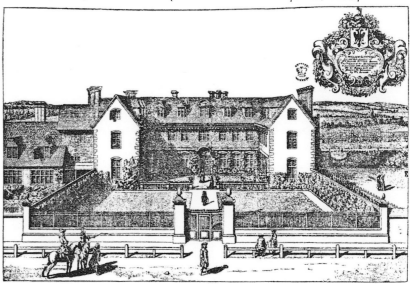

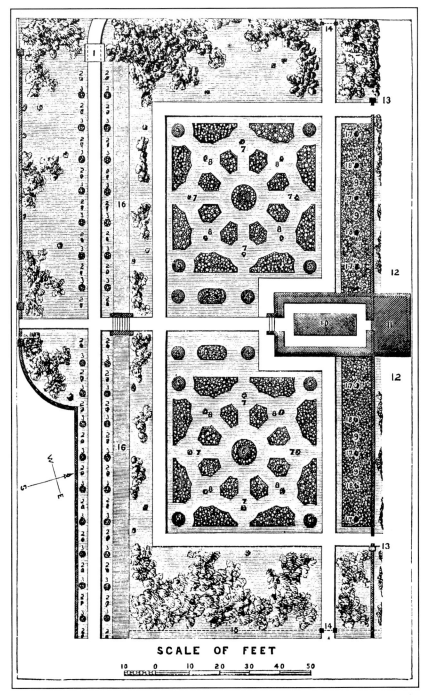

SCALE OF FEET

6. Acton Burnell, Shropshire: design for a flower garden. [From Edward Kemp, *How to Lay Out a Garden*, 1850]

From Tudor times up to the early Georgian period gardens had been predominantly regular and symmetrical after the Italian, French and Dutch styles. William Lawson recommended in 1618 that grounds 'be formal',[39] but by the time of the landscape movement the term was used disparagingly to describe the Jacobean garden.[40] In *How to Lay Out a Garden*, Kemp gave detailed descriptions of 'the old formal or geometric style' (Plate 6), although he advised against 'extreme formality' for small gardens;[41] but by the 1880s old gardens such as Brickwall, illustrated in *The Formal Garden* (see Plate 14), would have been generally referred to as 'old-fashioned',[42] or as 'pleasances'. Hence the widespread misunderstanding. Blomfield was aware of the shortcomings of his book's title: 'The Formal System of Gardening has suffered from a question-begging name. It has been labelled "Formal" by its ill-wishers; and though, in a way, the term expresses the orderly result at which the system aims, the implied reproach is disingenuous.'[43]

This reproach was not, however, directed only at formality; it was aimed also at the architect's incursion into the garden. In Robinson's mind 'formal' was a synonym for 'architectural'. He placed the lion's share of the blame for the Victorian formal garden squarely—but unfairly—on the shoulders of architects such as Barry. It followed that no architect was to be trusted in the garden. His role must be strictly curtailed:

> The architect can help the gardener much by building a beautiful house! That is his work. The true architect, it seems to me, would seek to go no further. The better the real work of the architect is done, the better for the garden and landscape. If there are any difficulties of level about the house beautiful, they should be dealt with by the architect, and the better his work and the necessary terracing, if any, are done, the pleasanter the work of the landscape or other gardener who has to follow him should be.[44]

Most of Robinson's exemplars were within landscaped parks, such as Goodwood, West Dean, Highclere, Westonbirt, Longleat. But he also praised Philip Webb's Clouds, with its gardens by Alfred Parsons, and the neo-Elizabethan Batsford Park (1888–93), described by him as 'one of the few really good new houses in England'. He added that it was 'not disfigured by the fashions in formality the authors wish to see revived',[45] although in fact it sat comfortably on the formal terraces—complete with garden pavilions—designed for it by Harold Peto (Plate 7). He agreed that terracing was desirable where the ground fell away steeply, and in *The English Flower Garden* expressed his admiration for the hanging gardens constructed in about 1700 at Powis Castle (see Plate 22).[46] But the type of garden he favoured most is demonstrated by his own layout for Golder's Hill, Hampstead, London, where a spacious, open lawn falls gently from the house and is surrounded by picturesque planting of trees and shrubs.[47] In short, the architect was needed to create terraces and sunny, sheltered spaces in and near his buildings, but 'Except for what is mostly a very small area near the house, the architect and garden-designer deal with distinct subjects and wholly distinct materials. They should work in harmony, but not seek to do that for which their training and knowledge have not fitted them.'[48]

Not to be outdone, the indefatigable Blomfield retaliated in the

Shrubland in mind. '*It is only where the plants of a garden are rigidly set out in geometrical design as in carpet-gardening and bedding-out that the term 'formal' is rightly applied.*'[36] This confusion between formal layout and formal planting lay at the root of the squabble, and Blomfield's book, which revived the term 'formal garden', did not help the situation. 'The very name of the book', wrote Robinson in his review, 'is a mistake. "Formal gardening" is rightly applied only to the gardens in which both the design and planting were formal and stupidly formal like the upper terrace of the Crystal Palace';[37] and he added later, 'For ages gardens of simple form have been common without anyone calling them "formal".'[38]

9

7. Batsford Park, Gloucestershire (Ernest George and Peto, 1888–93): south terraces. [RCHME 1892]

preface to the second edition (October 1892) of his book, pointing out, as he recalled in his memoirs, Robinson's 'unnecessary blunders as well as gratuitous discourtesy!' and boasting: 'I am still rather proud of that preface to the second edition of *The Formal Garden* as an exercise in destructive criticism, and Mr. Robinson accepted it all in the right spirit, for he afterwards asked me down to his beautiful place at Gravetye.'[49] By 1901, when the third edition appeared, he felt he could omit the preface as being 'no longer necessary'. The bitterness had subsided and both sides felt entitled to claim victory. Formal gardens certainly became the rule for Edwardian country houses, typical examples being Olantigh, near Wye, Kent (1906–11), by Burnett Brown and Barrow, 'an intensely Edwardian place, with its urns and statues about the close-clipped lawns'[50] (Plate 8); Sennowe Park, Guist, near Fakenham, Norfolk (1905–7), designed by George Skipper for a quintessential Edwardian client, Thomas Cook, grandson of the travel agent;[51] and Manderston, Berwickshire (1901–5), by John Kinross for Sir James Miller, Bt.[52] Ultimately it was Robinson's influence that was to prove the more enduring, but, at the time, the feud had the effect of dividing opinion into opposite camps, bringing to a head certain trends that had been developing since the 1870s. For whereas gardening had become more naturalistic, more rooted in sound horticultural principles, architecture was adopting a more orderly and academic approach. Blomfield's motive for writing his book was not just to defy the landscape gardener; he wanted also to align himself with the current revival of the English classical tradition. A resurgence of classicism was a key force in Edwardian architecture and *The Formal Garden in England* needs to be seen in this context.

The Revival of Classicism

Since the 1880s a fresh wave of classicism had been pervading all the arts, in painting led by the 'High Renaissance' artists, G.F. Watts and Frederic Leighton,[53] in architecture reaching a suave fulfilment in Richard Norman Shaw's 170 Queen's Gate, London (1887). Weary of the desperate search for a new style that had dominated the 1860s and reacting against the over-elaborate architecture of the times, many fell back on the English Renaissance. The standard of Wren was raised, and this was avidly followed by Blomfield. English country houses of the seventeenth and early eighteenth centuries became fashionable, but a demand for historical authenticity had to be satisfied. From 1895 to 1905 a flood of architectural literature appeared.[54] It was a field day for publishing houses and Blomfield's prolific pen was not idle. Albert Richardson said of him after his death, 'His monument exists in his writings... all will be agreed that no other man has done so much to inspire his fellow architects with a love of the great exemplars of the English classic tradition.'[55] Books and journals—including *Country Life* from 1897—provided the sources of details for new country houses, and also for old houses whose owners were ready to restore or enlarge, or create gardens of the kind evoked in *The Formal Garden*:

> Behind the lawyer's house, with its white sash-windows and delicate brick work, there may still survive some delightful garden bright with old-fashioned flowers against the red brick wall, and a broad stretch of velvety turf set off by ample paths of gravel, and at one corner perhaps, a dainty summerhouse of brick, with marbled floor and panelled sides; and all so quiet and sober, stamped with a refinement which was once traditional, but now seems a special gift of heaven.[56]

Blomfield's book could not, therefore, have been better timed. A reaction to Victorian eclecticism was well under way and the book was one of the earliest to focus attention on the seventeenth century, and the first to advocate forcefully a revival of the old, formal garden. It showed remarkable foresight on Blomfield's part and in later life he told Professor Reilly that 'he traced the growth of his practice in the early days largely to this book'.[57]

Blomfield's Historical Survey

Blomfield cared as little about horticulture as Robinson did about architecture. For him the issue at stake was that of overall control, and he looked back to the time before the advent of the Landscape School when a country house and its garden were determined by one unified set of principles. He therefore attempted to trace this design development and devoted a large part of the work to an historical sketch of the art of gardening up to the eighteenth century. Although it was a brilliant polemic, *The Formal Garden* suffered from the extreme bias of its viewpoint and from an inadequate knowledge of garden history. It was, for example, written as though the style of William Kent and Capability Brown had dominated the work of landscape gardeners up to the late nineteenth century, and it brushed aside all developments in Victorian formal layout. His selection of appropriate historical styles was heavily slanted in favour of his argument. He stressed the formal garden's distinguished ancestry, which reached back to Pliny's Tuscan Villa with its box-hedged enclosures and topiary,[58] later reborn with Alberti's view of the garden as an extension of the house.[59] These ideas were then brought back from Italy, acquiring their special native quality in the Elizabethan garden. The tradition, argued Blomfield, reached perfection in the early seventeenth century, and it was the simplic-

8. Olantigh, near Wye, Kent (Burnett Brown and Barrow, 1906–11): east front. [Author 1985]

9. Montacute, Somerset: north garden (remodelled between 1845 and 1890). Drawn by F. Inigo Thomas. [From *The Formal Garden in England*, 1892]

10. Hardwick Hall, Derbyshire: south garden (after 1868). [National Trust c.1973]

ity and practicality of the English garden of this period, as recorded by Gervase Markham and William Lawson, that Blomfield admired. In *The English Husbandman* (1614), Markham described what to Blomfield must have been the model of a compartmented, walled-in garden with its nosegay and herb garden, kitchen garden, orchard: 'Everything is to be laid out in comely order'.[60] Books such as these, and the smaller gardens of the period up to the English Civil War, represented 'the most charming side of the Renaissance in England'. After that a decline set in with a desire for more grandeur (foreshadowed from 1633 by Isaac de Caux's gardens at Wilton) and the ornamental influence of Dutch taste.

Like Morris's nostalgia for the Middle Ages, Blomfield's enthusiasm resulted in some misrepresentations and distortions. *The Formal Garden* included illustrations of Elizabethan and Jacobean gardens, but they were mostly conjectural reconstructions based on the evidence of seventeenth- and eighteenth-century books. By the time Blomfield's book appeared, most gardens of that period, if they had not already been destroyed by Cromwell or Capability Brown, had been altered in the nineteenth century. For instance, the north garden at Montacute (from 1598) (Plate 9) was remodelled from 1845 by Ellen Phelips and altered again before 1890; the so-called 'Sermon on the Mount' yew garden at Packwood House, Warwickshire, was a mid-Victorian re-creation of a Mannerist garden of the 1660s; and the south garden at Hardwick Hall, with its cross-alleys of yew and hornbeam (Plate 10), was laid out within Elizabethan walls by Lady Louisa Egerton after 1868. All these were regarded by Blomfield as authentic seventeenth-century gardens.[61]

Blomfield's avowed love of the modest English garden did not prevent his admiring the grandeur of Le Nôtre (1613–1700) whose influence was felt after the Restoration. Formal gardens reached their peak during the reign of William and Mary, recorded in the folios of views by Knyff and Kip, and Blomfield praised 'the masterly conception of the grounds as a whole' in front of Wren's building at Hampton Court, and included a detailed description of Badminton,[62] an extreme example of the grand manner, including immense vistas radiating in all directions and measuring nine miles across. To Robinson this was absurd, and even Blomfield had to admit that it was 'the first sign of the coming decadence'. Formalism had overstepped the mark (and become expensive to maintain) and 'The "natural" manner of gardening now became the rage'. In the words of Horace Walpole, 'Kent leapt the fence and saw that all nature was a garden', prompting Blomfield's bitter remark, 'It seems almost inconceivable that a man such as Kent, who could design fine and severe architecture, should have lent himself so abjectly to the fancies of the fashionable amateur.'[63] Capability Brown he dismissed in a dozen lines, Repton in even fewer: '[Brown] died in 1783, and was succeeded by Humphry Repton and other professors of landscape gardening, who between them irrevocably destroyed some of the finest gardens in England.'[64]

Victorian historicism, epitomized by Biddulph Grange, Staffordshire (1840s) and the work of landscape gardeners like Milner, was passed over quickly by Blomfield. In his view, George Devey and W. Eden Nesfield were the only recent designers who had made an 'effort to design the house and grounds in relation to each other'. H.H. Statham, editor of *The Builder* and a loyal supporter of Blomfield, agreed. Reviewing Milner's *The Art and Practice of Landscape Gardening* (1890), he wrote,

> The relation of the mansion to the garden is about the last thing [the landscape gardener] ever thinks of, except in regard to some pedantic notions about showing the house from favourable points of view in the approaches; and the ornamental erections which he inflicts on us in the way of summer-houses, bridges etc., as embellishments to the grounds, are only fit to grace a popular tea-garden.[65]

In the same review Statham praised Blomfield's book but criticized its antiquarian flavour: 'too much of the spirit of a revival about it', not enough guidance on the principles of 'what should be done in the modern garden…if the revival of formal gardening is undertaken merely as a fashion, the arbitrary adaption of the taste of a former period, it can have no other fate than has attended the revival of Gothic architecture'.

Francis Inigo Thomas

What would Statham have thought of the garden then being laid out at Athelhampton, near Dorchester? He would, perhaps, have found it too revivalistic. It included topiary of the kind he had in mind when he wrote, 'one of the favourite devices for lining a walk or surrounding a parterre was to place a row of small clipped trees in the shape of thin pyramids at regular intervals…it occurs over and over again in the views of the seventeenth and early eighteenth-century gardens. There is a disposition to revive it now, and it most certainly is not worth reviving, unless the object is merely to produce an imitation of an old garden, which is hardly a thing worth doing.'[66] Nevertheless, Athelhampton was a practical example of a new garden in the old manner, and the designer was none other than Blomfield's co-author, Francis Inigo Thomas (1866–1950). In the formal-garden revival Inigo Thomas has been overshadowed by his more demonstrative fellow-architect. Blomfield's book owed much of its success to Thomas's charming pen-and-ink illustrations which must have helped to lure owners thinking of enlarging or remodelling their gardens. His contribution did not, however, rest there. Although Blomfield's junior by ten years, he had begun laying out country-house grounds several years before the appearance of the book, and he played a substantial part in its preparation, scouring the country for information on the old gardens, some of which had to be reconstructed to show how they might have looked. Thomas's aristocratic connections helped to give him a head start over Blomfield. Both Sir George Sitwell (discussed in Chapter 7) and the future Marquess of Willingdon were his first cousins, and his self-portrait (Plate 11), painted in oils in 1903, shows him in the characteristic riding-kit of the country gentleman. Moreover, his uncle, William Brodrick Thomas (1811–98), was one of the leading landscape gardeners of the Victorian era, who, as Thomas described in 1926, 'gave up fox-hunting for laying out the places of country gentlefolk in the prevailing "landscape" manner. Forty years later, while he was still at work, I came down from Oxford to learn architecture with the late Mr Bodley, living the while with the aforesaid uncle.'[67]

11. Francis Inigo Thomas (self-portrait in oils, 1903). [AWG Album]

A son of the Reverend C.E. Thomas, Rector of Warmsworth, Yorkshire,[68] Thomas was educated, like Blomfield, at Haileybury and matriculated at Pembroke College, Oxford, in 1884. His apprenticeship with the Gothic Revival architects G.F. Bodley and Thomas Garner took place in about 1886–9, his fellow-pupils including C.R. Ashbee[69] and J. Ninian Comper. The ecclesiastically minded Comper developed a strong affection for Thomas and a high regard for his architectural work. Perhaps, being an agnostic, Thomas presented no rivalry, but in any event Comper could write in the 1940s: 'Inigo Thomas is a name which has not been known as it ought to be known, and the consequent loss to architecture has been great; of which his work at Hickleton Hall, Ufford House, Athelhampton and elsewhere, is proof. He is the pioneer of modern times in gardens.'[70] Significantly, Comper carried out work to the churches at all these places. While Thomas was with Bodley and Garner, the office was engaged in rebuilding Hewell Grange, Worcestershire (1884–91) for Lord Windsor, in neo-Elizabethan style, and with no expense spared. The gardens were laid out by the head gardener, Andrew Pettigrew, and included an elaborate, Jacobean-style, box-edged parterre based on an existing cross-pathed flower garden and enclosed by lime hedges and rose-covered arches.[71] Garner was responsible for the architectural work at Hewell Grange and would have furthered Thomas's knowledge of garden design;[72] while Bodley would have encouraged his life-long interest in painting and the crafts.[73]

From 1889 Thomas travelled widely on the Continent producing etchings in Chartres, Poitiers, Laon and the Vosges, also in Germany and Holland. He became proficient in various media and a talented artist, with a feeling for nature, as his 'The Yew Walk at Melbourne' in *The Formal Garden* bears witness.[74] In 1893–4 he was in Italy with the intention of compiling a book of surveys of Italian gardens, visiting many important examples.[75] Papers on gardens were read to the Society of Arts in 1896[76] and the Art Workers Guild in 1898,[77] but in the following year all this was left behind when Thomas departed for the Boer War, returning in 1902 'unscathed', according to Ashbee's journal,

> but a changed man to my thinking broader, bigger, and more human, though I noticed De Brett's [sic] Peerage was still among the most prominent of the books on his table...He is a fine fellow all the same though the caste mark is difficult to efface. He showed us his boer trophies Mrs. Botha's milk jug, which I begged him in chivalry to restore to her, the autograph of Paul Kruger, his own prison clothes...And the net result of the war to him? An unmitigated waste of time said the architect, but the *man* told a very different story.[78]

After his return from South Africa, Thomas bought 2 Mulberry Walk, Church Street, Chelsea, where he lived until his death in 1950.[79] In November 1914 Ashbee visited him there:

> a pleasant enough place for a bachelor, he has filled it with many charming drawings—gardens and dream buildings mostly, for like so many of us his best work is done in the imagination... He had been spending the morning bringing rolls of drawings &c from his office which he was shutting up...We agreed that during the last few years all the best work, and there was little enough of that, had been collared by Lutyens and Detmar Blow, we agreed that their genius helped them, but that the women helped them more. We discussed Bodley and Bodley pupils and the end of the great tradition for which Bodley stood...We did our reminiscent forgetting quite pleasantly over a mellow glass of port wine—it had about it a fine flavour of middle age.[80]

Thomas offered some technical advice on the laying out of grounds in his *Keystones of Building* (1912), a diverting account of the pitfalls likely to be encountered in a country-house practice,

12. Athelhampton, near Dorchester, Dorset (F. Inigo Thomas, 1891–3): the Coronet. [*CL* 1906]

and in a paper read at the RIBA in 1926 he outlined his design approach:

> After seeing the place the first thing I did was to make a series of sketch forecasts in oil of the ultimate effect...The next stage was a careful survey and then a drawing to small scale of the whole scheme. This was made solely for discussion, and I insisted on being allowed to finish it as I thought it ought to be. It was mounted on a stretcher and framed for hanging in the house as a guide for the next generation in carrying on the scheme which perhaps the present would leave uncompleted...For to design the garden is one thing, and to garden it so as to obtain the desired effect is another. The latter naturally falls to the occupants to do throughout the seasons and does not come to fruition till long after the designer is gone and forgotten.[81]

Thomas's first major commission, Ratton, in East Sussex, was not a fruitful start to his career. The old manor house had belonged to his grandfather Inigo Freeman Thomas, but after its destruction by fire in 1891 Thomas rebuilt it in time for the marriage the following year of his cousin, Freeman Freeman-Thomas (created Baron Willingdon in 1910, Viceroy of India, 1931–6, and 1st Marquess in 1936), to Lady Marie Adelaide, daughter of the 1st Earl Brassey, the dynamic and notorious Lady Willingdon, who fell out with Thomas over his designs for Ratton. Later, as Vicereine, she perpetrated the horrors to the interior of Viceroy's House at New Delhi that prompted Lutyens to tell her that 'if she possessed the Parthenon she would add bay windows to it'.[82] During the Second World War Ratton was commandeered, and burnt down again in 1942.[83]

Thomas's next garden scheme, Athelhampton, near Dorchester (1891–3), was the outcome of a more sympathetic designer/owner relationship and is probably his best-known work. The romantic, partly restored, mainly sixteenth-century manor house was bought in 1891 by Alfred Cart de Lafontaine[84] who employed Thomas to

13. Athelhampton: aerial view. [*The Studio* 1901]

advise on further restorations; also to add gardens between the house and the road to the south-east.[85] Thomas adopted a strongly architectural approach, using the warm, rust-coloured Ham Hill stone and subdividing the garden into a series of enclosures. As he said in his 1896 paper, 'Someone has described personal charm as an open secret, and that is precisely the character of an old garden. There is more left to the imagination where the whole cannot be seen at a glance.'[86] The three main compartments are arranged axially to produce vistas, the central, pivotal one being related to the entrance forecourt. Its circular enclosing wall is in the form of a coronet, crested with obelisks, clothed with *Clematis* and roses and backed by high yew hedges (Plate 12). On the cross-axis are Tudor arched doorways, and Thomas intended a sundial in the centre, but this was replaced by a circular fountain moved there from the forecourt. He described the original layout as illustrated in his aerial view (Plate 13):

There are three main lines on which the work is planned. One from the south garden gate in the foreground catches the reflec-

tion of the house in the long pool, passes through the doorway in the south front, and out into the court beyond; thence between the piers that are just visible it is continued down the centre of the tennis lawn, and across the pool at the end to a sculptured figure in the yew hedge by the river. Another line, centring with the window in the left wing, passes down the rose garden and through the circular coronet to a niche fountain between the two arches in the foreground. The third is taken from a summer house in the grove to the right, across the south garden, through the coronet, and up a flight of steps, with a wrought iron gate, to the sunk garden. Here it catches the fountain and continues up another flight of steps to end in a stone seat that projects from the back of the terrace.[87]

From this raised terrace, with its corner pavilions with masks representing the east and west winds over the doorways, there is an enticing vista back through the fountains (a play on the owner's name?) of the three enclosures (Plate 1). The square, sunk garden, which has a central pool and is surrounded by raised walks, was originally laid out with ornamental flower beds and statuary. It contained twelve yew pyramids which, as envisaged in Thomas's perspective, were typical examples of the topiary Statham had criticized.[88] However, they have now acquired a mysterious monumentality having reached a height of twenty-four feet, recalling those at the Elizabethan Brickwall at Northiam, Sussex, which Thomas drew for *The Formal Garden* (Plate 14).[89]

14. Brickwall, Northiam, Sussex. Drawn by F. Inigo Thomas. [From *The Formal Garden in England*, 1892]

Athelhampton is one of the most successful surviving examples of the formal-garden revival in its pioneering years. From the same period, but less well-known, is Thomas's garden at Barrow Court, Barrow Gurney, Somerset (1892–6) for Martin Gibbs. This also leant heavily on the old style and again the dominant note is architectural, with a preponderance of monumental stonework. Garden houses, gateways, balustrades, piers, balls, vases and obelisks abound, derived from local examples, such as Montacute, or with reference to Italy, as in the stone table for *al fresco* teas in the east court (reminiscent of Lante) or the semi-circular arrangement of figure terminals outlined against the landscape. All these denote the designer's vocabulary, but more important is the bold handling of spaces and the overall breadth and simplicity of treatment, complementing the Jacobean house and its adjoining church,[90] and befitting the situation overlooking the park (Plate 15). The garden is on descending levels to the north-east of the house. There was an existing terrace with formal garden below, centred on an old barn and consisting of a circular pool enclosed by yew hedges with flower gardens on either side (Plate 16). Thomas modified this and added a broad terrace walk with walled enclosures at either end to act as suntraps. The east court was aligned on the church tower with steps descending to a yew alley. Below these gardens, which also included a sundial court and iris pond, Thomas levelled the park to create a broad tennis lawn, closed at the north-west by a semi-circular balustrade. This has piers that rise from a bastion

wall and support busts of the twelve months, expressing the changing seasons and the passage of time (Plate 17). The eastern axis extends as a lime grove between shrubberies and is terminated by a circular recess with figure and flanking piers and ornaments.[91]

The gardens at Athelhampton and Barrow Court were designed to augment existing houses, but at his next two important commissions Thomas was able to design the layout in conjunction with the remodelling of the house itself. At Rotherfield Hall, Crowborough, Sussex (1897), for Lindsay Lindsay-Hogg (created baronet in 1905), he extended the house on the south under a long, tiled roof creating a pleasing breadth and balance to both entrance and garden fronts. The old house, built of the local stone, dated from 1535 but had been altered in 1666, a period from which he enthusiastically took his cue for both the remodelling and the garden design (Plate 18). The layout is axial with square entrance fore-

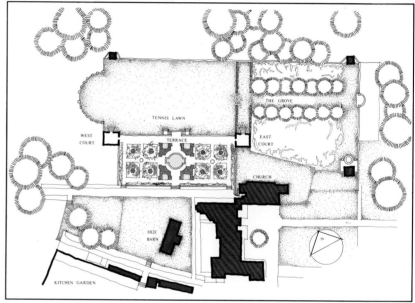

15. Barrow Court, Barrow Gurney, Somerset (F. Inigo Thomas, 1892–6): layout plan. [Miranda Ottewill]

16. Barrow Court: upper terrace. [Author 1984]

17. Barrow Court: the Twelve Months. [RCHME 1973]

court—following the precepts of *The Formal Garden*—and steps leading up through an archway in its east wall, past a fountain, to a transverse bowling green, beyond which a vista extends in a deep cutting through the woodland. The main pleasure gardens were laid out on descending levels to the west, a double stairway leading down eight feet from the terrace to a grass plat with box-edged beds and central lily pool. Beyond this parterre a grass bank slopes a further eight feet down to the lower lawn. The bank is contained at either end by garden houses with hipped roofs crowned by dovecotes, and the whole is enclosed by high walls, except at the western boundary where the parapet is swept down to allow a view of meadows and the Crowborough ridge (Plate 19). As Tipping wrote in 1909,

> The lay-out of this garden is perfectly apt to its site. That this was just the right thing to do under the circumstances is the feeling it produces. The drop from level to level and the width of the sections please the eye and consort with the natural slope. There is no hint of strain or difficulty about them . . . In giving to his scheme all that was needful to satisfy the trained eye, and nothing more, an unusual amount of judgment has been shown. There is always the danger that an inventive mind will overcrowd the canvas. The present race of garden architects need a warning against this pitfall, but Mr Inigo Thomas has successfully avoided it in the really delightful gardens at Rotherfield Hall.[92]

Thomas displayed commendable reserve at Rotherfield and treated the old house with respect. This is more than can be said of his handling of Nash's Ffynnone, near Boncath in Pembrokeshire. Built in 1793–5 for Colonel Colby, it consisted of a square block, with pediments to each façade, of great charm and simplicity. It had an east service wing, and in 1827 a Greek Doric entrance lobby was added. In 1904 Thomas vigorously remodelled the exterior for John Colby, improving the overall balance by the addition of east and west wings. However, his ruthless treatment of the façades

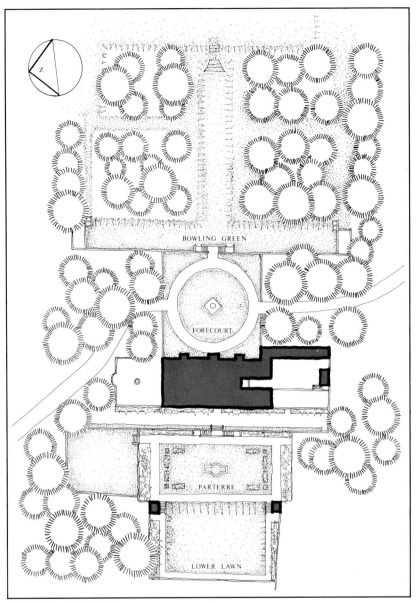

18. Rotherfield Hall, Crowborough, Sussex (F. Inigo Thomas, 1897): layout plan. [Miranda Ottewill]

revealed his true affections, the rusticated quoins and bold window surrounds, all in slate, being more reminiscent of his namesake, Inigo Jones, than Nash (Plate 21). The scheme included an elaborate and impressive series of hanging gardens—with a backward glance at Powis Castle (Plate 22)?—but only the upper terrace, including a semi-circular grotto at the eastern end, was carried out.[93] A terrace of a very different kind was added by him in 1902 to the grounds of the eighteenth-century Drakelow Hall, near Burton-on-Trent, Derbyshire, for Sir Robert Gresley. Situated overlooking the river, this was handsomely modelled with lawns, grass banks, statuary and a bastioned and balustraded river wall capped by urns (Plate 20).[94]

In 1910 Thomas produced possibly his finest garden scheme, at Chantmarle, Frome St Quintin, Dorset. The house was originally built in 1612–23, in Ham Hill ashlar, as an E-plan manor house by Sir John Strode, whose elder brother, Sir Robert Strode, lived at

19. Rotherfield Hall: view from the upper terrace. [*CL* 1909]

20. Drakelow, near Burton-on-Trent, Derbyshire (F. Inigo Thomas, 1902): river terrace. [*The Studio* 1908]

nearby Parnham (Plate 23).[95] However, by 1910, when it was bought from the Oglander family by F.E. Savile, Chantmarle had long since lost its wings and fallen into disrepair. Savile restored and enlarged the house and engaged Thomas to lay out the gardens. Its main pleasaunce, the South Garden, has much in common with the lower or north garden at Montacute, which was laid out before 1890 on the site of the main Elizabethan garden (see Plate 9). There is a similar cross-path, central, balustraded lily pool and north-south axis through the forecourt (Plate 24).[96] On the cross-axis, steps lead westwards to a box-bordered croquet lawn and raised grass walk, the vista being emphasized by four Irish yews flanking

the pool (Plate 25). The eastern end of this axis is marked by a pair of obelisks on the raised parapet of the retaining wall beside which runs a long canal—an echo of the original moat—bordered by a grass walk and yew hedge (Plate 26). This boundary wall, also in Ham Hill stone, is a striking feature of the garden, providing a strong base, softened by the planting which spills over from the border above. It incorporates certain details from the porch of the house, notably in a shell-headed niche on the axis of the pool; also the mouldings of the oriel are reproduced where the balustrade is corbelled out opposite the porch. This secondary cross-axis is also marked by obelisks and runs through the house to a circular lawn

21. Ffynnone, near Boncath, Pembrokeshire (F. Inigo Thomas, 1904): proposed hanging gardens, south elevation. [BAL]

22. Powis Castle, Welshpool, Montgomeryshire (c.1700): hanging gardens. [Author 1986]

fountains as focal points, and especially the division into compartments. In essence, Thomas was giving back to these old houses—for those who could afford it—the kind of formal gardens they had once possessed. They were not mere revivals, however; inevitably they reflected the special needs of the age: as he put it, 'a stage on which to play the drama of everyday life'.[98] The decline in their owners' affluence coincided with the end of Thomas's practice. One of his last schemes was at Otley Hall, a fifteenth-century timber-framed house near Ipswich, Suffolk, for Mrs Sherston. His proposed layout, rendered in oils in May 1915 (Plate 27), takes account of existing features and sets up radiating vistas both from

23. Parnham, Beaminster, Dorset: south terrace (from 1910). [Author 1985]

24. Chantmarle, Frome St Quintin, Dorset (F. Inigo Thomas, 1910): layout plan. [Miranda Ottewill]

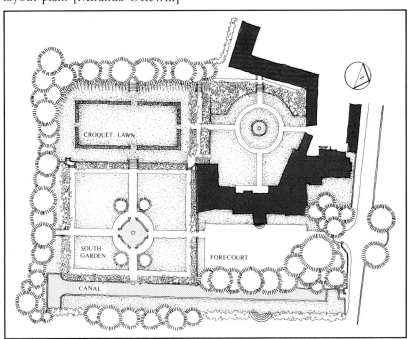

on the west side. Both Athelhampton and Chantmarle demonstrate Thomas's feeling for the *genius loci*. The earlier garden was appropriately inward-looking and intimate in scale, whereas Chantmarle, with its more open and sloping site, was treated with greater breadth.[97]

Although sometimes employing Elizabethan features, Thomas's gardens at Athelhampton, Barrow Court and Chantmarle have more in common with later seventeenth-century developments and can as a result seem too grand for their Elizabethan or Jacobean houses. They, nevertheless, give the appearance of being part of a natural evolution of the house and its grounds. Certain identifiable characteristics of the old gardens are accentuated in his work: changes of level, the use of axes and vistas with statuary and

25. Chantmarle: cross-vista looking west. [Author 1983]

26. Chantmarle: view from the south-east. [Author 1983]

the house and from a quincunx, through shaven alleys bordering a canal and 'wilderness' enclosures. According to Thomas's directions these enclosures were to be unkempt and their planting to include flowering nettles and brambles. Perhaps, in time of war, he had allowed his imagination to run a little wild, but in any event the scheme was abandoned and he carried out no further commissions.[99]

Blomfield's Gardens

Not so Blomfield; a pillar of the establishment, his practice flourished and continued into the 1930s. In his memoirs he recalled that *The Formal Garden* 'led to my being constantly called in for the design of grounds and gardens',[100] but in fact his important garden commissions did not arrive until after the turn of the century. In general his designs followed Thomas's example but were more pedestrian. His first new house and garden, Caythorpe Court, overlooking the Vale of Belvoir and built in 1899–1901 as a hunting lodge for the banker, Edgar Lubbock, did little more than provide a suitable base for the bland, neo-Tudor house; but at Brocklesby Park, also in Lincolnshire, which he reconstructed in 1899 for Lord Yarborough, a grand axial drive was enlivened by flanking topiary cones and ornamental pools.[101] Blomfield's conservative approach was appropriate for old buildings. At Knowlton Court, Kent, a somewhat nondescript, partly Elizabethan house, his east terraces and sunken gardens of 1904 followed the lines of the seventeenth-century garden and were at least unobtrusive; while at the Elizabethan Apethorpe Hall, Northamptonshire, laid out for Sir Leonard Brassey, also in 1904, the sunk garden was detached from the house and enclosed by yew hedges.[102]

It was a ground rule with both Blomfield and Thomas that there must be a clear demarcation between garden and surrounding landscape: 'there should be no question where the garden ends' wrote Blomfield,[103] and he demonstrated this very successfully at Godinton, near Ashford, Kent, where from 1902 to 1906, for George Ashley Dodd, he re-created formal gardens around the mellow, red brick, early seventeenth-century house (Plate 28). At the end of the eighteenth century the park had been landscaped almost up to the house,[104] but in the north-east corner, approximately on the site of the original geometric parterre, Blomfield laid

21

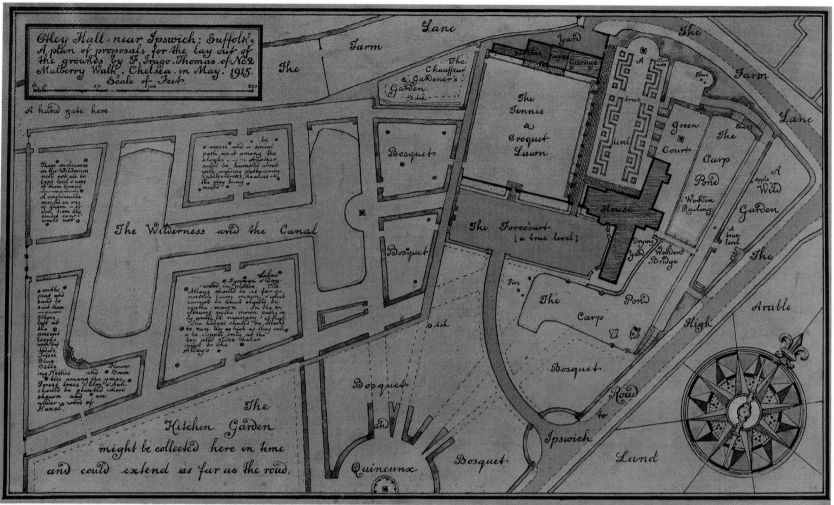

27. Otley Hall, near Ipswich, Suffolk (F. Inigo Thomas, 1915): layout plan by F. Inigo Thomas. [From the original oil painting, courtesy of John G. Mosesson]

out a box-hedged plat with central figure of Pan. The main axis extends southwards from this to a formal lily pool enlarged from an existing pond (Plate 29). The garden is enclosed by a massive yew hedge complete with buttresses, and Flemish gables reflecting those of the house, but low enough to permit views of the park (Plate 30), and broken on the southern boundary by a prospect towards the village of Great Chart.[105]

The same clear distinction between garden and open countryside occurs at Moundsmere Manor, Preston Candover, Hampshire, probably the best surviving example of a complete new house and garden by Blomfield. Built in 1908 for Wilfrid Buckley, a general merchant with American connections, it was 'Wrenaissance' in style as that master would have understood the term, being based on his work at Hampton Court. Although decidedly austere and assertive when photographed in 1910 for *Country Life*, it now has the complementary setting Blomfield intended, being handsomely framed by mature yew hedges. The principal formal garden on the south front has a sunken terrace with central canal surrounded by rose beds and flanked on either side by paths lined with clipped yews and flower borders (Plate 31). Beyond is a raised, gravel walk, with central viewing platform and well-head, and the garden is

29. Godinton: lily pool. [Author 1985]

30. Godinton: view of the park from the garden. [Author 1985]

31. Moundsmere, Preston Candover, Hampshire (R. Blomfield, 1908): south terrace. [Author 1986]

enclosed to east and west by hedges with shaped buttresses similar to those at Godinton. However, to the south, although the boundary is defined by a retaining wall and ha-ha, it is open to views of the distant hills.[106]

One of Moundsmere's best features was its pleasing relationship of garden to landscape, and Blomfield was able to pursue this more open treatment on a grand scale the following year at his most important garden commission, Mellerstain, near Gordon, Berwickshire, in Walter Scott country. The Adam house, whose gaunt, battlemented exterior conceals an elegant series of rooms, was begun in 1725 to designs by William Adam and completed by his son, Robert, in 1770–8 for George Baillie. In 1898 Blomfield carried out restorations for Lord Binning, but in 1909 was engaged to lay out gardens between the house and a canal that lay ninety feet below and about 450 yards to the south. As he wrote in his *Memoirs*,

As usual in Scotland there was an attractive walled-in kitchen garden at some distance from the house, but no garden near it. Lord and Lady Binning were enthusiastic on the matter of garden design, and with their help I laid out an important garden here with terraces, a crypto-porticus, parterres and water-pieces, and my scheme was to have been carried on to an immense grass hemicycle overlooking the lake at the foot of the hill, in the best manner of Le Nôtre, but we had to abandon this; indeed it would have required the resources of Louis XIV to carry out the whole of my design.[107]

The original, grandiose scheme, which aimed to link the house to the canal, was illustrated in a splendid bird's-eye view of 1910 by Adrian Berrington (Plate 32).[108] This shows two enormous terraces extending almost halfway down the hill, with massive retaining walls, loggias, bastions and a concave demi-lune in the lawn below. Although partly carried out, this scheme was fortunately abandoned in 1911 and executed on a considerably reduced scale. The lower terrace was omitted, the loggias altered, and the upper section revised to provide a broad, grassed terrace with topiary, from which a double stairway descends to the main geometric parterre. This was laid out in box with flower beds set into lawns on either side of a central paved area. A semi-circular staircase then leads to a broad expanse of lawn which sweeps down to the segmental wall forming the boundary with the lake. Viewed from below (Plate 33) the walls, buttresses, balustrades, stairways and portico, all in Black Pasture stone, appear excessively fussy, and one cannot help wondering with Mark Girouard whether 'the plain lawns they replaced were better suited to the castellated severity of

33. Mellerstain: view looking towards the house, c.1980. [Courtesy of the Curator, Mellerstain]

32. Mellerstain, near Gordon, Berwickshire (R. Blomfield, 1909): bird's-eye perspective by Adrian Berrington, 1910. [BALDC]

the house'.[109] However, the vista from the windows of the house is impressive, the parterre blending with the calm expanse of lawn, beyond which the lake nestles amongst beech woods below the misty, blue line of the far-off Cheviots (Plate 34).

The lake was a crucial element in this composition and Blomfield's treatment of it shows how much less doctrinaire he had become in the twenty years since writing his book. It had been formed originally from the River Eden and had a free outline, but when the new house was started in 1725 it was changed, probably by William Adam, into a 'Dutch Canal' measuring twelve hundred by four hundred feet. It had a segmental southern end and was 'surrounded by raised grass walks on which, at intervals, stood

34. Mellerstain: vista from the house looking south, c.1980. [Courtesy of the Curator, Mellerstain]

classical statues'.[110] In *The Formal Garden* Blomfield had lamented the enlargement of fish ponds to create Le Nôtre-type canals or basins, adding: 'the transition from this to the lakes of the landscape gardener was easy'.[111] But this was precisely what he did at Mellerstain. He restored the lake to its original shape, enlarging it and relating it in natural landscape style to the adjoining woodland, something he had condemned Milner for advocating. Milner had advised: 'The created character of a water feature must be consonant with the sourrounding land, for fitness to surrounding conditions is a measure of beauty to both; a lake expresses spaciousness, but much of its charm is due to its outline.'[112] The success of Blomfield's scheme as executed was largely due to the gradual transition from formal garden to the countryside beyond, a recommendation of Uvedale Price[113] which Blomfield had dismissed. Repton also had affirmed: 'I should condemn a long, straight water in an open park, where everything else is natural'.[114] Both Thomas and Blomfield had poured scorn on Repton, but by 1909 Blomfield possibly had a less jaundiced view of his writings.

In their gardens of the 1890s and 1900s, Inigo Thomas followed by Blomfield provided practical demonstrations of the arguments put forward in *The Formal Garden in England*. In general they drew their inspiration from seventeenth-century models, but their image of the old formal gardens was a predominantly architectural one. A garden to them was above all an extension of the principles underlying the design of the house, and thus it was the architect who should have sole responsibility for its layout.

2
Sedding and Garden-Craft

The old-fashioned garden…represents one of the pleasures of England, one of the charms of that quiet beautiful life of bygone times that I, for one, would fain see revived.

J.D. Sedding, 1891[1]

When William Robinson lauched his wholesale attack on architects trespassing in gardens, and on Reginald Blomfield's and J.D. Sedding's books in particular, he either ignored or was unwilling to acknowledge the older architect's wider and more tolerant views which stemmed from his love of plants and gardening. To take up *Garden-Craft Old and New* is to be aware of a different approach to garden design, one that was to have a more penetrating if less spectacular influence on the Edwardian garden. In the typical Inigo Thomas or Blomfield garden the purpose of the planting was to enhance the formal layout, and it was deliberately subordinated to the architectural features. Sedding substituted clipped hedges, shrubs and topiary and aimed for more variety of height and form to soften the overall geometry. He was not without praise for Robinson's *English Flower Garden:* 'Even the gardener who has other ideals and larger ambitions than are here expected', he wrote, 'heartily welcomes a book so well stored with modern garden-lore up to date'. His affirmation, 'A garden is first and last a place for flowers', could hardly have been further from Blomfield's definition; and in discussing their selection and arrangement for the geometrical garden—the only instance where he used the term 'formal garden'—he supported Robinson on the need for hardy flowers to provide a good appearance at all times of the year.[2] All this signified a more sympathetic attitude to garden design, to account for which one has only to look back over the very different context of Sedding's career.

John Dando Sedding (Plate 35) was born at Eton in 1838, the younger son of Richard and Peninnah Sedding of Summerstown, near Okehampton. In 1853 his elder brother, Edmund, entered the Oxford office of the emerging Gothic Revival architect G.E. Street, where his contemporaries included Philip Webb and, for nine months in 1855–6, William Morris.[3] In 1856 the office moved to London and Sedding became a pupil there in 1858. However, he found Street's work unsympathetic and left in 1863,[4] in 1865 joining Edmund who for health reasons had established a practice at Penzance. After Edmund's premature death in 1868 he took over the practice for a time, and the close contact with building of those early years 'inspired and coloured all his later works'.[5] In about 1872 he moved to Bristol where he married Rose Tinling, daughter of a canon of Gloucester, later settling in London and in 1880 moving his office to 447 Oxford Street, above t' showroom of Morris & Company. Sedding's practice was mainly ecclesiastical, and he was most at home in the little village churches of Devon and Cornwall, many of which he restored and altered following the local vernacular traditions. 'You must write on my gravestone' he said shortly before his death, 'He made the doors at Holbeton, and was an artist in his way.' Henry Wilson, his chief assistant, who took over his practice after his death in 1891, described him as 'a Romanticist born in an age of Stylists'.[6]

In 1888 Sedding moved his home out of London to 'a quiet old house with a beautiful garden', The Croft, West Wickham, where he spent the last three of his fifty-three years. It was there that he wrote his book, published a few months after his death and including a 'Memoir' by the Reverend E.F. Russell of St Alban's, Holborn, who wrote:

It seems to have taken some of his friends by surprise that John Sedding should write on Gardens. They knew him the master of many crafts, but did not count Garden-craft among them. As a matter of fact, it was a love that appeared late in life, though all along it must have been within the man, for the instant he had a garden of his own the passion appeared full grown. Every evening between five and six, save when his work called him to distant parts, you might have seen him step quickly out of the train at the little station of West Wickham, run across the bridge, and greeting and greeted by everybody, swing along the shady road leading to his house. In his house, first he kissed his wife and children, and then supposing there was light and the weather fine, his coat was off and he fell to work at once with spade or trowel in his garden, absorbed in his plants and flowers, and the pleasant crowding thoughts that plants and flowers bring. After supper he assembled his household to say evening prayers with them. When all had gone to rest he would settle himself in his little study and write, write, write, until past midnight, sometimes past one, dashing now and again at a book upon his shelves to verify some one or other of those quaint and telling bits which are so happily inwoven into his text. One fruit of these labours is this book on Garden-craft.[7]

The title of Sedding's book is revealing in itself. Like Morris he was imbued with a love of nature and the English landscape; his plea was also a manifestation of the revival of the crafts, a movement that reached back by way of 'Queen Anne', William Morris and Philip Webb to Ruskin and the Gothic Revival.

Sedding greatly admired Ruskin, a further example of common ground with Robinson. Both shared Ruskin's abhorrence of the artificiality of Victorian bedding. To Ruskin, speaking in 1837, a flower garden was an ugly thing, 'an assembly of unfortunate beings, pampered and bloated above their natural size, stewed and heated into diseased growth;...He who has taken lessons from nature, who has observed the real purpose and operation of flowers...will never take away the beauty of their being to mix into meretricious glare.'[8] In 1876 Sedding made drawings under Ruskin's guidance which helped to develop his feeling for texture and colour. 'Flowers were indeed passionately loved, and most reverently, patiently studied by him. He would spend many hours out of his summer holiday in making careful studies of a single

35. John Dando Sedding. [AWG Album c.1884]

36. Charles Collins, *Convent Thoughts*, 1851. [Ashmolean Museum, Oxford]

plant, or spray of foliage, painting them, as Mr Ruskin had taught him, in sienna and white, or in violet-carmine and white. Leaves and flowers were, in fact, almost his only school of decorative design.'[9] Ruskin told him that 'he must always have his pencil or chisel in hand', and Lethaby described how, from drawings of flowers, Sedding passed to designing wallpapers, embroideries and goldsmith's work.[10]

The Old-Fashioned Garden

Tennyson, by including them in some of his early poems, was one of the first to make 'old-fashioned' flowers fashionable, and they were passionately, if not always accurately, taken up by Morris in 'The Story of an Unknown Church' (1856), which includes a vision of an abbey garden filled with sunflowers, nasturtiums, hollyhocks and passion flowers (the latter not introduced into Britain until the early seventeenth century).[11] White lilies, symbols of purity and virginity, were beloved of the Pre-Raphaelites;[12] they appear, for example, in *Convent Thoughts* (Plate 36), painted in 1851 in the garden of the University Press at Oxford by Charles Collins. Through Edmund, Sedding would have been introduced to Morris and his circle, also to the Pre-Raphaelites with whom Robinson had links through his friend Vernon Lushington. However, nostalgia for the past was not something to which Robinson subscribed; neither would he have had much sympathy for the Morris group's idealization of the mediaeval pleasure garden or *hortus deliciarum* as described in *Le Roman de la Rose* and depicted in fifteenth-century illuminated manuscripts. With its orchards, fountains, trellises and crenellated walls, it influenced Morris's affection for the enclosed garden: 'Large and small, it should look both orderly and rich. It should be well fenced from the outside world. It should by no means imitate either the wilfulness or the wildness of nature, but

Penshurst.'[15] The Elizabethan garden, with its alleys and pleached bowers, became an important source of imagery. In 1866 Rossetti raved about his discovery of the yew topiary at the Elizabethan Brickwall (see Plate 14),[16] where in 1872, according to W.H. Godfrey, Devey enlarged and remodelled the house to suit the gardens.

'Old English', with its emphasis on vernacular materials in both building and gardening, had its roots in the country, where it was ably demonstrated by the picturesque houses of Norman Shaw. Its counterpart in the town emerged in the 1870s under the misleading title of 'Queen Anne'. Although Thackeray's novels such as *The History of Henry Esmond* (1852) had encouraged an interest in the time of Queen Anne,[17] the movement drew its inspiration not from her reign but from that of Charles I, with its architecture of Dutch gables and moulded brickwork typified by Slyfield Manor, Surrey (c.1630), where Renaissance features were grafted on to the indigenous building tradition. A necessary adjunct to those early

37. Penshurst Place, Kent (2nd Lord de L'Isle and George Devey, 1850). [From a watercolour by E. Arthur Rowe]

38. Queen's Garden, Royal Botanic Gardens, Kew (re-created seventeenth-century garden, from 1964). [Author 1981]

should look like a thing never to be seen except near a house. It should in fact look like a part of the house.'[13]

These romantic associations would have affected the young Sedding, but as well as absorbing ideas from writers and painters he would have been influenced by certain movements in architecture and garden design. An early development was the 'Old English' revival in which a leading figure was the architect George Devey (1820–86).[14] The style originated in and around Penshurst in Kent where in the 1850s Devey helped the 2nd Lord de L'Isle to put back the garden at Penshurst Place to something approaching what it had been in 1700 (Plate 37), following the formal layout shown in Kip's bird's-eye-view engraving of 1720. It seems all were united in approving Devey's work; even Robinson praised the gardens, and Blomfield wrote, 'Nothing can be more beautiful than some of the walks under the apple-trees in the gardens at

seventeenth-century houses was a trim formal garden with the 'daintie Herbes' and 'delectable Floures' so delightfully recorded by Lawson. Its spirit has been evoked at the Queen's Garden, Kew (Plate 38), laid out in 1964 behind the red-brick Dutch House of 1631. This attempts to re-create a number of contemporary features including a formal parterre planted with lavender cotton and edged with dwarf box, a pleached hornbeam walk, a mount and a nosegay garden containing mulberry, globe artichoke, chives and wormwood, also flowers for posies—pinks, heartsease and mignonette—surrounded by a raised walk and laburnum alley. 'Old-fashioned' gardens of this kind became one of the hallmarks of the 'Queen Anne' style. Their keynote was enclosure, with topiary, small beds edged with dwarf box, trees planted in tubs and an intimate scale which clearly distinguished them from the Blomfield and Thomas formal garden.[18] One of the pioneers of the movement was the architect William Eden Nesfield (1835–88), son of the landscape gardener, who inherited from his father a close interest in the layout of the grounds around his houses. When he remodelled Kinmel Park, near Abergele, Denbighshire (1868–74), and Bodrhyddan, Flintshire (1873–4),[19] he also laid out gardens with box-edged beds and yew topiary; and in about 1885 the principal founder of the style, J.J. Stevenson, added a small Dutch Garden at Ken Hill, Snettisham, Norfolk, the shooting box he built in 1881 for Sir Edward Green.[20]

39. Kate Greenaway, *Under the Window*, 1878.

The 'Queen Anne' garden played its part in book illustrations of the time, notably in the well-ordered world of children's books like Kate Greenaway's *Marigold Garden* (1885) and *Under the Window* (1878) (Plate 39) where afternoon tea is taken daintily from green-painted tables set on neat, hedge-bordered lawns. A more sophisticated interpretation formed the background of *La Belle Jardinière* (1896) (see Plate 52) by the Art-Nouveau pioneer, Eugène Grasset, a romantic set of illustrations depicting the calendar of the aesthetic lady gardener. From the 1890s several painters, including Alfred Parsons, E. Arthur Rowe, George S. Elgood, Ernest A. Chadwick and Beatrice Parsons, succumbed to the spell of the old-fashioned garden, capturing its changing seasons and recording its most appealing examples.

Garden-Craft Old and New

Sedding was one of the founding fathers of the Art Workers Guild and became its second Master in 1886–7.[21] Taking its cue from Morris, the Guild aimed to promote the unity of art, architecture and the crafts, a unity that Sedding had sought wherever possible in his church work. Good craftsmanship was the byword of the Guildsmen. It is significant that most of Sedding's assistants became

more distinguished in the crafts than in architecture: Ernest Gimson and Ernest Barnsley in furniture; Alfred Powell in ceramics; J. Paul Cooper and Henry Wilson as silversmiths. Not surprisingly, Sedding's office has been called the nursery of the Arts and Crafts Movement. Garden-craft fitted naturally into such a 'from-the-roots-up' approach to design. Whereas Blomfield had implied that the garden designer need have no knowledge of planting, for which he was justly castigated by Robinson, Sedding believed that, just as a knowledge of building materials was the only true basis for architecture, a similar understanding of plant materials was a prerequisite of garden-making.

On 3 May 1889 at Barnard's Inn Hall, with Walter Crane in the chair, Sedding read the first of a group of papers on 'The Architectural Treatment of Gardens' to his brethren of the Guild. Contributions followed by John Belcher, Halsey Ricardo, Somers Clarke and Mervyn Macartney, and the historical side was treated by Blomfield. Sedding's paper formed the basis of his book, the manuscript of which was completed just over a year later. This was well before the appearance of *The Formal Garden*, but in his *Memoirs* Blomfield recalled petulantly, 'J.D. Sedding also rushed out a book on *Garden-Craft* just in advance of mine, and I recollect feeling a little annoyed that, though I saw him every fortnight at the Guild, he had never said a word to me about it, and had stolen a march on me, though he knew that I had been working for some time on this subject.'[22] Although agreeing with many of Robinson's aims, Sedding wrote, like Blomfield, from the formalist side of the fence, and he, too, fired some volleys at the prickly gardener. He made it clear throughout *Garden-Craft* that he was putting forward the artist's view: 'It is not so much at what he finds in the landscape gardener's creations that the architect demurs, but at what he misses'.[23] It was the element of imagination that was lacking, and this was where he took issue with Robinson, calling his plan of a non-geometrical town garden in *The English Flower Garden* (Plate 40) 'a tortured horeshoe...No wonder he does not fear Nature's revenge, where is so little Art to destroy!'[24]—an accusation that Robinson angrily dismissed as 'false and confusing "Art" drivel'.[25]

Predictably, the subject of topiary generated strong feelings on both sides. Its Golden Age had come to an end at the beginning of the eighteenth century when it was ridiculed by Addison and Pope, but the Victorian era had brought signs of a renewal of interest, enough in 1837 to provoke Ruskin's objection to the practice mainly 'because the great beauty of all foliage is the energy of life and action, of which it loses the appearance by formal clipping'.[26] Yew hedges were an important feature at Biddulph Grange from 1849, and their use for architectural enclosure was common again by the 1870s. The revival of representational topiary followed and was well established by the time of Sedding's book. An elaborate example was at Ascott, near Wing in Buckinghamshire, where the old timber-framed house of 1606 had been enlarged from 1874 by George Devey for Leopold de Rothschild, who laid out gardens with the famous nursery, James Veitch & Sons of Chelsea. Alicia Amherst described how these included 'a remarkable collection of old cut yew and box trees. Some of these were transplanted from neighbouring cottage gardens but many were brought over from Holland.'[27] In 1895 a topiary garden was planted at Compton

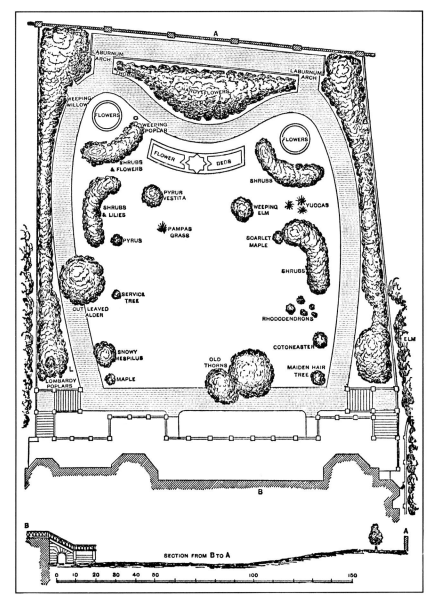

40. Plan of a non-geometrical town garden. [From W. Robinson, *The English Flower Garden*, 1883]

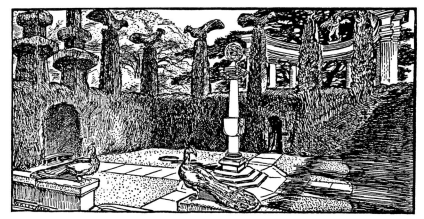

41. W.R. Lethaby, *A Garden Enclosed*, 1889. [From J.D. Sedding, *Garden-Craft Old and New*, 1891]

Wynyates, Warwickshire, perfectly complementing the irregular forms of the picturesque house.[28] Sedding had a weakness for topiary: 'I have no more scruple in using the scissors upon tree or shrub, where trimness is desirable, than I have in mowing the turf of the lawn that once represented a virgin world. There is a quaint charm in the results of the topiary art'.[29] At this, Robinson fulminated: 'here is a man delighting for its own sake in what he calls with such delicate feelings, "Vegetable Sculpture" in "cocked hats" and "ramping lions"!'[30] How, he asked, could anyone be so blind to the beauty of trees in their natural form?[31] It was a vivid instance of the perpetual art-versus-nature argument. Sedding had written:

> any garden whatsoever is but Nature idealised...*Real* nature exists outside the artist and apart from him. The Ideal is that which the artist conceives to be an interpretation of the outside

objects, or that which he adds to the objects. The garden gives imaginative form to emotions the natural objects have awakened in man. The *raison d'être* of a garden is man's feeling the *ensemble*.[32]

This was echoed in 1903 by an ex-pupil of Sedding, the Australian architect Walter Butler, who said in a paper,

> As you come back again from a lengthened stay on the Snowy River and your eye catches the outline of a clipt and stately hedge, it tells you that you are nearing home; and when you see a shape of ideal beauty cut in that hedge, it brings to your mind that in the midst of nature there is something that is above it all, and that something is the soul of man.[33]

Sedding's idealism was bound up with a deep, mediaevalizing taste for mystery and romance in gardens utterly absent from the pragmatism of Blomfield and Robinson. *Garden-Craft* included a drawing made in 1889 by Sedding's friend W.R. Lethaby, depicting a garden enclosed by yew hedges and topiary centred around a pillar with armillary sphere (Plate 41), probably inspired by the iconographic garden imagery of Francesco Colonna's romance, *Hypnerotomachia Poliphili* (1499).[34] This drawing expressed one of the themes of *Garden-Craft* (it was used as the frontispiece to the 1895 edition); it also reflected Lethaby's first book, *Architecture, Mysticism and Myth*, published in December 1891 and influential amongst Arts and Crafts designers. Blomfield confessed, 'none of us at that time made much of Lethaby's book',[35] and later in life Lethaby himself criticized his earlier interest in symbolism.[36]

Sedding's 'Historical and Comparative Sketch' was, like Blomfield's, mainly directed against the contemporary landscape gardener—who was blamed for everything—and he, too, fell into the trap of over-estimating the survival of the 'natural' school and ignoring all formal developments in Victorian garden design. He did, however, show a deeper appreciation of the qualities distinguishing English gardens from their 'rigid' and more elaborate counterparts on the continent:

> If we may speak our mind of the French and Dutch gardens, they in no wise satisfy English taste as regards their relation to Nature...In an English garden, as Diderot notes, Nature is

handled with more reverence, her rights are more respected...
even when we have idealised things to our hearts' full bent, they
shall yet retain the very note and rhythm of the woodland world
from whence they spring—'English in all, of genius blithely
free'.[37]

He was unstinting in his praise for Repton: 'a genius in his way—a
born gardener, able and thoughtful in his treatments, and distinguished among his fellows by a broad and comprehensive grasp of
the whole character and surroundings of a site, in reference to the
general section of the land, the style of the house to which his
garden was allied, and the objects for which it was to be used...
The best advice one can give to a young gardener is know your
Repton.'[38]

For the last third of his book Sedding turned to more practical
matters. Unlike Blomfield he favoured a gradual merging of the
garden with the landscape:

> It is of the utmost importance that Art and Nature should be
> linked together, alike in the near neighbourhood of the house,
> and its far prospect, so that the scene as it meets the eye, whether
> at a distance or near, should present a picture of a simple whole,
> in which each item should take its part without disturbing the
> individual expression of the ground. To attain this result it is
> essential that the ground immediately about the house should be
> devoted to symmetrical planning, and to distinctly ornamental
> treatment; and the symmetry should break away by easy stages
> from the dressed to the undressed parts, and so on to the
> open country, beginning with wilder effects upon the country-
> boundaries of the place, and more careful and intricate effects as
> the house is approached.[39]

He stressed the wisdom of following the characteristics of a site:
'every natural good point...shall be turned to good account',[40]
a principle conceded by both Robinson and Blomfield in later
editions of their books. In the 1898 edition of *The English Flower
Garden*, Robinson wrote, 'the best laid-out garden is that which is
best fitted for its situation, soil and climate, and without much
consideration as to any style';[41] and in the preface to the third
edition (1901) of *The Formal Garden*, Blomfield admitted that 'There
are, for instance, sites which make a purely formal garden out of
the question; and others in which, even if it were possible, it would
not be desirable.' He probably had in mind his own cottage, Point
Hill, on the outskirts of Rye in Sussex. This was situated on a cliff
edge which allowed him no option but to create an irregularly
shaped garden below, following the contours of the steep bank.[42]
A similarly informal, picturesque setting, in keeping with the
dramatic, rocky site, was called for at Norman Shaw's Cragside,
Rothbury, Northumberland (1869–85).

Sedding again drew inspiration from Repton who had written of
his designs for Brighton Pavilion, 'in the artificial garden, richly
clothed with flowers and decorated with seats and works of art, we
saunter or repose ourselves, without regretting the want of extent
any more than while we are in the saloon, the library, or the gallery
of the mansion'.[43] This was endorsed by Sedding's recommendation that the gardens nearest the house should be planted

42. J.D. Sedding, *Design for a Garden*. [From *Garden-Craft Old and New*,
1895 edition]

so that to step from the house on to the terrace, or from the
terrace to the various parts of the garden, should only seem like
going from one room to another. Of the arrangement of the
ground into divisions, each section should have its own special
attractiveness and should be led up to by some inviting artifice of
archway, or screened alley of shrubs, or 'rosery' with its trellis-
work, or stone colonnade...

and, taking his cue from Morris:

> A garden should be well fenced,...the provision of places of
> retreat has always been a note of an English garden. The love of
> retirement, almost as much as a taste for trees and flowers, has
> dictated its shapes. Hence the cedar-walks, the bower, the av-
> enue, the maze, the alley, the wilderness, that were familiar, and
> almost the invariable features of an old English pleasaunce,...
> The qualities to aim at in a flower-garden are beauty, animation,
> variety, mystery....At every turn the imagination should get a
> fresh stimulus to surprise; we should be led on from one fair
> sight, one attractive picture, to another; not suddenly, nor with-
> out some preparation of heightened expectancy, but as in a
> fantasy and with something of the quick alternations of a
> dream.[44]

The extensive gardens of his late friend Thomas Gambier Parry
at Highnam Court, Gloucestershire,[45] Sedding considered the best
modern gardens he had seen, but added, 'if there be a fault, it is that
Art has been allowed to blossom too profusely...We go about in
a sort of pre-Raphaelite frame of mind, where each seemly and
beauteous feature has so much to say for itself that, in the delight-
fulness of the details, we are apt to forget that it is the first business
of any work of Art to be a unit.'[46] This was a valid criticism of
Highnam where even the owner felt he had gone too far,[47] although
similar objections could be made about some of Sedding's own
designs (Plate 42).

Sedding's passion for garden design came late in his life. But as
early as 1867 he had laid out an important garden for W.J. Rawlings

laid in pigments in the beds before planting'.[49] Like most gardens of its time, The Downes has been much simplified, but, in its maturity, parts were illustrated in the *Architectural Review* and aptly described by one of Sedding's assistants, John Paul Cooper: 'The garden holds the house in a quiet embrace, and its levels fall by a series of steps and terraces till the garden melts away into the woods below. The house is linked with the site, wedded to its scenery, blended with nature.'[50] Arcaded yew hedges were also a feature of the garden at Killarney House, County Kerry, which Sedding laid out in 1877–80 for his friend George Devey who had designed the house in 1872 for the 4th Earl of Kenmare. The garden was subdivided into compartments and its many box-edged parterres, though Victorian in pattern, were planted with old-fashioned flowers.[51]

The Influence of Sedding

Sedding's influence on the younger generation of architects was considerable. Russell says in his *Memoir*, 'He was the living embodiment of all that an architect should be, he had the sacred fire of enthusiasm within, and he had the power of communicating that fire to others',[52] and the Secretary of the Art Workers Guild wrote at the time of Sedding's death, 'No member was ever more respected, none had more influence, no truer artist existed in the Guild.'[53] In garden design his more balanced outlook and understanding of plants helped to bridge the gap in the controversy between the formal and the free styles. In 1896 Gertrude Jekyll had this to say about the current debate:

> Both are right, and both are wrong. The formal army are architects to a man; they are undoubtedly right in upholding the simple dignity and sweetness and quiet beauty of the old formal garden, but they parade its limitations as if they were the end of all art; they ignore the immense resources that are the precious possession of modern gardeners, . . . they do not even concede [the gardener] the position of the builder of old, to whom the architect gave broad directions, leaving it to his traditional knowledge and personal wit to accomplish the details that the master knew he would find rightly done. Moreover, they do not suggest who is to play the very needful part of artist-gardener—who shall say what is to be planted where, and why and how . . . All who love gardens must value Messrs Blomfield and Thomas's excellent and beautiful book, . . . but those whose views are wider cannot accept their somewhat narrow gospel.[54]

The solution lay in mutual understanding and sympathy, and for that Miss Jekyll paid tribute to Sedding: 'His professional training as architect led him to favour the formal style, but it is strangely interesting to see throughout the book how the saintly simplicity of his character and the poetry of his nature made him forget his professional bonds and do justice to the best methods of the free garden.'[55]

Gertrude Jekyll had good reason to be sympathetic towards Sedding. Both had known Ruskin and been greatly influenced by him; both had an absorbing interest in the crafts. Furthermore,

43. The Downes, Hayle, Cornwall (J.D. Sedding, 1867–8): perspective view. [From *Garden-Craft Old and New*, 1891]

at The Downes, overlooking the town and harbour of Hayle, near St Ives in Cornwall. Designed initially by his brother Edmund, the style of the house reflected the move from High Victorian Gothic to 'Old English', and the garden had 'old-fashioned' features in the terraced treatment of the site and the central vista extending in an alley between clipped yews which, according to the perspective in *Garden-Craft*, were intended to be arcaded (Plate 43). The upper terrace contained beds of clipped holly and was enclosed to the north by a thick hedge of bay. It overlooked a geometrical parterre where Sedding and Rawlings departed from the customary Victorian bedding system and tried to implement the recommendations included in Sir Gardner Wilkinson's book, *On Colour* (1858), discussed later by Sedding in *Garden-Craft*.[48] A degree of permanence was aimed for in the colour combinations by ensuring a succession of hardy plants, and 'all the patterns were annually submitted to Mr Sedding for approval, the colours being actually

44. Robert Weir Schultz and penny-farthing in Edinburgh. [Keith Collection c.1878]

45. Sir George Clausen, R.A., *R.W.S. Weir, Master AWG, 1920*, 1925. [AWG] (NB Schultz added another 'Weir' to his name in 1915.)

enclosures (Plate 47). The first of these was a sunk lawn bounded at each end by low railings with piers capped by urns trailing ivy, and flanked to north and south by yew hedges scalloped to form recesses for seating and statuary. Semi-circular steps then led up to the main feature, a circular fountain garden, enclosed by a hedge and divided by grass cross-paths into quadrant beds filled with herbaceous plants, its centre-piece comprising a circular pool containing a large statue of the Marquess's patron saint, St John the

46. J.D. Sedding, *Perspective View of a Garden*. [From *Garden-Craft Old and New*, 1895 edition]

47. St John's Lodge, Regent's Park (Robert Weir Schultz, from 1891): view of the garden looking east from the house. [A.B. Waters Collection, late 1890s]

Sedding, in Ruskinian fashion, attempted to practise with his own hands what he preached. His book must have been prominent on the shelves of many of the Arts and Crafts architects who followed him. Enclosure, anticipation, mystery and surprise were important qualities of the gardens of, for instance, Schultz, Lorimer, Tipping and Ernest Barnsley.

An early example of Sedding's influence was the garden of St John's Lodge, Regent's Park, commissioned in the year that *Garden-Craft* appeared and designed by the young Scottish architect, Robert Weir Schultz (1860–1951) (Plates 44, 45). Born in Port Glasgow, Schultz was trained in Edinburgh under Rowand Anderson but in 1884 left for London and Norman Shaw's office. W.R. Lethaby was Shaw's chief assistant at the time and Schultz soon struck up a friendship with him that was to have a profound effect on his outlook. In 1890 he set up practice in Gray's Inn. The patron who made this possible was the 3rd Marquess of Bute,[56] and soon Schultz was busy at several of Bute's seats, including St John's Lodge, a Regency villa in the middle of Regent's Park. Lord Bute had taken a lease of the house in 1888, but for a Roman Catholic convert who was also both scholar and mystic, it lacked a chapel, a library and a 'garden fit for meditation'.[57] Such a garden is what in 1891 Schultz was employed to provide.

It was his first independent exercise in garden design and a bird's-eye view (Plate 49), prepared in 1897 by a fellow-Scot, J.J. Joass, showed how it would have looked when mature. Some features, such as the treatment of the yew hedges, resemble those in Sedding's 'Perspective View of a Garden' (Plate 46), but the design was determined mainly by the awkwardly shaped site (Plate 48) and the need to respect both the house and the eclectic tastes of his unusual patron. The approach was off the Inner Circle (opposite the Royal Botanic Society's garden where Robinson had worked), leading to a forecourt on the east side of the house from which the garden opened up as a grand, axial vista of formal

48. St John's Lodge: layout plan.

49. St John's Lodge: aerial perspective by J.J. Joass, 1897. [Bedford College]

Baptist, cast in block tin, by W. Goscombe John (1860–1952) (Plate 50).[58] Viewed from the forecourt, the statue appeared framed by a large and somewhat heavy-handed portico, possibly intended to reflect the triumphal-arched entrance to the house. Beyond this portico was an oval tennis lawn surrounded by pleached limes, the vista being closed, surprisingly, by a nymphaeum in the form of a semi-domed temple. From here a path connected with a broad walk extending along the north side of the house and leading to the west terrace with its sundial and tubs containing bay trees. The grand enfilade of compartments bore the imprint of the Victorian parterre, and some of the detailing, such as the awkward stone edging to the grass walks and the raised surround to the pool, displayed Schultz's lack of maturity as a garden designer. However, the beds had 'old-fashioned' planting, and further from the house, as the garden became more naturalistic and merged with the picturesque surroundings of trees and shrubs, some delightful Arts and Crafts touches were provided by the garden furniture. There was a curved seat and circular table at the end of the west terrace, and the ornamental rose garden beyond the tennis lawn contained a square seat around an old poplar (probably *Populus nigra*) (Plate 51), very like the seat in 'Mars' from Grasset's *La Belle Jardinière* (1896) (Plate 52); while nearby was a charming dovecote, bracketed out from an oak post and surmounted by a copper weather cock (Plate 53).[59]

Most of Bute's final years were spent at St John's Lodge and, after his death in 1900, F.W.H. Myers described them as 'a life simple and almost solitary; a life of long walks and long conversations on the mysteries of the world unseen'.[60] Bute himself wrote, 'Regent's Park is a *terra incognita* to a great many Londoners; and

51. St John's Lodge: seat in the rose garden. [A.B. Waters Collection, late 1890s]

52. Eugène Grasset, 'Mars' from *La Belle Jardinière*, 1896.

50. St John's Lodge: fountain garden, view looking west towards the house. [A.B. Waters Collection, late 1890s]

moor in Galloway, but St John's Lodge and Mochrum's walled garden had one thing in common: both were sanctuaries from the world outside; one a haven in the busy metropolis, the other a refuge from the wild Scottish moorland, in the words of Sedding, 'hidden happily and shielded safe'.[62]

53. St John's Lodge: dovecote in the rose garden. [A.B. Waters Collection, late 1890s]

54. St John's Lodge: general view west towards the house. [Author 1986] (NB The bronze group *Hylas* by Henry Pegram R.A. replaced the Goscombe John statue when the garden was remodelled after 1930.)

there is perhaps a certain piquancy about a place which almost simulates to be a country house and is yet only a shilling cab-fare from Piccadilly Circus.'[61] The garden of St John's Lodge reflected both Arts and Crafts ideas and the late nineteenth-century revival of classical art. Most of its features have disappeared, but the bones of the garden survive as part of the public park (Plate 54). Later, at Old Place of Mochrum (see Chapter 3), Schultz was to fashion a very different kind of garden for the 4th Marquess. It was a far cry from the sophisticated landscape of Regent's Park to a desolate

3
The Scottish Pleasaunce

Nothing is more completely the child of art than a garden. Its artificial productions are necessarily surrounded by walls, marking out the space which they occupy as something totally distinct from the rest of the domain.

Sir Walter Scott, 1828[1]

The Pleasure Garden

The important contribution that Scottish architects made to the formal revival of the 1890s reflected their country's tradition of walled gardens which had survived relatively unscathed since the seventeenth century. Scotland's climate and wild terrain did not encourage the grand manner, nor did it favour the English landscape style which made such a clean sweep south of the border. It had its own magnificent and picturesque scenery which did not suit the styles of either Le Nôtre or Brown. More desirable, and practical, were the small, sheltered enclosures which, partly owing to a native conservatism and detachment from foreign ideas, landowners had been reluctant to obliterate in favour of the latest fashion.[2] Any interruption this tradition had suffered was lamented as early as 1828 by Sir Walter Scott in his famous essay on landscape gardening published in the *Quarterly Review*. Scott—who, followed by Ruskin, was largely responsible for reviving the term 'pleasaunce'—described with affection a secluded garden, dating from the beginning of the eighteenth century, attached to a cottage in Kelso where he had once lived:

It was full of long straight walks between hedges of yew and hornbeam, which rose tall and close on every side. There were thickets of flowering shrubs, a bower and an arbour, to which access was obtained through a little maze of contorted walks, calling itself a labyrinth....There were seats and trellis-walks and a banqueting house.[3]

Revisiting it after an absence of many years he noted that, 'Its air of retreat, the seclusion which its alleys afforded, was entirely gone;...and the whole character of the place so much destroyed, that we were glad when we could leave it'. Earlier, Scott had deplored the destruction of the old gardens, especially of England, in his introduction to *Quentin Durward* (1823). Describing a visit in the early nineteeth century to a château whose gardens had previously boasted a succession of formal terraces, he continued,

Few of these scenes are now left in perfection; for the fickleness of fashion has accomplished in England the total change which devastation and popular fury have produced in the French pleasure-grounds. For my part, I am contented to subscribe to the opinion of the best qualified judge of our time [Uvedale Price], who thinks we have carried to an extreme our taste for simplicity, and that the neighbourhood of a stately mansion requires some more ornate embellishments than can be derived from the meagre accompaniments of grass and gravel. A highly romantic situation may be degraded, perhaps, by an attempt at such artificial ornaments; but then, in by far the greater number of sites, the intervention of more architectural decoration than is now in use, seems necessary to redeem the naked tameness of a large house, placed by itself in the midst of a lawn, where it looks as much unconnected with all around, as if it had walked out of town upon an airing.[4]

A famous example praised by Scott, where a formal garden had not 'degraded' the romantic situation, was Barncluith, near Hamilton in Lanarkshire (Plate 56), with its hanging gardens dating from the late seventeenth or early eighteenth century, carved out of a steep bank overlooking the Avon and Clyde:

Nothing can be more romantic than the scene around: the river sweeps over a dark rugged bed of stone, overhung with trees and bushes; the ruins of the original castle of the noble family of Hamilton frown over the precipice;...It might be thought that the house and garden of Barncluith, with its walks of velvet turf and its verdant alleys of yew and holly, would seem incongruous among natural scenes as magnificent as those we have described. But the effect generally produced is exactly the contrary. The place is so small, that its decorations, while they form, from their antique appearance, a singular foreground, cannot compete with, far less subdue the solemn grandeur of the view which you look down upon.[5]

A terraced garden like Barncluith was determined by the special nature of the site. More common was the inward-looking walled garden, usually a vegetable garden and, from the early eighteenth century, detached from the house though not banished from it as in England. A magnificent example was at Tyninghame, East Lothian, where the eighteenth-century walled garden of almost four acres was transformed into a flower garden in the 1890s (Plate 57).[6]

56. Barncluith, Hamilton, Lanarkshire (c.1700). Drawn by F. Inigo Thomas. [From *The Formal Garden in England*, 1892]

However, it was the seventeenth-century pleasure garden laid out adjacent to the house that provided the main source of inspiration for the garden architects of the 1890s.

A unique early example was the garden added to the traditional tower house of Edzell Castle, Angus in 1604 by Sir David Lindsay (d.1610), son of the 9th Earl of Crawford. The fruits of a rare period of calm, it was reconstituted in 1932 by Dr James Smith Richardson, Inspector of Ancient Monuments. The pleasure ground of just over half an acre has a double-storey summer-house at the south-east corner and is enclosed by massive walls, more for shelter than defence, excluding the surrounding landscape which extends right up to them. Inside, alternate bays have a heraldic chequer-pattern of recesses for wall planting, and mullets above with openings for birds to nest, while between are large rectangular recesses dished

for flowers. The motto of the Lindsays, DUM SPIRO SPERO, has been incorporated in box into the reconstructed parterre (Plate 58).[7] In 1954 Richardson was responsible for another conjectural restoration of a seventeenth-century garden at Pitmedden, Aberdeenshire, using King Charles I's layout of the gardens of Holyrood House as a basis for the design of the formal parterre.[8]

Historical Background to the Formal Revival

Although less formal, Scottish gardens of the seventeenth century tended to follow the English pattern, but from the 1660s there was an attempt at grander layouts and the influence of Le Nôtre could be seen, notably in the work of Sir William Bruce, the architect of Holyrood. From 1663 he remodelled Balcaskie, not far from Kellie, in Fife (Plate 59), laying out gardens in two main terraces

57. Tyninghame, East Lothian (Lord and Lady Haddington and R.P. Brotherston, 1890s): walled garden. [Author 1981]

separated by an eighteen-foot-high retaining wall with deep buttresses now surmounted by busts of Roman Emperors; while at Kinross, the house he built for himself in 1679–93, he created gardens on a larger scale. Such splendid schemes could not ignore the Scottish topography and in both instances Bruce focused them on a prominent feature of the skyline—at Balcaskie, the Bass Rock, and at Kinross, the ruins of a castle in Loch Levin—thereby linking the gardens with the surrounding landscape, an echo of that essential ingredient of the Italian garden, which Blomfield ultimately acknowledged at Mellerstain (see Chapter 1). The grandest garden of all was at Hatton, laid out towards the end of the century; but such magnificent estates were not typical of Scotland. Most seventeenth- and eighteenth-century houses and their gardens were modest in scale, reticent in their architecture—Carnock, Stirlingshire, being a fine example—with walled gardens,

59. Balcaskie, Fife (Sir William Bruce, from 1663). Pastel by Mary Wilson. [From H. Maxwell, *Scottish Gardens*, 1908]

lawns, orchards and belts of protective trees all within a stone boundary wall. At the compartmental garden of Crathes, Kincardineshire, the famous yew hedges were not planted until 1702, and formal gardens were the general rule throughout the reign of Kent and Capability Brown, although in the latter half of the eighteenth century a deeper recognition of local scenery and flora developed, and an ideal of Scottish natural landscape emerged.

In the nineteenth century the strong Scottish botanical interest in plants was reflected in the work of the Scottish landscape gardener and prodigious writer John Claudius Loudon (1783–1843), who published his mammoth *An Encyclopaedia of Gardening* in 1822. An admirer of Repton, in 1832 he coined the term 'gardenesque' which later came to imply the arrangement of trees and shrubs as botanical specimens, a garden 'calculated for displaying the art of the gardener'. The key word here was 'art', and Loudon's catholic views embraced many types of garden, from rustic and picturesque, as seen in the designs of his contemporary and fellow-Scot Charles M'Intosh, to geometric bedding patterns.[9] The Victorian parterre echoed its English counterpart but tended to be less garish in its display of bedding plants. At Dunrobin, near Dornoch, designed in 1845–51 for the second Duke of Sutherland, Sir Charles Barry replaced the old garden in Italianate manner with terraces and a circular parterre. There had been little interest in flowering trees and shrubs during the Victorian era: they were not sufficiently ostentatious. Country-house owners preferred evergreen shrubberies, plantations of laurel, bay, yew, holly and *Rhododendron ponticum*, and the inevitable, suffocating blanket of ivy covering trees, walls, pillars and summer-houses.

The reaction to all this in Scotland owed much to the example of Frances Jane Hope (d.1880) of Wardie Lodge, near Edinburgh, whose articles in *The Gardeners' Chronicle* in the 1860s and 1870s helped to coax the Scottish gardener away from artificial to more natural ways of planting, as Robinson and others were doing south

58. Edzell Castle, Angus (Sir David Lindsay, 1604): parterre. [Author 1981]

of the border. Her book, *Notes and Thoughts on Gardens and Woodlands*, published in 1881, a year after her death and two years before Robinson's *English Flower Garden*, included sections devoted to pleached alleys and arbours, but she did not go beyond making suggestions for their planting. For her 'the garden existed for the plants, not the plants for the garden'.[10] A sense of garden design was missing, but she did prepare the ground for the reception of Arts and Crafts ideas which aimed to strike a balance.

Although Blomfield had praised the old Scotch gardens in his book, it was the young Scottish architect J.J. Joass who first wrote an architectural description of some of the most notable examples, in an article of 1897 in *The Studio* entitled, 'On Gardening: with Descriptions of some Formal Gardens in Scotland'.[11] Joass suggested that the reason why a greater proportion of seventeenth-century gardens had survived in Scotland was one of economy: 'Being a poorer country, perhaps few proprietors could afford to go in for the expense of decorating their grounds in the new manner, levelling the terraces, uprooting the hedges, and forming the artificial lakes with belts and clumps that were then considered correct taste.' His examples, which included Edzell, Balcaskie and Barncluith, were illustrated by his own sketches and measured drawings made in 1893–6. The 'moderate scale' of these gardens, he wrote, made them 'most suggestive models for everyday application when the pleasaunce is becoming again a part of the English dwelling'.[12] Joass did not pursue garden design in his career; his steps took him to London's West End where he became a leading exponent of Edwardian mannerism.[13] It was Robert Lorimer, a young architect devoted to his country's building traditions and imbued with a strong affection for its old gardens, who was to take the leading part in the Scottish formal revival.

Robert Lorimer

The inscription over the entrance doorway of the romantic seventeenth-century castle of Kellie in Fife reads: 'HOC DOMICILIVM CORVIS ET BVBONIBVS EREPTVM HONESTO INTER LABORES OTIO CONSECRATVM EST A.S. MDCCCLXXVIII J.A.H.L.' ('This dwelling, having been cleared of crows and owls, has been devoted to honourable repose from labour'). In 1877 Professor James Lorimer, a distinguished lawyer, obtained a long lease of Kellie and set about lovingly restoring the derelict but virtually unaltered house as a holiday home and recreating the grounds with his family. By 1888 the gardens were complete and, true to the spirit of the seventeenth century, consisted of a series of compartments contained within a walled garth, with grassed alleys, archway of clipped yew, rose trellises and flower beds edged with box. The plan of this garden had been plotted by the Professor's younger son, Robert, and it was Kellie, with its mellow stone walls, turreted turnpike stairs and crow-stepped gables, that first inspired his future career and planted the seeds of his love of old gardens.[14]

Robert Stodart Lorimer (1864–1929) was born in Edinburgh and read Humanities, Greek and Fine Art at the University before entering in 1885 the office of Rowand Anderson, being articled to his partner, Hew Wardrop.[15] Robert Weir Schultz had left the office the previous year to work for Norman Shaw, and in 1889,

having completed his apprenticeship, Lorimer also set out for London, joining the office of G.F. Bodley, attracted by Bodley's close association with craftsmen. However, he remained with Bodley for less than a year, moving to an office with a strong Scots connection, that of the late James M. MacLaren. But, unlike his fellow-expatriates Shaw, J.J. Stevenson, Schultz, J.J. Burnet and J.J. Joass, Lorimer was too deeply rooted in his native land and its architecture to stay away for long. In 1892 he returned to Edinburgh, the immediate cause being to set up in practice on his own on the stength of the commission to restore the sixteenth-century tower house of Earlshall at Leuchars in Fife.

At Earlshall Lorimer was on home ground, for Kellie was only eleven miles away. Like Kellie it was in a dilapidated condition when it was bought in 1891 by R.W. Mackenzie, a friend of the Lorimers. In addition to restoring the house, Lorimer was asked to lay out gardens in the large walled enclosure, a chance for him to create the kind of garden he had admired at Edzell and had helped to recreate at Kellie. Of Kellie he wrote, 'the walled garden enters direct out of the house', and 'flowers, fruit and vegetables are all mixed up together. I always think the ideal plan is to have the park, with the sheep or beasts grazing in it, coming right under the windows at one side of the house, and the gardens attached to the house at another side.'[16] The enclosure at Earlshall was about four times larger than that at Edzell, and Lorimer broke it down into compartments comprising a central pleasaunce, bowling green, orchard and kitchen garden with espaliered fruit trees. As well as creating a series of separate spaces each with its own function and character, this subdivision helped to provide shelter. Even where the site had the potential for framed prospects, openings were seldom made in Scottish walled gardens, views being provided from two-storey garden pavilions or gazeboes—as at Edzell—two of which Lorimer planned originally for the south-east and south-west corners. However, enclosing walls afford only limited protection in a location such as Earlshall, and belts of trees were planted as a shield from the cold North Sea winds. In spite of this, the inscription over the doorway in the east wall reads, 'Here shall ye [sic] see no enemy but winter and rough weather', the quotation from *As You Like It* with which Sedding began his book.

Earlshall is approached through a fine gatehouse to a drive running along the west side of the enclosure, the high garden wall on one side contrasting with open meadows on the other which are bounded only by an open wooden fence. Halfway down this drive an arched gateway gives access almost casually to a cobbled courtyard between house and cottages from which there is an enticing glimpse of the main pleasure garden beyond. The house and garden were shown in a birds-eye perspective by Lorimer's friend, John Begg, in 1894 (Plate 60),[17] but the garden had been much simplified by 1900 when it was drawn by L. Rome Guthrie for Inigo Triggs's *Formal Gardens in England and Scotland* (1902) (Plates 61, 62).[18] The corner pavilions were omitted and the central parterre replaced by a lawn with clipped yews in groups of five and a central sundial in box; but this was revised yet again when the opportunity arose of moving some six-foot yew trees from an abandoned garden. These were arranged on the lawn like chessmen (Plate 63) and have now grown to such proportions that they complement

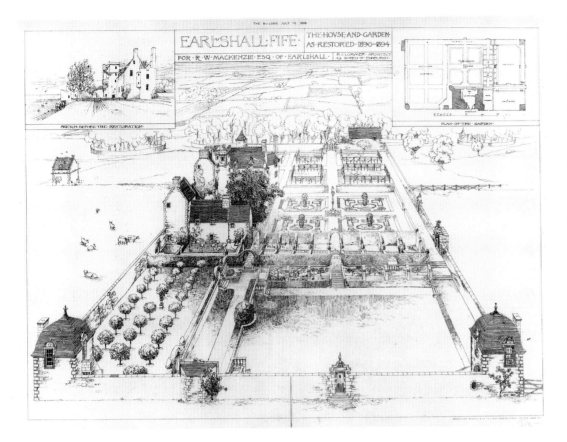

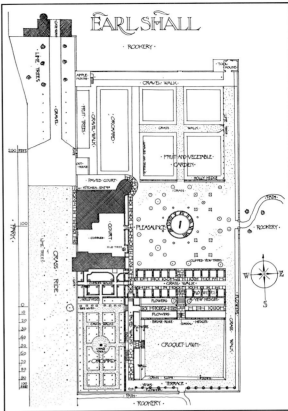

60 (above left). Earlshall, Leuchars, Fife (R.S. Lorimer, from 1892): perspective by John Begg, 1894. [RCAHMS; courtesy of P. Savage]

61 (above right). Earlshall: layout plan, 1900. Drawn by L. Rome Guthrie. [From H.I. Triggs, *Formal Gardens in England and Scotland*, 1902]

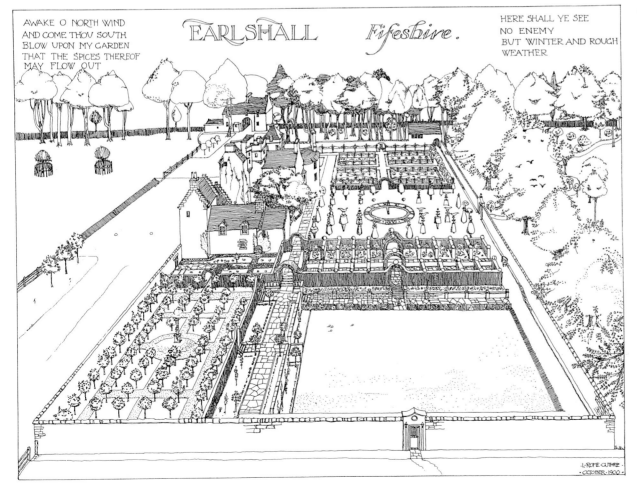

62. Earlshall: perspective by L. Rome Guthrie, 1900 [From H.I. Triggs, *Formal Gardens in England and Scotland*, 1902]

63. Earlshall: topiary garden. [Keith Collection 1900s]

nicely the austere vertical and rounded forms of the house, varying views of which are revealed as one walks between them (Plate 55). The effect must have appealed to Nathaniel Lloyd who provided a similar garden at his home, Great Dixter in Sussex, and who illustrated the Earlshall topiary in his book *Garden Craftsmanship in Yew and Box* (1925). Between this pleasaunce and a croquet lawn to the south was a yew alley or grass walk (Plate 64), bordered by flower beds divided into bays by low yew hedges, containing such old favourites as *Delphinium*, hollyhocks, irises, lilies and *Phlox*. This led to a miniature, box topiary garden crowded with figures, baskets, balls, finials, and so liberally peopled with chickens and ducks that Lloyd remarked, 'fancy has run riot in a whole poultry yard of box!'[19]

In 1898, with the experience of the by-now established garden at

64. Earlshall: the Yew Walk. Watercolour by J. Douglas, R.S.W., c.1905.

Earlshall behind him, Lorimer gave a talk on Scottish gardens to the Edinburgh Architectural Association, subsequently published in the *Architectural Review*.[20] He began by stressing the repose and seclusion that a garden should provide:

A garden is a sort of sanctuary, 'a chamber roofed by heaven.' Wherever intrusion is possible, and any movement other than that of birds is heard, we have no garden in the fullest, sweetest sense of the word....The garden is a little pleasaunce of the soul, by whose wicket the world can be shut out from us.... The true lover of a garden counts time and seasons by his flowers. His calender is the shepherd's calender. He will remember all the events of his years by the trees or plants which were in bloom when they happened. 'The acacias were in flower when we heard...' or 'the hawthorns were all out when we saw...'[21]

This is what Earlshall was intended to be, a haven, a world on its own. Lorimer's style recalls Sedding, whom he quoted in his paper: 'A designer, if his work is to have any freshness, should live and move and have his being in a garden, remembering the eager Sedding's aphorism that "an hour in the garden, a stroll in the embroidered meadows, is better than a month of sixpenny days in a stuffy museum."' On Barncluith he echoed Scott: 'It is the most romantic little garden in Scotland...such an atmosphere about the place. In the twilight or the moonlight destinies might be determined in this garden.' He shared the regret of the author of *Waverley* at the passing of such gardens and acknowledged Earlshall's debt to Edzell:

In Edzell and Earlshall are typical examples of the kind of place that came before the Renaissance had much influence. Here is the ideal for the man who wants to keep only one gardener. The natural park up to the walls of the house on the one side, on the other you stroll right out into the garden inclosed. That is all—a house and a garden inclosed; but what a paradise can such a place be made! Such surprises—little gardens within the garden, the 'month's' garden, the herb garden, the yew alley. The kitchen garden, too, and this no thing to be ashamed of, to be smothered away far from the house, but made delightful by its laying out. Great intersecting walks of shaven grass, on either side borders of brightest flowers backed up by low espaliers hanging with shining apples.

Walled gardens suited the terrian of Kellie and Earlshall, but sloping sites, of which Barncluith was an extreme example, needed terracing to anchor them to the land. This is what Lorimer provided for Frederick Sharp in 1906–7 when he remodelled Wemyss Hall (re-named Hill of Tarvit) near Cupar, Fife, a small classical house of 1696 attributed to Sir William Bruce. Here, Lorimer departed from his usual Baronial style. It is the most classical of his country houses and Blomfield would have appreciated the French flavour of the garden front with its attenuated French windows and balconies, 'apparently chosen to reflect the collection of French eighteenth-century furniture inside'.[22] The restraint, the horizontal mass of the house and the overall sense of repose are reinforced by the succession of terraces which weld the house to the landscape. They descend from the entrance forecourt on the west to a sunken

65. Hill of Tarvit, near Cupar, Fife (R.S. Lorimer, 1906–7): view from the south. [National Trust for Scotland 1980]

rose garden, while the main garden front has a central *perron* flanked by yew cones (Plate 65).[23]

Hill of Tarvit is not typical of Lorimer, but with his following three commissions he was able to arrange the gardens in the way he preferred—making the house open to the landscape on one side, while it gave directly on to an enclosed garden on the other. At Lympne Castle, Kent, restored and enlarged from 1907 to 1912 for F.J. Tennant, a terrace, retained by a curving wall linking old and new buildings, looks south over Romney Marsh, while on the entrance side outbuildings and some walls of old farm buildings enclose a series of courts, including a formal rose garden.[24] At Formakin, Renfrewshire, for the Glasgow stockbroker J.A. Holms,

one of the few completely new large country houses by Lorimer, the gardens were planned and planted in 1908, two years before the house was started. Walled gardens were arranged on ascending levels providing seclusion to the north of the house, while the main rooms looked south across the park and open country.[25] Finally, at Balmanno in Perthshire, the last tower house he restored, Lorimer achieved his ideal.[26] Built in 1916–21 for W.A. Miller, Balmanno is entered from the east through a lodge with central archway into a simple paved and grassed forecourt (Plate 66). Ahead rise the walls of the house with their ivory harling, grey dressings and roofs of Caithness slates. All is calm assurance. A doorway in the south-west corner of the courtyard reveals a chaste formal garden,

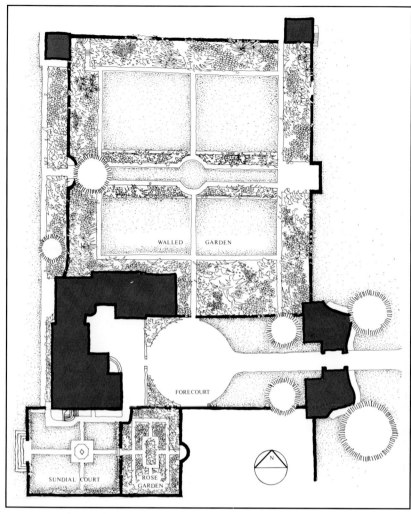

66. Balmanno, Perthshire (R.S. Lorimer, 1916–21): layout plan. [Miranda Ottewill]

67. Balmanno: sundial court. [Author 1981]

68. Balmanno: walled garden. [CL 1931]

exquisite in proportion and detail. Its eastern end contains a small rose garden protected by high walls. Stone steps lead down from the first-floor drawing-room to a sundial garden enclosed by low walls (Plate 67). To the west, across expansive lawns, is a prospect of trees, a pond and open landscape. Lorimer added a low, two-storey service wing to the north of the sixteenth-century tower and beyond this he laid out a large, square garden enclosed by high walls against which grew cordon apples and pears, a potting house and gazebo marking its north-east and north-west corners. Across the centre, flanked by trellises supporting espaliered apple trees, is a grassed alley, entered from a gateway at its western end and terminating in a covered sitting-place (Plate 68). Here is the perfect expression of that old-fashioned mixture of fruit, flowers and vegetables that Lorimer had known at Kellie. The restraint, breadth, scale and subtle colouring of the gardens of Balmanno show Lorimer at his mature best. Possibly the austere sundial court introduces a note of monumentality at the expense of domesticity, but this is not to deny its elegant and tranquil beauty. Of all his works, Balmanno was the house Lorimer would have chosen to live in himself.

Lorimer and his Contemporaries

Lorimer's devotion to the cause of creating a modern Scottish style rooted in tradition stands out by comparison with his contemporary, Charles Rennie Mackintosh (1868–1928). They shared an admiration for the Scottish Baronial, but Mackintosh was an individualist, with leanings towards continental art movements. He seems to have had little interest in, or at least opportunities for, garden design, being more preoccupied with the interiors of his houses, or their appearance as sculptural objects in a landscape of stylized shrubs and trees, which he stipulated were to be clipped in accordance with the *fin-de-siècle* manner of his drawings (Plate 69).[27]

69. Hill House, Helensburgh (C.R. Mackintosh, 1902): perspective by Mackintosh. [Glasgow School of Art]

Lorimer had more in common with Schultz, who had preceded him at Rowand Anderson's office, and who, although he did not return to his native land, carried out much work there after St John's Lodge, especially as architect to the Marquesses of Bute. Gardens featured in a number of these commissions such as House of Falkland, Fife, a Jacobean-style house of 1839 by William Burn, where from 1896 Schultz laid out ornamental gardens and designed garden buildings for the park including a circular, thatched summer-house.[28] His work for the Bute family did not end when the 3rd Marquess died in 1900. The 4th Marquess was interested in projects of his own and in 1903 employed Schultz to refurnish the interior and improve the grounds of Old Place of Mochrum, two miles from Port William on the west coast. Hunter Blair's description of Mochrum—'a queer two-storied tower set in the middle of a wild Wigtownshire moor, on the edge of a gloomy lake'[29]—hardly does justice to the beauty of moorland and loch of this corner of Galloway. Schultz refurbished the courtyard with diagonal paving and cobblestones and a wrought-iron well-head made in Ernest Gimson's workshop. To the south he laid out a new walled garden consisting of a square parterre with central sundial and diagonal paths bordered by grass strips enclosing triangular beds of shrubs and flowers (Plates 70, 71). The paths link rugged doorways in the rubble stone enclosing walls but by contrast with

70. Old Place of Mochrum, Wigtownshire (Robert Weir Schultz, 1903): parterre. [Keith Collection c.1906]

71. Old Place of Mochrum: garden front. [*CL* 1912]

the easterly exposure of Edzell and Earlshall, Mochrum's milder climate allowed a more open treatment for the south boundary, where the wall drops to a low, castellated parapet between raised platforms at each corner (Plate 72).[30] This south wall, with its primitive stonework and flanking prospects and stone seats, is an imaginative response to the site, a sense of communion with the wild moorland being maintained yet from within the safe confines of the pleasaunce.

Lorimer was sometimes seen as the 'Scottish Lutyens', probably owing to Lawrence Weaver who, as architectural editor of *Country Life*, did much to publicize the work of both architects.[31] In fact Lorimer anticipated Lutyens in certain garden features, such as the imaginative use of compartments, changes of level, intersecting axes, ground patterns, the design of garden buildings. Moreover,

72. Old Place of Mochrum: south-west prospect. [Keith Collection c.1906]

Lutyens was not always as successful as Lorimer, or Schultz, in creating subtle links with the adjoining landscape, a case in point being his Grey Walls, East Lothian (see Chapter 5).

Lorimer must have envied Lutyens's close association with Gertrude Jekyll. In his paper of 1898 he stressed the importance of working closely with horticulturists:

> provided the architect has sufficient tact not to try and teach the nurseryman his own business, he will very soon recognize him, not as his enemy, but as his friend, and come to see that the only way to arrive at a successful garden scheme, large or small, is for the two to work into each other's hands, and it is done like this: the architect roughs out his scheme, under the influence of the place if he is wise, then after the main lines have been settled, the nurseryman, with his knowledge of what happens to flourish best in that particular country-side, is called in. The whole affair is discussed and rediscussed, and after a certain amount of give-and-take the work quietly proceeds.[32]

He had been introduced to Jekyll in 1897 by E.P. Benson for whom he built Whinfold at Hascombe in Surrey, and he went to see her at about the time she was moving into her new house, Munstead Wood. 'She's a great authority on gardening and arts and crafts', he wrote, 'and a great character generally'.[33] It was Munstead that inspired Lorimer to plan the garden before the house at Formakin, an example that other zealous Arts and Crafts designers were to follow.

Gardens into Natural Landscape

The sympathetic chord that Gertrude Jekyll struck in Lorimer echoed a native interest in botany and practical gardening. But there was another Scottish thread that the architectural approach of Blomfield and Lorimer tended to disregard, namely a poetic and emotional response to nature which reached back to the age of Romanticism and was anticipated in 1763 by Kames's *Elements of Criticism*.[34] By the time the landscape style began to have an influence in Scotland,[35] an ideal had developed which sought to respond more positively to the wildness of the Scottish landscape, to that all-pervasive image of Highland scenery. The movement was boosted early in the nineteenth century by Loudon who advocated local flora 'proper for wild scenery'.[36] Combined with a new national awareness fostered by Scott's romances and the Victorian botanical interest in trees and plants, this led to wild gardens such as Inverewe, begun by Osgood MacKenzie in 1864. Not all Scottish gardens of the late nineteenth and early twentieth centuries retreated from the challenge of the hostile landscape and sheltered behind stone walls; some sought to come to terms with it, to gain inspiration from it, even to emulate it. Such a romantic approach reached its apogee at Corrour, in a desolate, rain-swept moorland north of Rannoch in Inverness-shire.

In this unpromising region, 1,250 feet above sea level on the water-logged shores of Loch Ossian, Sir John Stirling-Maxwell chose the site for his new shooting lodge and between 1894 and 1904 laid out a series of remarkable gardens, with the firm of L. and J. Falconer of Fort William as his architects. The house was built on a moraine of granite boulders, and along the south front a formal terrace was constructed. The alpines and herbs that flourished in the crevices of its walls and steps would have gladdened the heart of Miss Jekyll: the blues and purples of *Campanula*, gentians, forget-me-nots, *Cyananthus lobatus* and *Lithospermum gastoni* mingling with the pinks of *Acantholimum glumaceum* and *Dianthus neglectus* against a pearly-white background of *Oxalis enneaphylla*.

73. Corrour, Loch Ossian, Inverness-shire (Sir John Stirling-Maxwell, 1894–1904): alpine garden. Pastel by Mary Wilson. [From H. Maxwell, *Scottish Gardens*, 1908]

But it was as an integral part of the natural landscape between this terrace and the loch that the most memorable of Corrour's alpine gardens was made.

Six years after the gardens were completed, Maxwell's father-in-law, Sir Herbert Maxwell, described them in *Scottish Gardens*, published in 1908.[37] Although the book included also the most notable old formal gardens, Maxwell's preference for the natural approach is evident. For instance, in place of the ivy-covered walls, yew topiary and box edging to the Dutch beds at Barncluith, he would have preferred shrubs and 'the flowers of all seasons'. The ancestry of alpine gardening reached back to the eighteenth century, but it was associated with the rock garden, a contempt for which Maxwell shared with Blomfield: 'the effort of make-believe is almost always distressingly obvious' he wrote.

But is is otherwise at Corrour. No need to pile rocks in laborious imitation of a ravine; they lie here naturally in profusion as they were thrown down ages ago by the retreating glacier; and as for environment, let the broad flanks and towering crests of Carn Dearg, Beinn Bhreich and Beinn Eibhinn suffice for that, with the fair expanse of Loch Ossian at their feet. To turn this into an alpine garden little more has been necessary than to root out the heather and wild grasses from certain pockets and hollows, fill them with good soil and plant choice bell-flowers, globe flowers, primulas, saxifrages, speedwells, dianthus, and a rich variety of other flowering herbs.[38]

Scottish Gardens was illustrated by Mary Wilson, whose pastel of Corrour (Plate 73) depicts irises, *Spiraea*, and other water-loving plants that thrive at such altitudes, growing naturally amongst the boulders and native heaths and grasses, their drifts of muted yellow and purple set against the grey-blue background of loch, mountain and sky, a perfect union of the beautiful and the sublime. Nothing could be further from the formal Scottish pleasaunce, yet Corrour expressed equally important characteristics of the Scottish garden. It was the creation of an individual, with a special botanical interest, responding to a particular location; it was also an instance of that attitude to gardening, publicized by Robinson in 1870 with *The Wild Garden*, which seeks guidance in the spontaneity of nature.

74. Heale House, Woodford, Wiltshire (Hon. Louis Greville): Japanese garden (c.1901). [Author 1984]

4

The Naturalistic Garden

A garden must be spontaneous—allowed to spring from the ground in a natural way—otherwise it is devoid of that irresistible something called style, for style is born out of the shaping of use and beauty to environment. So I would make a plea for naturalness in gardens.

The Craftsman, 1911[1]

Most Edwardian gardens followed the precepts of Sedding, and Repton before him, in being formal near the house but naturalistic beyond. These 'natural' or wilder areas were often the more notable, providing scope for the increasing influx and cultivation of exotic flora such as alpine and water-loving plants. They might include rock, water, woodland or wild gardens. Sometimes the work of designers, more often they were the unself-conscious creations of amateurs or head gardeners whose interest was concentrated on the plants themselves, on nature's own forms. As outlined in Chapter 1, it was William Robinson (1838–1935) (Plate 75), the Irish gardener-cum-journalist and fierce opponent of formalism, who was the principal proselytizer of this so-called 'natural' gardening.[2]

William Robinson

When Robinson escaped to London in 1861 at the age of twenty-two, he went to the Royal Botanic Society's Garden in Regent's Park to work under its designer and curator, Robert Marnock (1800–89). Marnock had rejected the architectural gardening of the 1850s in favour of a development of the English Landscape School and the Gardenesque, and was to establish a reputation in the 1860s as the 'leading landscaper of the post-Nesfield period.'[3] Later, Robinson recalled,

> there was at that time a small garden of British plants, which had to be kept up, and this led me into the varied country around London, from the orchid-flecked meadows of Bucks to the tumbled down undercliffs on the Essex coasts, untroubled by the plough, and so I began to get an idea (which should be taught to every boy at school) that there was (for gardens even) much beauty in our native flowers and trees, and then came the thought that if there was so much in our own island flora, what might we not look for from the hills and valleys of the countries of the northern and temperate world?[4]

In 1863 he began writing articles for journals, including *The Gardeners' Chronicle* and *The Field*, and in 1866 left the Botanic Gardens to become a freelance writer and journalist. His first books, *Gleanings from French Gardens* (1868), and *The Parks, Promenades and Gardens of Paris* (1869), were the fruits of a period spent in France from January 1867 where he was horticultural correspondent of *The Times* for the Paris Exhibition. In 1870 *The Wild Garden* appeared and the following year he launched *The Garden*, the first of many periodicals founded by him, including the successful *Gardening* (from 1879), later called *Gardening Illustrated*. *The English Flower Garden* (1883) was his *magnum opus*, going through fifteen editions in his own lifetime. The first part included recommendations for every conceivable type of garden, and the second part comprised a dictionary of most of the hardy and half-hardy plants suitable for the British flower garden.

A shrewd businessman and literary magpie—substantial slices of his books were contributed by other authors, often unacknowledged, or were repeated from his previous publications[5]—Robinson's phenomenal success as a writer and propagandist enabled him in 1884 to purchase Gravetye Manor at West Hoathly in Sussex, a late Elizabethan, ironmaster's house, where he lived for the remainder of his life.[6] Here, he was at last able to put his ideas into practice, and gradually he acquired further adjoining land until by 1892 the Gravetye estate boasted over a thousand acres, its principal feature being five hundred acres of richly planted woodland. Although he had waged a crusade for wild gardening, the grounds were not free of formal elements. There was a vast, oval, kitchen and fruit garden; a massive pergola which curved in a gentle gradient from the flower garden up to the bowling green; and in 1902 Robinson replaced the west lawn with forty-six manageably sized rectangular beds for his roses, carnations and other favourite plants (Plate 76). For convenience of access and planting the beds were divided by walks paved with old York-stone slabs from London pavements, their appearance marred by edgings from the same flagstones.[7] Two years earlier he had enclosed the garden to north and west with an oak pergola and trellis, heavily clothed in summer with *Wisteria*, roses and vines (Plate 77). There was a central sundial and a shady south-west corner with stone table, near which, in 1910, he added a summer-house designed by Ernest George. Beyond the south retaining wall, the Alpine Meadow, planted with early bulbs, sloped down to the lake.[8]

Millais's *Ophelia* (1851–2) (Plate 78), which combined a faithful rendering of Shakespeare's 'crow-flowers, nettles, daisies and long purples [Loosestrife]', with a Pre-Raphaelite observation of nature, anticipated the theme of *The Wild Garden*.[12] The first edition contained an essay on 'The Garden of British Wild Flowers', expanded in the 1894 edition to include native trees. Robinson argued for the natural grouping of the flowers and trees of field and hedgerow and his words brought these ideas before a wide public.

Just as Morris had romanticized old-fashioned flowers, *The English Flower Garden* glorified the somewhat mythical image of the English cottage garden (Plate 79), with its roses, honeysuckle, madonna lilies, foxgloves, hollyhocks, marigolds, gillyflowers and primroses. John Parkinson described these in his *Paradisi in Sole Paradisus Terrestris* (1629), and they had grown in the 'old-fashioned' seventeenth-century borders. Somehow they had managed to survive the nineteenth-century mania for bedding-out, a few being relegated to the kitchen garden, others escaping to 'the little gardens of the rectories, the old maids' houses and the country convents'.[13] Robinson praised the unself-conscious, simple materials of these

75. William Robinson, photographed at Gravetye in 1909. [Courtesy of P. Herbert, Gravetye Manor Hotel]

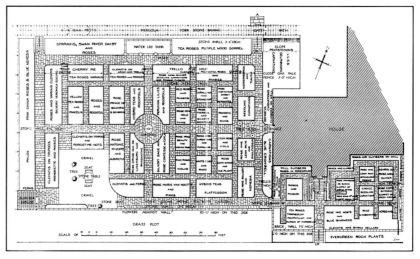

76. Gravetye Manor, West Hoathly, Sussex (William Robinson, from 1885): plan of paved west garden, 1902. [*CL* 1912]

77. Gravetye Manor: paved garden from the east. Watercolour by Margaret Waterfield. [From *Garden Colour*, 1905]

The Wild Garden, sub-titled 'or our Groves and Shrubberies made beautiful by the Naturalization of Hardy Exotic Plants', is Robinson's most enduring work. He explained in the preface that he did not have in mind a garden run wild, nor one that would 'interfere with the regulation flower garden', and even as late as 1903 he felt the need to explain to critics that his aim was 'to show that we could have all the joy of spring in orchard, meadow or wood, lawn or grove, and so save *the true flower-garden near the house* from being torn up twice a year to effect what is called spring and summer "bedding".'[9] The book was aimed at the owners of country houses with grounds that extended far beyond their gardens: 'among the ways of escape from the death-note of the pastry-cook's garden there is none more delightful to all who have any grass or fields or woods about them'.[10] The 1881 edition was beautifully illustrated by Alfred Parsons, depicting drifts of bulbs naturalized in woodland; plants growing amongst heather, in copses, beside streams or over cottage walls; wild roses covering a pollarded ash; and common trees were described: willow, poplar, wild cherry, medlar, crab and may. Movements in architecture and garden design often derive from literature or painting. Robinson admired the simple portrayal of nature of the English Landscape painters such as Crome, Constable and Turner,[11] and paintings like

78. John Everett Millais, *Ophelia*, 1851–2. [The Tate Gallery, London]

gardens, also of the cottages themselves which had 'braved several hundred winters'. In *The Wild Garden* he objected chauvinistically, 'The passion for the exotic is so universal that our own finest plants are never planted',[14] a view at variance with his definition of the essence of wild-gardening as 'the placing of perfectly hardy exotic plants from the northern and temperate regions under conditions where they will thrive without further care'. Robinson could sometimes run with the hare and hunt with the hounds!

Few of his ideas were original. Many of the reforms he advocated had been advanced by other writers including Shirley Hibberd who had attacked the exclusive use of bedding, advancing the hardly herbaceous border as the more important feature.[15] The botanist Forbes Watson, author of *Flowers and Gardens: Notes on Plant Beauty* (1872), argued for the treatment of flowers as individual living beings and praised both cottage gardens and wild flowers.[16] In the cultivation of plants from abroad, much of the pioneering spade work had been done by plantsmen such as Augustus Smith, who from the 1830s established his garden on Tresco, Isles of Scilly; also by Osgood Mackenzie, who in 1864 founded Inverewe, near Poolewe on the west coast of Scotland, transforming a barren peninsula into an exotic garden where plants from many countries flourished in luxuriant profusion. The naturalization of bulbs in woodlands, promoted by Peter Barr in the 1860s,[17] was another idea that anticipated *The Wild Garden*, but what Robinson did achieve was to put all this knowledge within the reach of many and thereby help to enlarge the gardener's vocabulary of foliage plants beyond what was generally considered acceptable for gardens.

But *The Wild Garden* was optimistic in its suggestion that the 'natural' garden needed virtually no control. In the words of Reginald Farrer, 'The ordinary wild garden is the very worst and most extravagant of frauds, requiring a supervision no less incessant and close than any parterre or border',[18] and Mrs Earle warned, 'In spite of all the charming things Mr Robinson says about it, "wild gardening" is, I am sure, a delusion and a snare,' and 'must be

taken with a great many grains of salt.'[19] None the less, the book was timely and its style eloquent and persuasive enough to establish Robinson as the oracle of a new concept of naturalness and 'permanent' gardening in the 1870s.

Robinson's emphasis on nature came at a time when it was guaranteed to have a strong appeal to his readers. The success of his books and journals is a mark of the wide influence he exerted, and the grounds of almost all late-Victorian and Edwardian country houses had their wilder regions. Nowhere were his ideas put to more dramatic effect than in his native Ireland. Sub-tropical vegetation was no newcomer to that country; at Fota, County Cork, James Hugh Smith-Barry began planting the arboretum and gardens in about 1810.[20] But in places like the southern coast of County Kerry off the Kenmare estuary, 'Robinsonian' gardens flourished beyond his wildest dreams.[21] They included Lord Lansdowne's at Derreen, and the island garden created by Samuel Heard at Rossdohan with its tree ferns and bamboos, both begun in the 1870s. Close by, from about 1900, the 4th Earl of Dunraven transformed Garinish Island at Parknasilla into another sub-tropical wild garden.[22] Robinson often visited Lord Dunraven's island which illustrated admirably many of his prescriptions for wild-gardening. Its reddish sandstone provided an excellent natural base for some of the plants he had described in *Alpine Flowers for English Gardens*, also published in 1870, the outcome of a walking excursion in 1868 in the Swiss Alps.

The Rock Garden

Blomfield may have ridiculed it, but an Edwardian country house would have been considered incomplete without its rock garden. Originating in the eighteenth-century grotto or cascade and in the aesthetic preoccupations of the Picturesque and the Sublime,[23] by the 1860s the purpose of a rock garden had become the cultivation of alpine plants in a setting resembling as near as possible their native surroundings; in short, 'a deliberate imitation of nature'.[24] The mounting appreciation for the delicate beauty of these plants

79. Cottage garden, Mattingley, Hampshire. [From *The English Flower Garden*, 1883]

80. Sandringham, Norfolk (W.B. Thomas and James Pulham): upper lake and rockery (1868–75). [Author 1984]

nicely complemented the Victorian love of mountains and rocks both for geological study and as a Ruskinian subject for art. Few gardens could boast the authentic setting of Corrour, but most rock gardens attempted to recreate similar mountainous habitats. The best material was weather-worn limestone, but since the whole thing was a pretence anyway, few had qualms about importing stone from one part of the country to another.

One of the earliest professional rockwork firms was that founded by James Pulham (1820–98) of Broxbourne, Hertfordshire, whose father had helped to pioneer Portland cement. Pulham devised a highly successful artificial stone called 'Pulhamite'. His enormous output included work at Highnam Court, Gloucester (1847–84), Battersea Park, London (1866–70) and Madresfield Court, Malvern (late 1870s).[25] A remarkably realistic example of his reproduction of geological strata can be seen at Sandringham, Norfolk, where the Prince of Wales virtually rebuilt the Georgian-cum-Victorian house in 1867–70 to the designs of A.J. Humbert. For the grounds he employed the professional landscape gardener, William Brod-

rick Thomas (see also Chapter 1), who later made alterations to the grounds of Buckingham Palace (of which Queen Victoria disapproved).[26] At Sandringham, Thomas removed the ornamental pool, laid out two lakes to the south, and brought in Pulham for cliffs, waterfalls, a rocky stream, rocky pathways (now planted with dwarf conifers), and a boat house in the form of a cave on the east side of the upper lake (Plate 80). 'I am very *much* pleased with your work', Thomas told Pulham, 'and I consider the Boat House quite a work of art. I will say again I was very *much* pleased with everything, and hope H.R.H. will be.'[27] When in the course of the work at Sandringham Thomas broke his leg, 'the Princess Alexandra showed him such kindness that he sent her white roses on her birthday for the rest of his life.'[28]

The strata system of rockwork can also be seen at Swaylands, Penshurst, Kent, an early nineteenth-century house remodelled by George Devey and with gardens laid out by the owner, George Drummond, from 1886 (Plate 81);[29] and at the Rock Garden at Wisely, built of Sussex sandstone in 1911 by Pulham's firm under

81. Swaylands, Penshurst, Kent (George Drummond): rock garden (from 1886). [RCHME; W.J. Day c.1906]

82. Friar Park, Henley-on-Thames, Oxfordshire (Frank Crisp): rock garden (from 1896). [RCHME; Newton c.1907]

the general direction of the landscape gardener, Edward White (1873–1952).[30] Some rock gardens were modelled on the moraine, a magnificent early specimen being that created in the 1850s by John Hutton Balfour at the Royal Botanic Garden, Edinburgh; an example of Pulham and Sons' work in this vein was the richly planted rockery of the 1890s at Gatton Park, Surrey, for Jeremiah Colman.[31]

The dominant figure of the Edwardian rock garden, and its chief chronicler, was the botanist Reginald Farrer (1880–1920), whose writing was as fearless as his zest for travel. Farrer's passion for alpines was engendered by an early interest in his parents' limestone rock garden at Ingleborough, West Yorkshire, and kindled further while at Oxford by visits to the rock garden at St John's College, the creation of the Bursar and alpine gardener, the Reverend H.J. Bidder (1847–1923). In 1908 Farrer published *Alpines and Bog Plants* followed in 1909 by *My Rock Garden*, and in 1912 he began the encyclopaedic *The English Rock Garden*, the peak of his achievement, published in 1919. In that year he made his last and fatal exploration to Upper Burma in search of new rock plants. His quest for *Primula* and other plants took him on several expeditions to the Dolomites with his friend, the renowned horticulturist E.A. Bowles (1865–1954). He dedicated *Among the Hills* (1911) to him, helped him to plan a 'moraine' at the rock garden at his home, Myddelton House, near Enfield, Middlesex,[32] and in 1914 wrote the preface to Bowles's *My Garden in Spring*.

Farrer took the opportunity of this preface for a dig at the more extravagant rock gardens like the one at Friar Park, Henley-on-Thames: 'the very rich are out to purchase the glories of the Alps at so much a yard', he wrote.[33] Friar Park's fantastic rock garden, consisting of 23,000 tons of rock, including a scaled-down Matterhorn, and harbouring about 2,500 different kinds of mountain plants (Plate 82), was begun in 1896 at the behest of the eccentric and wealthy solicitor, Frank Crisp (1848–1919). Crisp included microscopy and horticulture amongst his recreations and from 1881

to 1906 was Vice-President and Treasurer of the Linnean Society of London. The interior of his monstrous, 'French, Flamboyant Gothic'-style house incorporated various jokes on the theme of the friar. But it was in the grounds that eclecticism ran riot. Bewildered visitors were shown every type and style of garden, including eight medieval gardens based on fifteenth-century paintings.[34] In about 1905 Lady Ottoline Morrell was entertained there and described how, 'dressed in a long frock coat and top hat and with a large umbrella in his hands', Crisp showed visitors the 'sham Swiss mountains and passes, decorated by china chamois... and elaborate caves and underground lakes, lit up with electricity, and festooned with artificial grapes, spiders, and other monsters'[35] These gardens were divided into a patchwork of compartments, each one an entity in itself rather than part of a unified whole, a device that enabled owners to indulge a variety of fancies or whims. A popular and later example of this arrangement exists at Compton Acres, Poole, where, from 1919, seven distinct gardens were added to a neo-Tudor villa for Thomas William Simpson.

The Japanese Garden

Both Friar Park and Compton Acres included 'Disneyland' versions of the demented but short-lived craze for the Japanese garden.[36] More ambitious than the rock garden's straightforward imitation of nature, it attempted to recreate what was already a highly sophisticated interpretation of Japanese landscape. Being both naturalistic and alien, nothing could have been viewed with greater contempt by the Blomfield camp. How could reproducing and transplanting the motifs of the Japanese garden possibly hope to capture its esoteric spirit? Yet so irresistible and deceptively simple was its image that by the end of the Edwardian decade almost every self-respecting large garden had one in some form or another. The fashion reached Britain following the penetration of Japanese art to Europe in the 1860s, and the opening of trade with the west in the early seventies. By the time that Christopher Dresser's *Japan, its Architecture, Art and Art Manufactures* was published in 1882, Japanese prints, screens and fans had become requisite features of the 'Aesthetic' interior, as promoted by Liberty's and parodied in *The Mikado* in 1885 when the Japanese bonanza reached its peak.

Specimens of Japanese flora—if not its garden art—had been brought back by travellers such as Robert Fortune in 1860–62. A more important, and sometimes unwitting, influence came from diplomats serving in Tokyo, notably A. B. Freeman-Mitford (1837–1916, created Baron Redesdale in 1902), who was a member of the British diplomatic mission from 1866 to 1868. He developed a love of the country's culture and landscape and in 1871 published his classic *Tales of Old Japan*. His interest in botany dated from 1874 when, as Secretary to H.M.'s Office of Works in London, the Royal Parks came under his care. In his autobiography he described how he laid out the Dell at the lower (eastern) end of the Serpentine in Hyde Park 'as a sub-tropical garden with palms, tree ferns, dracaenas and other beauties, planted the little stream with water-lilies, royal fern and so forth, and made it from an eyesore and a den of horrors into what it now is'.[37] In 1886 he inherited Batsford Park, near Moreton-in-Marsh, Gloucestershire, and from 1887 to 1893 replaced the Georgian house with a neo-Tudor one designed by Ernest George and Peto. He then set about creating an arboretum and a number of wild gardens in the grounds.[38] These were by no means Japanese in style. To him the Japanese garden was 'a mere whimsical toy', a mystery of 'symbols hard to be understood'.[39] Batsford did, however, include many flora from China and Japan, notably a collection of fifty species and varieties of hardy bamboos which he described in *The Bamboo Garden* (1896), a *catalogue raisonné* of those then in British cultivation which attempted 'to focus such information in regard to them as could be obtained from Japanese as well as European sources'. The book was handsomely illustrated by Alfred Parsons who in the same year published *Notes in Japan*, the product of his own visit there from 1892 to 1894.

The first books to set down the principles and provide a proper vocabulary of the garden arts of Japan were by an English architect who settled there in 1877. Josiah Conder (1852–1920) was educated in Bedford and articled to Professor T. Roger Smith, after which he worked for William Burges, winning the Soane Medallion in 1875. The following year he joined the Public Works Department in Tokyo and in 1886 became a lecturer at the Imperial University. Conder formed a bridge between Japanese and Western styles of architecture through his buildings and his articles and books, the first of which, *The Flowers of Japan and the Art of Floral Arrangement* (1891) was followed in 1893 by *Landscape Gardening in Japan*. The danger with treatises of this kind is that they are open to literal interpretation, and those who had access to Conder's comprehensive manual would have lost no time in reproducing its conveniently illustrated descriptions. But, to do him justice, Conder did have another and higher purpose for his book: 'some may...hold that landscape gardening should be typical of the scenery of the soil, and regard the servile imitation of a foreign style as unnatural and purposeless,' he wrote in his preface. 'To this class the abstract principles of the Art may prove not totally

unworthy of attention, and may even supply suggestion for a modified form of Western gardening.'[40] The assimilation of the Shinto and Buddhist philosophies underlying oriental landscape architecture had to wait until the 1930s. Few Edwardians, even those who had set foot in Japan, were likely to appreciate the 'abstract principles' of the Japanese garden or the symbolism of its restrained planting and judiciously placed boulders reflected in calm water; and if they had aspired to such subtle effects, did not England have her own natural landscape school to turn to? They only wanted to stage an illusion of the style and that could be done with the aid of an oriental bridge, some rocks, stunted pines, bamboos and irises, a stone lantern or two by the pool, with the possible addition of a 'Garden Arbour' or 'Tea-Room'. And the great advantage of the Japanese garden was that it could be conveniently reduced to miniature scale and a corner found for it somewhere in the grounds. Conder supplied details for it all.

By the turn of the century the cult of the Japanese garden was well under way. Another dipolmat, Hon. Louis Greville (1856–1941), 2nd Secretary at the British Embassy in Tokyo in 1882–7, incorporated one into the grounds of Heale House, Woodford, Wiltshire in about 1901 after his return from abroad. Situated beyond the formal gardens laid out by Harold Peto, it includes a red-lacquered bridge and, also straddling the stream, a thatched tea-house complete with sliding walls, all made in Japan and put up by two Japanese carpenters. Happily, this garden survives together with much of the planting of Japanese maples, willow, *Magnolia soulangiana*, bamboos and irises (Plate 74).[41] Peto used his own free interpretation of Japanese wood construction for the tea-house (c.1902) at the edge of the lake at Easton Lodge, Essex, for Greville's sister-in-law, the Countess of Warwick.[42] It soon became the thing to use genuine Japanese gardeners. Heale was based on a plan prepared by one and they were employed at New Place, Haslemere (c.1901) (see Chapter 6) which had a Japanese temple, and where every plant was of Japanese origin.[43] At Fanhams Hall, Ware, Hertfordshire (1900–1), for Captain R.P. Croft, not only were two Japanese gardeners imported every summer but the garden was laid out by Professor Suzuki from Japan. As at Heale, this garden included an authentic Japanese tea-house, brought over from an exhibition in Paris.[44]

By about 1905 the Japanese garden was all the rage but, with increasing concern for authenticity, it became the custom to employ professional Japanese designers. A notable example was at Tully, Kildare, where Colonel W. Hall Walker (created Baron Wavertree in 1919), brought in an expert, Tasa Eida, to direct an army of Irish gardeners. It seems that he was not given a free hand, however, as the inscription states, 'devised by Lord Wavertree and made by Eida and his son Meiroru between 1906 and 1910'.[45] Herbert Goode, a wealthy china and glass merchant, whose shop was almost as important as Liberty's in spreading the taste for Chinese and Japanese goods, began by despatching stone lanterns and a tea-house back from Japan in 1905 for his garden at Cottered, near Buntingford, Hertfordshire, but in 1923 he commissioned the landscape architect, Seyemon Kusumoto to complete what was probably the most impresssive example of a Japanese garden in England. It has cascades and pools with specially imported stones, and a 'path of life' which leads across the bridge through a Shinto archway and up between *Kasuga* stone lanterns to a small shrine amongst the pine trees.[46] Most would-be Japanese gardens were not so successful. One was begun in 1908 at Powerscourt, County Wicklow, for the 8th Viscount Powerscourt; it had the regulation red bridge and stone lantern, with Japanese tortoises and bronze cranes,[47] but, as Lawrence Weaver pointed out in 1915,

> The importation of exotic motives into garden design in England is dangerous, not only because they are rarely understood, but because there are few sites where they can take their place at all naturally. The disposition of a few typical ornaments, of a bronze stork here and a stone lantern there, does not make a Japanese garden; it only makes an English garden speak with a Japanese accent.[48]

The Water Garden

Nevertheless, the influence of Japan during the Edwardian period provided a fresh impetus for the advocates of informality not only in planting[49] but also in the use of water, that indispensable feature of the Japanese garden. An important element of both the eighteenth-century landscape park and the formal garden, water also provided the ideal setting for the wild garden. Robinson devoted a chapter of his book to 'Brookside, Water and Bog Gardens'; 'many pictures might be formed by a brook on its way through glade or meadow',[50] he wrote, and he noted how the margins of lakes and streams could be enhanced by the natural grouping of hardy flowers—irises, lilies, *Gunnera*, meadow-sweet, ferns—with water-plants such as flowering rushes and *Nymphaea*. Some of his best writing described the aesthetic effect of small groups of water-lilies, and in *The English Flower Garden* he praised the pioneering work of B. Latour-Marliac, nurseryman at Temple-sur-Lot, 'who has added the large and noble forms and the lovely colour of the Eastern Water Lilies to the garden waters of northern countries'.[51]

Probably the most spectacular water garden of the period in the British Isles was developed as part of the garden paradise of Bodnant at Tal-y-Cafn, Denbighshire. Situated on a hillside looking west towards Snowdonia, the estate was bought in 1875 by Henry Pochin, MP, an industrial chemist from Salford. With the landscape gardener Edward Milner (1819–84), Pochin was largely responsible for the additional planting of conifers and other trees in the area deep below the house known as the Dell, a rocky gorge of the heroic scale beloved of the Victorians, down which the River Hiraethlyn plunges to the Conway. Beginning in the late 1890s a series of formal terraces was laid out west of the house. These were initiated by Pochin's daughter, Laura McLaren, but designed and constructed in 1904–14 mainly by her son, Henry Duncan McLaren (1879–1953), later to become the 2nd Lord Aberconway. Subsequently the Dell was transformed with an amazing collection of rhododendrons and azaleas, planted beneath the giant conifers, while the river was edged with lady ferns, irises, *Spiraea*, *Hydrangea*, *Primula* and other mosisture-loving plants, a realization of many of Robinson's suggestions (Plate 83).[52]

83. Bodnant, Tal-y-Cafn, Denbighshire (2nd Lord Aberconway): the Dell (c.1900). [The National Trust 1982; by kind permission of Lord Aberconway and the National Trust]

In 1905, while work was under way on the new terraces at Bodnant, Richard Grove Annesley, whose wife was a cousin of Lady Aberconway, began his gardens at Annes Grove, near Castletownroche in County Cork. It would be difficult to find a more enchanting wild water garden. Annesley's enthusiasm for planting, dating from a spell in British Columbia as a young man, lasted throughout his life, and Annes Grove is almost entirely his memorial alone.[53] Approached past a delightful castellated lodge, the house dates from the early eighteenth century and faces north on to a landscaped park. There are three separate gardens in the grounds: an old walled garden, made into a flower garden in Victorian times and complete with rustic, Gothic summer-house; a woodland garden extending along a belt of acid soil at the top of the cliff where, in the 1920s, a remarkable collection of Himalayan rhododendrons was planted amongst the native trees; and finally the water garden, situated behind the house where the ground falls steeply to a wooded gorge through which winds the River Awbeg, a tributary of the Blackwater. A tortuous path cut in the steep escarpment leads to a sheltered valley rich in alluvial soils and enclosed by mature trees. Here, Annesley planted poplars and willows, crab, dogwood and *Magnolia*. On the river bank the

84. Annes Grove, Castletownroche, County Cork (Richard Grove Annesley): water garden (from 1905). [Author 1984]

varied foliage of bamboos, pampas-grass, irises, skunk cabbages and the giant *Gunnera manicata* forms a lush background for orange *Hemerocallis* and red and white *Spiraea* and *Astilbe*. The glaucous leaves of *Orontium aquaticum* float languidly on the shallow rivulets, and naturalized Asiatic *Primula* abounds at the water's edge (Plate 84). Nothing disturbs the silence save the distant weir, the gentle rustle of bamboos, a retreating heron. It is a secluded paradise where the natural grouping of exotic and native plants approaches perfection.

Monet at Giverny

Annes Grove belongs firmly to the Robinsonian tradition and as a point of comparison it is worth looking briefly at the most famous western water garden of this period, Monet's at Giverny. Both were characterized by luxuriant naturalistic vegetation, but whereas one was the unsophisticated outcome of plants for plants' sake, Monet's purpose was to create pictorial effects of colour and light in the way that he applied paint to the canvas.

In 1883, after much searching along the Seine valley, Claude Monet (1840–1926) at last found the house at Giverny where he was to spend the second half of his life. He did not buy the house until 1890 but he began to transform the garden and orchards. Influenced by tulip fields seen on a visit to Holland, he planned his flower garden on a rectilinear basis with beds divided by raked gravel paths (Plate 85) but arranged asymmetrically and purely for convenience as Robinson was to do at Gravetye. Monet hated the French formal garden, and the beds almost vanished beneath a profusion of planting, as can be seen from paintings like *The Garden, Giverny* (1895). Stephen Gwynn recalled how they were 'so filled with flowers that you could hardly put your hand between them'.[54] They spilled across paths and cascaded from iron, trellised arches painted in the distinctive 'vert Monet'. In spring there were snowdrops, *Aubrieta*, jonquils and tulips, or broad masses of irises of single colour; while summer and autumn produced an array of lilies, foxgloves, *Delphinium*, *Campanula*, Californian poppies, willow herb, marigolds, backed by climbing roses and *Clematis*, and followed by dahlias, asters and Japanese anemones—a wild, glorious feast of colour harmonies and contrasts. Nasturtiums spread across the main walk; and near the house were beds edged with sage and filled with pinks—reflecting the walls of the house—or yellow *Oenothera*, or red and pink *Pelargonium* surrounding tall, bamboo frames up which climbed dark red nasturtiums (Plate 86). Gardening was second only to painting as a passion in Monet's life. Claire Joyes describes how he

gave daily orders, inspecting the garden several times a day. No detail escaped him; he would correct a vista, recompose a clump of flowers, alter a pattern, and he insisted on the removal of fading blooms. He planned his flower beds according to the principles that governed his palette, with light colours predominating and monochrome masses in juxtaposition.[55]

In 1893 Monet was able to buy an adjoining strip of land which included a stream. Water had always fascinated him and he began to create the water garden that was to provide a constant source of inspiration for his painting. Gradually the pond was enlarged and altered, and its banks planted with water-loving trees and plants: willows beside the poplars, weeping willows drooping into the water, grasses, irises, meadow-sweet. In common with his Impressionist friends Monet was profoundly influenced by Japanese art, and as soon as the pond was dug out he added a bridge inspired by a Japanese print. It was festooned with white and mauve *Wisteria*, while on the still surface of the water floated the delicately coloured water-lilies, Monet's *Nymphéas* (Plate 87). Monet's garden was a painter's canvas: as with the Japanese garden, nature followed art. It was the quality of light that absorbed him, the shimmering reflections of the sky mingling with those of the silvery green foliage: 'It was impossible to say where the gardener's work stopped and the painter's began, for the two were manifestly interconnected'.[56]

Gertrude Jekyll

An interdependence of nature and art is also a key to one of the outstanding English gardeners of the period and contemporary of Monet, Gertrude Jekyll (1843–1932). (Plate 88).[57] While the artist of Giverny was striving to capture on canvas nature's fleeting harmonies of form, colour and light, she was experimenting with her own varied and living pictures in her garden at Munstead Wood. But gardening is an ephemeral art, for where his paintings remain, their momentary flashes of inspired vision recorded for posterity, few of her gardens survive. Only the theories endure, the fruits of experience and close observation, preserved within her many books.

Gertrude Jekyll's first ambition was to become a painter. The seeds of her artistic talent having been planted by her parents, she managed to persuade them to let her take a professional course, and in 1861, at the age of eighteen, she enrolled at the Schools of Art attached to the South Kensington Museum. This was an independent step for a young woman at that time and was a foretaste of the courage and quiet determination that was to accompany all her activities. The lecturers at South Kensington included Christopher Dresser, who was both designer and botanist, and Richard Redgrave, the genre painter and campaigner for art education. Her two years there would have provided a sound visual training, but the emphasis was not so much on art as on design principles. She was soon made aware of its limitations in the Ruskin circle, to which she was introduced partly as a result of a tour of the Greek Islands in 1863–4 in the company of the orientalist Charles Newton and his artist wife Mary, eldest sister of Arthur Severn, a life-long friend of Ruskin. In 1867, following Ruskin's directions for students, she studied Turner's use of colour, copying some of

85. Giverny, Gasny-Eure (Claude Monet, from 1890): layout plan by Jean-Marie Toulgouat. [From Claire Joyes, *Monet at Giverny*, 1975]

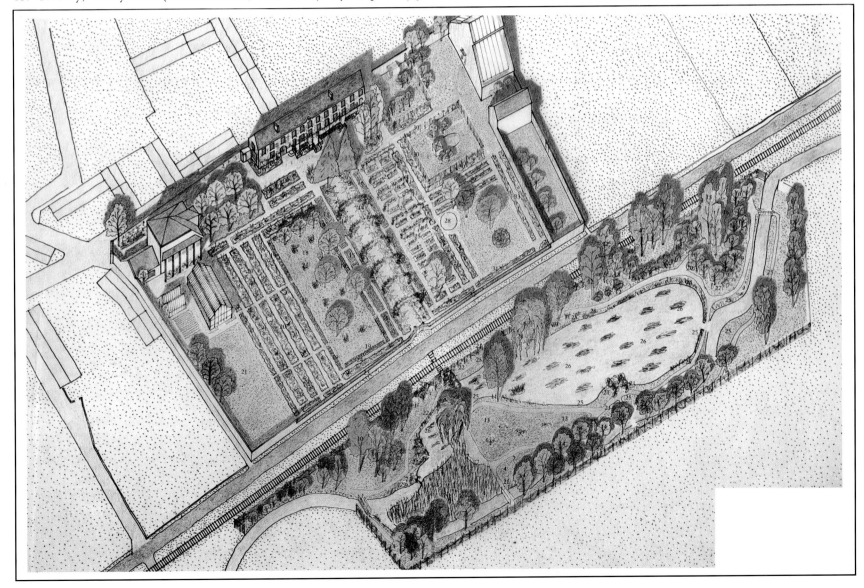

86. Giverny: Monet in his flower garden, c.1920. [From *L'Illustration*, 1927]

his paintings. An important and lasting influence was the friendship she established with the artist Hercules Brabazon Brabazon, and it was through him that in 1872 she met the remarkable and unconventional Madame Bodichon, formerly Barbara Leigh-Smith. A cousin of Florence Nightingale, she was a pioneer in the emancipation of women and one of the founders of both Bedford and Girton Colleges. She was also an intimate friend of George Eliot and the model for the heroine of *Romola*. In 1857 she had married Eugène Bodichon, a French surgeon and anthropologist, and it was at their home in Algiers that Gertrude Jekyll spent the winter of 1873–4.

Throughout her contact with this glittering, literary and artistic world she had been quietly pursuing her interest in nature and the crafts. In 1869 she visited Morris at Red Lion Square, but already she had become accomplished in interior decoration and in several crafts, notably embroidery.[58] Her delight in these traditions, recorded by her later in *Old West Surrey* (1904), derived from an early contact with village life at Bramley Park, Surrey, where she lived for twenty years from the age of four; and in a paper read to the Garden Club in 1927, she described how her interest in flowers also began in the gardens, shrubberies and woods of this country house.[59] The rustic idealism of the times was being expressed in this part of Surrey by the work of Myles Birket Foster who built an Elizabethan-style house at nearby Witley in 1861–3. His water-

87. Monet, *The Water-Lily Pond*, c.1899. [Reproduced by courtesy of the Trustees. The National Gallery, London]

The ground sloped gently from an area of heath and bracken, where a wood of Scotch pine had been felled, to a chestnut coppice and down to a small field at the north-west corner. Here she began to create a garden of her own where she could try out her ideas in practice, as Robinson was to do a few years later at Gravetye. Friends started to approach her for advice on garden schemes. In 1881 she had helped to make an alpine garden at Weybridge for G.F. Wilson and in 1884 prepared her first garden plan for a client, R. Okell of Manchester. Although she had little contact with professional gardeners, her knowledge of and interest in gardening was further strengthened through meeting many notable amateurs of the day; other visitors to Munstead included the botanist Sir Joseph Hooker, Eleanor Boyle, Sir Thomas Hanbury and, later, Theresa Earle. But the one she found 'the most valuable was Rev. C. Wolley Dod, scholar, botanist and great English gentleman, an enthusiast for plant life, an experienced gardener, and the kindest of instructors'.[64] She finally decided to give more of her attention to gardening in 1891 when she realized that, owing to her myopia, she would have to abandon all close work such as painting, embroidery and other crafts. By then she was well into her forties, but her remarkably rich and varied experience had engendered a profound feeling for nature and a knowledge and love of garden-craft. This was coupled with a painter's sense for colour and form, and it was this combination that determined her main contribution to gardening, namely, helping to elevate it to the status of a fine art.

88. William Nicholson, *Gertrude Jekyll*, 1920. [National Portrait Gallery, London]

colours depict pinafored children frolicking in a fantasy of perpetual summer outside cottages of picturesque poverty, or by hedgerows bedecked with wild flowers, specimens of which were conveniently planted outside Foster's studio window amidst the ferns, gorse and bramble.[60] In his wake came Helen Allingham (1848–1926) who, after she moved to the area in 1881, portrayed similar idyllic scenes of the cottage gardens that Miss Jekyll had found so instructive,[61] her paintings also helping to record many of the old cottages that were at that time rapidly falling prey to the 'improving' contractor.[62]

Miss Jekyll had to leave her beloved Surrey in 1868 when her parents moved to Berkshire, but she was able to return ten years later when, after the death of her father, the family built a house on Munstead Heath, near Godalming, designed by the 'Queen Anne' architect J.J. Stevenson and completed in 1878. Munstead House provided the first opportunity for her to lay out a garden on a virgin site. It included traditional elements, such as the cross-pathed kitchen garden, also many features that were to re-appear in her future work.[63] For advice on planting she turned from time to time to William Robinson. She had first met him in 1875, and he was taken to Munstead in 1880 by Canon S. Reynolds Hole, Dean of Rochester from 1888. Since 1872 she had subscribed to Robinson's *The Garden*, to which she began contributing articles in 1882 and for which she was joint editor in 1900–1 with E.T. Cook, who was also editing the *Century Book of Gardening* at that time. Then in 1883 she bought a fifteen-acre, triangular plot of poor, acid, sandy soil on the other side of Mustead Heath Road.

In 1899 Miss Jekyll published her first and most significant book, *Wood and Garden*, based partly on the 'Notes from Garden and Woodland' she had contributed to *The Guardian* from April 1896 to July 1897, and illustrated by her own photographs. Its sensitive observation of the seasons' activities at Munstead assured success, but there was a long tradition of books of this kind. Written by cultured amateurs, their detailed descriptions were usually interspersed with philosophical digressions generated while working or pondering their garden creations. Miss Jekyll acknowledged a debt to the most recent of these: to Dean Hole, whose *A Book about the Garden and Gardeners* appeared in 1893; and to Canon H.N. Ellacombe who published his *In a Gloucestershire Garden* in 1895, and whose garden at Bitton she visited.

The 1870s and 1880s had provided some earlier precedents. Henry Bright's *A Year in a Lancashire Garden* (1879) was first published in serial form in *The Gardeners' Chronicle* in 1874,[65] and Frances Hope's *Notes and Thoughts on Gardens and Woodlands* (discussed in Chapter 3) had appeared posthumously in 1881. A closer model was *Days and Hours in a Garden* (1884) by E.V.B. (Eleanor Vere Boyle, 1825–1916), a description, illustrated by her own woodcut vignettes, of her old-fashioned garden at Huntercombe Manor, near Taplow, Buckinghamshire,[66] which she transformed from 1871 adding close-trimmed yew hedges, green walks and an *allée verte*. Eleanor Boyle also had a 'Fantaisie', a woodland garden where her favourite flowers grew in wild profusion, for Huntercombe Manor was stamped with its owner's individuality: 'Long experience has taught me...to have nothing to do with principles—in the garden. Little else than a feeling of entire sympathy with the diverse characters of your plants and flowers is needed for "art in the garden". If sympathy be there, all the rest comes naturally enough.'[67] Her book was so popular it ran into eight editions by 1892 and encouraged a sequel, *A Garden of Pleasure* (1894).

Wood and Garden reflected the calendar form and lyrical style of Eleanor Boyle's books, also, to a lesser extent, *Pot-Pourri from a Surrey Garden* (1897),[68] by Mrs Earle, whose 'many valuable suggestions' Miss Jekyll acknowledged. Maria Theresa Earle, née Villiers (1836–1925), was the eldest sister of the Countess of Lytton. Intelligent and well-read, she had much in common with Miss Jekyll. In the late 1850s she, too, attended the South Kensington Schools of Art, and in the early 1880s Morris, Burne-Jones and Rossetti were among the wide circle of friends she entertained in London. Her interest in gardening began when she moved to Woodlands, her home at Cobham, Surrey. This housed her large collection of gardening books and an interesting feature of *Pot-Pourri* was her description of these, beginning with *Hortus Floridus* (1614) and ending, in the entry for 10 December 1897, with praise for her protégée Miss Jekyll's *Guardian* articles which she hoped would soon be published in book form. Where *Pot Pourri*—which went into over twenty editions—was liberally spiced with a medley of social and household hints, *Elizabeth and her German Garden* (1898) by Countess Von Arnim, also a best seller, contained asides on the equality of the sexes. It was apparently not enough for the formidable Countess that she could sit in her solitary Arcadia at Nassenheide in Pomerania, breathing the scent of lilacs, planning her yellow border of marigolds and nasturtiums, 'watching the lazy shadows stretching themselves across the grass', and forgetting the 'very existence of everything but green pastures and still waters'. 'I wish with all my heart I were a man', she professed, 'for of course the first thing I should do would be to buy a spade and go and garden.'[69] Such shortcomings did not deter Miss Jekyll from close contact with the soil. Although eventually the garden at Munstead needed eleven gardeners, in the introduction to *Wood and Garden* she could claim, 'I have lived among outdoor flowers for many years, and have not spared myself in the way of actual labour'.

Munstead Wood

Her fifteen years of devoted labour at Munstead had resulted in a diversity of gardens, each one suited to a particular time of year (Plate 89).[70] There were woodland gardens, a sheltered spring and peony garden, a secret garden enclosed by evergreens, a grey border, a June border (Plate 90) and a Michaelmas daisy border.[71] But in full summer the glory of Munstead's pleasure gardens was the main herbaceous border, facing south-east, two hundred feet long by fourteen feet wide, with an access alley behind and a narrow border for climbers and wall shrubs, all backed by a sandstone wall nearly eleven feet high. Here she was able to experiment with the colour harmonies first outlined in her article 'Colour in the Flower Garden', published in *The Garden* in 1882[72] and reprinted in a later edition of *The English Flower Garden*. These ideas on colour effects were developed in 'The Flower-Border and Pergola' in *Wood and Garden* and were finally set down in her important and influential book *Colour in the Flower Garden* (1908). They helped to transform the herbaceous border from its traditional regularity to an arrangement based on an informal progression of hues.[73] At South Kensington she would have been introduced to various colour theories, including those of Goethe and Chevreul,[74] also Beaton, Wilkinson and Owen Jones, all being widely debated in the gardening journals of the time.[75] Later, however, she probably agreed with Robinson when he wrote, introducing her contribution on colour in *The English Flower Garden*:

> Nature is a good colourist, and if we trust to her guidance we never find wrong colour in wood, meadow, or on mountain. 'Laws' have been laid down by chemists and decorators about colours which artists laugh at, and to consider them is a waste of time. If we have to make coloured cottons, or to 'garden' in coloured gravels, then it is well to think what ugly things will shock us least; but dealing with living plants in their infinitely varied hues, and with their beautiful flowers, is a different thing!

Although her studies of Turner's colour progressions had been an early influence, Miss Jekyll's appreciation of colour was ultimately the result of her own observation of nature, inspired by Ruskin, who as early as 1837 had proclaimed,

> Now, as far as we are aware, bluish purple is the only flower colour which Nature ever uses in masses of distant effect; this, however, she does in the case of most heathers, with the Rhododendron ferrugineum, and, less extensively, with the colder

colour of the wood hyacinth. Accordingly, the large rhododendron may be used to almost any extent, in masses; the pale varieties of the rose more sparingly; and, on the turf, the wild violet and pansy should be sown by chance, so that they may grow in undulations of colour, and should be relieved by a few primroses. All dahlias, tulips, ranunculi, and, in general, what are called florist's flowers, should be avoided like garlic.[76]

Above all, however, she acknowledged the support of her old friend Brabazon, 'to whom I owe, with deepest thankfulness, a pre-

90. Munstead Wood: June border. Autochrome by Gertrude Jekyll, 1900s [From *Gardens for Small Country Houses*, 1912]

89. Munstead Wood, Surrey (Gertrude Jekyll, from 1883): layout plan. [From Jekyll and Weaver, *Gardens for Small Country Houses*, 1912]

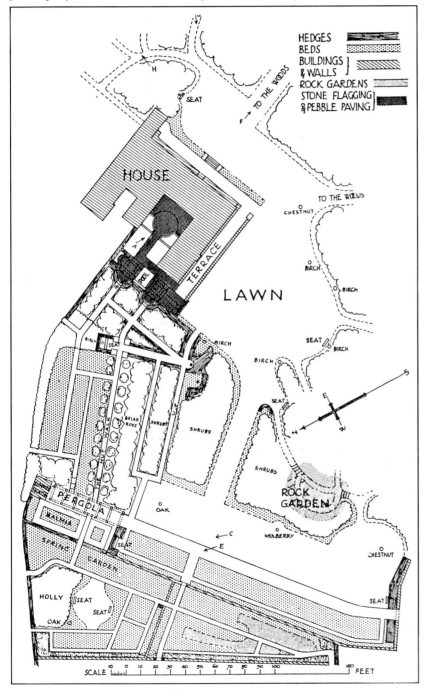

cious memory of forty years of helpful and sympathetic guidance and encouragement in the observation and study of colour beauty'.[77]

The colour scheme of Munstead's main border began at each end with white flowers amidst grey and silvery foliage. This was followed by warm white, pale pink and grey blue, progressing through pale blue and palest yellow to strong yellow, orange and mahogany, culminating in a glorious, central blaze of scarlet and crimson backed by hardy *Fuchsia* or the purple-leaved claret vine. White flowers were also used as highlights against dark foliage or to heighten the value of pale tints, and towards each end were accents: lavender, purple and pink at the east, blue with palest yellow at the west. The arrangement followed a sequence of drifts of analogous colours and satisfied certain basic optical principles. Cool hues were a preparation for the warmer masses, after which 'the eye has again become saturated, this time with the rich colouring, and has therefore, by the law of complementary colour, acquired a strong appetite for the greys and purples'.[78] Warm colours were always arranged in graduated harmonies, but she also valued contrast, especially in the case of blue: 'any experienced colourist knows that the blues will be more telling—more purely blue—by the juxtaposition of rightly placed complementary colour'.[79] She elaborated on this in a paper read for her at the Royal Horticultural Society in 1928:

There is some curious quality, not easy to define or to understand, about flowers of pure blue, such as Delphinium, Anchusa, Cornflower, and the useful dwarf Lobelia, that demands a contrast rather than a harmony; for though in a blue garden the colouring can, with more or less success, be made to pass from the pure blues into those of purpler shades, such as those of the Campanulas, yet it is a duller thing than if the pure blues only are used, with the companionship of something of white or pale yellow, such as white or yellow Lilies, white Phlox or pale

63

formal garden that is an architectural adjunct to an imposing building demands a dignified unity of colouring instead of the petty and frivolous effects so commonly obtained by the misuse of many colours'.[83] It was the planting and rigid patterns to which she objected, not the beds themselves. In the design of her marvellous flower border, the rectangular frame was a desirable discipline, even a catalyst. But a totally different kind of garden existed at Munstead, a woodland garden, situated on the upper land where the pines had been cut down. It was there that she was able to develop her ideas on wild gardening, a theme close to her heart, and one to which she was to return increasingly later in life. She let nature determine the broad grouping of this wood. Seedling trees had sprung up and these became areas of birch, oak, beech, chestnut, pine. They were divided by mown grass paths, radiating from the garden, to which they were joined by limited groups of flowering plants, merging almost imperceptibly into the woodland. In the spring, primroses abounded beneath the oaks and hazels; there were stretches of daffodils, one kind after another, and azaleas beneath the chestnuts. Running due south from the lawn was the main Green Walk, 'the most precious possession of the place' with its cathedral-like 'illusions of distance and mystery', bordered first by groups of rhododendrons, then by the smaller *Andromeda* and *Lithospermum prostratum*. Lesser walks brushed past wild ferns and bracken, 'with here and there a flowery incident—a patch of trillium, and further a little bank of the lovely little trientalis and a bold back grouping of Solomon's seal and white foxglove'.[84] Restraint was maintained throughout, planting being carried out only where it seemed to call for it: 'I thought where the copse looked well and complete in itself it was better left alone'.[85] It must have given the appearance of being spontaneous, as though the woodland had merely been coaxed and encouraged to reveal its intrinsic beauty, had 'happened' rather than been planned. A reverence for nature was Gertrude Jekyll's abiding philosophy together with a view of art as work well done:

> No artificial planting can ever equal that of nature, but one may learn from it the great lesson of the importance of moderation and reserve, of simplicity of intention, and directness of purpose, and the inestimable value of the quality called 'breadth' in painting. For planting ground is painting a landscape with living things; and as I hold that good gardening takes rank within the bounds of the fine arts, so I hold that to plant well needs an artist of no mean capacity.[86]

The Influence of Gertrude Jekyll

In the professional-amateur division in gardening there is a distinction between the professional gardener's practical bias and the amateur artist-gardener's attempt to bridge the gap between art and horticulture. Although Gertrude Jekyll belonged to the latter category, her example helped to make gardening an acceptable profession for women in the years up to the First World War. In the 1880s gardening ladies had begun 'to supplement the labour of their staff as well as to direct them',[87] but it was not easy for women to take up such work professionally. To garden for love was one thing; for money another. However, in the early 1890s

91. Munstead Wood: main border. Watercolour by Helen Allingham, 1900. [From M.B. Huish, *Happy England*, 1903]

yellow Snapdragon; or the creamy white of *Artemisia lactiflora* or *Clematis flammula*.[80]

The stone wall formed a backcloth to the Munstead border and was 'clothed for the most part with evergreen shrubs—Bay and Laurustinus, Choisya, Cistus and Loquat'.[81] These were placed to harmonize with the sections of the border in front, while the foreground was of *Bergenia* or the grey foliage of *Santolina*, *Stachys lanata*, *Cineraria maritima* and sea kale, silvery-leaved plants forming an edging to purple flowers. The border in its heyday was recorded in watercolour by Helen Allingham, in 1900 and 1902 (Plate 91), and its colour harmonies became the archetype of the herbaceous border. More subtle than Monet's flower garden, its complexity defies description; but, as she wrote in *Wood and Garden*, 'The whole thing sounds much more elaborate than it really is; the trained eye sees what is wanted, and the trained hand does it, both by an acquired instinct. It is painting a picture with living plants'.[82]

Miss Jekyll recognized the place of formality and was not always opposed to the bedding system. Her 1882 article had included a section on 'Colour in Bedding-Out' in which she wrote, 'The

horticultural colleges began to admit women as students and soon several courses specially for women gardeners were pioneered. The Countess of Warwick took the first step in 1898 when she established the Lady Warwick Agricultural Association for Women at Reading. This provided hostels for the training of women in horticulture and agriculture and its success led to the founding in 1903 of Studley Castle College in Warwickshire.[88] The following year Frances Wolseley (1872–1936) began her Glynde School for Lady Gardeners near Lewes in East Sussex. Like Lady Warwick she was motivated by a humanitarian concern to open up career prospects for women, but where Studley College had a more practical basis with an emphasis on market gardening and opportunities for posts abroad, Glynde was directed more towards employment in private gardens, the curriculum including even the history of garden design. Together with Robinson, Mrs Earle and Miss Willmott, Gertrude Jekyll became a patron of the Glynde School. In 1919 Viscountess Wolseley described her as the 'one great pioneer',[89] and students were recommended to read her books.

Ellen Willmott (1858–1934), elected the first woman member of the Linnean Society in 1904, also acknowledged her debt. Her sumptuous *The Genus Rosa* (1910) was inspired by Miss Jekyll's *Roses for English Gardens* (1902). In 1909 Miss Willmott published *Warley Garden in Spring and Summer*, an account of the rare collection of plants at her home, Warley Place, near Brentwood, Essex, described by Miss Jekyll as 'a garden that stands alone in beauty and interest'.[90] Through her books Miss Jekyll's influence extended abroad, especially to America where many of her principles of garden design were faithfully applied. She even prepared designs for three gardens there: an architectural garden (unexecuted) at Perintown, Ohio (1914) for Grace Groesbeck; a wild garden at Greenwich, Connecticut (1925) for Helen Resor; and an old-fashioned garden for the Old Glebe House, Woodbury, Connecticut (1926) for Annie Burr Jennings.[91] Her ideas also inspired many American writers on gardens, including Grace Tabor, Mabel Cabot Sedgwick and especially Mrs Francis (Louisa) King (1863–1948) of Alma, Michigan, a founder member in 1913 of the Garden Club of America.[92] Her books included glowing references to Miss Jekyll, who wrote prefaces for *The Well-Considered Garden* (1915) and *The Flower Garden Day by Day* (1927). *The Beginner's Garden* (1927) contained plans in the Jekyll style. They became close friends and Mrs King dedicated her *Chronicles of the Garden* (1925) to the one who 'more than any other has made the planting of gardens in the English-speaking countries one of the Fine Arts'.

In 1895 Beatrix Farrand (1872–1959), one of the most notable landscape gardeners in the United States, visited Gertrude Jekyll while on a tour of Italy and England. She became a great admirer of her work and was instrumental later in preserving her garden plans for future study.[93] In particular, Miss Jekyll's ideas on colour in flower borders influenced her, although, as a landscape designer, Farrand showed more awareness of the total effect of the planting, including the colour, texture and form of the foliage.[94] This is clearly demonstrated at her finest garden, Dumbarton Oaks, Washington D.C., for Robert Woods Bliss, which, beginning in 1921, gradually evolved as a progression of formal and naturalistic areas. In its fusion of the planting with the architectural elements, Dumbarton Oaks stands in the tradition of the Lutyens and Jekyll garden, just beginning to appear at the time of Farrand's visit to Munstead.

5

The Lutyens and Jekyll Garden

Every gardener must needs desire the support of some backbone of experience...some basis of form on which to rest...his own realisations of natural beauty.

J.D. Sedding, 1891[1]

Gertrude Jekyll had always intended to build a house for herself, and in 1892 she asked the architect Edwin Lutyens, whom she had met three years before, to design a cottage for her. They began collaborating on plans of gardens for the houses he was building or altering mostly in that part of Surrey, and so started a remarkable association whose products were to become the symbol of a new concept of home and garden. The Lutyens and Jekyll garden represents a synthesis of formal layout and natural planting unique in garden art. To his youthful genius for architectural form and geometric invention, she brought a mature understanding of the crafts and an enthusiasm for vernacular and old-fashioned plants, which together produced a succession of enchanting designs, original in concept, perfect in scale and exquisite in colour and material.

Edwin Landseer Lutyens (1869–1944) (Plate 93), was born at Thursley, only seven miles south-west of Munstead, the son of an army officer turned painter.[2] He was not sent to boarding school and was often left to fend for himself in Thursley where he could observe the traditional crafts still being practised. Later in life he told Sir Osbert Sitwell, 'Any talent I may have was due to a long illness as a boy, which afforded me time to think: and to subsequent ill-health, because I was not allowed to play games and so had to teach myself, for my enjoyment, to use my eyes instead of my feet. My brothers had not the same advantage'.[3] He taught himself to draw, being influenced by the style of Randolph Caldecott's nursery books, and on his bicycle rambles in West Surrey, mastered the art of making rapid perspective sketches. After studying architecture in 1885–7 at the South Kensington Schools of Art, he entered, at the age of eighteen, the office of Ernest George and Harold Peto, where he met Herbert Baker and Robert Weir Schultz. He did not stay long, however, having secured his first sizeable commission, additions to a house at Crooksbury near Farnham for Arthur Chapman, and in 1889, when barely twenty, set up his own office in Gray's Inn Square.

While he was working on Crooksbury the celebrated meeting with Miss Jekyll took place at the house of a mutual friend, Harry Mangles, the rhododendron-grower, who was a brother of Mrs Chapman, and for whom Lutyens was building a cottage at Little-

worth Cross.[4] Lutyens described the meeting thus: 'It was in 1889 that Mr Harry Mangles asked me to meet his remarkable friend, Miss Jekyll. I eagerly accepted the privilege. She was already celebrated in the gardening world, and by her ever-growing circle of devoted and appreciative admirers. We met at a tea-table, the silver kettle and the conversation reflecting rhododendrons'.[5] Shortly after began the series of weekend visits to Munstead and forays of discovery through the lanes of Surrey and Sussex in Miss Jekyll's pony-cart, looking at old houses and unsophisticated cottage gardens. In the words of the architect Harold Falkner (1875–1963), a godson of Gertrude Jekyll, trained under Blomfield, 'Miss Jekyll had a knowledge of the very finest building practices which she transferred to Lutyens, and that "sense of material" made him different from all other architects of his time'.[6] A link was thus forged between an architecture of natural materials, traditional craftsmanship and vernacular forms, and the naturalistic gardening being pursued by William Robinson, Miss Jekyll and others. The direct contact between the waspish Robinson and waggish Lutyens[7] was not so successful. In April 1897 Lutyens wrote from Gravetye, 'Been out for a long walk, W.R. went on, I left him, he bores so...his conversation is wayward and contradicts himself every two minutes, until one feels inclined to explode!...He is very anxious...to marry Conny! [Lady Constance Lytton (1869–1923), Lutyens's future sister-in-law]...It is delicious the idea of brilliant Conny marrying such a foozle headed old bore'.[8] These sentiments did not, however, prevent Lutyens designing in 1906 Robinson's new editorial offices for *The Garden* at 42 Kingsway in London.

Munstead and Orchards

The cottage that Lutyens designed for Miss Jekyll in 1892 became known as 'The Hut' and was built in 1894–5 in the Surrey vernacular of brick, roughcast and tiles on the south-west side of her land at Munstead. She gave an idyllic account of it in *Home and Garden*, and Lutyens's sketch designs are preserved in the 'Munstead Wood Sketchbook' at the British Architectural Library.[9] It had a large, open-roofed workshop-cum-living-room

siting in the clearing close to the woodland created a series of picturesque views from the winding paths (Plate 94). Munstead Wood grew out of a perfect understanding and sharing of aims between owner and architect. With it Lutyens reached maturity as a designer. Indeed, it could be said that at Munstead, owing in no small part to Miss Jekyll's restraining influence, he achieved an unassuming yet noble simplicity encountered only rarely in his subsequent work, for example at Lambay. In the opening chapter of *Home and Garden*, Miss Jekyll described how the house was built in the spirit of the local traditions with Bargate stone walls, hand-made tiles, mullioned windows and joinery of locally grown oak, an early and enthusiastic example of the application of Arts and Crafts principles inspired by the writings of Ruskin and Morris and the work of Philip Webb. The only formal garden was on the north between two wings of the house, consisting of a paved court

94. Munstead Wood: view from the south-east. [*CL* 1900]

93. Edwin Landseer Lutyens, photographed in 1897. [From Lady Emily Lutyens, *A Blessed Girl*, 1953; courtesy of Mary Lutyens]

with inglenook fireplace, and was planted front and back with the simple cottage flowers that became her June Garden. She loved the primitive rusticity of her life at The Hut, but in 1895, when her mother died and her brother Herbert took over Munstead House, she needed somewhere more permanent to house her possessions and receive her friends. It was then that, with the help of her architect, she was able to turn her attention to creating the house she had dreamed of for so long and where she was to spend the rest of her life.

She had always known approximately where it would go, but it now needed to fit in with the well-established gardens (see Plate 89), with the result that, as she remarked later, 'there are portions which meet at awkward angles'[10] and 'the garden has less general unity of design than I should have wished'.[11] Nevertheless, its

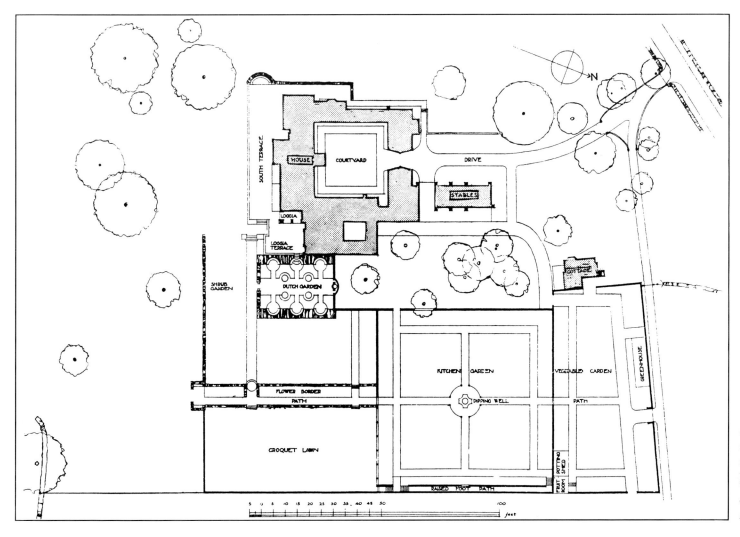

95. Orchards, Godalming, Surrey (1897–1902): layout plan. [From L. Weaver, *Houses and Gardens by E.L. Lutyens*, 1913]

bordered by lilies, bellflowers and *Hydrangea*, the flanking walls being festooned with *Clematis montana* and vine. North of this, a tank was enclosed by a double flight of steps which led to the Nut Walk (planted in about 1885), also to the pergola and the main flower gardens. Elsewhere the house was surrounded by lawns and woodland.

The building of Munstead Wood took place in an eventful period in Lutyens's life. During the summer of 1896 he met Lady Emily Lytton (1874–1964), and took her on a surprise visit to The Hut on 21 September;[12] the following August they were married. In October 1897 Miss Jekyll moved into her new house, but already in May it had landed Lutyens a much larger fish, the commission to design Orchards (1897–1902), on a site nearby, for William and Julia Chance.

The partnership's formal garden *début*, an addition to Woodside, Chenies, Buckinghamshire, for Adeline, Duchess of Bedford, had taken place four years earlier in 1893,[13] but Orchards was their first opportunity to combine their talents on an entirely new house and garden and was an important landmark in their work. How the Chances' friendship with Miss Jekyll began was described later by Lady Chance herself. Being dissatisfied with their first architect's plans, they were on the way to re-visit their site:

Passing through a sandy lane we saw a house nearing completion, and on top of a ladder a portly figure giving directions to some workmen. The house was a revelation of unimagined beauty and charm, the like of which we had never seen before, and we stood entranced and gazing until the figure descended from the ladder, and we found ourselves, after due explanation, being welcomed as future neighbours and shown over the wonderful house. Later, as a result of this meeting, we became the owners of a Lutyens house with a Gertrude Jekyll garden.[14]

Located on the wooded, sandstone hills near Godalming, looking east towards the North Downs, Orchards, like Munstead, was built of the honey-coloured Bargate sandstone quarried on site, with openings embellished by lintels or voussoirs of red, roofing tiles in a sophisticated version of the local vernacular. The house was approached from the north through a gatehouse into a courtyard (Plate 95) (in the manner of Norman Shaw's Leyswood), and, for the principal rooms, aspect took precedence over prospect. They faced south across the existing bracken-covered land which was modified only by the occasional planting of shrubs forming a transition between the lawns and the wild woodland.[15] To the east the ground fell away and it was there that a series of formal

96. Orchards: the 'Dutch Garden'. [*CL* 1901]

gardens was laid out, their enclosing yew hedges forming the foreground to the magnificent view across the valley towards New-
lands Corner beyond Chinthurst Hill. From the loggia terrace,
steps descend to the so-called 'Dutch' garden, a *tour de force* of
garden architecture (Plate 96).[16] One of Lutyens's earliest exercises
in geometry, it employed his characteristic motif of York stone
loops enclosing circles of planting or brick on edge laid herringbone pattern flanking a central area of stone paving. On either side
stand dark walls of yew with semi-circular bays seemingly
hollowed out of the seven-foot high hedges, and seats formed by
raising the semi-circular paving on dwarf walls of horizontally laid
tiles. On the side nearest the house the central circle forms first a

convex step, then a flight of concave steps, with dark risers of the
same horizontal tiles, ascending to the terrace. The garden is
enclosed on the north by a tile-coped wall with central fountain
where, from a lion's head mask designed by Julia Chance, water
trickled into a circular basin. The planting was of the utmost
simplicity: white China roses against the dark green yew, pale
dwarf lavender blending with stone, brick and tile. As in a mediaeval pleasance, sound and scent combined with sight and touch
for the delight of the senses. It had much in common with the
'Italian' Garden designed at about the same time by Lutyens at The
Pleasaunce, Overstrand, near Cromer, Norfolk (1897–9), for Lord
Battersea, and described by Marie Luise Gothein in 1913 as 'one of

70

the distinctive gardens of modern England',[17] although there the planting was not by Miss Jekyll but by the Batterseas themselves.

Beyond the 'Dutch' garden at Orchards, a north-south cross-axis is marked by a yew-enclosed alley with herbaceous border, at the end of which a massive archway with tiled voussoirs forms the entrance to the kitchen garden. Square, like that at Munstead House, it had cross-paths edged with an abundance of the flowers one might see in a cottage garden. There was a central dipping well ringed by rambler roses on posts and chains, and along the east wall a Tudor-style, raised walk, terminated by the fruit house, commanded a view of the Surrey countryside. Beyond the kitchen garden was the vegetable garden proper and, banished to the northernmost boundary, the greenhouse. Glass was not a material dear to Lutyens's heart, and Miss Jekyll considered greenhouses to be strictly utilitarian. One looks in vain for conservatories in a Lutyens-Jekyll house and garden, even when the owner belonged to a family of glass manufacturers!

Working Relationship

Orchards was the first masterpiece of garden design to spring from the partnership and is especially notable for its unity with the house. A new-found confidence was apparent, and materials, both plants and paving, were treated with restraint. Already the main formal characteristics of their style were established: the projection of the lines of the house outwards along routes and vistas; the multiplication of the forms and materials of the house thereby increasing its apparent size; and the subsequent breaking down of these forms by clothing them with luxuriant, informal planting. In the 'Dutch' garden especially, as A.S.G. Butler observed, not only does the planting 'blur the outlines of both the house and the terraces and so combine them' but also 'the counter-curving steps are in scale with and reflect in form the loggia arches'.[18] Both house and garden appear to grow out of the ground, and, as Sedding had advised, the same materials are used throughout: 'if the house be of stone; as at Haddon, or Brympton, or Claverton, the balustrade is of stone; if the house be of brick as at Hatfield or Bramshill, the walls and balustrades will be of brick and terracotta. The advantage of this agreement of material is obvious, for house and terrace, embraced at one glance, make a consistent whole.'[19]

The garden at Orchards was the outcome of a fruitful collaboration between architect, gardener and enthusiastic clients. In 1901 Miss Jekyll wrote, 'The truth appears to be that for the best building and planting...the architect and the gardener must have *some* knowledge of each other's business, and each must regard with feelings of kindly reverence the unknown domains of the other's higher knowledge.'[20] On Lutyens's part there was probably more 'kindly reverence' than knowledge of gardening. As Hussey observed, 'It was a strange and rather tragic circumstance that the architect of so many entrancing gardens never had one of his own. But he was neither a garden lounger nor a garden grower by temperament. For him a garden was an occasion for a work of art that, once designed, he had no wish to see again until its components had reached maturity.'[21] The 'little white house' of

the betrothal casket of 1896 never materialized (although its spirit was revived later at Marsh Court). His general views on gardens reflected Miss Jekyll's. Proposing a vote of thanks (an ordeal for him) to a paper by Thomas Mawson on 'Garden Design' at the Architectural Association on 8 April 1908, he said, 'The true adornment of a garden lies surely in its flowers and plants. No artist has so wide a palette as the garden designer. No artist has greater need of both discretion and reserve'; and echoing Sedding, 'A garden scheme should have a backbone—a central idea beautifully phrased.'[22] He would have found little fault with Blomfield's book; the garden he added to The Hoo, Willingdon, East Sussex (1902), with its terraces and gazebos, was very much a tribute to the seventeenth century.

When Miss Jekyll turned to gardening, she already possessed a keen aesthetic sense, and her short-sightedness and consequent blurred vision may even have given her a better grasp of the broad picture, especially with regard to tones and colour massing.[23] Lutyens had at an early age acquired the ability to memorize details, gleaned mainly from drawings and photographs, and to visualize the effect of a completed building; but for a gardener it was even more important to form a picture in the mind's eye of a garden that would take many years to mature. As Miss Jekyll attached considerable importance to 'place' in planting and design, when she was unable later to visit sites herself, this visual imagination must have been a great compensation. Whereas in the early days the partners would go off from Munstead together to decide where the house should be placed and how the garden should be laid out, after the turn of the century, due to her advancing years and failing sight, she rarely ventured further than the range of her pony-cart, an exceptional visit being the train excursion they made together to Lindisfarne in 1906. She had to rely upon Lutyens and other architects to provide surveys of information such as soil, contours, aspect and prospect, and she always asked her own clients to provide a surveyor's plan; moreover, apart from the early Surrey gardens and Folly Farm which she visited in 1916, she never saw her work in its maturity. As she became less mobile, and he the busy establishment architect, their joint undertakings decreased. By 1908 he could send a note concerning Middlefield at Great Shelford, promising her that the garden was ready for her attention; but a Jekyll garden never materialized.[24]

One gets close to the Lutyens-Jekyll ideal with the description in *Gardens for Small Country Houses* (1912) of Millmead (1904–6), the small house and garden she built—but let to tenants—on a plot in Snowdenham Lane, Bramley, near the grounds of her old family home. She had resolved to build a house that would be 'worthy of the pretty site' and 'the best small house in the whole neighbourhood'. The entrance was 'quiet and modest' as at Munstead, through a doorway directly off the lane into a small forecourt (Plate 97), as recommended by her in 'Gardens Past and Present':

When a small house of a good type...stands a little way back from the road on the outskirts of a country town, it is usual for the entrance to be through a door into a walled forecourt....A good plan in such a case is to have a flagged path from the road door to the house entrance with plain unbroken turf on each

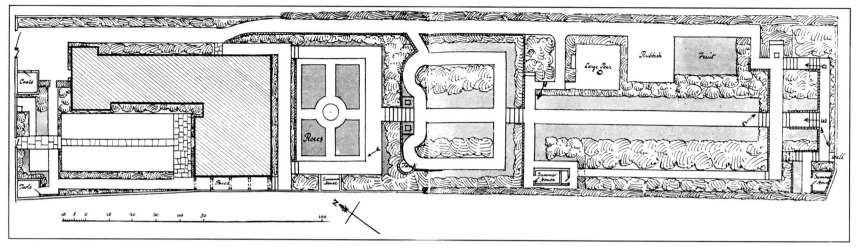

97. Millmead, Bramley, Surrey (1904–6): layout plan. [From *Gardens for Small Country Houses*, 1912]

98. Millmead: view from the south-east. [From *Gardens for Small Country Houses*, 1912]

(1909). Harold Falkner was much taken with Millmead: 'In colour, texture, form, background, setting, smell and association...it was perfect...(By the word "association" I mean that it was English—typical of the English village; owing something perhaps to a hundred foreign influences, but having so absorbed them that their origin is lost and they have become our own.)'.[28] It was the perfect proportions of the terracing, and the planting, framing the central vista, that gave the garden its special quality (Plate 98). *Wisteria* grew over the garden front and the base of the wall was planted with *Escallonia*, *Iris stylosa*, the sweet-scented *Choisya*, rosemary and lavender. At each successive level of the garden a particular note was struck, the upper level consisting of a formal rose garden with central sundial and perimeter borders of shrubs and flowers, the border on the shady side including a summer-house flanked by greenery with a suggestion of muted colour (Plate 99).[29] The steps

99. Millmead: planting plan of north border at upper level. [From *Gardens for Small Country Houses*, 1912]

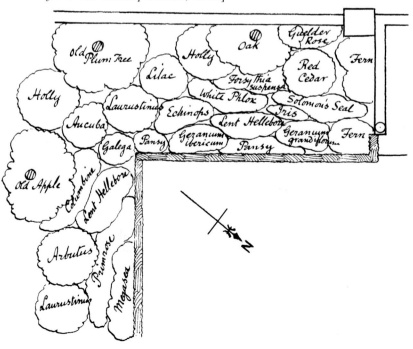

side, and to keep any planting, and that of a quiet green character, against the side walls, with perhaps, only a few white Lilies or one or two China Roses, but to avoid anything of strong colour. To come into such a forecourt, passing directly from a busy street or more or less populous road, is like stepping into another world—a comforting world of sympathetic restfulness that shuts out all bustle and hurry, and induces a sense of repose and invigorating refreshment.[25]

The walls of the forecourt were covered by a vine, *Clematis montana* and traveller's joy, with 'arbutus, laurustinus and spiraea lindleyana treated as wall plants, and the borders at the foot have acanthus, megasea, Lent hellebore, Solomon's Seal and hardy ferns'.[26] A pergola at the side of the house led to the main garden which was subdivided into three parts (like Tintinhull in Somerset[27]) and descended in terraces with connecting flights of steps on the axis of the symmetrical garden front of the house. This garden elevation was an early example of Lutyens's 'Wrenaissance' style which he was to develop at Folly Farm (1906) and Great Maytham

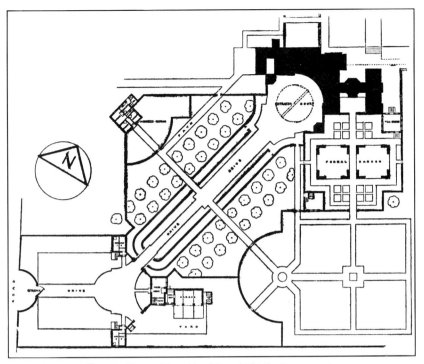

100. Grey Walls, Gullane, East Lothian (1901): layout plan.

and retaining walls dividing the sections of the garden enabled Miss Jekyll to indulge her love of dry-wall planting, and they were adorned with *Aubrieta*, stonecrops, snapdragons, catmint, rock pinks and saxifrages. At the bottom of the garden there was a secluded area comprising a second summer-house, a dipping well, and planting of low shrubs affording a 'pleasant prospect of mead and millstream' (from which the house derived its name). Only vestiges of the garden remain, but early photographs record its sympathetic union of architecture and planting. Millmead would acquire greater significance after the First World War as a model for the suburban house, but, at the turn of the century, gardens of far greater magnitude were being demanded of the partnership.

Floruit

An early example of Lutyens's romantic phase was Berry Down, near Overton in Hampshire (1897) for Archibald Grove.[30] Its gardens were not a conspicuous success, but the layout is notable for the axial approach from the stable block on the road—in Caldecott, yeoman-farmhouse style—through a walled enclosure into a forecourt with fig trees growing against the roughcast walls. Lutyens developed the courtyard theme further as a means of creating a transition between road and house at Grey Walls, Gullane, East Lothian (1901), for the MP Alfred Lyttleton, a golfing-holiday house on an awkward site overlooking the Muirhead Golf Links and the Firth of Forth.[31] Two walled forecourts were contrived at an angle, the concave entrance front of the L-shaped house being approached diagonally along a north-south axis (Plate 100). The main forecourt screens a formal garden centred on the south-east front of the principal rooms—an ingenious division of public and private zones—the traditional lowland materials of creamy rubble sandstone and grey-pantiled roofs providing an effective background for the rose garden, which is sheltered from the northerly winds, and which, if not planted, was at least inspired by Miss Jekyll (Plate 101). From this garden a vista continues south-east between hedge-bordered courts and is closed by a stone *clair-voyée*, a witty conceit which nevertheless interferes with the view of the Lothian hills it is intended to frame.

Grey Walls provided a grand vehicular approach, but this was not typical of Lutyens's houses of this period. Unlike their Victorian predecessors, which were usually set back in extensive grounds with the inevitable serpentine drive affording occasional glimpses of the house between massed rhododendrons, they often had only the barrier of a single open forecourt, as for example at Tigbourne Court (1899), which was situated directly off the road. Another recurring device, evocative of Morris's Kelmscott Manor, and not inappropriate to those pre-motor-age days, was the provision of a doorway in the boundary wall from which one entered the transitional space of an intimate court, vehicular access being accommodated elsewhere. This was the case at Millmead and later at Folly Farm, but the most celebrated example was Deanery Garden (1899–1901) for Edward Hudson, a bachelor's retreat in the Thames-side village of Sonning in Berkshire.

Lutyens owed this commission to Miss Jekyll's introduction. In 1897 Hudson had founded *Country Life*, to which Miss Jekyll contributed garden notes and which exerted a strong influence on the revival of the old-fashioned garden. Mary Lutyens has described him as 'a tall man, very kind, but unattractively plain... He was very good natured. We had a fire-screen in the nursery, the bottom part of which could be moved up leaving a gap at the bottom. It was perfect for playing French Revolutions, and Hudson was most obliging in kneeling on the floor and putting his head through the gap so that we could guillotine him.'[32] In spite of these attempts on his life Hudson became a life-long friend and admirer of Lutyens. He publicized his principal buildings in his

101. Grey Walls: view from the south-east. [Author 1981]

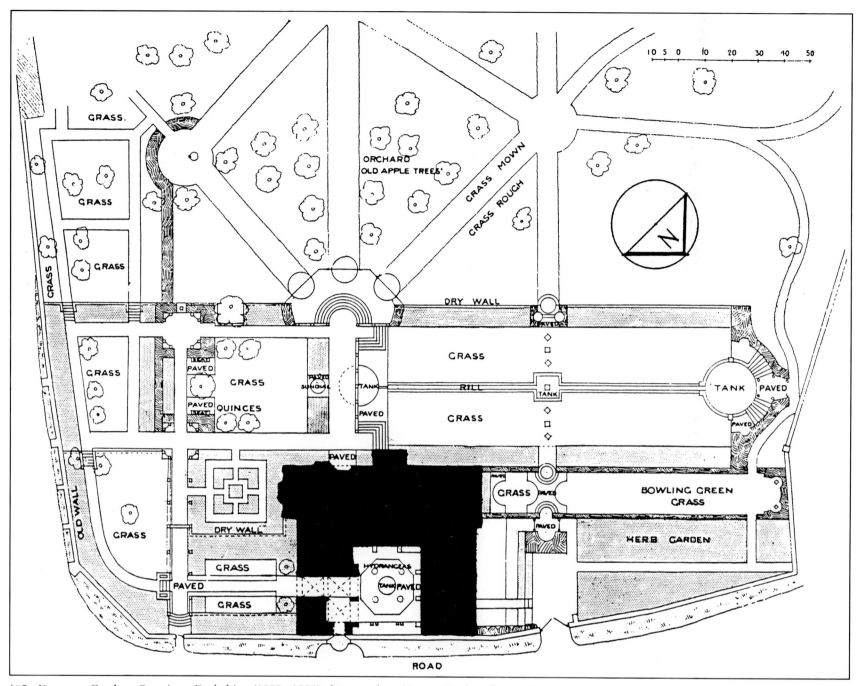

102. Deanery Garden, Sonning, Berkshire (1899–1901): layout plan. [From *Gardens for Small Country Houses*, 1912]

journal and employed him for all his subsequent projects, including his new offices for *Country Life* (1904) in Tavistock Street. In 1902 he bought Lindisfarne Castle on Holy Island and got Lutyens to restore it and, in 1911, to design with Miss Jekyll an intriguing little garden there based on two vanishing points.[33]

The site of Deanery Garden was an old orchard and garden with a rich loamy soil in the centre of the village, surrounded by an ancient, mellow brick wall. Lutyens was determind to preserve this wall, and the entrance is a modest arched doorway penetrating it directly off the street. As at Munstead Wood he used a U-shaped plan and the house was positioned up against the north-east boundary (Plate 102), partly to allow maximum space for the garden

in the manner of French and Italian villas where the site was restricted. The entrance doorway leads into a low passage, groin-vaulted in brick and chalk. To the right is an inner courtyard with central pool and statuary creating a cross axis, while a hint of the garden is revealed through an archway to the left which frames a pergola beyond. There is a feeling of ambiguity about this space, anticipation but uncertainty as to whether or not one has entered. It introduces the dominant theme of Deanery Garden which is the interpenetration of inside and outside by means of intersecting axes. The structural geometry of the house is extended outwards setting up a direct relationship with the garden and thereby making the house appear larger than it is, a constant device of Lutyens. The

103. Deanery Garden: garden front. [Author 1982]

104. Deanery Garden: tank garden from the west. [*CL* 1903]

entrance axis, placed asymmetrically to the mass of the house, continues through a quasi-screens passage and out on to a paved walk ending in a flight of semi-circular steps (Plate 103). This marks the south-west boundary of the unified house and formal garden and is clearly delineated by a retaining wall. From this vantage point mown grass paths radiate out into the orchard, the diagonal path to the west providing a view of the church tower. A *patte d'oie* of radiating steps and paths was a recurring feature which Lutyens used again at The Hoo and Great Dixter. To the south-east a path leads to a rose-covered arbour on the axis of the pergola, which was glimpsed from the entrance court. Thus a circulatory walk is provided, echoing the plan of the house but offset from it diagonally by shifting the axes in a southerly direction.

A second theme was introduced at Deanery Garden. From the upper terrace steps lead down to a tank garden, its longitudinal axis marked by a narrow rill which connects a circular pool at the north-west end to a fountain pool—developed from that at Orchards—half of which is bridged by a segmental arch supporting the terrace above (Plate 104). The garden front, with its splendid double height bay window, its deeply embrasured garden doorway, and massive chimney with three stacks placed diagonally, all in brick, tile and English oak, is a romantic allusion to Tudor architecture, the effect being heightened by the upper terrace reading as a bridge when viewed from the 'moat' of the tank garden beneath.

Gertrude Jekyll described her planting for Deanery Garden in *Gardens for Small Country Houses*. Above the semi-circular steps were masses of 'The Garland' rose which cascaded down almost to the level of the orchard, while the adjacent retaining walls were given earth joints and planted with pinks, saxifrages, stonecrops, sandworts, rock-cresses and other alpines. For the water garden—their first important design in this medium—they may have had in mind the old gardens of Spain, with their Moorish associations, such as the Patio de la Acequia in the Generalife gardens at

Granada, which Miss Jekyll illustrated in *Wall and Water Gardens*.[34] At Deanery Garden the narrow channels have flat stone kerbs flush with the lawn and are planted with the water forget-me-not, water plantains, flowering rush and *Iris pseudacorus*. The borders were filled with flowers which could be varied from year to year including many old-fashioned varieties in Miss Jekyll's characteristic restrained and delicate pale blue, pink, and occasional touches of purple: *Delphinium*, hollyhocks, *Nepeta*, snapdragons, irises and mignonette, offset by her favourite grey-greens: *Yucca, Santolina, Stachys,* lavender and rosemary. From the 'Great Hall' one could gaze down across smooth lawns and calm water to banks of flowers, with fruit trees standing in a carpet of daffodils, fritillaries and meadow saffron, or draped in rambling roses. Already, at the dawn of the Edwardian age, the Lutyens-Jekyll art had reached a sophistication to be surpassed only at Hestercombe. In his thirtieth year Lutyens had secured an unassailable position which he was to command up to the First World War; but his architecture owed much to Miss Jekyll's sensitive, informal planting which softened the uncompromising lines of his obsessive geometry.

In 1898, between Orchards and Deanery Garden, Lutyens designed Le Bois des Moutiers, at Varengeville in Normandy, for Guillaume Mallet, a Huguenot who, though not a banker himself, belonged to an old banking family. He probably obtained this commission through Mme Mallet whose aunt, Mrs Grunelius, knew Mrs Earle, Lady Lytton's eldest sister, who had just published the first in her series of *Pot-Pourri* books. The Mallets became close friends of the Lutyens family (they introduced Lady Emily to theosophy in 1910).[35] The house is approached from the south through gates off the village street, but, unlike Deanery Garden, whose secrets are withheld, the nature of this garden is revealed at once. Ahead stretches a long drive paved in brick and enclosed by roughcast walls with tiled copings similar to those at Berry Down (Plate 105). It is a direct, axial approach at the end of which one might expect a formal, French front, but instead one is

75

105. Le Bois des Moutiers, Varengeville (1898): entrance approach. [Author 1985]

presented with an asymmetrical composition flanked by informal borders of shrubs and flowers. The picturesque tiled roofs, battered, Voysey-style chimneys and homage to Norman Shaw in the porch and attenuated oriel windows, belong more to English than to French soil, and indeed this is what the anglophile Mallets wanted. There is nothing French about Le Bois. But its English-ness lies less in its grey roughcast walls than its Arts and Crafts interiors and delightful gardens. M. Mallet was already familiar with Robinson's writings, and Miss Jekyll's books were about to make their timely appearance. In 1904 Miss Jekyll prepared plans for him which, although superseded by Lutyens's later addition of walls, determined the spirit of the subsequent planting.

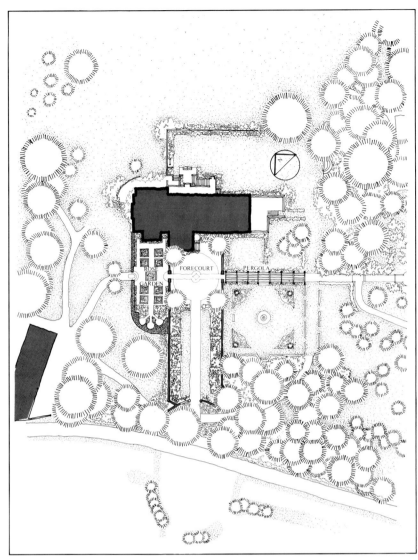

106. Le Bois des Moutiers: layout plan. [Miranda Ottewill]

Varengeville-sur-Mer, a few kilometres west of Dieppe, does not enjoy as favourable a climate as the south of England, hence the high forecourt walls which provide some protection from gales, and the subdivision of the garden into compartments. The entrance drive has twin borders filled with roses, tree peonies, *Deutzia* and *Hosta*, and edged with saxifrages, *Hebe* and *Stachys lanata*. It leads to a small forecourt with formally placed cypresses and a circle of brick paving divided across the centre by a stone path announcing a cross-axis (Plate 106). To either side are arched doorways, with the familiar Lutyens 'voussoir' tiles (Plate 107), leading on the left to a formal rose garden, its beds now edged with box and filled with white flowers—'Iceberg' roses, *Eremurus elwesii* 'Albus', foxgloves, *Spiraea, Hosta* and *Hydrangea petiolaris* (Plate 108)—its southern end containing circular seats and benches backed by yew hedges. To the right of the forecourt a pergola walk leads to a garden house, while, to the north, lawns slope down from the house providing vistas and glimpses of the sea. Here, too, Le Bois des Moutiers looks devotedly across the Channel, the planting of the surrounding woodland bearing the unmistakable stamp of William Robinson.[36]

The compartmental approach was developed further at one of Lutyens's finest houses, Little Thakeham (1902), where the principal rooms overlook a protective inner ring of gardens each with its distinctive character (Plate 110). Tudor in style and built of local stone with russet tiled roofs, it was designed for Ernest Blackburn, himself a skilled amateur gardener, which explains why Miss Jekyll was not brought in. Located in the Sussex weald, the site slopes gently southwards with views of the Downs, the approach drive running along the north boundary and continuing on to the stables. As though off a country lane, the house is set back behind an entrance forecourt laid out chastely with flagged paths, grass and flower beds (Plate 109). On the south, the central axis is extended down a stepped ramp to a raised pergola overlooking a large rectangular lawn, the perfect foil to its surroundings, bounded to south and west by orchards and to the east by a line of elms, the principal existing feature of the site. Beyond is a nut walk

107. Le Bois des Moutiers: view across forecourt. [Author 1985]

108. Le Bois des Moutiers: rose garden. [Author 1985]

109. Little Thakeham, Sussex (1902): view across forecourt. [Author 1984]

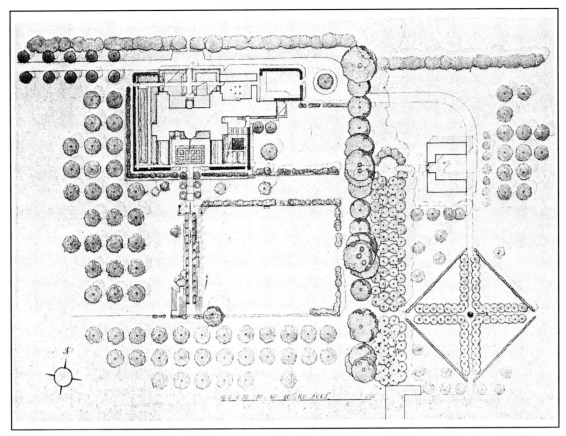

110. Little Thakeham: layout plan. [From Shepherd and Jellicoe, *Gardens and Design*, 1927]

111. Little Thakeham: garden front. [*CL* 1909]

and a square kitchen garden similar to that at Orchards but placed with diagonal cross-paths. As a general rule Lutyens's early houses had symmetrical entrance fronts but were informal at the rear, examples being Berry Down, Tigbourne Court, Daneshill and Marsh Court. At Little Thakeham, however, the plan is a double Elizabethan 'E' with both elevations treated symmetrically, a huge polygonal bay marking the centre of the garden facade and lighting the double storey 'Great Hall'. This hall—whose interior is a portent of Lutyens's Palladian games—interrupts movement from entrance to garden, access being arranged modestly from a door under the staircase at which steps descend to a paved flower garden with enclosures on either side filled with climbing roses. A second garden door from the dining-room gives on to a raised terrace from which steps and platforms cascade down to a lily pool and iris garden. The central walk leads from these secluded outdoor rooms to the pergola, the principal formal feature of the gardens. Of noble yet rustic simplicity, it continues the materials and architectural presence of the house out into the garden but without intrusion (Plate 111). Here, as at Orchards, stonework and foliage merged harmoniously: alpine pinks and Shirley poppies spread at one's feet; roses hung from the oak beams and clamboured over the sturdy masonry pillars, alternately square and round, between which, across the orchards, one glimpsed the distant Downs.

The key to Little Thakeham's enchantment lies in its restraint and simplicity. There is none of the elaborate detail of the Blomfield or Inigo Thomas garden; neither does it possess the self-consciousness of most Lutyens houses of this period: the garden has received no more than an architectural framework. As Shepherd and Jellicoe remarked, 'It settles into its surroundings as though it had been there always.'[37] Lutyens himself thought Little Thakeham the 'best of the bunch', and after visiting it in July 1904 he wrote to Lady Emily,

> I got to Thakeham about eight. A most divine evening. The great Downs bathed in reflected light and the garden wonderfully good. Blackburn is very slow, apparently, but is really an artist and he does little at a time but what he does is singularly good I think. He has made the pergola delightful—in a way quite his own—with hollyhocks—and to enjoy the effect he postpones planting the more permanent things....I do wish we could have a garden and a country house.[38]

Most of the early gardens of the Lutyens-Jekyll partnership were in situations that favoured enclosure, but Marsh Court at Stockbridge (1901–4), for Herbert Johnson, was located on the spur of a hill, enjoying views to south and west over the River Test and its bordering meadows. Here was just the site, in the Hampshire chalk downland (with trout fishing thrown in), calculated to kindle Lutyens's fertile imagination. What is more, Johnson was able and willing to give Lutyens free rein, to encourage his flair for the dramatic. His acumen for the Stock-market had earned him an early fortune, a sizeable chunk of which Lutyens now helped him to spend on this romantic extravaganza, his final fling in the Tudor manner, picturesque in composition, its walls built of the chalk escarpment from which it arose clifflike above the east side of the river.

Marsh Court is approached up a long drive to the half-moated forecourt of a symmetrical block with wings spreading low and wide under its blanket of russet tiles. This entrance front awakens memories of the 'little white house', but inside the symmetry

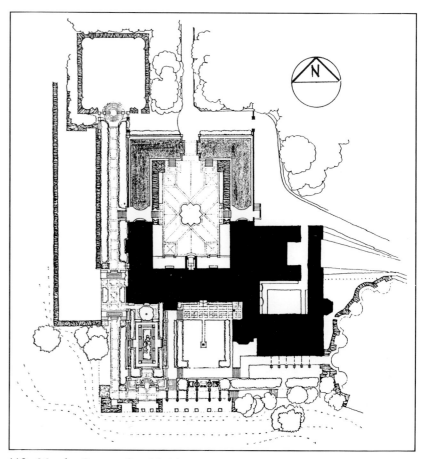

112. Marsh Court, Stockbridge, Hampshire (1901–4): layout plan. [From Shepherd and Jellicoe, *Gardens and Design*, 1927]

113. Marsh Court: view from upper terrace. [*CL* 1913]

breaks down to take account of the service wing and the prospect (Plate 112). The axis shifts to a 'screens passage' centred on a sundial lawn which can also be reached through a loggia from which there is an uninterrupted view to the south-west, protection being provided by wide flower beds in place of balustrades (Plate 113). From here steps descend to the lower terraces and enclosures, their descending planes helping to wed the house to its site.

But there is a more intriguing approach to these gardens, around the west and south sides, which takes advantage of the views and provides a dramatic experience of the exterior of the house. From an enclosed lawn to the right of the approach drive, two flights of semi-circular steps lead down to a long alley paved in panels of herringbone brick, bordered with flower beds, and separated by a hedge from a bowling green to the west. Further steps descend to a sunken court where the massive south-west chimney stack rises up organically out of its base of chalk and flint, its random-squared clunch walling enlivened by accents of brick and tiles until it merges into a chequerboard supporting triple, twisted stacks. A gateway on the left gives an enticing hint of an enclosed garden, and a gap on the right opens up the first view across the valley, but this is immediately closed by yew hedges where the walk is turned to the left. Then, unexpectedly, through an opening between classical piers, the sunken water garden is revealed (Plate 114). Steps lead down to a pool, the lowest point of all, behind which twin bay windows rise up majestically, a dramatic contrast with the spreading horizontality of the entrance front. Further glimpses of the landscape open up as the path continues under a pergola with massive piers of horizontal tiles supporting cambered oak beams, and past an exedra of exquisite lily pools let into the stone paving. At this point one is a complete storey below the upper terrace which is finally reached up steps beneath trees at the eastern end.

The idea for the sunken pool garden (completed in 1904) may have come from Miss Jekyll who had described her ideal 'Lily Tank in a Formal Garden' in *Wall and Water Gardens* (1901). This was inspired by her memories of the 'good old gardens of Italy', also by the 'beautifully coloured forms of the newer Water Lilies' which she felt 'would exactly accord with masonry of the highest refinement, and with the feeling of repose that is suggested by a surface of still water'. The plan she included showed a sunken court with, as at Marsh Court, a wide flagged path all round backed by flower borders and an eight-foot-high wall, and with steps leading down into the water on all sides. Her description reveals the artist's eye and deserves to be quoted at length:

> a beautiful effect is gained by steps leading actually into water. In this case I would have the two lowest steps actually *below* the water-line. Although steps are in the first instance intended for the human foot, yet we have become so well accustomed to the idea of them as easy means of access from one level to another that in many cases they are also desirable as an aid to the eye, and in such a place as I think of, the easy lines of shallow steps from the level of the path to that of the water-surface and below it, would I consider, be preferable to any raised edging such as is more usually seen round built tanks. It would give the eye the pleasant feeling of being invited to contemplate the Lilies at its

114. Marsh Court: sunken pool from the south. [M. Hill 1978]

> utmost ease, instead of being cut off from them by a raised barrier. . . . Coming down the steps you see the level lines of water-surface jewelled with the lovely floating bloom of white and pink and tender rose colour, the steps into the tank on the near and far sides still further insisting on the repose of the level line. . . . In the flower borders next the wall I would have Lilies, and plants mostly of Lily-like character, Crinums and Funkias, and of the true Lilies a limited number of kinds—the notable White Lily, *L. Harrisi, L. longiflorum, L. Browni*, and white and rosy forms of *L. speciosum*. These would grow out of the groups of the beautiful pale-foliaged *Funkia grandiflora* and of the tender green of the Lady Fern and of Harts-tongue. I would not let the walls be too much covered with creepers, for I hold that wherever delicate architecture marries with gardening, the growing things should never overrun or smother the masonry; but in the

Lily court I would have some such light-running creeping things as can be easily led and trained within bounds, such as *Clematis Flammula*, blue Passion Flower, and, if climate allows, *Rhodochiton volubile*, *Cobaea scandens*, and *Solanum jasminoides*. These would be quite enough, and even perhaps too many.[39]

No plans survive earlier than 1905 but her description is a clue to the original planting, and early photographs show *Santolina*, lavender and *Stachys lanata* in the borders and *Clematis* and *Wisteria* on the walls. Perhaps these were considered 'quite enough', but the same cannot be said for the steps and platforms of which there are 'too many' in Lutyens's intricate design (Plate 115). Although a brilliant richness of effect has been obtained, it is at the expense of the 'feeling of repose' that Miss Jekyll had in mind. Lutyens's exuberance needed sometimes to be held in check.

115. Marsh Court: sunken pool from the house. [From *Gardens for Small Country Houses*, 1912]

The integration of house, gardens and landscape displayed by Marsh Court was developed further by Lutyens at Lambay Castle (1905–12), considered by Hussey to be 'the most sustained expression of his poetic genius'.[40] In 1905 Cecil Baring, director of Barings Bank and later 3rd Baron Revelstoke, asked Lutyens to advise on the rehabilitation and enlargement of a derelict fortress (built in 1575–95) on Lambay Island about three miles off the coast of County Dublin. The subsequent success of Lambay owed much to the close relationship that developed between the Lutyens and Baring families; according to Mary Lutyens, 'Father always seemed at his happiest with the Barings'. The island was a desolate, green and rocky square mile inhabited mainly by gulls, guillemots, fallow deer and grey seals, the fort being situated on a slope that rose gently from the jetty on the north-west. In March 1910 Lutyens was stranded there for two days in rough seas and wrote

to his wife: 'the weather has been bad and getting material to the place well nigh impossible. I do wish you could come to Lambay. It is such a delicious aloof place alone in its wash of waters.'[41] In an effort to provide some protection for this windswept retreat, Lutyens planned a new service and guest court and farm buildings to the north-east, a plantation of ash and sycamore to the south-west and enclosed it all within a circular rampart in the manner of a

116. Lambay Castle, County Dublin (1905): general view north-west towards the mainland. [*CL* 1929].

117. Lambay Castle: west forecourt looking north-west. [*CL* 1929]

fortified castle (Plate 118). Behind this *enceinte* the ground rises to its highest point of four hundred feet to the east (Plate 116).

The approach is by foot from the jetty across an open field to a bastioned entrance with gates suggesting a portcullis. This section of the rampart is constructed of double walls filled with excavated

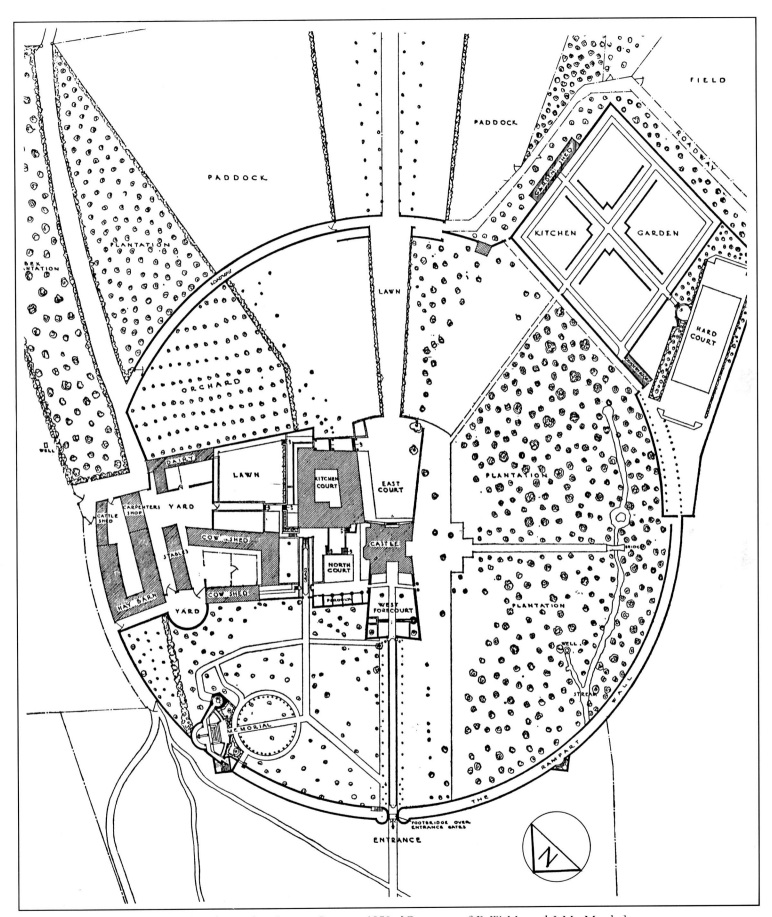

FIELD

ROADWAY

PADDOCK

KITCHEN GARDEN

HARD COURT

PADDOCK

PLANTATION

ILEX PLANTATION

LAWN

WELL

PLANTATION

ORCHARD

DAIRY

LAWN

CARPENTERS SHOP

CATTLE SHED

KITCHEN COURT

EAST COURT

COW SHED

STABLES

YARD

HAY BARN

COW SHED

NORTH COURT

CASTLE

PLANTATION

WEST FORECOURT

BRIDGE

WELL

STREAM

THE RAMPART WALL

MEMORIAL

FOOTBRIDGE OVER ENTRANCE GATES

ENTRANCE

118. Lambay Castle: Layout plan drawn by George Stewart 1950. [Courtesy of R.W.M. and J.M. Monks]

material forming a grass walk along the top, connected over the gates by a footbridge. Inside is an avenue—originally lined with mulberry trees until torn out of the ground by gales in the late 1930s—placed axially on the fort and consisting of a mown grass path edged with stone flags. It leads to the West Forecourt, the first of three walled courts or gardens clustered around the house, entered through the gates of a lattice screen-cum-*clair-voyée* in an inverted, segmentally arched wall echoing the circular rampart (Plate 117). Within, the path is of stone, and a rill crosses under it to feed a sunken tank on the left, another playful allusion to a castle moat. Then, before the entrance to the castle is finally reached, there is another cross-path, leading on the left to the North Court, which has a pergola to one side supported by massive round piers from an old farm shed, and from which steps ascend between raised flower beds towards a lawn and orchards to the east. These sheltered walled enclosures are a further instance of the way Lutyens expanded his houses by the addition of large, roofless outdoor rooms. The enclosing walls of the West Forecourt and East Court are splayed, their lines radiating out to the south-east to form lawns and avenues rising up the hillside, further anchoring the castle to its site, an idea that must have been triggered by the enfiladed corner towers of the fort.

In 1907 Miss Jekyll prepared planting schemes for Lambay that included a wide herbaceous border on the south-facing wall of the East Court. For this she optimistically suggested peonies, lilies and snapdragons amongst the rosemary, lavender, *Santolina* and *Yucca*.[42] Sections of the rampart were clothed with *Cotoneaster*, *Escallonia*, buckthorn and *Fuchsia* which prospered in places; but walls on their own without the support of thick belts of trees provide limited protection in a situation exposed to salt-laden winds.[43] The gardens and landscaping of Lambay were primarily a tribute to Lutyens's chaste handling of planes of mown grass and stone paving. The peak of his romantic phase, the buildings were roofed throughout with grey pantiles, the walls being of the island's porphyry, 'coppery green and coppery brown with purple streaks, like a stormy sea, shot with feldspar crystals'. The interior was of the utmost Arts and Crafts simplicity: whitewashed walls and scrubbed oak floors relieved by rugs. Outside, all is bleached and washed by the elements and, as Hussey observed, 'the buildings are of much the same colour as the rosemary that flowers below them and the sea on a misty day'.[44]

Gardens added to Existing Houses

As gardens and gardening became more fashionable and the partners' reputation grew, they were increasingly approached by owners wanting new gardens for their country homes. More often than not the existing houses lacked distinction, the gardens being designed independently of them, to be seen from but not necessarily to harmonise with the house itself. This was the case at Heywood, Lutyens's most important garden in Ireland, carried out in 1909–12 for Lieutenant-Colonel William Hutcheson Poë[45] and situated at Ballinakill, near Abbey Leix, County Laois. Old photographs testify to the unexceptional exterior of this eighteenth-century house, which was designed in 1773 by its owner, Michael

Frederick Trench. He showed more ability, however, as a landscape gardener, laying out a chain of artificial lakes and embellishing the demesne with picturesque features including temples, a mausoleum, a stone cross and reconstructed ruins from the Friary at Aghaboe. The house overlooked a landscape park, the ground falling away sharply towards the lakes to the south-west. Part of Lutyens's brief was to provide a large lawn on the garden front, but this had to be contained—at considerably greater expense than Poë had contemplated—by a massive stone wall complete with battered buttresses. When formal gardens were added to Georgian houses in landscape parks the appearance of the house in its setting often suffered, and at Heywood this retaining wall rears up in a most ungainly fashion when seen from the lake walk. Between the lawn and the house Lutyens arranged terraces on two levels (Plate 119). From the lower terrace steps lead down to a pergola walk, almost concealed below the flower border at the north-west end of the lawn—a delightful feature, wreathed in *Wisteria*, honeysuckle and the occasional climbing rose. It is constructed of Ionic columns taken from a Temple of the Winds that once stood in the park, and, though somewhat slender supports for the heavy cambered oak beams, they contrast with the rugged stonework of the retaining walls, whilst framing the view down to the lake, glimpsed through trees beyond the flower-bordered parapet. The upper terrace continues south-east in a long vista through a pleached alley to the main feature of Heywood: the Fountain Garden.

The elliptical form of this garden (which echoes that at the Villa Donà delle Rose, Valsanzibio, Venetia) was prompted by an existing stone wall, which ran from the south corner of the house, then curved round to the entrance gates. In the residual space to the north Lutyens laid out a yew garden and added oval niches containing lead busts in the old wall. At the eastern end of the alley, gates admit to the large, bowl-shaped sunk garden which consists of three concentric, oval tiers connected by flights of steps: an upper walk between flower borders, then a lower border, and finally a pool within a band of grass (Plate 120). Eight bronze tortoises faced into the pool which had as its central feature a pedestal in Antwerp stone supporting a bronze group by John Hughes. Lutyens shared Miss Jekyll's dislike of elaborate fountain centrepieces and complained in a letter to his wife from Grasse in 1911, 'Col. Poë writes from Paris. He is having a hideous fountain made in Paris for my garden.'[46] Fortunately, he managed to persuade Poë to abandon this and accept his own design. Closing the vista on the far side, a pantiled garden house adds an Italian note to the garden, the fine details of its limestone dressings contrasting with the dark grey brown of the local, sandstone walling, which is used throughout, its crevices harbouring plants in characteristic Jekyll manner. In 1910 she prepared schemes for the borders but no plans have survived. Early photographs show the garden house clothed in jasmine; shrubs and creepers growing against the perimeter walls; and the second tier filled with perennials and annuals including irises, *Alchemilla mollis*, foxgloves and tobacco plant.

Heywood was a difficult commission for Lutyens, but several features bear witness to the care he took over its three-dimensional effects: the prospect from the pergola; the ingeniously contrived counter-curving steps which link the yew garden directly with the

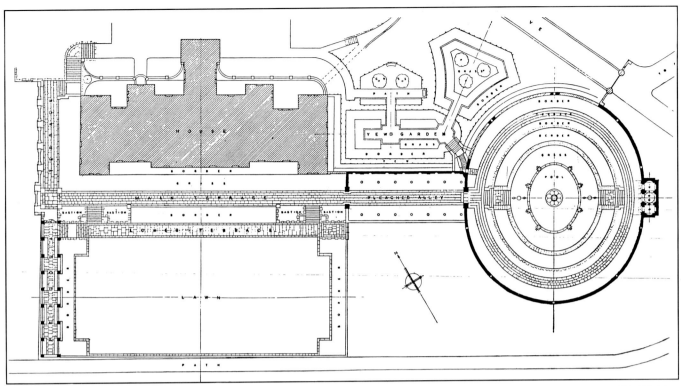

119. Heywood, Ballinakill, County Laois (1909–12): layout plan drawn by George Stewart 1950. [Courtesy of R.W.M. and J.M. Monks]

120. Heywood: Fountain Garden. [*CL* 1919]

121. Heywood: steps linking Yew and Fountain Gardens. [Author 1984]

garden below (Plate 121); and the oval *clair-voyees* in the enclosing wall of the sunk garden which provide framed views of the landscape beyond. Early in June 1909 Lutyens spent two days at Heywood, work beginning soon after, and he made further visits between then and August 1912.[47] Lawrence Weaver summed it up well in his *Country Life* article of 1919: 'In some gardens of marked beauty there comes sometimes the chilling sense that they were brought to life on paper and translated into stone and hedge and turf. Here they seem to have been carved by a skilful hand straight from the hillside without intent to make an architectural gesture or to phrase a theory of design. And the result is a very gracious garden.'[48] Usually it is the gardens of country houses that are the victims of time, but at Heywood the reverse is true. In 1950 the house burned down and only a levelled grassed area remains where it once stood; but the gardens are being lovingly restored by the present owners, the Salesian Fathers.[49]

Lutyens's most dramatic Italian-inspired garden was devised in 1902 at Ammerdown Park, near Radstock, Somerset, for the 3rd Baron Hylton. Earlier he had added an Italian garden (with a sideways glance at Nesfield's East Parterre of c.1851), at Eaton Hall, Chester (1897–8) for the 1st Duke of Westminster (Plate 123).[50] That commission probably came through Miss Jekyll who in 1874–5 had designed some curtains and fittings for Eaton.[51] There is no evidence that she collaborated at either Eaton Hall or Ammerdown, although Lutyens would have benefited from her first-hand knowledge of the historic gardens of Italy. She had first begun sketching there back in 1868, and in 1896 she wrote, 'In what other country of the world can one receive such impressions of poetry and mystery as among the waters and groves of Italy?[52] The Villa d'Este she considered 'one of the noblest of the gardens of the Renaissance', although when Lutyens saw it for himself on his first visit to Italy in October 1909 he was disappointed: 'Some

122. Ammerdown, near Radstock, Somerset (1901): circular parterre. [Author 1984]

of the work—the terrace balustrades—lovely, but more...was horrible and ugly....It wants to be seen with great discrimination. Yet, there is a real god-given loveliness.'[53]

The idea for the Italian garden at Ammerdown probably came from the Hyltons themselves. Lady Hylton was both artist and gardener. She had visited Italy after her marriage in 1896 and had a special interest in Italian history.[54] Ammerdown House (1788–93) was designed by James Wyatt and, in keeping with the times, stood in a landscape park; deer could be fed from the windows. In 1902 a revival of sympathy for the eighteenth-century park had not yet occurred, and it would have been generally felt that the house lacked a formal garden. There was a large, walled kitchen garden on higher ground to the north-east, with a fine stone orangery of 1793, also by Wyatt, in the centre of its south wall, but being at an angle to the house, it posed a problem for Lutyens to design linking gardens that would resolve the disparity between its axis

123. Eaton Hall, Chester (1897–8): Italian Garden. [*CL* 1901]

and that running east-west from the south front of the house. His solution was to contrive a pivotal rotunda at the intersection of the axes, embedded within a rectangular mass of yew lying parallel with the east front (Plate 124). From the south terrace a path descends in three stages to this circular parterre, its axis continuing out and beyond as a vista through an avenue of limes. Elaborate box-edged beds, scarlet flowers in the ascendant, echo in minor key the yew walls, while the sound of water playing in the central fountain marks the point where balanced axes meet, those to the south leading down steps to the lake garden, while to the north one path ends in a secret rose garden with central astrolabe, the other and principal vista passing through a square court and up to the orangery (Plate 125).

The walls of these gardens appear to have been hollowed out of the solid yew to imply rooms and linking passageways or doorways, as at the Villa Bernardini at Saltocchio near Lucca (1590), where a series of garden rooms were laid out amidst *boschi*.[55] Lutyens was to create other gardens with a strong Italian flavour, including the elegant, London town garden for Sir Hugh Lane at 100 Cheyne Walk (1910),[56] but at Ammerdown he was able to pursue the theme begun in the Dutch Garden at Orchards. Designing in yew appealed to him (in the 1930s he had great fun drawing up plans for a huge, semi-serious 'green mansion' for Saxton Noble[57]), and at Ammerdown he placed statuary *à l'Italienne* within scooped-out niches and exedræ, highlighted against the dark *terre verte* of the twelve-foot-high yew hedges

124. Ammerdown: layout plan. [Miranda Ottewill]

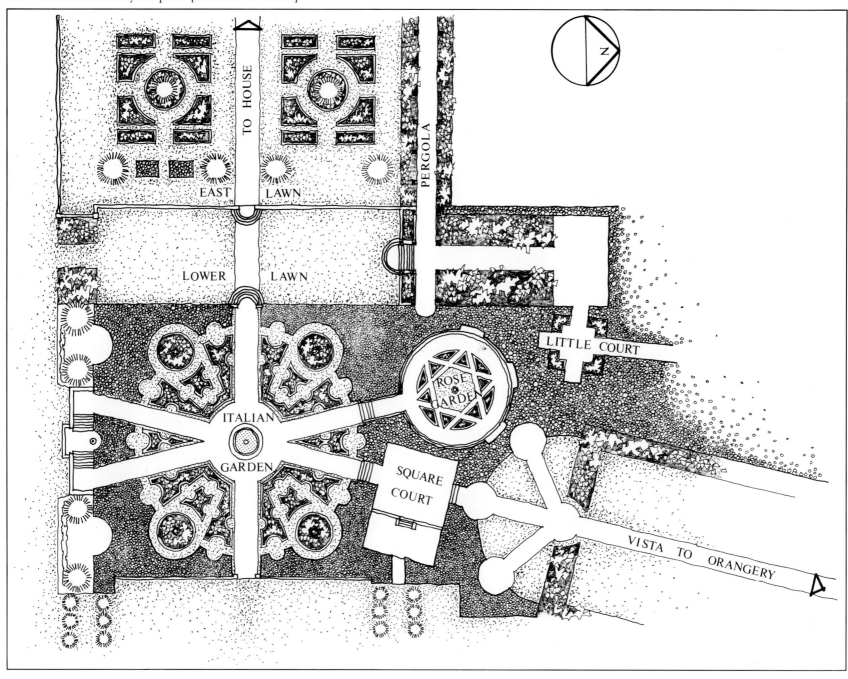

125. Ammerdown: vista north towards orangery. [Author 1984]

126. Abbotswood, Stow-on-the-Wold, Gloucestershire (1902): view from the lower lawn towards the house. [From a Lumière autochrome c.1910; RCHME]

(Plate 122).[58] The garden also contained another characteristic Italian feature, a little 'green theatre', forty-five feet by thirty feet with raised platform and intriguing canted exit leading to another avenue in the park.[59]

In the same year as Ammerdown Lutyens remodelled the house and laid out gardens at Abbotswood, near Stow-on-the-Wold, Gloucestershire. There, too, it appears Miss Jekyll took no active part, although, as with so many of his commissions, she did introduce him to the owner, the banker Mark Fenwick (1860–1945), himself an amateur gardener. To increase the scale of the Victorian house Lutyens added a lily-pool court on the west front, focusing on an alcoved fountain recess, while to the south he laid out an elaborate terraced garden divided equally into a formal parterre, with pergola on the east (now demolished), and a lower lawn with pool and corner garden house, all richly planted and

magnificent in its prime (Plate 126).[60] Less successful was the effect of the garden when viewed from the house, the terraces obtruding into the Cotswold landscape. As Robinson had complained in his *English Flower Garden*, 'to make delightful gardens in or near [houses] is quite a different thing from cutting off the landscape with vast flat patterns'.[61] That criticism does not, however, apply to what is generally agreed to be the culmination of Lutyens's collaboration with Miss Jekyll: the gardens of Hestercombe (1904–9).

In 1903 Hon. E.W.B. Portman (1856–1911), eldest son of the 2nd Viscount Portman of Bryanston, engaged Lutyens to add an orangery and parterre at Hestercombe House, situated four miles north of Taunton, Somerset, and commanding a superb view south over Taunton Dene to the distant Blackdown Hills. The property had acquired distinction in the eighteenth century as the home of the landscape painter C.W. Bampfylde (d.1791), who designed the combe behind the house in accordance with picturesque theory. In the 1870s the estate was bought by the 1st Viscount Portman, who laid out the upper terrace and whose unfortunate remodelling of the Queen Anne house gave Lutyens some justification for turning his back on it.

The garden was laid out in two sections (Plate 127): the Great Plat below the existing terrace; and, connected to it by a pivotal rotunda pool, the Orangery and Dutch Garden, set an an angle determined by existing trees and overlooking the site of Bampfylde's lawn to the south. Exploiting the steep fall in the site, Lutyens created a succession of six levels descending first to a rose garden, which provides an 'outdoor room' close to the house, and then to the grassed Grey Walk immediately beneath the old terrace, bordered with the Jekyllian grey and blue foliage of lavender, *Nepeta*, pinks, *Yucca* and the blue elymus grass. Except for dressings of Ham Hill ashlar, the walling throughout is of self-splitting, unworked rubble stone, quarried nearby; and selected stones

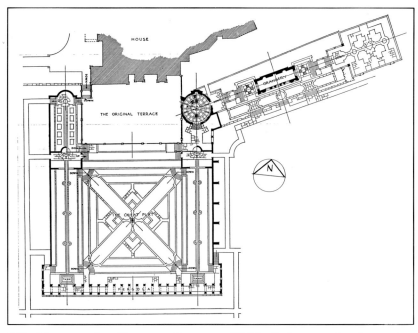

127. Hestercombe, Taunton, Somerset (1904–9): layout plan drawn by George Stewart 1950. [Courtesy of R.W.M. and J.M. Monks]

from the same quarry are used for the paving. The mortar joints of retaining walls are as usual set back to allow plants to take root, and the *Erigeron* daisy has become naturalized there. Below each end of the Grey Walk are landings containing circular pool alcoves feeding the West and East Rills, which convey water to tanks at the southern corners. These channels and small pools, set in a carpet of grass flanked by flower borders, are a development of the theme introduced at Deanery Garden and were filled with irises, forget-me-nots, arum lily, water plantain and arrowhead. Their edging is of Ham Hill ashlar stone and, as described by Miss Jekyll, 'at even intervals they turn, after the manner of the gathered ribbon strap-work of ancient needlework, and enclose circular tanklets giving the opportunity of a distinct punctuation with important plants... (Flowering Rush)' (Plate 128).[62] At the far end, steps lead down to a pergola supported by massive piers, alternately round and square, up which climbed vines, *Forsythia* and old-fashioned roses. It runs along the southern boundary providing a view of the Vale between the piers, and broken only to provide vistas from the Rill Gardens. Within, one looks down on to the pattern of the parterre, 125 feet square with central sundial and entered from quadrants of steps at each corner. It was this arrangement of corner entrances that precipitated the garden's most striking feature (similar to Schultz's earlier parterre at Mochrum): the diagonal division of the Great Plat by broad grass walks. These have apsidal ends and enclose triangular flower beds of China roses, peonies and *Delphinium*, their outline strengthened by stone surrounds and an edging of *Bergenia cordifolia*.

There was nothing revivalistic about Hestercombe; it was an original work of garden art. Here was the repose of the garden enclosed, drifts of luxuriant foliage spilling over wall and terrace to a mosaic of enchanting colour beneath, the raised walk and pergola, though rising from a bastion wall below, providing no

more than a gentle demarcation between its verdant lawns and the bordering meadows (Plate 92). The relationship of formal garden to natural landscape reached joyful resolution in these gardens. As Tipping remarked, 'They prove that an architect can be in unison with nature, that a formal garden can form part of a landscape'.[63]

'Wrenaissance'

By the time of Hestercombe, Lutyens had begun to turn away from the vernacular and Tudor modes towards classicism, and by 1910 his conversion was complete. The early houses had contained classical elements, but it was in the garden designs that classical planning first appeared; at Orchards, Le Bois des Moutiers and Marsh Court, for example, the gardens are more formal than the houses. Lutyens had his first opportunity of working entirely within the classical orders in 1906, with Heathcote, Ilkley, for J.T. Hemingway, a rich Yorkshire cotton-broker. Built of Guiseley stone with red pantiled roofs, the house is united with the garden in one, grand, axial sequence from entrance court, through the hall to the terrace, where a distant view of Ilkley Moor is revealed beyond an elliptical lawn.[64] Lutyens was to pursue this classical 'High Game' in his banks and offices culminating in New Delhi, but for the bulk of his domestic work from this period he evolved a more sober manner, his 'Wrenaissance', which he introduced to London in the *Country Life* building (1905). This urbane style was a forerunner of the ubiquitous 'neo-Georgian' of the post-war years, invoking the late seventeenth-century house with its hipped roofs, white-painted cornices and sash windows; and it was accompanied by an equally restrained treatment of the gardens.

Its first appearance on a grand scale was at Great Maytham, Rolvenden, Kent (1909), where from 1898 to 1907 the remnants of the original eighteenth-century house had been let to Frances Hodgson Burnett, its old walled garden inspiring *The Secret Garden* (1911), in which a magical and symbolic restoration was wrought amongst roses, evergreen alcoves, stone seats and moss-covered urns. In 1909 the house was bought by H.J. Tennant[65] who engaged Lutyens to rebuild it and re-design the grounds. A new clock-house was built at the road to the north-east, and an avenue of limes planted leading to the forecourt. Lutyens remodelled the old walled gardens, and on the garden front he added a magnificent planted terrace to provide a strong plinth to the house. His treatment of the ground to the south reflected the trend in garden design towards more openness of prospect.[66] Except for flagged paving following the line of the old garden wall, the layout consisted merely of descending planes of lawn acting as a foil to both the foreground and the distant view of the Kent countryside (Plate 129). The contrast with Abbotswood could hardly be greater. The house is a clear tribute, writ large, to its Georgian predecessor, but the grounds too, though in essence formal, seem to revive the spirit of the early eighteenth-century vista.

A similar restraint is evident at two other 'Wrenaissance' houses: The Salutation at Sandwich, Kent (1911), for two bachelor brothers, Gaspard and Henry Farrar; and Ednaston Manor, Brailsford, Derbyshire (1912–13) for W.G. Player. The Salutation (its

128 Hestercombe: West Rill Garden. [RCHME 1982]

129. Great Maytham, Rolvenden, Kent (1909): view to the south. [Author 1984]

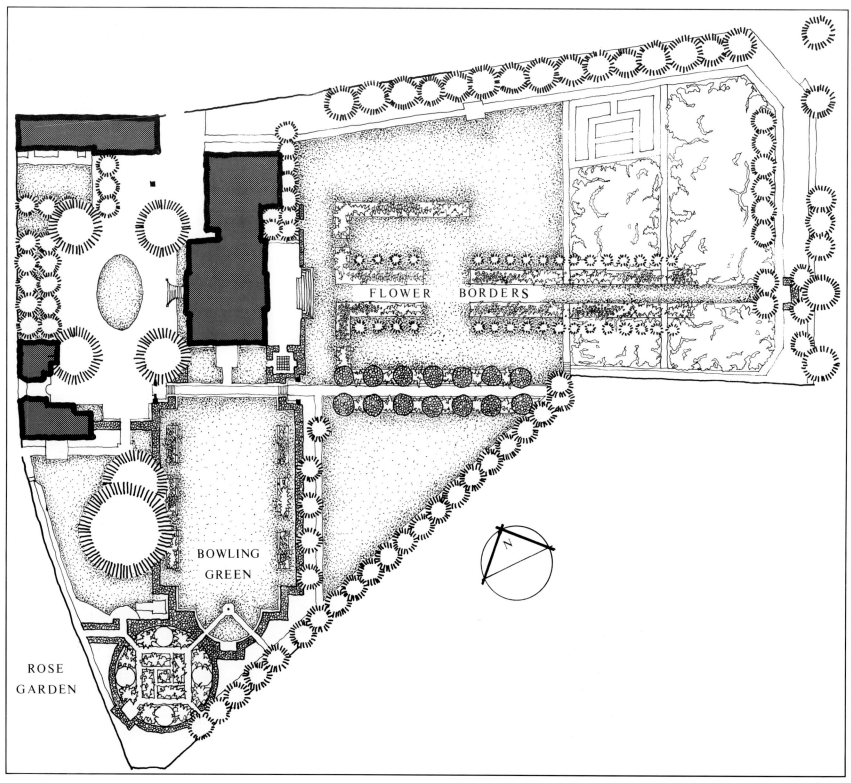

130. The Salutation, Sandwich, Kent (1911): layout plan. [Miranda Ottewill]

name came from an inn which once stood there) is situated at the edge of the town on an irregularly shaped site surrounded by high walls (Plate 130). Lutyens gave the house bi-axial symmetry, its south and east elevations being centred on two separate garden compartments. To the south is a bowling green, raised to the level of the reception rooms, enclosed by thick yew hedges and pro-

viding a view of the church tower. It has an apsidal southern end with sundial from which a path radiates south-west to the circular rose garden. The main entrance is off the street through a gatehouse, its axis extending across the raised garden to a path bordered by clipped cylinders of *Quercus ilex*. The east lawn, approached from a wide terrace off the dining room, has a long vista between herbaceous borders and rose pillars. Ednaston, also bi-axial, has stepped terraces on the east, their architectural severity now pleasantly submerged beneath Jekyll-style planting.[67]

Lutyens laid out the gardens of all these 'Wrenaissance' houses on his own, but Folly Farm was designed in close liaison with Miss Jekyll and provided a fitting conclusion to their work before the intervention of the First World War. Located at Sulhamstead, six miles west of Reading in the Kennet Valley, the site included an old timber-framed farmhouse to which in 1906 Lutyens added for H. Cochrane, an exquisite, H-plan 'William and Mary' house built of narrow, blue-grey Reading bricks with red dressings under a hipped roof. Like Millmead it was approached from an arched doorway off the road into a walled entrance court. A further court to the right was centred on the classic form of a terracotta oil jar, both courts having the required flagged paths between 'plain un-

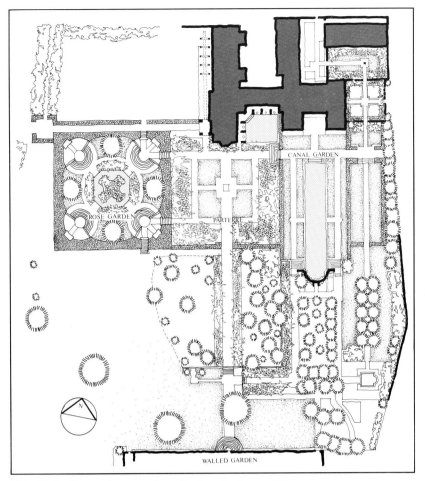

132. Folly Farm: layout plan. [Miranda Ottewill]

131. Folly Farm, Sulhamstead, Berkshire (1906, 1912): vista from the entrance court. [Author 1982]

broken turf' edged with box, relieved by borders of old-fashioned flowers and backed by climbing roses, *Clematis*, jasmine and laurustinus. To the left, the axis continued as the first of Folly Farm's many vistas, a raised walk leading to an avenue of limes (Plate 131).

In 1912 Zachary Merton, a wealthy mine-owner, commissioned Lutyens to provide additional accommodation at Folly Farm. His solution to this was a *tour de force* of architectural contrast. So as not to disturb the earlier house, he planned the new block at right angles joined by a splendid extravagance, a two-storey corridor in his vernacular manner which, viewed from the south, has a barnlike appearance, its enormous roof sweeping down to within five feet of a tank court, whose still, dark water reflects a cloister of massive battered piers. It was at this stage that the main gardens were designed, continuing the compartmental theme of the earlier layout (Plate 132). On the axis of the 1906 house they added, appropriately, a Dutch canal garden enclosed by low, yew hedges. It was an object lesson in simplicity and repose incorporating many of the principles that Miss Jekyll had set down in *Wall and Water Gardens*. The impeccably detailed surrounds were set flush with the adjoining lawns and the water level was high, giving mirror-like reflections (Plate 133). At the southern end of the 1912 addition, a two-storey bay closed another vista from the walled garden, and on its axis a *parterre à l'anglaise* was laid out in grass and paving, its

133. Folly Farm: view from the south showing the Reflecting Pool. [From L. Weaver, *Houses and Gardens by E.L. Lutyens*, 1913]

stark simplicity accentuated by a central, altarlike block of Purbeck marble. West of this, steps led down through thick, scalloped yew hedges to the sunken rose garden. This had circular platforms at each corner from which semi-circular steps descended to rose beds around an octagonal pool with central lavender bed (Plate 134).[68] It was a direct descendant of the Dutch garden at Orchards, but the geometry had become self-consciously elaborate with little of the charm of that early masterpiece. Perhaps it was a portent of the diminishing influence of Miss Jekyll.

In the summer of 1916 Folly Farm was the setting of a rare holiday which the whole Lutyens family spent together; even Miss Jekyll was persuaded to leave her beloved Munstead for a while. Mary Lutyens has written of her father on that occasion: 'His happiness that summer was like a blessing on the house. I have a very clear picture of him in my mind, facing me on the croquet lawn at Folly Farm, wearing his usual London clothes, his pipe in his mouth, his mallet poised between his legs for a shot.'[69] The entire vocabulary of the Lutyens-Jekyll garden was marshalled at Folly Farm: compartmentation, vistas, the use of levels, steps, paving patterns, water, planting, the herbaceous border. But there were signs that the partnership was beginning to fade. Although Lutyens continued to consult Miss Jekyll (for example at Amport

134. Folly Farm: Sunken Pool Garden. [Author 1978]

and Gledstone, described in Chapter 8), they were drifting apart in their interests. He was becoming obsessed with the classical language of architecture. In his garden designs, the 'backbone' was becoming a dominant skeleton entirely dependent on the relieving effect of her planting. This is particularly noticeable today when gardens on that scale are impossible to maintain. As he moved away from her restraining and humanizing influence, away from his Arts and Crafts roots, his designs became more assertive, instead of providing a basic framework to be embellished by her hand. They lacked the restraint of, for instance, some of the old Italian gardens, which retained their beauty, were even enhanced by the passage of time. The formula expressed by Vita Sackville-West, 'maximum formality of design with maximum informality of planting', no longer worked its magic. By the close of Edward's reign Lutyens had moved irrevocably to a system of rationalized proportion and rhythmical design summed up in his motto, *Metiendo vivendum*: 'By measure we must live'. But he never lost his feeling for natural materials, something fostered by Miss Jekyll on those early pony-cart excursions in the Surrey lanes.

As the focus of Lutyens's practice moved from country houses to important public buildings, Miss Jekyll was less occupied with his large formal layouts. Her attention was directed more to the 'natural' garden, what she called 'the free and less costly ways of gardening, such as give the greatest happiness for the least expenditure.'[70] However, her growing reputation, based on both her planting schemes and her books, meant that she was increasingly in demand from private clients; also from other architects who, though probably less fun to work with than Lutyens, were more practical, and sometimes offered her more scope. Most of these architects had been nurtured in and remained faithful to the Arts and Crafts cause. To them she represented a link with Ruskin, Robinson and the 'natural' school, while, on her part, she must have welcomed any association with a movement that sprang from the same roots as her own.[71]

135. Snowshill Manor, near Broadway, Gloucestershire (Charles Wade, 1919–23): general view looking south-west. [Author 1981]

6

The Arts and Crafts Garden

Green yew chambers and ash pavilions; with orchard glades and nut alleys, with chequers of flower-beds and borders of rose trellis; with summer-house, fountain and sundial...a sunny wall, a pleasant shade, a seat for rest, and all around the sense of the flowers, their brightness, their fragrance.

E.S. Prior, 1901[1]

Central to the Arts and Crafts creed was a reverence for nature combined with a belief in organic design based on traditional crafts. C.F.A. Voysey expressed this in a lecture in 1909: 'Now, how does nature go to work? Everywhere we find her making the best possible use of immediate conditions, evolving beauty out of fitness, and wisdom out of regard for requirements, materials and conditions all in exquisite harmony with established law.'[2] He was speaking of building, but since a further aim of the movement was to bring together all the arts and crafts, especially those associated with the home, it was but a short step from the house to the garden; this deserved equal attention, not in the Victorian way but with the new-found feeling for materials that embraced plants as well as brick and stone. A house could not be designed without due regard for site, materials and climate; likewise some knowledge of garden-craft was needed, of the natural habitat of trees and plants, if both house and garden were to be seen to belong to the soil.

Certain specific aims derived from this ideological base, and although the Arts and Crafts garden resists definition as a style, a number of common characteristics can be identified. A sacred principle was the use of local materials in the construction of the garden and this extended as far as possible to the plants themselves. Hence a preference for old-fashioned flowers and traditional trees and shrubs indigenous to the locality in place of the sophisticated and exotic plants and specimen trees favoured by the Victorians. Hedges and topiary excepted, more freedom of growth was allowed in the planting, and just as a mellow patina of age was viewed as a positive asset on an Arts and Crafts house, so too was nature encouraged to become established in the paving and walls of the garden and generally to clothe and subdue the underlying architectural form. Colour schemes were more naturalistic, being restricted to subtle and muted hues or monochrome masses embracing the colour and texture of both flowers and foliage. The various enclosures of the garden were defined less by walls and garden architecture than by clipped yew hedges, trellis screens, pergolas or alleys of pleached lime or hornbeam. Such elements helped also to merge house and garden, while further from the house the boundary was often broken down with judicious placing of trees or areas of wild planting to create a transition with the surrounding landscape. Finally it is significant that the most important Arts and Crafts designers were themselves amateur gardeners, constantly gaining knowledge of the craft in their own gardens and thereby able to establish good working relationships with both professional gardeners and owners.

Morris, Webb and the Old-Fashioned Garden

The inspiration behind many of these attitudes can be traced back to William Morris. His own gardens, beginning with Red House, Bexley Heath (1859), were filled with old-fashioned flowers, the principle of their growth forming the basis of many of his wallpapers and chintzes.[3] 'The garden came into the house'[4] with his designs, as it had earlier in Pre-Raphaelite paintings such as Millais's *Mariana* (1850–1), and as it did almost literally at Red House. Its garden was a constant source of joy to Morris:

> in his knowledge of gardening he did...with reason pride himself. It is very doubtful whether he was ever seen with a spade in his hands; in later years at Kelmscott his manual work in the garden was almost limited to clipping his yew hedges. But of flowers and vegetables and fruit trees he knew all the ways and capabilities. Red House garden, with its long grass walks, its mid-summer lilies and autumn sunflowers, its wattled rose-trellises inclosing richly-flowered square garden plots, was then as unique as the house it surrounded. The building had been planned with such care that hardly a tree in the orchard had to be cut down; apples fell in at the windows as they stood open on hot autumn nights.[5]

Although notoriously untidy himself, Morris liked order in the garden and wrote from Kelmscott House in 1882, no doubt with a touch of irony, 'we are hard at work gardening here, making dry paths and a sublimely tidy box-edging; how I love tidiness!'[6]

Morris met Philip Webb (1831–1915), the architect of Red House, in the Oxford office of G.E. Street in 1856 and they became life-long friends and associates, Webb's buildings expressing an attitude to design similar to that which Morris brought to the crafts.[7] Webb's ideas on garden design favoured the 'old-fashioned', compartmented approach. At his *magnum opus*, Clouds (1876–85), situated on the wooded edge of the Wiltshire Downs near East Knoyle, he seems to have won the approval of the natural as well as the formal school. Even Robinson singled it out for praise: 'As regards the best new houses, Clouds, so well built by Mr Philip Webb, is not any the worse for its picturesque surroundings, which do not meet the architect's senseless craving for order and balance.'[8] In fact, Clouds was not without its formal gardens, but Robinson would certainly have approved of the care Webb took over the placing of the house. After visiting the site with his client, Hon. Percy Wyndham, a younger son of Lord Leconfield, he agreed to undertake the work but spoke of the 'absolute necessity of preserving the fine yew trees'.[9] One of these was retained at the south-east corner of the new house and acted as a pivot between the south lawn and the gardens enclosed by yew hedges on the east. Clouds was 'one of the houses that set the style for a particular way of country-house life',[10] a venue for gatherings of a circle that aimed to combine politics with art and literature. Through the Wyndhams' romantic and aesthetic progeny (the three Wyndham sisters were competently recorded in Sargent's group[11]) it became a popular haunt of the Souls—a group reacting against the philistinism of the 'Marlborough House Set' which surrounded the Prince of Wales—being perfectly planned for their particular kind of informal house-party. There was always a room to adjourn to 'where confidences could be exchanged behind the scenes and cabinet decisions anticipated'.[12] The garden compartments also ministered to this function and like the decorations of the house they received the personal attention of the hostess, Madeline Wyndham, of whom Wilfred Scawen Blunt wrote, 'not a rose blossoms but with the owner's knowledge, not a lily withers but to the owner's grief'.[13] Webb took enormous care over both house and gardens; it took three years before the final design was agreed and the work was not finished until 1886. In 1889, fulfilling a strange prophecy, the house was gutted by fire, but rebuilt in 1892.[14]

The circumstances at Webb's last major country house, Standen, East Grinstead (1892–4), were not particularly favourable to a sympathetic garden scheme, for not only had a landscape designer, G.B. Simpson, already been appointed and work begun, but the owner's wife had colourful ideas for the planting which ran counter to Webb's quiet taste for old-fashioned flowers.[15] Probably his most fruitful collaboration with both owner and gardener took place in 1885 at Great Tangley Manor, near Guildford, a sixteenth-century, half-timbered house which had been bought in a derelict condition in 1884 by Wickham Flower.[16] Webb repaired and enlarged the house, and gardens were laid out within and beyond an old moat which was cleared and whose banks were planted with bog-weed and the large water saxifrage, *S. peltata*. The house was entered from the south through a long, oak-framed covered way with tiled roof which formed a bridge over the moat and partially screened a walled garden (Plate 136). To the right of the forecourt a pleached lime walk led to a rustic pergola clothed in vines, roses and *Clematis*. This beckoned to the wilder regions which included a rock garden and dell filled with a profusion of alpine plants (Plate

136. Great Tangley Manor, near Guildford, Surrey (Philip Webb, 1885): moat and bridge from the south-east. [*CL* 1905]

137. W.R. Lethaby with his wife, Edith, under the rustic pergola in the Nut Walk at The Barn, Hartley Wintney, c.1919. [Keith Collection]

138. Great Tangley Manor: the Dell. [RCHME 1892]

138). Great Tangley Manor was familiar to Gertrude Jekyll from childhood, and Lutyens probably assimilated much from its expert handling of traditional materials. Webb's close association with the gardener, Mr Whiteman, was a foretaste of the kind of working relationship that would underlie the Lutyens-Jekyll partnership.

The Influence of the Art Workers Guild

An architectural *eminence grise*, Webb never allowed his work to be illustrated while he was in practice, and, although young architects

worshipped at his feet from about 1890 at the Society for the Protection of Ancient Buildings, he was not involved in the founding of the Art Workers Guild. It is, however, to the influence of the Guild that one must return to pick up the threads of the Arts and Crafts garden as seen in the work of several founder members, all of whom, inspired by Sedding, contributed to the revival of the old-fashioned garden in the 1890s.

Webb's most ardent disciple, and the acknowledged teacher and spokesman for Art and Crafts architecture, was W.R. Lethaby (1857–1931) (Plate 137) whose few but significant buildings spanned a period of only ten years.[17] These began with Avon Tyrrell in the New Forest (1891) for Lord Manners which was designed to take full advantage of the view, its long garden front being anchored to the site by a broad, grassed terrace. By contrast the gardens at Lethaby's High Coxlease (1900) at nearby Lyndhurst, for Thomas Eustace Smith, were wilder in character, befitting their setting in a clearing on the edge of the forest, the main feature being a rock and water garden, planted with water-lilies and saxifrages and merging with the fern-carpeted woodland.[18]

Lethaby considered Melsetter in Orkney his best work, and, with touches of arcane symbolism beneath a reticent exterior, it in some ways reflected his own character. Situated on the remote island of Hoy, it was built from 1898 as an Arts and Crafts retreat for Thomas Middlemore, a retired Birmingham industrialist with artistic interests. To May Morris, a friend of Mrs Middlemore and a gardener herself, 'It seemed like the embodiment of some of those fairy palaces of which my father wrote with great charm and dignity...a very lovable place.'[19] Lethaby enlarged the existing laird's house in the local vernacular of green-grey Caithness slates and harled walls with red sandstone dressings. It nestled in the lee of a hill protected to the north by a belt of trees, and the gardens were laid out as walled enclosures (Plate 139). There was a dual approach to the flagged entrance courtyard: one road ran alongside the existing kitchen garden, a shrubbery, and a new rose garden enclosed by outbuildings on the site of the steading; the other approach was from the south, past a 'rookery' and the old, cross-pathed walled garden to which Lethaby added a pavilion to match the existing one at the south-west corner. Along the south terrace,

139. Melsetter, Hoy, Orkney (W.R. Lethaby, 1898); layout plan. [Redrawn by Elizabeth Brandon-Jones from the original sketch design dated 5 October 1898]

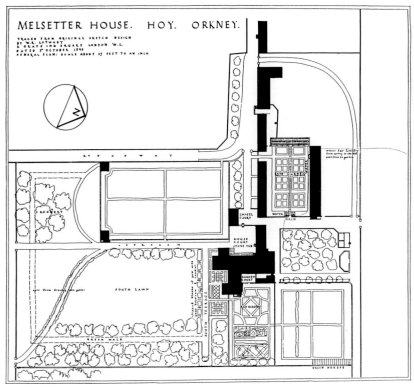

140. Melsetter: east parterre, 1942. [Courtesy of J. Brandon-Jones]

a serried row of guns and clipped yew overlooked a lawn flanked by a green walk, and a parterre was laid out east of the house. All was contained within a walled rectangle fitting into the pattern of the fields beyond, for unlike Lorimer's houses Melsetter was entirely surrounded by its gardens, giving the protection and security its location demanded. The exterior was appropriately severe, but inside could be found all the homely ingredients of Arts and Crafts living, including Morris materials and oak furniture designed by Lethaby himself. In the brief northern summer you could look down from the dining-room on to his east parterre and ponder its mystical patterns of daisies and red tulips (Plate 140).[20]

Leading the 1890s revival of the traditional domestic architecture of the English Renaissance were two ex-pupils of Norman Shaw, Ernest Newton (1856–1922) and Mervyn Macartney (1853–1932) (Plates 141, 142), whose urbane houses were accompanied by equally restrained and elegant formal gardens. Modest and unassuming, Newton was the antithesis of Blomfield, who described

141. Ernest Newton. [AWG Album c.1884]

142. Mervyn Macartney. [AWG Album c.1884]

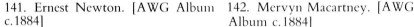

garden compartments grow, and the corridor from which they and house are entered. Beyond its enclosing walls of yew are, first, lawns, grass walks and a sunken bowling green, then a rose-

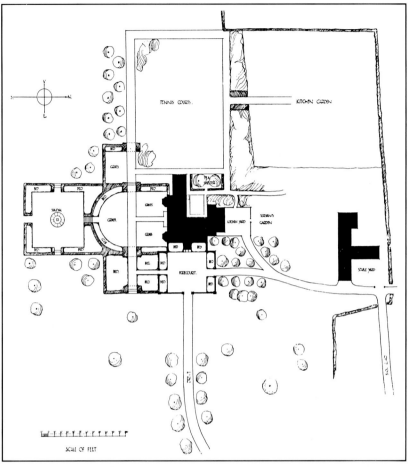

143. Redcourt, Haslemere, Surrey (Ernest Newton, 1894): layout plan. [From W.G. Newton, *The Work of Ernest Newton*, 1925]

144. Fouracre, West Green, Hampshire (Ernest Newton, 1901): entrance forecourt, drawn by T.H. Crawford, 1902. [BALDC]

him as 'an excellent architect, of fastidious taste. . . but not the man to lead a charge of cavalry'.[21] Newton believed the garden to be an essential complement of the plan of a house, and he demonstrated this in 1894 at Redcourt, Haslemere, for Louis Wigram (Plate 143). Its linked succession of yew-hedged enclosures showed a clear debt to *Garden-Craft*, especially in the entrance forecourt which echoed Sedding's quadrangular courtyard; 'the place for a walk on bleak days' he had written, 'in its borders you are sure of the earliest spring flowers, for the tender flowers can here bloom securely, the myrtle, the pomegranate will flourish, and the most fragrant plants and climbers hang over the door and windows. What is more charming than the effect of hollyhocks, peonies, poppies, tritomas and tulips seen against a yew hedge?'[22] Such forecourts became a common feature of Newton's houses (Plate 144).

Macartney established himself as a leading authority in the revival through his books such as *Later Renaissance Architecture in England* (with J. Belcher; 1898). Later, he published *English Houses and Gardens in the Seventeenth and Eighteenth Centuries* (1908), notes on views reproduced from Kip, Badeslade, Harris and others, and he also exerted much influence as editor of the *Architectural Review* from 1906 to 1920. His Irish background and love of gardening may have influenced Robinson's choice of him as architect of Holms Cottage at Gravetye.[23] Lawrence Weaver said of him, 'Nowhere is he more in his element than in garden design',[24] and a good example was Rosebank, the home he created for himself from 1895 on the site of a burnt-down cottage at Silchester Common in north Hampshire. No sign of classicism here, but it was an early work, and architects generally chose the modest vernacular when building for themselves. Rosebank was so enveloped in greenery that it became almost submerged by the garden. From the gate on the common a long vista extends to a sundial against a back-drop of pines. The bird's-eye view (Plate 145) shows this path to be the central stem off which the various covered pergola and trellis leading to the house, followed by the kitchen gardens and, to the left, a diminutive old cottage retained for garden use. Herbaceous borders flank the path where it continues between hedges of holly; the sundial marks a cross-path, while beyond, the garden merges with the heather which originally covered the site. All is unsophisticated cottage charm and simplicity, except for an Italian garden tucked away to the east of the house where a square of low fruit trees encloses a sunken circular pool.

Of all Shaw's pupils, the one most committed to forging links between the artist-architect and the craftsman was E.S. Prior (1852–1932) (Plate 146).[25] In a paper given at Edinburgh in 1889 he stressed the importance of natural materials: 'There are Nature's

145. Rosebank, Silchester Common, Hampshire (Mervyn Macartney, 1895): bird's-eye view. [From L. Weaver, *Small Country Houses of Today*, 1910]

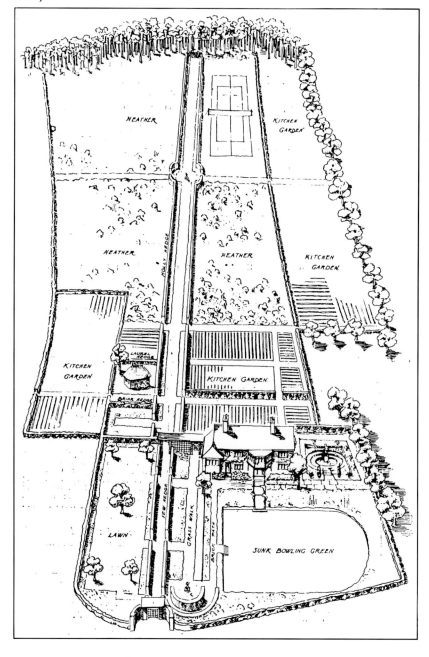

146. E.S. Prior [AWG Album c.1884]

own Textures for us to use . . . we may borrow from her and show the natural grain and figure of her work'; also of craftsmanship: 'our plaster may show the impress of the loving hand that laid it'.[26] But in spite of Ruskin's insistence on the liberty of craftsmen, neither Prior nor any other Arts and Crafts architect ever delegated much responsibility to them either in the house or the garden. To profit from the gardener-craftsman's practical experience was one thing, to allow him a say in the design quite another, and this applied as much when Miss Jekyell was brought in, her schemes always giving detailed planting instructions.[27]

In 1895, at the Royal Academy, Prior exhibited a model of a house in Dorset, one of the first of the 'butterfly houses' that were so fashionable in the Edwardian age,[28] and this led to the commission to build The Barn, Exmouth (1896–7) for H.B. Weatherall. A seminal house of the period, it was built with thatched roof and

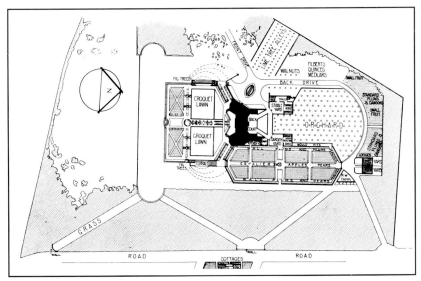

147. Home Place, Holt, Norfolk (E.S. Prior, 1903–5): layout plan. [*AR* February 1906]

used to build the house, the larger flints for the external facing of the walls, the smaller for the mass concrete'.[31] These cobbles and pebbles were also used for the retaining and dwarf walls of the garden, and for the risers of steps which thus appear to have grown from the ground under the sympathetic hands of the craftsmen. The layout (Plate 147) recalls Lutyens's play with diagonals at Grey Walls, gardens and approach drive being based on hexagonal lines related to the wings of the house which are set at 30 degrees to the central block. The sunk garden on the south front is approached off a terrace whose tapered ends lead down to pergolas supported on massive round piers. These were backed by flower-borders and high walls protecting the garden from northerly winds. On the central axis a double flight of steps descended past stepped stone tanks filled with water-lilies, irises and forget-me-nots. 'Italian' steps then led down to a double row of almond trees terminating in

walls of local sandstone interspersed at random with huge pebbles found on the site. Both house and walled garden affirmed his belief in symmetry. The wings of the house enclosed a verandah from which steps led south to the kitchen garden and west to formal flower beds overlooking the sea and protected on the north by a thatched wall and circular summer-house.[29] In 1901 Prior contributed a series of articles on 'Garden-Making' to *The Studio* which illustrated his strongly formal stance. 'The more regular the general form of the layout', he wrote, 'the more economical will it be in every respect. And since man walks straight from point to point—unless intoxicated—a bend or a curve certainly requires excuse for its eccentricity.'

Prior exemplified this at his next large house, Home Place, Holt, Norfolk (1903–5), which developed the 'butterfly' theme on a grander scale. The Norfolk coast near Cromer (the setting for L.P. Hartley's *The Shrimp and the Anemone*) was a popular Edwardian seaside resort, and Home Place was not the first 'butterfly' to arrive in the area. In 1900 Detmar Blow had built Happisburgh Manor, and others followed up to 1912 when Edward Maufe designed the last pre-war example, complete with axially planned garden, at Kelling Hall, only two miles from Holt, for Henry (later Sir Henry) Deterding, a director of Shell. Some of these were holiday homes where the garden was of minor importance, but at Home Place the extent of both house and garden, combined with Prior's highly personal and eccentric detailing, so drained the resources of the owner, the Reverend Percy R. Lloyd, that he was unable to live in it and it was let to another clergyman.[30] The house was built without a contractor but with the architect Randall Wells as resident master of the works. Prior's conviction that buildings be 'racy of the soil' dictated the materials for the walls: gravel, flint pebbles and cobbles. Furthermore, 'It was desired to furnish Home Place with a garden of such richness as would form a suitable setting for the house. The site was wind-swept and the soil not kindly. A sunk garden was indicated, and an acre was excavated to a considerable depth. The materials so obtained were graded and

148. Home Place: sunk garden from the south, 1905.

149. Home Place: pergola in kitchen garden. [*CL* 1909]

A.M. Stedman. Situated in the Surrey hills above Haslemere, the ground sloped to the west with views across a combe, but Voysey stepped the house up across the contours with the principal rooms facing south on to an ascending succession of terraced gardens. This anchored the house to the site and allowed the garden enclosures to be directly linked at various levels with the house, from whose windows a variety of vistas were obtained (Plate 151). The lowest level of the garden, a sunken lawn with sundial, was reached down a stairway from the south side of the forecourt through wrought-iron gates decorated with vine leaves. This compartment acted as a foil to its surroundings and had that quality of repose so sought after by Voysey, an object he shared with Gertrude Jekyll who in 1902 prepared a planting plan for a rose garden south of the lawn. Voysey's sympathy for her views was apparent from

150. C.F.A. Voysey. [AWG Album c.1884]

a central circular basin (Plate 148). On either side yew arches separated croquet lawns from flower beds crossed by diagonal paths, and the southern boundary was marked by a retaining wall with low arched fountains. The geometrical theme continued into the kitchen garden, whose walls supported plums and peaches, the central flagged paths being lined with espalier apples and pears either side of a central pergola (Plate 149).

The use of symmetry, axes and vistas seems to surprise those who associate the Arts and Crafts Movement with naturalness and everything informal.[32] The softening effect of planting may have made it more acceptable, but formality went back to the mediaeval garden, long before the influence of Renaissance Italy. C.F.A. Voysey (1857–1941) (Plate 150) considered himself the last disciple of Pugin, so one would expect to find echoes of the *hortus conclusus* in his garden layouts.[33]

The best surviving example is New Place (1897–1901), built for

151. New Place, Haslemere, Surrey (C.F.A. Voysey, 1897–1901): layout plan, dated 6 December 1897. [BALDC]

his 1909 lecture which observed of Nature, 'She furnishes with an abundance of the most soothing colour, viz., green; she uses her red most sparingly. In the spring she feasts us with delicate greens, greys, blues, purples, and, later on, yellow, gradually warming and strengthening her colour as the summer sun increases its power over the eye;...nature never allows her colours to quarrel.... Harmony is everywhere.'[34] The east retaining wall of the sunk garden formed a background for shrubs including *Abutilon vitifolium* which harmonized with white and pale blue flowers against the grey stone. From this lower level the gardens stepped up eastwards, first to a long walk between flowering shrubs ending in a rustic summer-house, then to the bowling alley with its screen wall of huge, semi-circular arches between piers. These arches were reflected at the northern end by an unusual thatched arbour, while beyond, at the uppermost level, was the tennis lawn—*de rigueur* by then—and the cross-pathed vegetable garden, the vista being terminated by a niche with statue in the enclosing east wall. Below these formal gardens the site retained its natural form, the rose garden leading to rock and water gardens and finally to a miniature Japanese garden (see Chapter 4).[35]

C.E. Mallows and 'Architectural Gardening'

Most Arts and Crafts architects were less uncompromising—and less individualistic—than Voysey and were able to reconcile their beliefs with the indigenous classical styles. Of those who aimed to combine a feeling for traditional materials with a classical discipline in garden design, few displayed more energy, flair and devotion than Charles Edward Mallows (1864–1915). Trained in the wake of what he later termed that 'ridiculous movement', the Gothic Revival, he was articled to F.T. Mercer in Bedford before working in various offices including that of William Flockhart. In about 1886 he began to practise independently, but much of his time during the following few years was devoted to the preparation of a series of remarkable drawings of English and French cathedrals, many being illustrated in *The Century Magazine*, and in 1889 he won the RIBA Pugin Studentship. Throughout his career Mallows retained a passion for drawing. For him it held the key to architecture, and he rapidly established a reputation as an outstanding perspective artist, something that tended to eclipse his achievement as an architect and garden designer.[36] In common with most architects at that time, he soon fell in with the English Renaissance revival, to free himself, as Alfred Cross insisted, 'from the pernicious and soul destroying effects of false doctrines inculcated in his youth. "Ruskin says this—*therefore* it is so."'...Had his intense devotion to art—his genius—his amazing energy— been rightly directed from the very first day he entered an architect's office, who shall say that Mallows would not have gained a reputation world-wide and imperishable?'[37]

Ruskin's influence had nevertheless contributed, through Sedding, to the new doctrines of garden design which were enthusiastically endorsed by Mallows in a series of articles on 'Architectural Gardening' published in *The Studio* in 1908–10: 'Today, thanks to the doughty warriors in art of some twenty to thirty years ago, with Sedding in the front rank, we are slowly, but it is to be hoped

surely, taking up once more the thread of the classic tradition, and with it, naturally, the old tradition in garden design.' Then the extravagant and somewhat sanguine claim: 'in England and in America at least—the principles that Sedding fought for are being slowly established, and in both countries the "landscape" man has been reduced to such small proportions that he is scarcely visible.'[38] Mallows illustrated the articles with his own work, which included some theoretical schemes prepared during slack periods in the office such as a symmetrical semi-butterfly house near Sherborne (1908) (Plate 152),[39] and a Wrenaissance 'Brick House in Kent' (1909–10). Jekyll and Weaver praised the layout of the latter[40] and noted especially the steps leading from the forecourt down to the rock garden, whose uneven edges were sensitively portrayed by Mallows's pencil.[41]

Significantly, the first example in *Gardens for Small Country Houses* of 'the right relation of the garden to the house' was Mallows's Three Gables, Biddenham, Bedford (1900–1) (Plate 153). The year 1900 was an exciting one for Mallows for it included his marriage, his election as a Fellow of the RIBA, the opening of an office in London and the commission for Three Gables. Built originally for his father-in-law, H.J. Peacock, it became his own home from 1904 until his untimely death eleven years later, and most of his creative work was done there, the London office being merely administrative. It was the closest expression of his Arts and Crafts approach to domestic design,[42] and, as illustrated in *Country Life*, it evoked that movement's fusion of vernacular building materials and natural planting (Plate 154).[43] The exquisite pencil drawings were not by Mallows but by his pupil, Frederick Landseer Griggs (1879–1938). Griggs had worked in Mallows's Bedford office in 1896–8[44] but soon abandoned architecture for illustration, nevertheless remaining a close friend of Mallows, helping him with the *Studio* articles and continuing to do perspectives for him.[45]

Mallows's London office was at 28 Conduit Street, next to that of the garden designer Thomas Mawson (see Chapter 7), with

152. Project for a house near Sherborne, Dorset (C.E. Mallows, 1908): perspective view. [BALDC]

whom he collaborated on a number of projects. One of the earliest of these, additions and formal gardens at Dalham Hall, Suffolk (1901) for Sir Robert Affleck, was abandoned, whereupon a further scheme was prepared for the new owner, none other than Cecil Rhodes (1853–1902), who died the following year.[46] This was a foretaste of much of Mallows's practice. Even his most important commission, Tirley Garth, was beset with problems initially. Situated near Tarporley, about eight miles east of Chester, this picturesque mansion (originally called Tirley Court) was planned around a central cloister and built of roughcast walls and Cheshire stone dressings, with the gables, mullions and chimneys in his much-favoured neo-Tudor style. It was begun in 1906 for Bryan

Leesmith of the chemical firm Brunner Mond, but he left it unfinished and it lay dormant until 1911 when it was leased to a textile manufacturer, R.H. Prestwich, subsequently chairman of Burberrys. As his daughter Irene recalled later, 'For years the architect had waited while its fate hung in the balance. Now was his chance! He rushed home from abroad, delighted to find a family in sympathy with his conception. Together we began to plan and work to make a perfect whole of house and garden.' The Prestwich family moved into the house in August 1912 (Plate 156) and it was then that the layout of the grounds was finally settled and the main garden work carried out.

The Edwardians often considered aspect more important than

153. Three Gables, Biddenham, Bedford (C.E. Mallows, 1900–1): south front, with Mrs Mallows and her sister in the verandah, c.1908–10. (The seat is one of the 'Peacock' seats made by J.P. White for Mallows and Baillie Scott.) [Courtesy of E.W.N. Mallows]

154. Three Gables: view from the north-west. Drawn by F.L. Griggs. [*CL* 1910]

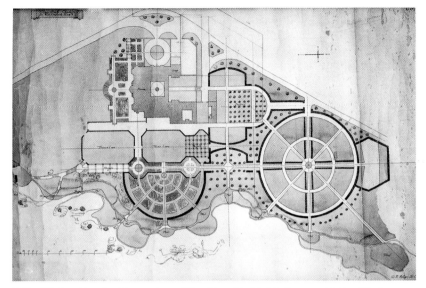

155. Tirley Garth, Tarporley, Cheshire (C.E. Mallows, 1906–12): layout plan. [Courtesy of the Tirley Garth Trust and Jonathan M. Gibson]

prospect, but Tirley had the benefit of both, since the site faced south towards the distant outline of Beeston Castle. The principal rooms were placed to take advantage of this, the foreground being limited to a planted terrace beyond which lawns swept down to merge with trees and shrubberies. The formal gardens were concentrated to the east, arranged geometrically, but ingeniously taking account of the contours (Plate 155). They step down the hillside, first to two tennis lawns on different levels, then to a north-south walk which extends in a long vista through octagonal enclosures to a one-acre, circular kitchen garden with a cross-fall, like a gigantic plate tipped on one side. Tirley is a garden of vistas, and the most dramatic occurs between the tennis lawns, focused on the east bay window of the dining-room and framed by cypresses (Plate 157). Below the north-south axis a fan-shaped rose garden

was laid out descending in tiers to where steps led down to a wild garden in the dell (Plate 158). Along this eastern boundary a stream wound its way, occasionally widening into lily pools, and bordered, as at the spectacular approach drive, with crimson, pink and purple rhododendrons which flourished in the acid soil (Plate 159). Although Mallows was responsible for the layout at Tirley, horticulture was not his strong point, and in the summer of 1912 he enlisted Mawson's help with the planting, meeting him several times on the site and visiting him at his home, as recorded in his diary: 'To Mawsons re scheme for Tirley greater part of the afternoon. Also advised on scheme for buildings at Vancouver B.C. Stayed at Hest Bank with Mawsons.'[47]

Mallows's only other substantial country house, and one of his most pleasing works, was Craig-y-Parc at Pentyrch in South Wales. Built in 1913–15 for Thomas Evans, a colliery-owner, it was situated on a wooded hillside, overlooking the Vale of Glamorgan, from which he could watch trucks taking his coal to the Cardiff Docks. Constructed of stone quarried on the site, it was Tudor-vernacular in style, reminiscent of early Lutyens. The plan was strongly axial and the sketch scheme of March 1913 (which demonstrates Mallows's flair for rapid pencil and wash presentation) shows a grand, symmetrical layout, inspired by his recent visit to Italy, with formal enclosures and circular walks and glades cut out of the *bosco* (Plate 160). This ambitious scheme was, however, reduced in execution to take closer account of the site and the oblique view to the south-east. The gardens were formed in a descending succession of levels, beginning with a terrace off the colonnaded atrium from which flights of steps descended to herbaceous borders and a croquet lawn, thence to a rose garden with belvedere and sunken amphitheatre below. To the west, where the ground fell away steeply, there were woodland and water gardens forming a transition with the natural scenery beyond.[48]

There is a danger in categorizing garden designers too rigidly. Weighing the merits of landscape and formal gardens, Mallows wrote, 'it is not wise…in approaching the question of design today to be too prejudiced in favour of any one particular school'.[49] Each had its place, and similarly, in his 'architectural gardening' he saw no obstacle to designing within several stylistic modes. For an Arts and Crafts man this was not the apostasy it might appear, as that movement had less to do with style than with an attitude of mind, the search for an ideal. Called upon to lay out gardens at Canons Park, Edgware, Middlesex, he entered enthusiastically into the spirt of the place. The original house, built in 1713–25 by the Duke of Chandos, boasted in its time the most extravagant formal garden in England, its radiating avenues, laid out by A. Blackwell, prompting Pope's 'Grove nods at grove, each alley has

a brother, and half the platform just reflects the other'. Canons was, however, short-lived, and the modest house that replaced it was subsequently acquired by Arthur Du Cros, MP (1871–1955), founder of the Dunlop Rubber Company, who in 1910 commissioned Mallows to enlarge it and recreate some of the garden's former grandeur. As though making up for all his abortive projects, Mallows went a trifle far on the north and south fronts, laying out elaborate paving, steps, flower beds, lily pools, urns and statuary (Plate 161). 'The shade of "Princely Chandos" seems to have inspired the designer with a touch of his own lust for unrestrained splendour', commented H. Avray Tipping.[50]

Little survives of this garden. Alas for Mallows, his legacy to

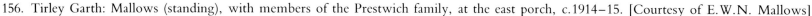

156. Tirley Garth: Mallows (standing), with members of the Prestwich family, at the east porch, c.1914–15. [Courtesy of E.W.N. Mallows]

157. Tirley Garth: vista west towards dining-room bay. [Author 1985]

158. Tirley Garth: view from the wild garden looking west. [Author 1985]

159. Tirley Garth: the Dell.
[Author 1985]

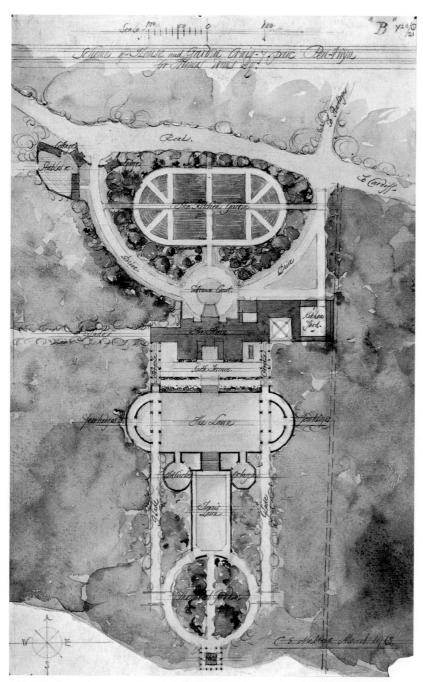

160. Craig-y-Parc, Pentyrch, near Cardiff (C.E. Mallows, 1913–15): layout plan, dated March 1913. [BALDC]

his premature death as a 'serious loss to the world of art...it is a matter of common knowledge in the profession that very few prominent living architects have been less favoured by fortune.'[52]

The Continent

By the early 1900s Arts and Crafts ideas had begun to reach the Continent. *The Studio* had been widely read in Europe since it first appeared in 1893 and schemes like Baillie Scott's for the Grand Ducal Palace at Darmstadt of 1897 had been well publicized. German architects began to take an active interest in the new formal garden movement, especially after the publication in 1904 of *Das Englische Haus* by the architect Hermann Muthesius (1861–1927). This zealous anglophile's three weighty volumes aimed to convert the German middle classes—or at least the educated denizens of the suburbs of Berlin—to the reasonableness (*Sachlich-*

161. Canons Park, Middlesex (C.E. Mallows, 1910–12): north garden. [*CL* 1916]

garden design lies more in his drawings than on the ground. In 1913 he had the unenviable task of designing a terrace garden for Sir George Sitwell at The Green, Eckington, on the edge of the Renishaw estate (Plate 162). Surprisingly, this particular scheme—'The Folly' as it was known in the Sitwell family—appears to have at least partially materialized. In *Great Morning*, Osbert Sitwell described how his father had been spending 'eight or ten thousand at Eckington, on making a fantastic garden, with enormous stone piers, and monoliths—one, with a flaw in it—for the entrance'.[51] It was one of Mallows's last works, for he died suddenly—working to the very last—the year after the outbreak of war. His obituary spoke of his 'masterly examples of the garden-maker's art', and of

162. The Green, Eckington, Derbyshire (C.E. Mallows, 1913): sketch design for terrace garden. [From Osbert Sitwell, *Great Morning*, 1948]

keit) and cosiness (*Gemütlichkeit*) of the English home. They represented the fruits of his research into English building carried out while he had been attached to the Imperial German Embassy in London from 1896 to 1903. The Arts and Crafts Movement was then at its peak, and he had become captivated by all aspects of English bourgeois life, in particular the arts of domestic design, including the way 'house and garden are treated as one closely integrated unit'. His book attacked the orderless naturalism of the eclectic landscape garden still in vogue in Germany at that time, and he held England up as a model of how to replace it, drawing heavily on the work of Sedding, Blomfield, Lorimer, Lutyens, Voysey and Mawson. It was, however, an exclusively architectural viewpoint and, like Blomfield, he cut a formal path through the English scene, completely ignoring Robinson and mentioning Gertrude Jekyll only in passing as 'a celebrated writer on gardens' with 'a strong preference for the woodland garden'.

After his return to Germany, Muthesius led a band of like-minded architectural warriors in making dramatic formal inroads into the professional landscape gardener's domain. Inspired by the English example, these architect-designers seized upon the concept of 'outdoor rooms' or *Freilufthäuser*, as they came to be known. Not surprisingly, however, the strongly architectural nature of their early schemes left little room for plants. Exhibitions of such gardens were held at Düsseldorf (1904), Darmstadt (1905) and Mannheim (1907),[53] and in 1908 the periodical *Woche* sponsored a competition for private gardens with Muthesius as one of the assessors. True to the message of *Das Englische Haus*, the entries, published in *Hausgarten*,[54] featured hedge, trellis, pergola and summer-house, but, apart from a continuing weakness for rows of mop-headed trees, the use of the shears was by then less in evidence than in Britain. A greater sympathy for natural foliage could be seen for instance in the designs of Leberecht Migge, who laid out the Reinhardt garden at Reinbeck in about 1910.[55]

Vienna produced a more abstract and monumental interpretation of the new garden, exemplified in the work (c.1905–8) of Franz Lebisch. An agricultural college graduate, he had also studied under Josef Hoffmann, founder of both the Viennese Sezession in 1898 and the Wiener Werkstätte (modelled on Ashbee's Guild of Handicraft) in 1903. Stylized trees, shrubs and flowers became almost a *leitmotif* of the Sezession[56] (Plate 163) and were displayed in Lebisch's brilliantly coloured designs at the 'Gartenkunst' exhibition in Vienna in 1907, some being reproduced in the postcards

163. Poster by Johann Viktor Krämer for 11th Vienna Secession Exhibition, 1901. [Royal Museum of Scotland]

164. André and Paul Vera, *Le Nouveau Jardin*, 1912.

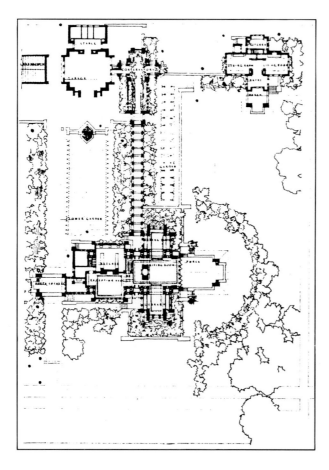

165. Darwin D. Martin House, Buffalo, N.Y. (Frank Lloyd Wright, 1904): layout plan. [Copyright The Frank Lloyd Wright Foundation 1942, Courtesy of the Frank Lloyd Wright Memorial Foundation]

ing for a garden that would be in keeping with the intimate scale of the modern house, but their vision of pleached walks, beds, pools and statuary, while embodying Arts and Crafts forms and textures, maintained their country's strong formal tradition (Plate 164).

All these European formal revivals were destined to be replaced by a return to naturalism after the First World War. In 1907 Muthesius played a leading part in the foundation of the Deutsche Werkbund, a forerunner of the Bauhaus, which led to the International Style of the 1920s. The Arts and Crafts ethos had helped to purge continental design of its eclecticism, but there is a certain irony in the subsequent abandonment of the garden as a formal adjunct to the house (see Chapter 8), a situation not foreseen by Muthesius when he wrote in his book, 'The old garden, from which the English are now eagerly learning, was the product of a different society and a different philosophy. The new garden will quite naturally become something different. We cannot tell from the present phase of development what the end product will be. But one thing is certain: it will be formal and orderly.'

The United States

Compared with the Continent the influence of the Arts and Crafts Movement in the United States was wider and lasted longer even than in Britain itself. If *Das Englische Haus* was the catalyst in Germany, this function was fulfilled across the Atlantic by readers of *The Studio* and its American edition, *International Studio*; also by American journals such as Charles Sprague Sargent's *Garden and Forest* (from 1888), *The House Beautiful* (Chicago, from 1896), *House and Garden* (Philadelphia, from 1901), and Gustave Stickley's *The Craftsman* (from 1901). All these helped to transmit both Arts and Crafts ideals and the natural gardening principles of william Robinson and Gertrude Jekyll. The flow of ideas in general was not of course one-way; the English, for instance admired the Shingle Style in the 1880s, and the revival of the Italian garden began in New England in the 1890s (see Chapter 7). Arts and Crafts issues took root most dramatically in helping to establish a number of regional aesthetics. These included landscape styles relating to the various regions and climates of America: colonial traditions on the East Coast and in the south-west; Japanese, as well as Mediterranean, in California;[58] 'Pueblo' vernacular in New Mexico; and, in the Midwest, native planting echoing the horizontality of the landscape. From the turn of the century this last theme was characteristic of the Prairie School of design which was marked also by close harmony between house and garden. By 1902, with Frank Lloyd Wright's Ward Willits house at Highland Park, Illinois, a pronounced integration between the house and its surroundings was apparent. The plan was opened up and extended into the garden on three sides, and Wright developed this further in 1904 at the Darwin D. Martin house, Buffalo (Plate 165), where the horizontality is accentuated by axes which link loggia, porch, pergola and flower garden.[59] This preoccupation with spatial interpenetration reflected the wide, open spaces of the Midwestern landscape, contrasting with the intimacy and sense of enclosure of the typical English countryside and garden.

published in 1907–8 by the Wiener Werkstätte.[57] France was slower to respond to the new movement, her interest at first being confined to the restoration of her historic gardens in which the leading authority was Alphonse Duchêne (whose son, Achille, laid out the water terraces at Blenheim in 1925–30; see Chapter 8). A plea for a style that would express modern thought and art was not made until the publication in 1912 of *Le Nouveau Jardin* by André Vera in collaboration with his brother, the painter Paul Vera. They demanded a complete break with the grandeur of Le Nôtre, argu-

Garden Features

Of all the features to make their way to America at that time, none was more enthusiastically received than the pergola.[60] A common Edwardian device for linking house and garden, it originated in Italy as a support for vines and was relatively unheard of in England after the seventeenth century until the revival of rustic-work in the 1870s. In Arts and Crafts hands it usually took the form of sturdy masonry piers supporting oak beams which might display *Wisteria* or *Laburnum* on the inside, roses or *Clematis* outside,[61] and like the Tudor pleached alley it could provide a shady walk, serve as a covered way, or link the levels of a terraced garden (Plate 166).[62]

Muthesius drew attention to the revival not only of the pergola but also of topiary, 'an indispensable means of establishing form', but, echoing Bacon's objection ('I for my part do not like images cut out of Juniper or other garden stuffe; they be for children'), he considered its purpose to be architectural, not for shaping figures.

167. Country Homes: Gardens Old & New. Title panel from *Country Life*. Drawn by J. Byam Shaw, 1898.

Trim yew hedges enclosed the formal garden that Rudyard Kipling (1865–1936) added to his home, Bateman's, in Sussex. His link with the Arts and Crafts was through his aunt, Georgiana Burne-Jones. Before his return to India in 1882 he had stayed at the Burne-Jones's holiday home, North End House at Rottingdean, and in 1897 he became their neighbour at The Elms. He would have known the flint-walled garden divided with trellis and 'snail-haunted pergola', which their granddaughter, Angela Thirkell, recalled with its orchard, espaliers and two-storey summer-house where 'the smell of sweetbriar on a hot afternoon filled the air and permeated everything'.[65] In 1902 Kipling at last put down roots of his own in the English soil he loved after discovering Bateman's 'down an enlarged rabbit-hole of a lane',[66] and it was there that he brought the Edwardians down to earth with 'The Glory of the Garden' (c.1907–8).[67] In 1906, near an existing double row of pleached limes (planted in 1898), he laid out a pond and rose garden[68] whose ordered simplicity reflects the honest-to-goodness solidity of the seventeenth-century ironmaster's house. This quality was captured in the watercolour (Plate 168) painted in 1913 by Kipling's uncle, Sir Edward Poynter,[69] and was aptly described by one of the Kipling family: 'The house stands like a beautiful cup on a saucer to match.'[70]

166. Acremead, Crockham Hill, Kent (Cecil Brewer, 1906): stepped pergola. [Author 1984]

Nevertheless, representational topiary became a trademark of the Arts and Crafts garden and was incorporated into the decorative vignette, designed by J. Byam Shaw, which served as a title for the *Country Life* articles 'Country Homes: Gardens Old and New', from 1898 to 1940 (Plate 167).[63] Revived in Inigo Thomas's sober pyramids at Athelhampton in 1891, topiary could also lend itself to the bizarre and fanciful, but most garden architects used yew mainly for their enclosing walls, accompanied by such unashamedly masonry derivations as batters, piers, buttresses, archways and crenellations. As Shepherd and Jellicoe noted, used in this way 'a yew hedge has great beauty from varying shades of surface that mark each tree.'[64]

168. Bateman's, Burwash, Sussex (Rudyard Kipling, 1906): Watercolour of the pond garden by Sir Edward Poynter, 1913. [National Trust]

169. H. Avray Tipping, photographed in about 1914. [Courtesy of Gordon Singleton]

H. Avray Tipping

The same analogy could have been made about the gardens of H. Avray Tipping (1855–1933) (Plate 169) at his three successive homes in Monmouthshire,[71] but being the work of one whose first and last love was gardening they had the added dimension of their exuberant planting. His gardens were planned to provide large masses of colour at all seasons of the year, and he was likened to Kipling's artist who aimed to 'splash at a league of canvas with a brush of a camel's tail'.[72] Known to the general public in later years for his column 'On Gardens' in the *The Observer*, he had begun by contributing to Robinson's *The Garden*. This was followed from 1907 by a regular series of articles on country houses and gardens for *Country Life* which became that journal's most important feature and formed the basis of his monumental *English Homes*, published in nine folio volumes between 1923 and 1935, also of his

English Gardens of 1925. Tipping's consequent reputation as a leading historian of English houses and gardens has overshadowed his achievements as a garden architect. As he observed in his last book, *The Garden of Today*, published in the year of his death, he was given a garden when he was seven and had been a gardener for seventy years.

In 1894 Tipping bought the ruins of Mathern Palace, near Chepstow, which had been the home of the Bishops of Llandaff since 1406. He restored and enlarged it sympathetically, taking care also to create a garden that would enhance its picturesque qualities. To the west and south he laid out a series of enclosures, including, on the site of an old quadrangle, a paved garden with yew arbour, overlooking terraced bowling greens (Plate 170). To the south, a grass walk, tulip-bordered in spring, was enclosed by a cut yew hedge sporting foxes, cocks and pheasants, almost mature when photographed for *Country Life* in 1910 after only ten years' growth. To the north the land fell away to naturalistic rock and water gardens.

Tipping took equal care over the design of both formal and

170. Mathern Palace, Chepstow, Monmouthshire (H. A. Tipping, 1894): paved garden. [*CL* 1910]

natural gardens at his next and most ambitious project, Mounton House, not far from Mathern. 'The best of gardening', he wrote in 1900, 'is perhaps to lovingly tend one of nature's choice spots; to remove what injures, and to heighten what improves its form, to vary and stimulate its flora, to retain the grace and feeling of the wild, while adding the eclectic richness and reasoned beauty of the cultured.'[73] In 1907 he put this into effect, buying part of a nearby gorge and stream in which to create a natural-style water garden. On the death of the last of his three elder brothers in 1911 followed a year later by that of his widowed mother, Tipping inherited the family estate and was able to buy a sixty-acre plateau above the gorge on which to construct a new house and garden. By 9 September 1912 he could write in his diary, 'Pavement laying and other garden work in progress', followed six weeks later by 'Pergola garden being planted and dry wall beginning.'[74] The house was approached down a long vista between buttressed walls on the north-east leading to a colonnade and entrance forecourt (Plate 171). A broad, flagged terrace ran along the south-west wall of the house against which grew Tipping's favoured vines and *Solanum*, myrtle and pomegranate, *Abutilon* and jasmine. From this terrace, steps descended to the bowling green and thence to the rock garden. As at Mathern the gardens were compartmented: 'Set high on the bare arable field that edged the tree-clad limestone gorge, enclosure was the keynote of the scheme of the formal layout.'[75] There was a parterre, glorious with peonies in June and *Aster thomsonii*, a great favourite of his, from August. Adjacent was a lawn, a rose garden, and what must have been Mounton's crowning glory, the pergola garden. Entered off the dining-loggia at the south corner of the house, it was enclosed on three sides by walls, but open to the south-west above a parapeted retaining wall. Here, the central bays were draped with the American pillar rose, with the profusely flowering *Carpenteria californica* between, framing a view down across the bowling green to the woodland

171. Mounton, Chepstow, Monmouthshire (H.A. Tipping, 1911): layout plan. [Miranda Ottewill]

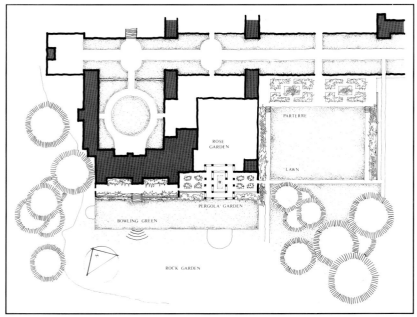

gardens beyond. The pergola itself, measuring fifty-five by forty feet, occupied the centre of the garden and was constructed of massive, square, limestone piers with plain caps. These noble piers were ten feet high to allow rambler roses and *Wisteria* to hang down from the beams, and they also formed an open cloister around a lily pool with a nicely scaled central figure supported on a column pedestal (Plate 172).[76]

172. Mounton: pergola garden. [*CL* 1917]

Tipping lived in grand style at Mounton up to the First World War, his guests including the future Prime Ministers, Lloyd George and Stanley Baldwin. It was at this time that he was commissioned by the MP Arthur Lee (created Lord Lee of Fareham in 1918) to lay out gardens at Chequers in the Chilterns. Blomfield had designed a south terrace there in 1892 for the previous owner, Bertram Astley, and in 1909–12 remodelled the house for Lee.[77] Tipping's subsequent improvements to the grounds included a paved walk to the north and a new east forecourt, but his principal achievement was to create a walled garden south of the house. This was arranged with broad grass walks around the perimeter and steps leading down to a paved parterre, similar to Mounton's, each of its beds being planted with a single variety of rose, and sunk just enough to

173. Chequers, near Princes Risborough, Buckinghamshire (H.A. Tipping, c.1912–14): sunk garden. [*CL* 1917]

provide privacy from the road through the park (Plate 173). In 1917 the Lees established a trust to preserve the house for the nation as the country residence of British Prime Ministers, and in the same year Lady Lee wrote to Tipping,

> everyone agrees that your treatment of a difficult and delicate problem could not have been bettered, and that you have been singularly successful, not merely in giving Chequers what it most lacked—an adequate frame for an old and beautiful picture—but in reviving, in an ingenious and happier form, the ancient setting of the house.[78]

Tipping was never content to stay long at his houses once the garden was mature but was restless to take up the challenge of another site. After the First World War, following the advice of Sir George Sitwell that 'we should abandon the struggle to make nature beautiful round the house and should rather move the house to where nature is beautiful',[79] he began a wild garden on a wooded hilltop near Trellech above Monmouth, commanding a distant view of the Welsh mountains. By 1923 he had built a smaller house there, High Glanau, his country home until about 1930, after which he lived mainly at Harefield House, Middlesex, which he had bought in 1921 as a London residence.[80] Unlike Voysey's New Place, High Glanau was set along the contours taking advantage of the magnificent prospect to the west. To the south was a broad grass walk between richly coloured herbaceous borders and separated from a lower border by *Lonicera nitida*, the earliest example of its use as a protective hedge. At the far end of the walk, a pergola of sturdy round piers stood against the kitchen-garden wall. West of the house the hillside was terraced with planted, dry stone retaining walls, and a central flight of steps descended to an octagonal pool (Plate 174). This marked a transition between the formal and the wild, and from it paths led amongst bracken and boulders, through oaks and hazels into a wooded dell. It was a perfect example of the blending of formal and natural which he urged in 1928 at a Royal Horticultural Society conference: 'Let there be some formalism about the house to carry on the geometric lines and enclosed feeling of architecture, but let us step shortly from that into wood and wild garden.'[81]

Detmar Blow

Tipping's architect at Mounton and High Glanau was Eric Carwardine Francis (1887–1976) of Chepstow. They collaborated on the gardens at Chequers, also at Wyndcliffe Court, Chepstow, where Tipping designed a sunken garden in the 1920s. Francis was already acquainted with garden design, for in 1909 he had been articled to Guy Dawber and subsequently worked in the office of Detmar Blow (1867–1939). Blow, whose career illustrated that turn-of-the-century tension between professionalism and romantic idealism, was one of the most fascinating figures in the world of Edwardian country-house building. His first substantial house was Happisburgh Manor (later St Mary's), Norfolk, another Edwardian butterfly, built in 1900 for the Cator family. The garden was planned within concentric ovals with low, flint and brick walls enclosing forecourt, flower gardens, an angled south garden facing a formal vista, and an east terrace flanked by thatched pavilions looking across the sand dunes to the sea.[82]

In 1893 Philip Webb wrote to Percy Wyndham praising Blow's assistance on the repair of the church tower of East Knoyle, the birthplace of Sir Christopher Wren.[83] This auspicious introduction led to several commissions in Wiltshire in the 1900s including Wilsford Manor, Woodford (1904–6) for Sir Edward Tennant (later Lord Glenconner) who married Percy Wyndham's youngest daughter, Pamela. Built on the site of an earlier house, it preserved elements of the former garden including ilexes and some old yews, two of which were retained to flank the steps leading up to the West Garden.[84] Further down this beautiful valley where the Avon meanders between water meadows and downland, Blow skilfully restored and enlarged the seventeenth-century Heale House for Hon. Louis Greville. In 1906 and 1911 formal gardens were added, but these were by Harold Peto who had worked for Greville's

174. High Glanau, Trellech, Monmouthshire (H.A. Tipping, 1923): view west towards the octagonal pool. [Author 1984]

sister-in-law, the Countess of Warwick, at Easton Lodge (see Chapter 7). Splendid new formal gardens, based on the lines of the original layout and complete with double-arched loggia, were added at the sixteenth-century Hatch House, near Tisbury, which Blow enlarged in 1908 for Lieutenant-Colonel Bennett Stanford Fane;[85] and on the nearby Fonthill estate he built Little Ridge (1904, demolished 1972), for the art collector Hugh Morrison. After he went into partnership with Fernand Billerey in 1906 (see Chapter 7) the house was enlarged and a delightful round pavilion, with elliptical arches and ogee roof, was added in the corner of the walled formal garden (Plate 175).[86]

In 1910 Blow married Winifred, granddaughter of the 1st Lord Tollemache, and from 1914 began building his own house at

175. Little Ridge, Tisbury, Wiltshire (Detmar Blow, from 1904): pavilion in the walled garden. [From *Gardens for Small Country Houses*, 1912]

Harescombe in Gloucestershire which overlooked his own farm, for Hilles was intended to be the realization of his dream of a benevolent rural community. At William Morris's funeral in 1896 the farm cart had been 'driven by a man who looked coeval with the Anglo-Saxon Chronicle';[87] that man was Blow dressed in a waggoner's smock. Hilles was inspired by Morris's ideals of the Simple Life, which were, however, doomed to failure after the war.

An Arts and Crafts Architect-Gardener

Blow went some way towards reconciling his Arts and Crafts beliefs with the demands of practice, and in this respect he can be compared with Robert Weir Schultz, his equally committed but more down-to-earth contemporary. After the death of the 3rd Marquess of Bute in 1900, Schultz's practice widened, his *magnum opus* being Khartoum Cathedral (1906–13), but he also acquired a reputation for garden design. An early challenge came in 1902

176. The Lodge, Felixstowe, Suffolk (Robert Weir Schultz, 1902): arched gateway to pergola. [Keith Collection c.1904]

177. The Lodge: dip-well and fountain. [Keith Collection c.1904]

when he was approached by the MP, banker, and bursar of King's College, Cambridge, Felix T. Cobbold (1841–1909) to add a terraced garden at The Lodge, the commodious 'Old English'-style house he had built for himself at the north end of Felixstowe.[88] Situated south-east of the house on a clifftop facing the sea, the garden was approached through its principal feature, a fine, brick and oak pergola, which rose from a buttressed retaining wall pierced by arched pockets for wall plants. It overlooked a sunken flower garden whose eastern boundary was marked by chains looped between a row of massive oak posts on top of which sheet copper seagulls swivelled in the sea breezes. Flanking the parterre, wide paths patterned in brick and pebbles led up to raised sections of the pergola. To the right was an arched gateway (Plate 176), while on the left the vista was closed by a dip-well and fountain, its cusped arch and half-dome niche in brick headers and knapped flints creating an almost Byzantine decorative richness (Plate 177).

A pergola walk was an important element of the formal gardens that Schultz added at Cottesbrooke Hall, north of Northampton, in 1911–14 for Captain R.B. Brassey. Built in 1702–13 for Sir John Langham and altered in about 1795 by Robert Mitchell, the house is one of the contenders for the model for that in *Mansfield Park*. Consisting of a central block linked by quadrant walls to twin pavilions, its axis is aligned on the distant tower of Brixworth church to the south-east. Besides carrying out renovations and a complete reconstruction of the interior, Schultz laid out a series of garden enclosures south-west of the house, fitting neatly between the west pavilion and two magnificent Lebanon cedars on the edge of the park. Beneath one of these, steps descended to a paved sunken garden with lily pool and flower beds from which stretched a long terrace with herbaceous borders and a view across the park (Plate 178). On the other side, the pergola screened the largest of the compartments, a square parterre enclosed by brick walls and an old brewhouse (Plate 179). This was laid out with geometrical

178. Cottesbrooke Hall, Northamptonshire (Robert Weir Schultz, 1911–14): the terrace from the south-west. [Author 1985]

179. Cottesbrooke Hall: the parterre. [Keith Collection c.1914]

flower beds, circular perimeter path, alcoves for seats, all centred on a sundial of unusual design and embellished with decorative leadwork by one of Schultz's artist-craftsman collaborators, Herbert Palliser.[89] Cottesbrooke was characteristic of Schultz's work and a good illustration of an Edwardian formal garden added unobtrusively to a Georgian house without destroying its setting in a landscape park.[90]

It is in their own gardens that one gets closest to the work of garden designers. For those who believed in the Arts and Crafts Movement it was almost a religious duty to design the whole environment in which they lived, and The Barn, Hartley Wintney, Schultz's home for fifty years, was a prime example of this. His friend Ernest Newton had already built a cottage for himself at nearby Hazeley Heath, but he probably got to know this part of North Hampshire through a client, Dr W.S. Playfair, a Scottish obstetrician. In 1897 Playfair bought West Green House, a fine example of the smaller Georgian house, and commissioned Schultz to remodel the south front and provide a small formal garden. Schultz added bay windows looking into a parterre which displayed many of the Arts and Crafts hallmarks: box edging, rose arches, a pigeon-cote recalling that at St. John's Lodge and ornamental leadwork (probably by his friend Troup), including an inscription over the bay similar to that at Kellie: 'HOC DOMICILIUM EX SITV LONGO ET RVINA EREPTVM HONESTO INTER LABORES OTIO EST CONSECRATUM MDCCCXCVIII'.[91]

West Green must have sharpened Schultz's resolve to have a garden of his own, for the following year he bought some land a mile away at Phoenix Green consisting of about ten acres of fields relieved only by a fine old oak and two sixteenth-century barns, one of which was to form the nucleus of his future home. In 1901 he laid out a sunk flower garden which was reached directly through a verandah, following Morris's dictum that a garden should 'look like a part of the house' (Plates 180, 181). Its square

180. The Barn, Hartley Wintney, Hampshire (Robert Weir Schultz, from 1900): layout plan. [Miranda Ottewill]

lawn was bordered on three sides by raised, box-edged beds divided geometrically at the front into brick pockets for alpines, backed by box topiary and standard roses, with climbing plants beyond—flowering quince, roses, honeysuckle—trained against diagonal trellis, the whole creating an organic fusion of architecture and planting. The focal point of this garden was the sundial of 1906 (Plate 182), supported by a lead putto and bearing the inscription, 'Life has many shadows but the sunshine makes them all'. This reflected the theme of the bookplate, 'Shadows Pass' (Plate 183), designed for Schultz in 1899 by his life-long friend, Lethaby.

Over the years Schultz extended the garden into a patchwork of hedge-bordered compartments, each with its own identity.[92] South of the sunk garden were ornamental rose beds and espalier fruit trees on either side of a mulberry, while, to the west, an archway through the skittle alley led to a croquet lawn with, at its far side, a raised walk above bastioned, brick planting boxes. Schultz shared Sedding's affection for topiary. At the gate from the common, peacocks confirmed the Arts and Crafts world within (Plate 184); a cat reclined above the yew arbour; while along the clipped yew hedge enclosing the lawn, squirrels hesitated, their bushy tails mingling with the pyramids, crowns and cheeses. An arched alley continued west, past the orchard, to the Nut Walk (taken straight from *Wood and Garden*), and thence to the Green Walk, vegetable gardens, woods and meadow. Not sufficiently established to feature in *Das Englische Haus*, in its maturity no better example of an Arts and Crafts architect's garden could be found, complete with old-fashioned plants and every accessory from terracotta oil jars down to cob-and-*pisé* potting shed and brick incinerator.

For Schultz it was not sufficient to be, like Lutyens, merely a designer of gardens; he needed to experience the craft himself, with

his own hands. When he established The Barn as his permanent home he became a devoted gardener. The idea of the nobility of labour, preached by Carlyle and Ruskin, was an important article of the Arts and Crafts faith. When Schultz got back from his London office, he changed into corduroy breeches and leather leggings, donned an old straw hat and, like Sedding, disappeared into the garden until dinner. And guests were not allowed to escape; jobs were duly allotted, for, in the words of Kipling,

> There's not a pair of legs so thin, there's not a head so thick,
> There's not a hand so weak and white, nor yet a heart so sick,
> But it can find some needful job that's crying to be done,
> For the Glory of the Garden glorifieth every one.

A frequent visitor at The Barn but, being no gardener, a reluctant helper, was the architect Francis W. Troup (1859–1941) (Plate 185).[93] Born at Huntly, Aberdeenshire, Troup worked for J.J.

181. The Barn: sunk garden. [Author 1979]

182. The Barn: sundial (1906). [Author 1979]

183. R.W.S. bookplate by W.R. Lethaby 1899. [Keith Collection]

184. The Barn: entrance topiary. [Author 1984]

185. Francis W. Troup at The Barn, c.1927. [Keith Collection]

Stevenson and met Schultz at the Royal Academy Schools in 1885. He was distantly related to Joseph King who, together with his wife, was active in the Haslemere Peasant Arts Society begun in 1896 by Mrs King's brother-in-law, Godfrey Blount.[94] For these ideal Arts and Crafts clients Troup designed Sandhouse, near Witley, Surrey, in 1902. It was built of wood-burnt bricks from a nearby kiln with grey, vitreous flare-end headers worked into a diaper pattern on the walls; and it had elaborate formal gardens, contrived with vistas on an irregularly shaped, sloping site (Plate 186)[95] and including an octagonal rose garden, a green walk and a large sunken lawn screened from the kitchen garden to the east by a pergola roofed by a curved trellis. Jekyll and Weaver criticized this pergola for being too narrow for its height compared with one of generous width at Walter Cave's Ewelme Down, Oxfordshire (c.1910).[96] Another pergola they singled out for praise was constructed simply of larch poles with angle braces,[97] and was similar

124

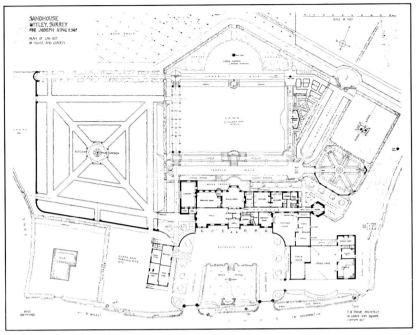

186. Sandhouse, Witley, Surrey (F.W. Troup, 1902): layout plan. [Courtesy of Freda Levson]

188. Tylney Hall: herbaceous borders. [Keith Collection c.1907]

to the rustic pergolas that once stood in the slendid gardens of Tylney Hall, Rotherwick, Hampshire, designed by Schultz in 1901–5.

The eighteenth-century Tylney Hall was rebuilt in 1878 for Charles Edward Harris who planted most of the trees in the grounds, but in 1897 the whole estate was bought by the Rand millionaire, Lionel Phillips (created baronet in 1912). A buccaneering adventurer, Phillips made his fortune as one of the 'Uitlanders' in Orange Free State. A leader of the Transvaal Reform Movement

187. Tylney Hall, Rotherwick, Hampshire (Robert Weir Schultz, 1901–5): sunk rose garden. [From a Lumière autochrome c.1910; RCHME]

189. Tylney Hall: rustic loggias. [Keith Collection c.1907]

in 1895–6, he was involved in the Jameson Raid and sentenced to death. This was commuted to a fine of £25,000 and he returned to England, exiled but with his fortune intact.[98] For the rebuilding of Tylney he chose Ralph Selden Wornum (1847–1910), who had designed Lord Wimborne's villa at Biarritz and a summer palace for the Queen Regent of Spain. Wornum did a competent revamping of the 1878 'Jacobethan' house, its most noteworthy feature being the giant water tower. At this stage there was a Victorian parterre to the north-west of the principal rooms overlooking the park and lake, and a sunk garden at the south corner (Plate 187). But these were not enough, and in 1901, at the instigation of Phillips's wife, 'the exuberant Florence Phillips', Schultz was approached to provide more gardens. His work

190. Tylney Hall: rose garden with antique well-head. [Keith Collection c.1907]

191. Tylney Hall: pond and wild garden. [Keith Collection c.1907]

included an orangery to the south-west of the stable block, green-houses, a row of 'bothies' and, to supply the garden, a second water tower, built of brick in Arts-and-Crafts-cum-German-mediaeval style with oak-framed belvedere. Most of these buildings survive, but of the fruit gardens beyond, where once herbaceous borders flowered abundantly to either side of broad grass walks stretching between thatched loggias (Plates 188, 189), nothing remains. Elsewhere one chanced upon rustic rose trellises, a thatched summer-house, and a circular rose garden forty yards wide, enclosed by a yew hedge and with *treillage* and iron archways centred on an antique well-head (Plate 190). There was a tea-house, an aviary, a boat house by the lake. In its prime, Tylney boasted thiry-five gardeners amongst its hordes of servants; in 1907 John Buchan, who dedicated *Prester John* to Phillips, spent his honey-moon there.[99]

After the Boer War Phillips was able to go back to South Africa. There, in 1909, Schultz, in collaboration with Herbert Baker, designed a house for him, Arcadia, Johannesburg. He sold Tylney in 1916. Like the age that begat them, the gardens of Tylney were short-lived. But one ornamental feature has survived: Schultz's hexagonal summer-house near the orangery, constructed of brick with oak columns supporting a shingled, bell-shaped roof capped by a copper weathercock. And it has another claim to attention, for it overlooked the upper pond of a wild garden designed in 1906 by Miss Jekyll (Plate 191). Working from Schultz's survey of the existing ponds and wood,[100] she produced an exquisitely flowing design unified with winding and diverging paths, creating the anticipation of an unfolding series of garden pictures (Plate 192).[101]

Schultz set great store by Miss Jekyll's books and must have valued her expert guidance at Tylney. It was one of the few in-stances where she collaborated with an architect on the layout of a naturalistic garden. A later example was Vann, Hambledon, Surrey, not far from Munstead, where in 1911 she advised W.D.

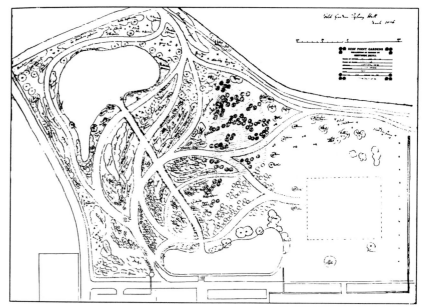

192. Tylney Hall: plan of wild garden by Gertrude Jekyll. [RPG 1906]

Caröe (1857–1938) on the lower water garden. In 1907–8 Caröe had enlarged this old house, incorporating, like Schultz, the exist-ing barn and creating additional garden enclosures to the east filled with old-fashioned flowers and divided by a pergola. This led to a pond, with the water garden below planted with the characteristic Jekyll foliage of *Hosta, Rodgersia*, ferns and irises, blending into the natural woodland.[102]

Gertrude Jekyll's Commissions from other Architects

Miss Jekyll's work for architects consisted usually of planting schemes for their formal designs, typical examples being the gardens at Bishopsbarns, York (1905) and at Dyke Nook Lodge, Accrington (1907) for the York architect, W.H. Brierley (1862–1926).[103] Most impressive of all was her work at Barrington Court, near Ilminster, Somerset. When this Tudor house, with its fine stable quadrangle of 1666, was acquired by the National Trust in 1907, the buildings were in poor condition and completely bereft of their old gardens. To Blomfield it was a prime example where nothing 'of the quality of the house' was to be found in the grounds: 'There is a gaunt, famished, incomplete look about these houses, which is due quite as much to the obvious want of relation between the house and its grounds, as to any associations of decay.'[104] As though inspired by Blomfield's words, the Trust's tenant, Colonel A.A. Lyle, set out to remedy the situation. In 1917

the architects Forbes and Tate prepared ambitious plans for an elaborate series of garden compartments which utilized some existing walls within the five-sided moat. The plans were sent, together with biscuit tins full of the limy soil, to the seventy-four-year-old Miss Jekyll, and the result was one of her finest and most richly coloured planting schemes. Not all her designs were adopted, but the Jekyllian spirit is still in evidence today, especially in the Lily Garden. This has a central lily pool and in the perimeter borders a rich tapestry of *Crinum*, lilies, *Hosta* and *Bergenia* can be seen framed against the mellow brick walls and paths (Plate 193).[105]

Not all Miss Jekyll's commissions were for private houses. One of her largest schemes, prepared in 1907, was at the King Edward VII Sanatorium north of Midhurst, West Sussex, founded by the

193. Barrington Court, Ilminster, Somerset (Forbes and Tate, 1917): lily garden. [G.S. Thomas c.1978]

194. King Edward VII Sanatorium, Midhurst, Sussex (Charles Holden, 1902): view of the chapel with 'Lady Gardeners', 1907. [Courtesy of The Francis Frith Collection]

King in 1902 with funds provided by Sir Ernest Cassel (1852–1921), a wealthy banker from Cologne and intimate friend. It was built from 1903–6 to designs by the young Charles Holden (1875–1960) of Adams, Holden and Pearson. At this early stage in his career Holden was inspired by the 'free' ideas of Walt Whitman and had one foot in the Arts and Crafts camp, having worked from 1897–9 for C.R. Ashbee. There are monumental overtones in the massing of the sanatorium, but the use of Sussex vernacular materials imparts a touch of domesticity. The site was on high ground backed by pine woods, with a view over the South Downs, and the symmetrical design, long and spreading to capture the sunlight, its central communal spaces flanked by separate blocks for men and women, set the pattern for sanatoria up and down the country. Fresh air and outdoor activities were the order of the day (Plate 194), and accordingly the buildings were surrounded by a series of garden enclosures. Internal courts were given beds of *Magnolia*, roses and *Fuchsia* with, against north-facing walls, guelder rose, *Weigela* and *Clematis montana*. The light, sandy soil suited some of Miss Jekyll's favourite plants such as *Cistus*, *Stachys*

and *Santolina*, and ornamental beds were edged with rosemary and lavender. On the south front the canted wings embraced terraced lawns whose retaining walls and steps were built of the lower greensand, quarried on the site. It was the planting of these that particularly interested Miss Jekyll, as she wrote to an American friend:

The garden is laid out on several levels, each level carried by retaining walls built with earth joints for planting. I make out detailed planting plans, and send the plants for every section. There are 1200 feet of the dry walling, and I hope, in a year's time—for nothing shows so quickly as this type of planting— that it will be a good example of wall gardening. It is intended that the garden should provide light and interesting work for the patients and keep them a great deal in the open air. The King takes a great interest in the place and goes there often.[106]

Here was ample scope for her harmonizing colours, the clustered grey, pink and purple of *Nepeta X faassenii*, lavender, *Campanula*, rock pinks, *Aubrieta* and *Cerastium* leading through white, and the pale yellows of *Alyssum*, stonecrops, asphodel, *Verbascum phlomoides* and columbines, to a warm grouping of red valerian, snapdragons and *Sedum spurium*.[107]

Most of Miss Jekyll's schemes for memorial gardens came after the First World War, but one that she found especially interesting, the Phillips Memorial, Godalming, was prepared in 1913 for the Arts and Crafts architect, Thackeray Turner. Erected in honour of a local resident, John George Phillips, the chief wireless operator of the SS *Titanic*, who died at his post in the disaster of April 1912, it took the form of a brick-paved court enclosed on three sides by a cloister and arcaded wall but open to a view of the church to the south through an oak pergola. It had a central octagonal pool and suitably restrained planting of *Bergenia*, irises, evergreen shrubs and *Wisteria* (Plate 195).[108] Hugh Thackeray Turner (1853–1937) (Plate 196) is best known as the long-serving secretary of the Society for the Protection of Ancient Buildings, founded by Morris in 1877.[109] A great friend and admirer of Miss Jekyll, his own house, Westbrook (1899), perched on a hill above Godalming

195. Phillips Memorial, Godalming, Surrey (Thackeray Turner, 1913): general view. [Author 1985]

196. H. Thackeray Turner. [AWG Album c.1886]

Church, expressed the same love of traditional Surrey crafts and was built of the same materials as Munstead Wood. He was a dedicated and experienced amateur gardener himself, and Miss Jekyll considered his garden at Westbrook good enough to warrant a chapter to itself in *Gardens for Small Country Houses*.[110] Subdivided into compartments (Plate 197), its lawn was bounded on the east by a wall screeening the kitchen garden and on the west by a pleached lime walk. Behind this was a shrubbery laid out with winding paths leading to a concealed circular enclosure, apparently designed as an escape route from unwanted visitors but no doubt also for the benefit of Turner's children. The more serious attractions of Westbrook were, however, to the west of the house. Here was an intriguing arrangement of spaces, each with its own distinct architectural form and character, borrowing the plan forms of a rotunda and a church and with yew hedges for walls. Its main feature was a circular sunk garden in three concentric tiers with octagonal lily pool and descending cross-paths connected on the north to a cruciform enclosure with broad grass walks and flower borders. In the residual spaces were fitted a small sunk garden near the house for summer flowers, a rose garden and a delightful

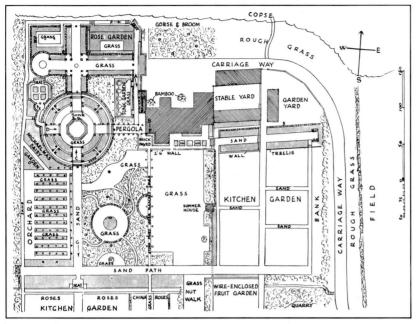

197. Westbrook, Godalming, Surrey (Thackeray Turner, 1899): layout plan. [From *Gardens for Small Country Houses*, 1912]

walled winter garden, a *giardino segreto*, sheltered and secluded, approached by a narrow, twisting path from the circular garden and containing beds of rhododendrons, *Erica, Daphne* and Lent hellebores, with jasmine, pyrus japonica, *Garrya* and laurustinus against the walls. The planting throughout showed the influence of Miss Jekyll, especially in the colour scheme of the sunk garden. At the foot of the enclosing yew hedge was a narrow border containing mostly low plants: rock roses, *Nepeta, Lithospermum, Sedum, Veronica,* saxifrages, *Artemisia, Omphalodes verna*, while the lily tank was bordered with ferns, hardy grasses, irises and *Hosta*; but the outer and inner flower borders—their corners marked by Irish yews and junipers—were gradated from warm colours facing the midday sun, including oriental poppies, peonies and bergamot, round to the cooler hues of *Delphinium, Campanula, Nepeta,* on the shadier side.

In 1913 Thackeray Turner spoke at a meeting on 'The History and Making of Gardens' held at the Art Workers Guild,[111] but the main paper was delivered by Oswald P. Milne (1881–1968). Milne had worked in Lutyens's office and later laid out the terraced gardens at Coleton Fishacre, Kingswear, Devon (1925–6) for Rupert D'Oyly Carte (1876–1948).[112] The mantle of principal speaker at such a gathering ought to have fallen on Miss Jekyll herself, but she was a solitary worker, speaking only through her books and articles, and, in any case, the Guild was a male domain to which women were not admitted as members until 1964.

The Cotswolds

One of the last gardens Miss Jekyll designed for an architect member of the Guild was at Combend Manor, Elkstone, Gloucestershire. The Cotswolds was a focus of the Arts and Crafts Movement, Morris himself taking the first step when in 1871 he rented

Kelmscott Manor, its front garden immortalized in *News from Nowhere*: 'my hand raised the latch of a door in the wall, and we stood presently on a stone path which led up to the old house... the garden between the wall and the house was redolent of the June flowers, and the roses were rolling over one another with that delicious superabundance of small well-tended gardens'.[113] Morris found the perfect expression of his ideals of life and handicrafts in the Cotswolds, epitomized in a cottage he saw in Broadway in 1876, 'a work of art and a piece of nature—no less'.[114] In 1893 Sidney and Ernest Barnsley and Ernest Gimson set up workshops at Pinbury Park, near Cirencester; and they were followed by C.R. Ashbee and his Guild of Handicraft who moved to Chipping Campden in 1902.[115] The seventeenth-century Combend Manor was enlarged for Asa Lingard from 1921 by Sidney Barnsley (1865–1926), who also laid out a series of terraced, walled enclosures to the south of the house. In 1925 Miss Jekyll did planting schemes for the borders of these formal gardens, but of greater interest was the semi-wild garden below, where, as at Tylney, she transformed the existing pond with a curvilinear design planted with flowering shrubs, ferns, irises and hogweed.

Morris may have been one of the first to discover Broadway, but it was a group of illustrators for *Harper's Magazine*, including the Americans Edwin Abbey and Frank Millet, who virtually colonized it from 1885. Spellbound by its as yet unspoilt rusticity, they were soon joined by the expatriate American, John Singer Sargent (1856–1925), who worked away in Millet's garden at *Carnation, Lily, Lily, Rose* (1885–6), endeavouring to capture the fading light of that late summer.[116] The following year Edmund Gosse and Henry James (1843–1916) arrived, the latter hastening the end of Broadway's rural calm by describing it and its community of artists and cultured anglophiles in *Harper's* three years later.[117] Amongst the team of illustrators was the landscape painter Alfred Parsons (1847–1920) (Plate 198), who lived with Abbey in Campden Hill, London, where they had adjacent studios. Parsons was

198. Alfred Parsons. [*Harper's* 1889]

199. Hartpury House, near Gloucester (Thomas Mawson, 1907): lower terrace and gateway. [Author 1985]

another founder member of the Art Workers Guild, and he assisted Webb with the enclosed gardens on the east side of Clouds. Best-known for his illustrations, which included the 1880 edition of *The Wild Garden* and Ellen Willmott's *The Genus Rosa* (1910), he was also an enthusiastic gardener and a skilful garden designer, his country-house work including formal gardens (c.1890) at Wight-wick Manor, Staffordshire.[118] At Worcester College, Oxford, in 1904, he remodelled the garden for the Provost, the Reverend Dr Charles Henry Daniel, filling the borders with a broad and colour-ful canvas of the old-fashioned flowers he loved.[119] Cotswold rubble walls were to stike an alien note amongst the Oxford ashlar, but the cottage garden settled happily within the mellow walls of the colleges.

In the late 1890s Parsons decided to settle at Broadway. Soon after, he designed gardens at the late-Georgian Hartpury House,

north of Gloucester, but, as at Wightwick in about 1910, these were gone over in 1907 for Mrs Gordon Canning by Thomas Mawson who observed of Parsons's work, 'The plantations...were well and artistically arranged. The rhododendron beds in particular were planted in large masses, rising out of a surrounding irregular carpet of choice ericas.'[120] However, Mawson had a low opinion of landscape-painters-turned-garden-designers and felt the need to 'infuse a little form and order into the garden, and to bring it into character with the house'. The upper terrace had a formal rose garden whose axis was not centred on the garden front but was determined by two large elms (subsequently victims of Dutch elm disease).[121] Mawson extended this axis to create a vista through a gateway in a balustraded retaining wall with steps descending to a lower terrace marking the boundary of the old gardens (Plate 199). This terrace was in Mawson's Arts and Crafts mode, the walls consisting of local rag-stone planted with alpines, and the gates being made by Mrs Ames Lyde, a blacksmith who divided her time between her palace in Florence and her estate at Thoram, Norfolk. Below stretched a grass glade which was flanked by clipped blocks of yew backed by woodland, and beyond were Parsons's rhododendron beds.[122]

In 1895 Hartpury had been enlarged and substantially remodelled by E. Guy Dawber (1861–1938) whose country houses were invariably accompanied by sympathetic formal gardens. Dawber built up a large practice mainly in the Cotswolds, whose tradition of fine domestic architecture captivated him while he was acting as clerk of works to George and Peto at Batsford Park (1887–93). He expressed his admiration for this undocumented tradition in *Old Cottages, Farm-Houses, and other Stone Buildings in the Cotswold District* (1905), illustrated with his own notes and sketches. His reticent houses fitted perfectly into the countryside and were surrounded by gardens to match, examples in the Cotswolds including Nether Swell Manor (1904), Burdocks, near Fairford (1910), and Eyford Park, Upper Slaughter (1912).[123]

Alfred Parsons derived several other garden commissions for Americans through his Broadway connexions. In 1895 the American actress Mary Anderson bought The Court Farm at Broadway where he laid out the garden for her and her husband, Antonio de Navarro. He also advised Henry James on a new layout for the walled garden at Lamb House when James moved to Rye in 1897.[124] A friend of the Navarros and one whose family could have walked straight out of James's novels, Lawrence Waterbury Johnston (1871–1958) created the best-known of all Edwardian gardens, Hidcote, about six miles north-east of Broadway. Born of well-to-do American parents but brought up mainly in France, Johnston became a naturalized British subject in 1900. His mother, Gertrude Winthrop, had bought him the farm of 280 acres and the hamlet of Hidcote Bartrim, and he decided in 1907 to make gardening his hobby.

Located on the northern edge of the Cotswold Hills, the site consisted of a heavy, alkaline soil over limestone which Johnston transformed in his lifetime into a labyrinth of magical gardens, ranging from the trim and orderly to the rampantly 'wild' (Plate 200). From a magnificent Lebanon cedar near the old manor house, Johnston set down a principal axis—the 'backbone' of the scheme—consisting of a grassed walk rising gently westwards. To the south of this axis—like transepts and chapels off a cathedral nave—are smaller enclosures, each with its own colour theme: the Maple Garden, the White Garden, the Fuchsia Garden, Mrs Winthrop's Garden with yellow and blue flowers, and the Pillar Garden of English yew with verdant borders including *Philadelphus*, tree peonies, *Magnolia* and *Yucca*. Hidcote is not particularly local in character. Johnston travelled widely in search of rare plants and is supposed to have imported vast quantities of lime-free soil for his rhododendrons. The red-brick garden houses would also be more at home in Hampshire. But what gives it an Arts and Crafts flavour is the subtle blending of 'old-fashioned' formality with the seeming artlessness of the cottage garden. The arrangement of linked outdoor spaces divided by hedges is 'architectural', but it is free from any rigid paper layout; it evolved by stages, growing

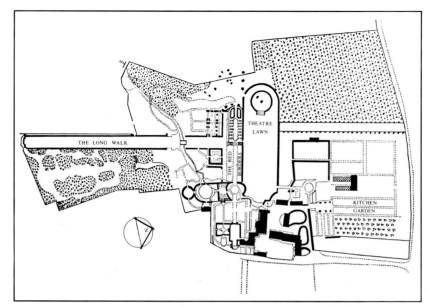

200. Hidcote, Hidcote Bartrim, Gloucestershire (Lawrence Johnston, from 1907): layout plan. [National Trust]

from the natural features of the site, without any predetermined master plan. First and foremost it is a plantsman's garden, filled with varied and luxuriant planting. There are some details which do not bear comparison with their forerunners: the out-of-scale steps and narrow paths; the addition of the bathing pool with its raised surround; the over-wide, unrewarding Long Walk. But there is a fine overall sense of colour and form, highlighted in its most striking and memorable feature, the view west up the main axis (Plate 201). Here the foreground is woven with a rich tapestry of the Jekyll-inspired red borders, the mingled scarlets and purples of roses, peonies, dahlias and *Hemerocallis* massed against the copper purple *Prunus* and *Berberis*. Beyond, the summer-houses mark the ascending planes and receding forms of the pleached hornbeam walk, and the vista is terminated only by the delicate wrought-ironwork of the gates, flanked by *Quercus ilex*. Flowers, shrubs and trees almost touch, divided by the grass and steps which rise to meet the open sky. In this noble duality dwells an element of mystery. One feels compelled to climb those steps, to discover what lies beyond, an invitation rewarded by an entrancing glimpse of the distant Vale of Evesham. For this *tour de force* of anticipation alone Hidcote deserves its place in garden histroy.[125]

Hidcote's inward-looking compartments were partly determined by the exposed site. This need for shelter was an important feature at another Cotswold garden begun soon after Hidcote, Rodmarton Manor, situated between Cirencester and Tetbury; but here the 'outdoor rooms' had a direct link with Sedding's *Garden-Craft*, for Rodmarton's architect, Ernest Barnsley (1863–1926) had trained in Sedding's office in 1885–7. In 1901 he enlarged an old cottage at Sapperton as the basis of his own home, Upper Dorvel House. From its hall you stepped into an intimate plat of little box-bordered beds of old-fashioned flowers with miniature clipped yews *à la* Kate Greenaway.[126] Later the garden was extended almost to the site of an old manor house with yew hedges and topiary in abundance. The commission for Rodmarton came in

201. Hidcote: principal vista. [M. Hill 1981]

1909 from Claud Biddulph, a stockbroker. Not only was the house to be built using local materials and craftsmen, but, aided and abetted by Mrs Biddulph who was a trained horticulturist,[127] its gardens were to be laid out as an integral part of the whole scheme. Indeed, as Lorimer had just done at Formakin, and Miss Jekyll earlier at Munstead, Ernest Barnsley persuaded the Biddulphs to start the garden at the same time as building began.[128] The manor is long, rambling and accretive, bringing to mind the country houses of George Devey, designed to look as though they had evolved naturally over several generations. It is also deliberately low-style, unlike Dawber's traditional Georgian houses, yet formal gardens went with both. There is nothing particularly remarkable about the layout at Rodmarton (Plate 202). The garden compartments are entered off an east-west path like rooms off a long corridor. Immediately south of the house is a series of descending terrace gardens, enclosed by thick yew hedges decorated with topiary, from which steps lead down to a long border devoted mainly to white flowers. This white border is separated by a dry-stone wall from a daffodil-filled meadow, and it marks an axis that extends westwards past a succession of separate gardens on the south. At the end is a wild garden bounded by an avenue of hornbeams leading in true Sedding style 'on to the open country'.

But there is a further tribute to Sedding: a concealed garden, of whose presence one is at first hardly aware. Sandwiched between the southern suite of compartments and the vegetable gardens is the Long Garden, enclosed on one side by a massive yew hedge and on the other by a high south-facing wall. Sedding had written, 'Nothing is prettier than a vista through the smooth-shaven green alley, with a statue or sundial or pavilion at the end, or an archway framing a peep of the country beyond.'[129] At Rodmarton the alley

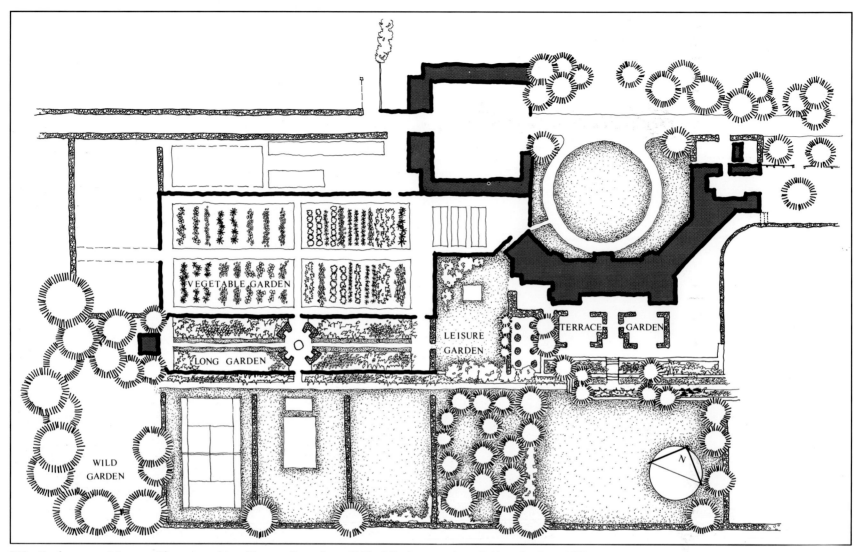

202. Rodmarton Manor, Gloucestershire (Ernest Barnsley, 1909–29): layout plan. [Miranda Ottewill]

takes the form of a central path flanked by grass and twin herbaceous borders. At its eastern end is a yew archway with the manor rising up behind, while to the west the vista ends in a perfectly proportioned, stone summer-house with hipped roof of mellow Stonesfield slates (Plate 203).[130]

The building of Rodmarton was interrupted by the First World War, and both Ernest and Sidney Barnsley died in 1926, their architectural work being taken over by Norman Jewson (1884–1975), who completed Rodmarton in 1929.[131] In the summer of 1907 Jewson had gone on a sketching tour of the Cotswolds with donkey and cart. He had been taken on by Gimson, married Ernest Barnsley's daughter and stayed at Sapperton for the rest of his life. His sympathetic repair of old buildings included both Hidcote and the romantic Owlpen Manor,[132] famous for its colossal cylinder yews and mysterious yew parlour, just the kind of garden to capture the imagination of Edwardian garden designers. Its dark green complements the manor's pale limestone, and its bold, sombre masses suit the Cotswold landscape in the way that colourful herbaceous borders and rose-clad pergolas seem to belong to the red brick, tile-hanging and intimate scale of Kent and Sussex. A

203. Rodmarton Manor: The Long Garden. [Author 1981]

garden can turn its back on the landscape, as at Hidcote, and create a world of its own, but if the genius of the place is to be consulted, then the broad sweep of folded hills of the Cotswolds and its closely knit stone villages suggest a more restrained and sculptural approach to garden design.

To find such a garden one need only climb the hill above Broadway to where the architect Charles Paget Wade (1883–1956) (Plate 206), made his home at Snowshill Manor. Serving in France during the First World War, Wade saw an advertisement in *Country Life* for the semi-derelict Snowshill and bought it in 1919. He restored the house, which dates from c.1500 and, on the site of an old farmyard where the hillside falls steeply to the west, created between 1920 and 1923 a succession of mysterious and enchanting walled enclosures (Plate 204). They descend in terraces and are

approached down a flagged path between columnar yews which form a vista closed by a mediaeval dovecote. The upper garden consists simply of a square lawn surrounded by flower borders displaying a preponderance of Wade's favourite purples and blues, and with a central column supporting a gilded armillary sphere (Plate 205) (which echoes Lethaby's frontispiece to *Garden-Craft*; see Plate 41). From here, steps descend to reveal a further enclosed court overlooked by a gallery on the south and with a Venetian well-head as its centre-piece. Roses spill over the east retaining wall, mingling with the luxuriant planting of the raised bed at its base. At the north end of the Well Court is a square lily pool backed by a garden house, while to the west, past the dovecote, semi-circular steps lead down to the kitchen garden. Describing his garden in 1945 Wade nailed his colours firmly to the formal mast:

204. Snowshill Manor, near Broadway, Gloucestershire (Charles Wade, 1919–23): layout plan. [Miranda Ottewill]

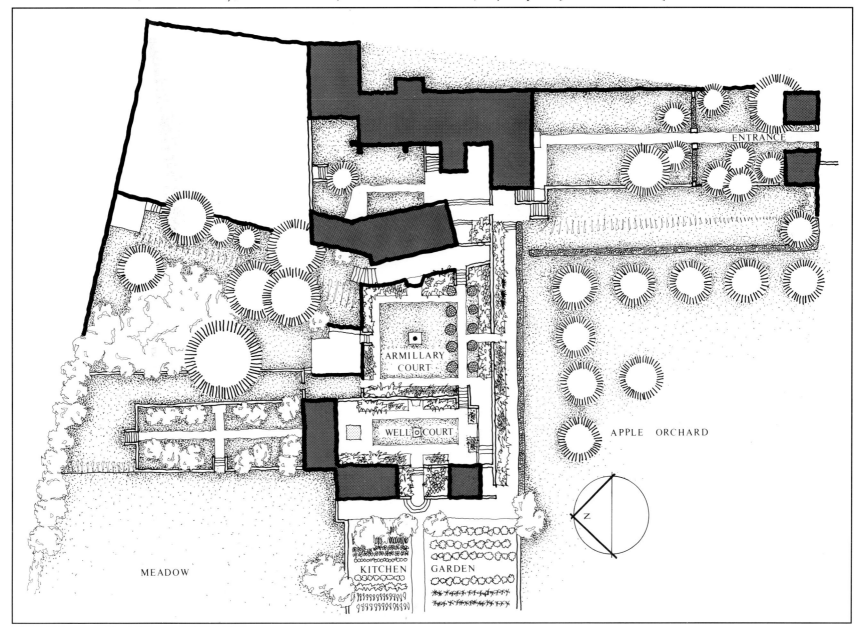

205. Snowshill Manor: Armillary Court. [Author 1981]

A garden is an extension of the house, a series of outdoor rooms, the word garden means—garth—an enclosed space, so the design was planned as a series of separate courts, sunny ones contrasting with shady ones, courts for varying moods. The plan of a garden is much more important than the flowers in it; walls, steps and alleyways give a permanent setting so that it is pleasant and orderly in summer and winter. Mystery is most valuable in design, never show all there is at once. Plan for broad effects of light and shade, unbroken stretches of grass are an asset, but do not cut up with flower beds as so often seen. Indeed a delightful garden can be made in which flowers play a very small part, by using effects of light and shade, vistas, steps to changing levels, terraces, walls, fountains, running water, an old well head or a statue in the right place.[133]

On summer evenings—to Wade 'the loveliest part of the day'—the garden of Snowshill is a magical, green and honey-coloured mosaic of descending planes within a framework of paths and walls; the dark yew casts its matching shadows over smooth-shaven grass, while house and garden merge in perfect harmony with village, apple orchard and meadows (Plate 135). Snowshill is the apotheosis of the architectural garden, one that is ordered and controlled by the architect alone. Wade was determind to dispense with expert gardening advice. He described how at his family home at Yoxford, Suffolk, the retired coachman took over the job of gardener,

But he became such an autocrat, it ceased to be our garden any more, it became his garden in which we were allowed to walk. If asked to move a plant, we were always told it was the wrong

136

206. Charles Paget Wade, photographed in 1954 by James Cramb, FRPS. [Courtesy of The National Trust]

garden in which I was allowed to walk. When the workmen were here repairing the old house I noted a labourer who was a good worker and very tidy in all he did. I liked his name, which was Hodge, his hat, which was mauve, and having asked him, I was satisfied that he knew nothing about gardening beyond cabbages and cauliflowers, so here was the very man. The garden has remained my garden these 25 years, and at my wish plants are moved in spite of the time of year, in spite of their age or the age of the moon, nor do they invariably die, but flourish abundantly.[134]

time of year, or the plant was too old or too young, or the moon not old enough, in any case it would die if moved. He ordered all the seeds and plants and put them where he wished, our only part was to pay. I took warning from this when I came to Snowshill, preferring to have my own garden and not a gardener's

Wade had a high regard for the work of M.H. Baillie Scott (1865–1945), who in 1906 brought out *Houses and Gardens*, illustrated by his own work both built and projected. Describing a typical scheme Scott explained, 'It is not a case of first designing a house and then laying out its immediate surroundings as a garden bearing a certain relation to it, for house and garden are here the product of a single initial idea which comprehends the whole.' As far as flowers were concerned he took the opposite view to Frances Hope's,[135] arguing, 'The possessor of such a little garden will find scope enough within its boundaries to create a little paradise of flowers. But it should always be borne in mind that the flowers are for the garden, not the garden for the flowers.'[136] His chapter on 'The Garden' introduced nothing new, but it anticipated the growing demand for the smaller suburban garden, one that required little maintenance.[137] Gertrude Jekyll was an important influence: 'To those who wish to study the subject I would recommend a

207. Heather Cottage, Sunningdale, Berkshire (M.H. Baillie Scott, 1904): watercolour by Baillie Scott. [From *Houses and Gardens*, 1906]

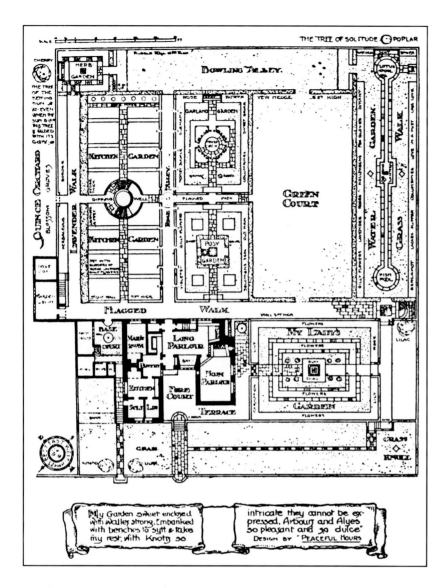

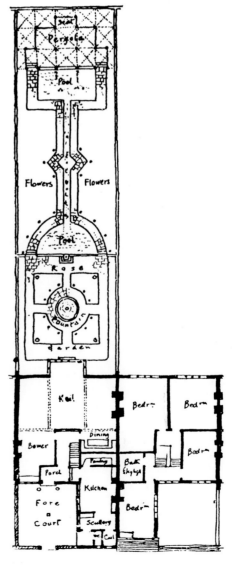

208 (far left). Charles Wade, Design for a small garden, 1907. [National Trust]

209. M.H. Baillie Scott, Spring-cot, project for a cottage, 1903. [From *Houses and Gardens*, 1906]

210. M.H. Baillie Scott, Design for a terrace house (B), c.1904. [From *Houses and Gardens*, 1906]

careful perusal of Miss Jekyll's books which may be taken as an infallible guide.' His houses retained a 'Munstead Wood' cosiness and he was much closer to her ideals of the simple rustic 'home' than Lutyens.[138] At Heather Cottage, Sunningdale (1904) (Plate 207), although there was a debt to nearby Deanery Garden, a plain, home-spun quality is apparent and the formal layout of the garden soon disappears into the gorse and heather of the hillside.

Wade's competition entry for the design of a small garden organized by *The Studio* in 1907, for which he won second prize (Plate 208), included a number of features derived from *Houses and Gardens*, in particular the rose garden and water garden of Spring-cot (1903) (Plate 209). It also developed Scott's theme (similar to that of Deanery Garden) whereby axes and vistas are projected outwards so that the house appears merely as one element in a total garden scheme. Not surprisingly, therefore, Wade sought guidance on the layout of the garden at Snowshill from Scott, who prepared a rough sketch plan in 1920, simplified by Wade in execution.[139] Wade drew also on his own competition plan, for instance its green court and sundial garden filled with old-fashioned flowers. The latter included, at opposite borders, 'Carnation, Lily, Lily, Rose', presumably in homage to Sargent's masterpiece.

Within the illustration:

Four Houses built by the Garden Suburb . . .
Development Company (Hampstead) Limited.

· View from corner of Meadway ·
· · Hampstead Way · · ·

· M·H·Baillie Scott · Archt ·
· Fenlake · Manor · Bedford ·

211. Terrace houses, Meadway, Hampstead Garden Suburb (M.H. Baillie Scott, 1908): general view. [From *Garden Suburbs*, 1910]

Garden Cities

Scott was one of the independent architects working at Hampstead Garden Suburb where Wade was one of Raymond Unwin's team in 1907–11.[140] In the 1900s the garden cities and garden suburbs were strongholds of the Arts and Crafts, their gardens nestling happily amidst cottages in vernacular style. The longing to escape from the smoke and compression of the cities had become an obsession by the close of the century, and such communities, applying the teachings of Ruskin and Morris to a social purpose, came closest of all to realizing Arts and Crafts ideology. Influenced by Octavia Hill, Dame Henrietta Barnett conceived Hampstead Garden Suburb as a balanced community set in an arcadia of woods, tree-lined roads, hedges and gardens, although for Central Square she agreed with her consultant architect, Lutyens, on the necessity for an axial layout with radial avenues (as Unwin had planned for Letchworth in 1904) and public buildings acting both as terminal vistas and cultural symbols. These public gardens embodied certain Arts and Crafts characteristics, in the details of steps, paving and pergolas for instance, and in the trees which were originally pleached into rectangular shapes. The influence of the style was apparent also in some of the private gardens.

At Bournville in 1897, as much for reasons of self-sufficiency as for personal recreation, the provision of private gardens for workers' housing aimed to give everyone the opportunity of creating a garden of their own, no matter how small. With the spread of owner-occupied suburbia in the 1920s, a garden became an inalienable right, and gardening a national occupation.[141] In the garden cities, however, even though personal involvement was supposed to be an important article of the Arts and Crafts faith,[142] the delegation of garden-making was sometimes limited to the planting, the layout being indicated by the garden-architect. At Letchworth, garden designs like that for 34 Sollershott West (1908) by Barry Parker (1867–1947) were symmetrically planned after the manner of Baillie Scott.[143] Such designs were for the larger plots, but in the same year Scott designed a groups of terrace houses in Meadway, Hampstead Garden Suburb (Plate 211), based on his influential scheme of c.1904 illustrated in *Houses and Gardens* (Plate 210). This proposed a square rose garden, overlooking a semi-circular pool with sundial, connected to a lower pool and rustic pergola.

Gardens have always been subject to the wheel of fashion. Due largely to the influence of Robinson and Jekyll, the unsophisticated flowers of cottage, hedgerow and woodland had transformed Edwardian garden design. Now some of the features of the country-house garden were in turn beginning to percolate down to the trim, little gardens of the new artisans' dwellings.

212. Plas Brondanw, Penrhyndeudraeth, Merionethshire
(Clough Williams-Ellis, from
1908): *clair voyée* towards
Sowdon. [Author 1982]

7

The Italian School

[The Renaissance architect] had now three problems to deal with: his garden must be adapted to the architectural lines of the house it adjoined; it must be adapted to the requirements of the inmates of the house, in the sense of providing shady walks, sunny bowling-greens, parterres and orchards, all conveniently accessible; and lastly it must be adapted to the landscape around it. At no time and in no country has this triple problem been so successfully dealt with as in the treatment of the Italian country house from the beginning of the sixteenth to the end of the eighteenth century...

Edith Wharton, 1903[1]

Lutyens's grand layout for Central Square, Hampstead Garden Suburb, was a sign of the inability of the Arts and Crafts Movement to stem the tide of Edwardian classicism. A similar trend was apparent in garden design for although the Arts and Crafts was ideal for the smaller house and struck the right note for a particular cultural milieu of professionals, politicians and artists, the more affluent section of society, from landed aristocrat to up-and-coming businessman, demanded something grander and more historically evocative. Why not, therefore, it was felt, turn again for inspiration directly to the age that first saw the rise of a wealthy, cultured class? What better models could be found than the creations of those garden-makers of the second half of the sixteenth century who, filled with a new-found love of nature, revived the spirit of antiquity in the villas of Renaissance Italy?

This new and more authoritative interpretation of the Italian garden was not confined to one country. Ideas were exchanged across the Atlantic, and the principal scene shifted between America, Britain, the French Riviera, even Italy itself. The movement originated in the 1870s when Victorian moral earnestness began to give way to a revival of interest in humanism. Aesthetic awareness —'the power of being deeply moved by the presence of beautiful objects'—was the keynote of Walter Pater's *Studies in the History of the Renaissance*, published in 1873. By 1878, with the first English edition of Burckhardt's *Civilisation of the Renaissance in Italy*, the worship of Italian art had received a new impetus, and this was followed in 1884 by W.P. Tuckermann's *Die Gartenkunst der Italienischen Renaissance-Zeit*, a study of Italian gardens complete with plans and engravings.[2] In art the general emphasis was once more on form and aesthetics, but allied to a Pre-Raphaelite concern for nature and realism; while in garden design a more penetrating interest in antiquity and sixteenth-century Italian garden art paralleled the new naturalism in horticulture. Although the Italianate gardens of Barry, Paxton and Milner had provided models for many Victorian country houses, they were based on little or no first-hand knowledge of Italian garden-craft.[3] Garden designers of all persuasions reacted against such artificiality but the spell of the genuine old Italian gardens was not lost upon them. Even Sedding, devoted follower of Ruskin and Morris, could write,

Of the garden of Italy, who shall dare to speak critically. Child of tradition: heir by unbroken descent, inheritor of the garden-craft of the whole civilised world. It stands on a pinnacle high above the others, peerless and alone: fit for the loveliest of lands ...and it may be seen upon its splendid scale, splendidly adorned, with straight terraces, marble statues, clipped ilex and box, walks bordered with azalea and camellia, surrounded with groves of pines and cypresses—so frankly artistic, yet so subtly blending itself into the natural surroundings—into the distant plain, the fringe of purple hills, the gorgeous panorama of the Alps with its background of glowing sky.[4]

Such romantic descriptions must have appealed to the Edwardian sybarite with a taste for the pleasure-loving modes of these sixteenth-century residences, but there were differing views on how far it was possible to recreate them in Britain. Blomfield was in no doubt about the matter: 'our climate and the quality of light in England make it impossible to obtain the effect which is actually attained in the great Italian gardens such as those at Tivoli'.[5] There, the climate precluded all but the minimum of grass and flowers, and called for the cooling effects of shady evergreen avenues and alleys, of stonework, and of the sight and sound of water.

Sir George Sitwell and Renishaw

None the less, some were determined to try to capture their spirit in this country, foremost amongst whom was Sir George Sitwell, who in 1887 began to remodel the park at his family seat, Renishaw Hall, near Chesterfield in Derbyshire. Sir George Reresby Sitwell (1860–1943), 4th Baronet, succeeded to his estate at the age of two. Reacting against his Victorian upbringing, he pursued scholarly tastes inherited from his distant forbears, developing a love of Italy combined with an insatiable appetite for building and landscaping.[6] He began in earnest a study of Italian gardens in the early 1890s, visiting over two hundred, and the fruits of his research, which accompanied his development of Renishaw over a period of thirty years, were contained in *An Essay on the Making of Gardens*, subtitled *A Study of Old Italian Gardens, of the Nature of Beauty, and the Principles Involved in Garden Design* (1909). Written in a lyrical style not unlike Sedding's, it drew from Ruskin, and from studies in psychology which he maintained held the secret of the 'garden-magic' of Italy. The emphasis was on the aesthetic perception of the garden, its appreciation by all the senses: sight, sound, scent and touch. While commending the work of Sedding, Blomfield and Thomas, he added, 'the formal garden in England falls short of the great examples of the Italian Renaissance; it is seldom related as it should be to the surrounding scenery; it is often wanting in repose and nearly always in imagination'.[7] In his view the Renaissance impulse ended with Bacon's essay *Of Gardens* (1625), and by the time of Sir William Temple's *Gardens of Epicurus* (1685) decadence had set in; thereafter, 'For more than two centuries the gardens of the Italian Renaissance lay under a cloud.'

Paramount was the relationship of the garden to the landscape:

we may find the eye returning again and again, not to fountain or lawn or parterre, but to some object so trivial that it can be hidden by a single finger of the outstretched hand; some tiny cloud of blue which tells of a far-off mountain, some gleam of distant water half seen between the trees, or green depth of a forest glade...the whole lay-out should be subordinated to them, and on no account should they be cut off by a rigid boundary, the 'good high wall for choice' of the English architects.[8]

He stressed also the importance of wonder and surprise, the value of contrast, and not least the element of water, 'the principal source of landscape beauty', whose virtues lay not only in its form and sound but in the poetry of colour.

According to Sir George, the three great gardens of Italy were the Villa d'Este at Tivoli, begun before 1540 by Pirro Ligorio; the Villa Lante at Bagnaia, Vignola's masterpiece, begun in 1566; and the Giusti garden at Verona, c.1585, attributed partly to Sanmicheli. 'These old Italian gardens, with their air of neglect, desolation and solitude...have a beauty which is indescribable, producing upon the mind an impression which is difficult to analyse, to which no words can do justice. In all the world there is no place so full of poetry as that Villa d'Este which formalist and naturalist united to decry.'[9] Though of inferior architectural detail, the grandiosity of this most famous Italian garden was calculated to appeal to Sir George on several counts. Firstly, it was one of the most dramatic representations of man's mastery over Nature; secondly, it was a symphony in water, complete with cascade and water organ; and thirdly, it had acquired a quality of pleasing decay. When Italian-style gardens of the 1900s were conceived, it took not only patience but vision to imagine them in their maturity. If Miss Jekyll could remark of d'Este, 'Kindly Nature clothes the ruin with her own beauty; were it stripped of this gracious mantle, and all its mutilation and decay laid bare, how much of its mysterious, poetical charm would be lost!',[10] how much more stark must these Edwardian gardens have looked when new compared with their crumbling predecessors. Lante was also linked by water: 'pool, cascade and water-temple are threaded like pearls upon a string...a colour harmony of cool refreshing green and brighter flowers, of darkest bronze, blue pools and golden light'.[11] But it had a different character, its succession of gardens unfolding from the dark

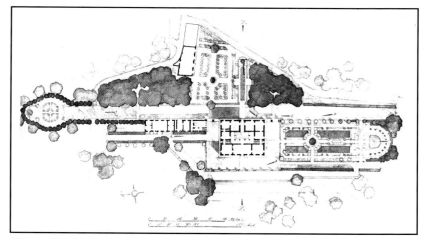

213. Villa Gamberaia, Settignano, Florence (School of Ammanati, from 1610): layout plan. [From Shepherd and Jellicoe, *Italian Gardens of the Renaissance*, 1925]

bosco of plane and ilex, culminating in the elaborate, sun-drenched parterre and water garden, the final stage in the transition from the natural woodland to the town below, its twin casinos being merely elements in one sublime garden scheme. Landscaped in the nineteenth century, little survives of the terraced gardens of Giusti, but the approach vista remains, framed by ancient cypresses.[12] 'For pure sensation there is nothing in Italy equal to this first glimpse through the Giusti gateway', and it is this 'narrow alley, girt in by sheer precipices of green' with its 'grave and haunting beauty' to which the memory returns.[13]

These three gardens were not, however, the most appropriate models for the Edwardian garden designer. There were others more modest in scale, such as the garden of the Villa Piccolomini at Frascati (c.1560), which had the character of a noble salon; and most instructive of all, the Tuscan Villa Gamberaia at Settignano, begun in 1610 for the Lapi family (Plate 213). This skilfully incorporated a diversity of elements within an awkwardly shaped site, the whole being tied together by axes and vistas (a device used by Lutyens at The Salutation), also by the bowling alley and the grass walk that extends from one end of the garden to the other. Its southern end commands a magnificent view over the Arno, while to the north is a *giardino segreto*, a grotto enclosed by cypresses. The largest enclosure is the water parterre to the south front, laid out at the end of the nineteenth century, but the most delightful feature is on the east axis, between terraced woods, a narrow, sunken grotto garden from which double flights of steps lead up to a lemon garden with box-edged beds alongside the *stanzone* (Plate 214). At Gamberaia, assembled into an area of only three acres, was a complete design vocabulary and many important lessons for the Edwardian garden designer: disposition of outdoor rooms, treatment of levels and of water, contrast of sunlight and dense shade, simplicity of form, human scale and controlled use of colour.[14]

Renishaw profited from all these examples, but the long lines of the house and the nature of its setting called less for qualities of mystery, wonder and surprise, or of dramatic contrast between enclosure and distant prospect, than for an outward-looking breadth and spaciousness. The battlemented house, built of the local, grey-

214. Villa Gamberaia: grotto garden from the east. Watercolour by Maxfield Parrish. [From E. Wharton, *Italian Villas and Their Gardens*, 1904]

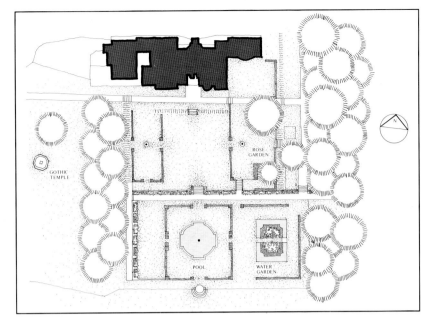

215. Renishaw Hall, Derbyshire (Sir George Sitwell, from 1890): layout plan. [Miranda Ottewill]

brown sandstone, dated from 1625 and had been extended in 1793–1808 by the 1st Baronet, Sir Sitwell Sitwell. At that time the grounds were landscaped and the original garden enclosures swept away, and it was partly to remedy their loss that Sir George laid out his gardens. Sir Osbert Sitwell (1892–1969) has described the garden created by his eccentric father: 'The garden would be beautiful—and is beautiful—with no flower blooming there...Its architecture does not consist so much in stone walls and paved walks, as in green walls of yew and box.' He recorded also the painstaking care with which his father determined the prospect and the exact proportions of its various elements:

He walks up and down, surveying his work, which will never be finished, his head full of new projects of sun and shade, but never of flowers, measuring the various views with a stick to his

eye or a pair of binoculars. Sometimes he is planning a boat of stone upon the lake, or a dragon in lead, writhing for a quarter of a mile through its level waters, or a colonnaded pavilion upon another island, or a Roman aqueduct in counterfeit to frame the prospect with its elongated arches, or a cascade to fall down a stone channel for a hundred and fifty feet, from the water to the garden below: and, for projects such as these, though most of them never materialised, he would cause wooden towers, built up of planks and joists and beams—like an early machine for siege warfare or a drawing by Piranesi—to be erected here and there at the right points of vantage.[15]

The keynotes at Renishaw were simplicity, restraint and unity with the landscape, the main vista presenting a series of gently descending terraces whose lawns merged with the park, the circular pool acting as a visual link with the lake. It was a 'gallery of foregrounds' with the marvellous view over the valley of the Rother for its backdrop. The gardens were divided into compartments, including rose garden, secret garden, pool and the water garden, his last project, carried out in the 1930s (Plate 215). As in Italian gardens, the transverse axes were contained, by the woodland to the east and by an old avenue of limes and elms to the west (Plate 216); but the principal Italian note was struck by the statuary which marked the central vista. Mid-way in the layout stand figures of Diana and Neptune, reputed to be by Caligari, which replaced the earlier piers set with obelisks (similar to those that frame the view of the Giusti gardens[16]). They are echoed by the two giants, Samson and Hercules, guarding the southern boundary overlooking the park. Particular attention was given to the scale and placing of these statues, which as well as evoking the past add interest to the otherwise bland design. The dividing walls of the gardens consist of yew hedges punctuated by pyramids, of which Sir Osbert recalled, 'I never remember a time between the ages of three and

216. Renishaw Hall: view from the south-west. [Author 1985]

seventeen when we were not the same height',[17] but whereas in Italian gardens figures were either raised and silhouetted against trees or sky, or seen against massive walls of yew, the hedges at Renishaw, although preserving the view, form a restless background for the statues.

These yew pyramids derived from seventeenth-century Dutch and English precedent rather than Italian and recalled Athelhampton. Inigo Thomas—who designed the cupola at the west end of the house—is credited with some of the box-edged flower beds (now removed).[18] Being a first cousin, he was doubtless consulted on other matters, although it seems unlikely that he, or any other architect for that matter, could have long survived the exacting demands and vacillations of the autocratic baronet.[19] Sir George cared little for flowers. Bright colour, anathema to him, was confined to these box-edged beds and the terrace borders.[20] 'Such flowers as might be permitted, had, like all else in good taste, to be

unobtrusive, not to call attention to themselves by hue or scent',[21] and only white flowers were tolerated in some areas, including the Rose Garden. The old Italian gardens were not without their displays of tulips and irises, although the bright sun called generally for cooling hues. Gamberaia was a green monochrome in grass, box, yew, cypress and ilex, and at Renishaw, too, the aim was for repose, 'the counterpoint of bright, mown grass and deep shade, of water and of trees'.[22] With much of this Miss Jekyll would have agreed. She was consulted, from 1910, on the planting of some flower beds,[23] which, partly filled with brightly coloured annuals, were unlikely to have appealed to Sir George. In spite of this, Osbert Sitwell remembered the richness of the mature garden in the summer of 1911: 'The heads of dahlias and zinnias and carnations and roses were heavier and more velvety than in the previous decade, and the scent of the box hedges and of the various flowers was wafted up to the window, while at dusk the fragrance

217. Kingston Maurward, near Dorchester, Dorset (Cecil Hanbury, 1918–20): view of the formal garden. [Author 1985]

218. Eden Garden, Giudecca, Venice (Frederic and Caroline Eden, from 1884): lily pergola. [*CL* 1900]

of the tobacco plants and the stocks became overwhelming.'[24] As Sir George developed his theories of design based on studies of Italian villas, the gardens of Renishaw took shape. However, someone with such a love for Italy and its historic gardens could not— to paraphrase Blomfield—be content for long with a faint echo of their style but would want the real thing. In 1906 he bought the Castello di Montegufoni in the Tuscan Hills and took up permanent residence there in 1925, making over Renishaw to Osbert.

In settling at Montegufoni, Sir George was following in the wake of others who had long succumbed to the lure of the Mediterranean, including many British and American expatriates who bought up Italian estates. Owing to the enthusiasm of Dorothy Hanbury, La Mortola on the Italian Riviera was developed into an exotic garden paradise in the 1900s, its network of richly planted paths joined by an impressive avenue of Mediterranean cypresses flanking the stairways that descend the steep hillside.[25] The Palazzo Marengo at La Mortola had been bought in 1867 by her father-in-law Thomas Hanbury, who had made his fortune trading in the Far East, and who presented the gardens at Wisley to the Royal Horticultural Society in 1903. In 1918–20 formal gardens were added to Kingston Maurward House, near Dorchester (Plate 217),[26] for his son, Cecil Hanbury, but again it was Dorothy Hanbury who was the principal instigator.

The exotic was not the aim of Frederic Eden. Where Sir George sought to bring the spirit of Italy to England, the Edens embellished their palazzina in Venice with reminders of an English flower garden. Gertrude Jekyll's elder sister, Caroline (1837–1928), married Eden in 1865.[27] In 1870 they settled in Venice, living in an apartment in the Palazzo Barbarigo, and in 1884 acquired a small house on the Giudecca. Its old and neglected garden was partly enclosed by walls and had a view of the lagoon and the dome of the Redentore. They set to work to restore it and to fill it with plants in Robinsonian style: 'our individual taste loves vegetation as Nature grows it rather than as man clips it'.[28] Nevertheless, the garden had

a formal structure consisting of a network of vine pergola walks constructed from the traditional *pali*, *cordoni* and *traversi* made from willow poles, with paths of crushed sea shells and flower borders edged with old bricks. These pergolas were notable for the white madonna lilies, *Lilium candidum*, growing in the shade in the borders (Plate 218), of which Miss Jekyll wrote: 'If one might have only one lily in the garden, it would have to be the beautiful old White Lily that has been with us since the end of the sixteenth century.' She included a view of her sister's pergola in her *Lilies for English Gardens* (1901), and it was also illustrated in an article in *Country Life* by Alethia Wiel who wrote, 'The beauty of the garden at this time is beyond description. In every direction the eye is carried along lines of pure white lilies to some fresh vision of loveliness.'[29] The Edens' Venetian garden included also lawns, courts, a cypress walk and a pool inspired by the Generalife at Granada. The existing cabbages and artichokes were replaced by flowers, which, if the soil happened to suit them, were allowed to ramp in a mass of bloom. Statuary raised on pedestals was silhouetted against cypresses, mulberry trees, pomegranates, *Magnolia* and oleanders —the 'Garden of Eden' became an earthly paradise where they entertained their large circle of friends up to the 1920s.[30]

The Italian Revival in the United States

Before considering other gardens created by those, principally Americans, fortunate enough to settle amongst the cypress avenues and olive groves of Italy, one must look at the work of two leaders in the Italian revival, the American landscape painter turned architect Charles A. Platt (1861–1933) and the English architect Harold A. Peto (1854–1933). The cult of the Italian garden received its first impetus on the other side of the Atlantic where the artistic climate had long been receptive to Renaissance styles. In the last quarter of the nineteenth century many writers and artists, particularly Bostonians, came increasingly under the spell of Italy, a movement vividly portrayed by Henry James in his early novels, beginning with *Roderick Hudson* (1875). Nevertheless, it was not until 1894 that Platt's *Italian Gardens* appeared, the first illustrated study of the subject in English.[31] The product of a six-month tour of about twenty-five villas in 1892, it signalled the revival of the formal garden in America, presenting, as Sedding and Blomfield had done with the English Renaissance, the formal and aesthetic viewpoint as distinct from the natural and picturesque approach advocated by Frederick Law Olmsted (1822–1903), the designer of Central Park, New York.

In 1893 Platt had been able to try out his knowledge of Italian gardens at his summer residence at Cornish, New Hampshire, dividing the garden into an informal arrangement of geometric units related axially to the house; and from 1895 he began to take up architecture and landscape design as his main profession.[32] His first major garden and landscaping commission, in which he replaced the Olmsted firm, came in 1897 at Faulkner Farm,

Brookline, Massachusetts, for a wealthy member of Congress, Charles F. Sprague. In its approach alley, raised terraces and flower garden, the layout (Plate 219) displayed marked similarities to Gamberaia (Plate 213), and the pavilion, the 'Casino', flanked by quadrant pergolas at the apsidal end of the flower garden (Plate 220) was inspired by the twin lodges at the top end of Lante.[33] As in Victorian Britain, there had been earlier, so-called 'Italian' gardens in America, but Faulkner Farm was the first to show a grasp of the formal principles of the Italian villa, combined, moreover, with a 'painter's sensitivity to the landscape'.[34]

Harold A. Peto

This pioneering activity was followed in Britain by Harold Peto (Plates 221, 222), who had visited America in 1887 and subsequently must have known about Platt's work, from American publications at least. His career was in some ways the reverse of Platt's, since he

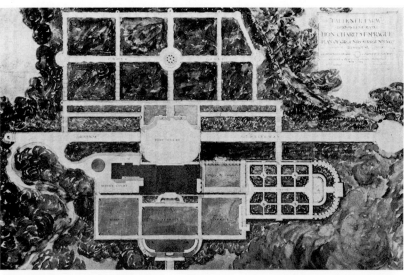

219. Faulkner Farm, Brookline, Massachusetts (Charles A. Platt, 1897): layout plan. [Boston Athenaeum]

220. Faulkner Farm: flower garden. [Courtesy of Graduate School of Design Library, Harvard University]

221. Harold Ainsworth Peto, from a photograph taken in Venice by Fratelli Vianelli. [*Building News* 1890]

222. Harold Peto on the bridge at Iford, c.1930. [Courtesy of Hilary Grainger]

had begun as an architect but had changed by the late 1890s largely to interior and garden designer. Peto was the fifth son of Sir Samuel Morton Peto, Bt (1809–1889), one of the great Victorian railway contractors, whose own estate, Somerleyton Hall, Suffolk (1844–51), boasted an enormous winter garden and gardens by W.A. Nesfield.[35] He failed in the financial crash of 1866, but his sons were brought up in comfortable circumstances, owing to their mother's independent wealth. In 1871 Harold Peto followed an 'architectural training' with J. Clements of Lowestoft as well as working in the joinery workshop of Lucas Bros, and in 1876 he went into partnership with Ernest George (1839–1922). In the

223. Iford Manor, near Bradford-on-Avon, Wiltshire (H.A. Peto, from 1899): view of the main stairway. [Author 1981]

1880s the office of George and Peto became one of the most fashionable in London, much sought after by young assistants: Lutyens, Schultz, Herbert Baker and Guy Dawber all worked there. Ernest George was the prolific designer of the firm, while Peto was more important in the decorative work and on the business side by virtue of his connections. By 1892 Peto was able to terminate his partnership with George, and a few years later he began the independent professional career which allowed him to pursue his special interest in garden and interior design.[36] From the 1880s he had made regular studies of Italian gardens, and this was combined with a practical interest in gardening unusual in an architect, enough to earn him the admiration of Miss Jekyll, who included his work in *Garden Ornament* (1918). His schemes were always well related to their surroundings and gave the impression of having been determined on the site rather than planned on paper. Thus he formed an

important bridge not only with the Italian garden but also the Picturesque, and, as Tipping wrote in 1910, 'If the relative spheres and successful inter-marriage of formal and natural gardening are better understood today than ever before, that desirable result is due to the efforts of no one man more than to Mr Peto.'[37]

These qualities were admirably demonstrated in his own garden at Iford Manor, near Bradford-on-Avon, Wiltshire, his home from 1899 until his death in 1933. This limestone manor house, Elizabethan but with a fine Georgian front of c.1725, nestled beneath woods in the valley of the Frome, and behind it and to the east were hanging gardens containing many fine trees largely laid out in the first half of the nineteenth century. Over the years Peto transformed these gardens into a series of enchanting terraces, reached from the east end of the house by a succession of stairways forming a vista up to an oval lily pool—originally surrounded by

224. Iford Manor: main terrace. [Author 1981]

147

225. Iford Manor: vista across pool towards valley. [Author 1981]

broad walks with seats and statues and tall cypresses. If more of our English gardens could have an increase of this influence it would be well instead of their running riot in masses of colour irrespective of form.[38]

An Italian note is struck also by the Tuscan colonnade marking the southern side of the terrace and recessed above the lily pool, creating the effect of a romantic ruin and reminiscent of the classical fragments from Leptis Magna erected at Virginia Water in 1826.[39] It recalls also the colonnade at the top of Lante, but whereas that marks the transition from *bosco* to formal garden, at Iford it acts as a foreground to the distant view. The terrace is flanked to one side by the dark woods, but on the other side, between vertical accents of column and cypress, a soft, green backcloth is provided by the meadows rising across the valley (Plate 225). Iford is a memorial to Peto's love of architecture, horticulture and history. As he wrote in

226. Wayford Manor, near Crewkerne, Somerset (H.A. Peto, 1902): central vista. [Courtesy of R.L. Goffe, 1930s]

227. Wayford Manor: central vista. [Author 1984]

pillars and chains supporting *Wisteria*—and beyond to the main terrace (Plate 223). This delightful promenade, set high on the hillside, dates from the eighteenth century, as does the octagonal summer-house that closes its eastern end. Peto re-paved the terrace with Westwood stone and bordered it with antique sculpture and architectural fragments, collected on his travels (Plate 224). To the west the terrace leads past a loggia or casita with coupled columns of pink Verona marble of c.1200, to a well-head, originally a Theodoric capital, and finally to a curved stone seat overlooking the orchard. The planting at Iford was varied and informal and there was no lack of colour, but it was chosen to complement the basic architectural form. There is an abundance of green foliage—cypress, juniper, yew, *Phillyrea* and *Acanthus*—borders are planted with scented herbs, and the main terrace has bay trees in tubs, bush roses and pale blue *Agapanthus*; *Wisteria* abounds. All this follows the Italian example of which Peto wrote,

> The entirely subordinate place in the scheme that flowers occupy gives a breadth and quietude to the whole which is sympathetic, the picture being painted with hedges, canals and water tanks,

his manuscript *Boke of Iford*, 'old buildings or fragments of masonry carry one's mind back to the past in a way that a garden of flowers only cannot do. Gardens that are too stony are equally unsatisfactory; it is the combination of the two in just proportion which is the most satisfying.'[40]

Peto created another hillside garden at Wayford Manor, near Crewkerne, Somerset (1902) for his sister, Helen Baker (1860–1929). Built in 1602 of the golden Ham stone, it was bought in 1899 by Ingham Baker who in 1902 employed George and Yeates to add the missing north wing of its E-shaped plan.[41] The site, of lime-free loam, faced south across the River Axe towards the North Dorset Downs and included an upper terrace, which was all that remained of the original Elizabethan garden (Plate 228). Below this, Peto laid out two additional terraces and formed a central vista, marked by columnar cypresses and junipers, from the entrance forecourt down to a wild garden (Plates 226, 227). The upper level was enclosed by farm buildings to the west and was

228. Wayford Manor: layout plan. [Miranda Ottewill, based on a plan prepared by Howard Bolton, 1976]

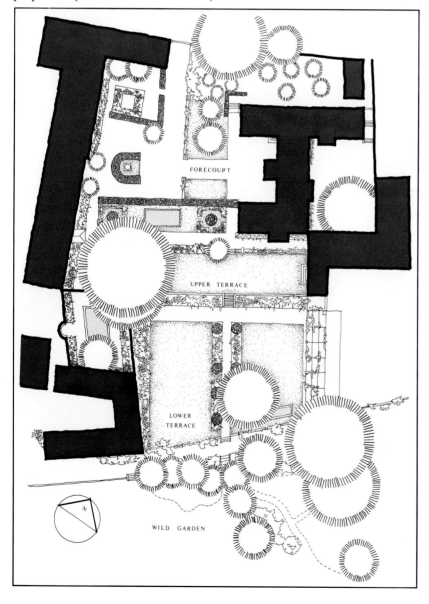

229. Walter Crane, frontispiece to *Flowers from Shakespeare's Garden*, 1906. [From the Art Collection of the Folger Shakespeare Library]

subdivided further with yew hedges to create several intimate enclosures with figs and flowering quince growing against the east-facing wall. Steps then descend to a long, grassed terrace or bowling alley bounded on the south by a stone balustrade (Plate 230). At its eastern end Peto added a characteristic arched loggia linked to the house, balanced at the western end by two enormous horse-chestnuts, beneath which a stone staircase connects to a *giardino segreto* in whose sequestered shade grow lilies, *Hosta*, irises and Solomon's seal around a fountain pool. By contrast the third and lowest terrace is a simple lawn, traversed by the central path lined with yew cones and open to the sky except for a magnificent *Magnolia soulangiana* in its south-east corner. Wayford owes much to the Italian garden, yet there is nothing revivalistic about its design, which appears to have grown naturally from its English rural setting.[42]

It has been said of Peto's most important client in the early 1900s, 'If a single Edwardian romantic can represent the whole epoch, then Daisy, Countess of Warwick, must be chosen.'[43] Frances Evelyn Maynard (1861–1938) was only four when her father died, followed a few months later by her grandfather, the last Lord Maynard, leaving her sole heiress to his estates. She married Lord Brooke in 1881, becoming Countess of Warwick in 1893. Although a prominent member of the 'Marlborough House Set'—that pleasure-loving circle which from the 1860s had revolved around the Prince of Wales—in 1895 she suddenly became converted to socialism, soon losing, reluctantly, her favoured place both in Society and as the Prince's recognized mistress, and concentrating her passions on charitable causes. Philanthropist, guardian of all animals and birds, author, Lady Warwick numbered also gardening amongst her diverse interests, including founding the Studley College for women gardeners (see Chapter 4). Easton Lodge, near Dunmow, Essex, where she was brought up, had been the seat of the Maynards since Elizabethan times, but its brick mansion of 1595 was largely destroyed by fire in 1847, and a three-

storey addition, designed by Thomas Hopper in a grey stucco, bastard Jacobean, was built alongside.[44] In the 1890s her romanticism extended to a range of gardens on the Easton estate, including the Dairy Garden, the 'Roserie', the 'Border of Sentiment' and the 'Garden of Scripture'. Near the 'gothick' Stone Hall there was a topiary sundial with yew gnomon and box numerals,[45] a Garden of Friendship, consisting of concentric circles of plants given to her by friends (notably the Prince of Wales) whose names were recorded on heart-shaped pottery plaques,[46] and last, but not least, her Shakespeare Border, full of scented herbs, marigolds, gillyflowers, eglantine, musk- and damask roses and other flowers associated with him (and approved by Ruskin), each labelled with a pottery butterfly containing the relevant quotation.[47] Later a sympathy with socialism brought Walter Crane to Easton and in 1906 he inscribed his *Flowers from Shakespeare's Garden* to his hostess and depicted her in the frontispiece kneeling before the immortal Bard (Plate 229).

230. Wayford Manor: upper terrace. [Howard Bolton, 1976]

231. Easton Lodge, Dunmow, Essex (H.A. Peto, 1902): general view [RCHME c.1906]

Set in a thousand-acre park noted for its herds of deer, Easton Lodge lacked any pleasant and sheltered formal gardens, and these are what in 1902 Peto was commissioned to provide. Bacon's essay had inspired other gardens and may have been the model for the layout at Easton, this being just the kind of romantic notion to appeal to Lady Warwick.[48] The gardens were laid out north of the house and comprised first a lawn corresponding to Bacon's 'green'. Next, an old croquet lawn was bordered on two sides by arched pergolas evoking Bacon's 'covert alley upon carpenter's work' and displaying Peto's knowledge of wood construction. Their central *treillage* domes derived from seventeenth-century French patterns, and their timber arches were covered with jute netting and wreathed in climbing plants, creating galleries of green architecture. The sunken water garden north of this agreed with Bacon's fountain

and occupied the site of an existing pond. Carried out in Ham Hill stone, it had a central balustraded pool over a hundred feet long, resplendent in summer with water-lilies and surrounded by broad, grass walks (Plate 231). Beyond was a maze, and to the east a tree house substituted for one of Bacon's 'mounts'.[49] The construction of these gardens provided an opportunity for Lady Warwick to promote the cause of practical socialism, sixty-seven inmates from a Salvation Army Inebriates' Home being employed for some of the labourers' work.

In 1906 Peto laid out formal gardens for Lord Warwick's brother, Louis Greville, at Heale House, Woodford, Wiltshire, which had been restored and enlarged by Detmar Blow. These included a stone terrace to the east by the river, and, on the south-west front, a grassed parterre with ornamental fish ponds either side of a

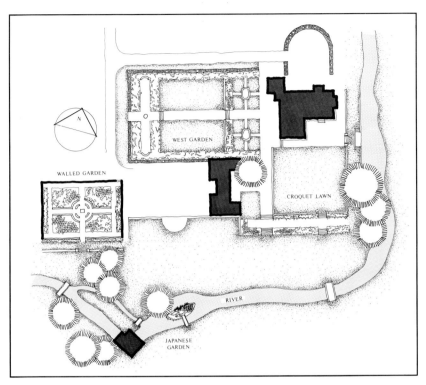

232. Heale House, Woodford, Wiltshire (H.A. Peto, 1906): layout plan. [Miranda Ottewill]

233. Heale House: west garden. [Author 1984]

broad, flagged walk which sloped up to a terrace with a semi-circular, stone seat at either end (Plates 232, 233).[50]

At Buscot Park, Berkshire (now in Oxfordshire), Peto had the opportunity, denied to other Edwardian architects, to design a water garden on a grand scale. The estate, with its Georgian house of c.1780, was acquired in 1885 by the financier and connoisseur Alexander Henderson (1850–1934), created Lord Faringdon in 1916.[51] In 1892–7 he employed George and Peto for the picturesque model village of Buscot and in 1899 to add a wing to the house. In 1904 Peto was approached to lay out a garden that would

connect the house with the twenty-acre lake lying at a considerably lower level to the north-east. A narrow vista was created partly through woodland, consisting of a succession of formal spaces enclosed by box hedges and terminating in a garden temple on the opposite side of the lake. From the house, steps descend to a grassed walk leading to a long canal which begins as a circular pool with a 'Boy and Dolphin' fountain, the water then falling via a narrow rill with broad steps and miniature cascades to a rectangular pool. It then narrows again, widens to a second circle, and passes under a little stone bridge before finally coming to rest in the lake (Plate 235). Buscot recalls the Mughul gardens of Kashmir, not only in its layout, but also in being a garden in its own right, independent of the house. Its haunting beauty owes much to the still reflections of sky, trees and Roman 'terms' which guard the perimeter, also to the contrast between the foliage and the precise lines of the pool surrounds, and between the pale stone and dark water.[52]

Similar qualities are found in Peto's designs for smaller, enclosed water gardens on level sites, but the feeling engendered is appropriately one of greater breadth and tranquillity. Notable examples were Bridge House and Hartham Park. H. Seymour Trower, a friend of Peto, bought the Victorian stucco Bridge House at Weybridge, Surrey in 1890 and developed the grounds over a period of twenty years with the help of Peto.[53] The water garden was added in 1906 to the south of the house, its main feature being a T-shaped canal, recalling the Dutch-inspired, seventeenth-century garden at Westbury Court. At its head an arcaded garden house was flanked by quadrant colonnades linked by creeper-clad chains (Plate 234), all strongly reminiscent of Platt's Faulkner Farm (see Plate 220). Wide, stone surrounds divided the canal, with its random pattern of white, yellow and pink water-lilies, from the adjoining grass plats which were enclosed by a semi-circle of pleached limes backed by tall yew hedges.[54] A few years earlier Peto had designed a similar arrangement of canal and loggia, more intimate and less

234. Bridge House, Weybridge, Surrey (H.A. Peto, 1906): water garden. [CL 1908]

235. Buscot Park, Berkshire (H.A. Peto, 1904): water garden. [Author 1982]

sophisticated, within an old walled garden at Hartham Park, near Corsham, Wiltshire, for Sir John Dickson-Poynder, Bt. Its canal was set within informally planted paving and herbaceous borders (Plate 236), and the loggia was based on the Lante lodge theme, with lofty central arch and steeply pitched roof of local stone slates.[55] This enclosed garden was for contemplative moods, but Hartham boasted another more outward-looking garden. The house, originally by James Wyatt of 1790–5, was set in the customary landscape park, but Edwardian taste demanded more formality. To satisfy this, Peto laid out the raised South Terrace, approached up steps from the parterre on the south front, and extending outwards to the south-west like a pier into the park. It consisted of a long walk enclosed by low yew hedges and, like the grassy walk at Gamberaia, ended in a balustraded enclosure with semi-circular stone seat overlooking the park.

The concave seat, conducive to conversation and placed at a vantage point on the boundary of the garden, was a recurring feature in Peto's gardens. Besides those at Iford and Heale, a version with carved ends and pedestals supportig *amorini* terminated the vista to the terrace he added at Hinton Admiral, near Christchurch, Hampshire (c.1905) for Sir George Meyrick.[56] Such curved seats resemble those marble exedrae that often appeared in the paintings of Lawrence Alma-Tadema,[57] who even designed a pair himself in 1909 for Sandringham, facing across a Venetian well-head in the central bay of the massive rustic pergola erected in 1905 (Plate 237).[58] Alma-Tadema belonged to that band of Victorian Olympians including Lord Leighton, E.J. Poynter and Albert Moore, who looked to ancient Greece and Rome and to sixteenth-century Italian art for inspiration.[59] Their paintings, which sometimes included re-creations of classical gardens, were another source of imagery for the Italian revival in garden design. Examples were Moore's *A Garden* (1869) and Leighton's *The Garden of the Hesperides* (1892) which evoked that other Eden in the west, with its tree of golden apples and hedonistic air of voluptuous opulence.

A reinterpretation of the classical ideal, forming a climax to Peto's career, was also situated in the west, although not in the sunny mediterranean but on the cloudy south-west coast of Ireland. Garinish Island, lying in the sheltered harbour of Glengarriff at the head of Bantry Bay in County Cork, was bought in 1910 by John Annan Bryce (1874–1924), a Belfast-born East India merchant

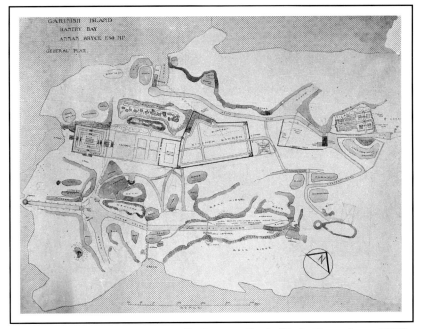

238. Garinish Island, Glengarriff, County Cork (H.A. Peto, from 1910): layout plan. [National Parks and Monuments Service, Office of Public Works in Ireland]

236. Hartham Park, Wiltshire (H.A. Peto, c.1903): water garden. [RCHME c.1906]

237. Sandringham, Norfolk (Sir Lawrence Alma-Tadema, 1909): seats in a rustic pergola. [Author 1985]

and Scottish MP. Inspired by the tranquil beauty of the bay—a haven for seals, its inlets backed by the grey-blue Caha Mountains—and encouraged by the almost sub-tropical climate, Bryce resolved, with the help of Peto, to transform the thirty-seven acres of barren rock and scrub into an island paradise. An Italianate mansion was designed for the highest point near an old Martello tower but was never built, an enlarged gardener's cottage sufficing and the creation of the garden becoming the principal object. Bryce began by having additional soil transported from the mainland and a protective belt mainly of pines was planted around the perimeter, up to one hundred men being employed before and after the First World War.

Peto based his layout (Plate 238) on a circuit linking a succession of open and enclosed spaces, merging effortlessly between natural and formal gardens and punctuated by vantage points providing views across and from the island. The visitor arrived at a landing stage at the north-west creek from which a drive led to the house. Nearby is a walled kitchen garden with a clock tower and a garden house at opposite corners. Climbing plants flourish against its walls—flowering quinces, jasmines, *Clematis*, roses, *Ceanothus* and *Wisteria*—while the central path is lined with herbaceous borders backed by espalier apples. From its north-east gateway a pathway climbs to the Martello tower, commanding a prospect of the whole island, then continues down to a grassy woodland glade between outcrops of rock and planted with a rich variety of trees and shrubs. The average annual rainfall at Garinish is seventy-three inches, but the mild, equable climate and rapid drainage enabled plants from many parts of the world to be imported, especially after the shelter belts matured. Australasian genera that thrive include *Dacrydium*, *Callistemon*, *Grevillea* and *Leptospermum*. *Griselinia* grows luxuriantly in many parts of the island and is used as a

239. Garinish Island: sunken garden (Author 1984)

hedge-plant. Of special note is the exuberant growth of myrtles, *Hoheria*, *Eucryphia*, variegated *Pittosporum* and *Abutilon*. This 'Robinsonian' wild garden extends along the south-east of the island to a point where flights of steps formed from roughly hewn slabs of the local blue shale ascend between Italian cypresses to a hexagonal temple structure overlooking the bay. From the base of this stairway the route continues to the north-west amidst further exotic plants and trees until it emerges into a large, rectangular, open expanse of lawn. This is closed at the far end by the walled garden and at the other by a casita with an open verandah. Behind lies the jewel of Garinish: the sunken pool garden (Plate 239). It is the ultimate development of the theme employed at Hartham and Bridge House, here placed in a dreamlike setting. The lily pool, framed by paving, flower beds, raised grass walks and shrubs, mirrors both the constantly changing sky and the perfectly proportioned Ionic pavilion with its *rosso antico* marble columns, central arch and hipped roof set against the misty silhouette of the Sugarloaf Mountain. Italian Renaissance gardens were rarely by the sea, and rectangular pools have Moorish associations. Peto's formal garden at Garinish echoes a more distant age, recalling Pliny's description of Roman seaside villas and evoking the eternal spirit of antiquity.[60]

The 'Mediterranean' Revival

The mild, humid climate of Garinish was ideal for the enthusiastic plantsman, but it was not the most appropriate setting for a house in the Italian manner. Nevertheless, it was probably Peto's reputation as the architect of several villas in the south of France that had commended him to Bryce, as well as his skill as a garden designer. Peto's agreement with Ernest George, which precluded his practising as an architect in Britain, partly explains his Riviera practice, although he was well known in France long before then. In 1902, for Ralph Curtis, he designed the Villa Sylvia at Cap Férrat in the Alpes Maritimes, the first of a string of commissions which lasted up to the First World War. The Côte d'Azur had for long been the resort of the itinerant leisured classes, but its congenial climate also attracted those seeking to establish a more permanent home. Most houses occupying this idyllic stretch of country reflected more wealth than taste and their gardens were either flamboyantly exotic or perpetuated the worst of Victorian gardenesque or bedding. It fell to Peto to respond more sympathetically to the special character of this hilly terrain by the sea and to revive the Italian-garden tradition.

All the examples of his work described so far were either attached to existing houses or were completely separate entities, but with these villas he was able to aim for a unified total composition. The Villa Sylvia was laid out on a steeply sloping site facing west towards Villefranche Bay. Loggias, those desirable transitional spaces linking house and garden, were provided on the south, connecting with an enclosed parterre, also on the west where steps descended to a terrace beyond which formality melted into luxuriantly planted olive groves overlooking the azure sea. The Villa Maryland (c.1904), for Mrs Arthur Wilson, had a similar hillside

240. Villa Maryland, Alpes Maritimes (H.A. Peto, c.1904): central alley to the upper garden. [*CL* 1910]

241. Villa Rosemary, Alpes Maritimes (H.A. Peto, c.1910–11): pergola garden. [*CL* 1912]

242. High Wall, Headington, Oxford (H.A. Peto, c.1912): pergola. [Author 1985]

site sprinkled with old olive trees on the Cap St Jean. The garden was laid out with cross-axes. One marked a shallow descent through the lower garden; it was bordered with lavender bushes and the grey-leaved *Echium*, framed by tall cypresses and terminated in a temple on the southern boundary. The other vista extended west from the house through the long, central alley of the upper garden, between antique columns, to a square parterre and garden house with quadrant pergola arms on the Faulkner Farm model (Plate 240). Peto was a master of the classical pergola, notable examples in England being at West Dean Park, West Sussex (1910)[61] and High Wall, Headington, Oxford (c.1912) (Plate 242).[62] The Mediterranean provided the ideal context for such pergolas, and Peto could give them the opulence of the oval colonnade at Isola Bella, Cannes (1910) or the dignity of the pergola garden at the Villa Rosemary, Alpes Maritimes (c.1910–11) for Arthur Cohen (Plate 241), whose serried ranks of square stone piers and graceful beams could well have inspired Tipping's at Mounton.[63]

157

Peto's work on the Côte d'Azur was not the only Mediterranean example of the revival, and the movement took root also in places with similar climates and cultural links such as California and parts of Australia. Moreover, Italy itself had rediscovered its historic gardens, previously considered old-fashioned, many having been supplanted by the *giardino inglese* with its serpentine paths and irregularly shaped flower beds. The awakening of interest owed much to English writers for whom Italy had been a fashionable resort throughout the nineteenth century, notably at Pisa, Bagni di Lucca, and Florence, where there was a flourishing Anglo-Italian community. The appreciation of Italian Renaissance gardens was pioneered partly by Julia Cartwright,[64] and also by Violet Paget (1856–1935), who lived at the Villa il Palmerino at Maiano, Florence, and wrote from 1875 under the pseudonym of Vernon Lee.[65] A prolific writer on the Renaissance, her sensitivity to the *genius loci* of the Italian landscape was vividly displayed in essays such as 'Old Italian Gardens'[66] and was later evoked in Percy Lubbock's description of a visit with her to an old garden near Siena 'whose grave and noble beauty had been saved by poverty and neglect'.[67]

It was to Vernon Lee that the New York novelist Edith Wharton (1862–1937) turned for guidance in 1903 when she was gathering material for her book *Italian Villas and Their Gardens*.[68] Her first book had been *The Decoration of Houses* (1897), written in collaboration with a young Boston architect glorying in the Jamesian name of Ogden Codman. A plea for simplicity in interior design, it pointed to Italian models and epitomized the American pursuit of elegance and 'good taste' of the 'eighties and 'nineties. The Italian garden was one facet of this humanist revival. Rose Standish Nichols had included a chapter on 'Italian Villa Gardens' in *English Pleasure Gardens* (1902), but whereas she described the more 'princely' examples and their Italianate successors such as Wilton and Shrubland Park (see Chapter 1), it was to the more modest and less familiar villas that *Italian Villas and Their Gardens* was directed. Based on articles published the previous year in *The Century*, it was accompanied—through no choice of its author—by a series of romantic watercolours by Maxfield Parrish (see Plate 214) and was dedicated, inevitably, to Vernon Lee, 'who better than anyone else has understood and interpreted the garden-magic of Italy'. It had the rare distinction of receiving praise from none other than Sir George Sitwell who wrote in the preface to his *Essay*, 'During the last few years several sumptuous volumes have appeared illustrating the old gardens of Italy, yet except for a few hints given by Mrs Wharton in her most valuable and charming book, little or nothing has been said about principles.' These she stressed in her Introduction:

> The garden-lover should not content himself with a vague enjoyment of old Italian gardens, but should try to extract from them principles which may be applied at home. He should observe, for instance, that the old Italian garden was meant to be lived in—a use to which, at least in America, the modern garden is seldom put. He should note that, to this end, the grounds were as carefully and conveniently planned as the house, with broad paths (in which two or more could go abreast) leading from one division to another; with shade easily accessible from the house, as well as a sunny sheltered walk for winter; and with effective transitions from the dusk of wooded alleys to open flowery spaces or to the level sward of the bowling-green. He should remember that the terraces and formal gardens adjoined the house, that the ilex or laurel walks beyond were clipped into shape to effect a transition between the straight lines of masonry and the untrimmed growth of the woodland to which they led, and that each step away from architecture was a nearer approach to nature.[69]

She had in mind the mere striving after effects of many gardens at home, 'a marble bench here and a sun-dial there'; she also wanted to answer those critics who insisted that the Italian garden could never be translated to another age, landscape and climate. Some, like the reviewer of Platt's book in *Garden and Forest*, had strong reservations, maintaining that only in the American South would such gardens be possible.[70] Miss Jekyll agreed: 'I think the true Italian character is only suitable or completely possible in a corresponding climate such as that of California and others of the Southern States.'[71] This was in a letter of c.1913 to Mrs Francis King who had sent her a book on American gardens, probably *Old Time Gardens* (1901) by Alice Morse Earle, which included illustrations of an Italianate garden at Drumthwacket, New Jersey. Italian and Spanish styles thrived in Santa Barbara, which boasted many such villas after the turn of the century,[72] and in her *Chronicles of the Garden* (1925) Mrs King included an illustration of one at Pepper Hill, Montecito, the *Clematis*-draped balustrade of its broad terrace outlined against the sierra and framed by oak and eucalyptus.

Australia provided another sympathetic habitat for the Italian garden, although some felt that natural, even wild gardens were more appropriate. The great debate was pursued there, a discussion taking place in 1903 in Melbourne at the Royal Victorian Institute of Architects at which the formal viewpoint was presented by the architect Walter Richmond Butler (1864–1949) who had worked in Sedding's office before sailing to Australia in 1888.[73] He inherited Sedding's view of the garden as an extension of the house, a transition with 'primeval wilderness'; but the opposite speaker, the horticulturist Charles Bogue Luffman, favoured something more 'Gothic', with more shade and greenery, 'winding glades', even some 'wayward growth'.[74] Both favoured greater partnership between architect and gardener, and the marriage of Italianate design with rich, informal planting was apparent in Butler's work, a notable surviving example being Marathon, Mount Eliza, Victoria, laid out in 1913–14 for Lieutenant-Colonel H.W. Grimwade on a dramatic clifftop site overlooking Port Phillip Bay. In contrast to the romantic, gabled house, the main garden was laid out axially as a succession of terraces, with steps leading down first to a balustraded croquet lawn, then descending to a central walk between flower gardens, and finally to a niche fountain and lily pond. The formality was softened by luxuriant planting that included *Wisteria*-draped pergolas and *Bougainvillea*-clad trellis screens (Plate 243).[75]

After the First World War naturalistic planting and Jekyllian

243. Marathon, Mount Eliza, Victoria, Australia (Walter R. Butler, 1913–14): general view. [Peter Watts 1981]

colour schemes were used by Edna Walling (1896–1973) to blur the architectural lines of her Italian-inspired gardens in Victoria, such as Warrawee at Toorak, a suburb of Melbourne, originally laid out by Butler in 1906–10.[76] The same happy union could be seen in America in the work of Edith Wharton's niece, Beatrix Farrand, who, though guided by the principles outlined in *Italian Villas and Their Gardens*, was also influenced by Robinson and Miss Jekyll (see Chapter 4). 'The work of the architect and landscape gardener should be done together from the beginning' she wrote, 'not, as too often happens, one crowding the other out.'[77]

In 1910 Edith Wharton settled in France, and in 1919 she too bought a house in the Mediterranean, the Château Sainte Claire, above Hyères, whose gardens she later recreated.[78] Her neighbour was the celebrated gardener, the Vicomte de Noailles (1891–1981), who laid out a modern garden there in the early 1920s and then, from about 1925, restored an eighteenth-century villa at Grasse,

adding terraced gardens with architectural hedges in box and a half-size replica of one of the water spiral columns at the Villa Aldobrandini. Both were close friends of Lawrence Johnston who in the early 1920s created a formal, sub-tropical garden at his winter retreat, La Serre de la Madone, above Mentone in the Alpes Maritimes.[79]

Cecil Pinsent

Most gardens on the Riviera had to be newly formed out of the olive-planted hillsides, but usually all that the new owners of old Italian villas had to do was to restore what was already there. An exception was I Tatti, which Edith Wharton began to visit regularly from 1910. This Tuscan villa, situated above Florence at Settignano, was typical of the kind of villa she had praised in her book. In 1900 it was rented by the American art historian Bernard

and naturalistic teachings of Ruskin, and argued for design based on aesthetics and space as exemplified by the Baroque.[82] In the chapter entitled 'The Romantic Fallacy', he wrote of the Picturesque,

> 'Formal' architecture is to the 'picturesque' as the whole body of musical art to the lazy hum and vaguely occupying murmur of the summer fields....Like a coarse weed, not unbeautiful in itself, [the picturesque] tends to stifle every opportunity of growth.

Though opposed to Blomfield's architectural views, Scott, too, dismissed the cult of Nature:

> There is a beauty of art and a beauty of Nature....Taken in isolation, made hostile to the formal instincts of the mind, Nature led, and can only lead, to chaos...by the romantic taste the artificial was scorned, though art, whatever else it is, is necessarily that; and it was scorned simply because it was not natural, which no art can hope, by whatever casuistry, to become.[83]

From May 1909 Pinsent commenced practice in Florence, sharing a flat with Scott at the top of an old palazzo in the Via delle Terme.

The commission for I Tatti, which Scott had obtained from Berenson, was their first important joint undertaking. The villa, which was in a desolate state, lacked formal gardens, and these were laid out in a succession of terraces on the sloping ground to the south. Immediately below the house, and occupying its full width, is a parterre, boldly designed in box, below which is the *limonaia*, with a central archway through which the main garden is revealed, an intricate green cascade of clipped box, descending in tiers, each with its own geometrical pattern (Plates 245, 246). A central path in pebble mosaic divides into a double stair around a pool and then steps down, flanked in summer by serried rows of lemon trees, to twin pools surrounded by stone benches. The entire garden is enclosed by gigantic cypress hedges of great textural beauty, broken only where the central vista continues, punctuated by statuary, past a balustraded double stair to the ilex grove. A cypress avenue formed the approach to the house by foot and the grounds also contained a jasmine-covered, trellis cupola over a round pool and 'as English a meadow in springtime as one might ever hope to see south of the Alps'.[84] In 1949 the fastidious Berenson wrote of his villa, 'Although I had so gifted an architect as Cecil Pinsent, who often understood my wants better than I did, it half killed me to get it into shape...now after many years I love it as much as one can love any object or complex of objects not human'.[85] Later he added, 'Though I have travelled all over the world and seen many lovely places, I now find all the beauty I need in my own garden.'

In 1911 Pinsent carried out alterations at La Pietra for Arthur Acton who had bought the fifteenth-century villa in 1902 and was modifying its seventeenth-century gardens. His next major commission was the Villa Le Balze, Fiesole (1912–14) for the American philosopher Charles Augustus Strong; here he designed both house and garden. Situated on a narrow strip of land following the contours of the steep hillside just below the Villa Medici, Le Balze was perfectly blended into the landscape, the house enjoying an unobstructed prospect over the valley of the Arno. The gardens, how-

244. Geoffrey Scott and Cecil Pinsent in Battery Park, New York, 5 August 1929. [Courtesy of Dr John Scott]

Berenson (1865–1959), who bought it in 1905 and in 1909 commissioned the writer Geoffrey Scott (1883–1929) and the English architect Cecil Ross Pinsent (1884–1963) (Plate 244) to restore it and to provide new gardens embodying the spirit of the old.[80] Berenson was one of the protégés of the art collector Isabella Stewart Gardner ('Mrs Jack'), and, partly sponsored by her, he had set off in 1887 for Europe, from which, apart from brief visits, he was never to return. Later he became the principal agent in assembling the collection housed at her pseudo-Venetian palace-cum-museum, Fenway Court, Boston. Incorporating architectural details shipped from Venice, and with an adjoining Monk's Garden, it was begun in 1899 and opened in characteristically flamboyant style at the beginning of 1903 at a *fête de Nouvel An*, the climax of which came when guests were admitted to its lofty, glass-roofed garden court and were rendered spellbound by the 'gorgeous vista of blossoming summer gardens...with the odor of flowers stealing toward one as though wafted on a southern breeze'.[81]

While on a study tour of Italy in 1907 Pinsent began to acquire commissions from American and English emigrés who were buying villas in the hills around Florence and looking for someone to advise them on alterations and additions. In Pinsent they were to find the ideal architect for their needs. In the same year he also met Scott who had become Berenson's secretary-cum-librarian at I Tatti. In 1914 Scott was to secure a place for himself in the history of architectural theory with his book, *The Architecture of Humanism*. This attempted to explode various theories, including the ethical

245. Villa I Tatti, Settignano, Florence (Cecil Pinsent, from 1909): view from the *limonaia*. [Harriet Parsons 1974; Florence, Berenson Collection, reproduced by permission of the President and Fellows of Harvard College]

246. Villa I Tatti: view looking towards the house. [Florence, Berenson Collection]

247. Villa Le Balze, Fiesole (Cecil Pinsent, 1912–14): walled camellia garden (1986). [Courtesy of the Provost's Office, Georgetown University]

ever, were treated as a series of external ante-chambers through which the house was approached (Plate 247) and were enclosed by walls or orange trees allowing only occasional framed views of the countryside.[86]

Although exhibiting a sensitive understanding of the historic traditions, Pinsent's gardens incorporated a number of distinct differences, including the greater sense of enclosure provided by tall cypress hedges and the architectural use of wide box borders. Their bold, sculptural quality reflected his method of working up his designs by means of plasticine models. This had the added advantage of giving his clients a better idea of the ultimate form of the garden. His parterres derived from Renaissance patterns, but in place of the traditional, brightly coloured beds they were usually filled with plain areas of grass with restrained planting in terracotta pots. Characteristic also was the more sophisticated use of decorative features, including fountains, vases, statuary and encrusted grotto-work. Some of this Pinsent carried out himself, notably at

Le Balze where in 1921–2 he added Baroque stairs opposite the entrance with a sponge-stone grotto fountain decorated with shells and stalactites and a self-portrait bust.

I Tatti and Le Balze, though based on Italian villa theory, were modern interpretations of the style, but at the Villa Medici (1912) the problem was to re-create an historic garden. Situated opposite I Tatti, the villa was built c.1450 for Cosimo de' Medici by Michelozzo, architect of the Palazzo Medici-Riccardi. In 1911 it was bought by Lady Sybil Cutting (1879–1943), daughter of the 5th Earl of Desart and widow of William Bayard Cutting (d.1910), Secretary of the American Embassy in London. She commissioned Scott and Pinsent to make alterations, including the reconstruction of the parterres of the lower and west terraces, based on old drawings and descriptions.

Pinsent's practice flourished after the First World War, other gardens in Florence being Villa Papignano (1925) for H.S. Whitaker, the less formal Villa Piazza Calda (1931–5) for Richard Blow, and the better-known Villa Ombrellino re-designed in 1926 for Mrs Keppel, the popular hostess and favourite of Edward VII, who was called to his bedside by Queen Alexandra just before he died.[87] Between 1924 and 1939 Pinsent designed several formal gardens and garden buildings for Lady Sybil's daughter, Marchesa Iris Origo, at La Foce, her remote country estate not far from Chianciano Terme, south of Siena, which is described in her delightful autobiography, *Images and Shadows*. It includes a less formal flower garden,

> with wide borders of flowering shrubs, herbaceous plants and annuals, big lemon-pots on stone bases, a shady bower of wisteria and banksia roses, and a paved terrace with a balustrade, looking down over the valley, on which we would dine on summer nights when, just before the harvest, the whole garden would be alight with fireflies and the air heavy with nicotiana and jasmine.[88]

248. Villa La Foce, Chianciano Terme (Cecil Pinsent, 1924–39): chapel and cemetery garden (1933). [Courtesy, Marchesa Origo 1986]

In 1933 Pinsent added the chapel and cemetery which he considered one of his finest works. Situated in woodland at some distance from the house, the cemetery was enclosed by cypresses and walls, against which grew *pittosporum*, and it was planted by the Marchesa with blue periwinkle and roses amongst the graves so that it formed a garden, a thing unknown in Italy at that time (Plate 248).

The Influence of the Beaux-Arts

Much of Pinsent's work was for Americans sufficiently enchanted with Italy to adopt voluntary exile. Others, like James and Sargent, chose to settle in England, but of these, some needed to surround themselves with reminders of Italian art. None did this with more determination and extravagance than William Waldorf Astor (1848–1919), created Viscount Astor in 1917, who in 1903 bought Hever Castle in Kent. Not for him the sensitive refinement of Platt, Peto or Pinsent; when he began planning his colossal garden he aimed for something more monumental to display his amazing collection of Italian statuary and sculpture. It was no wonder that the most spectacular Edwardian classical garden in England, epitomizing both the romantic nostalgia and the opulence of the age, should have been at the behest of such an ambitious and eccentric multi-millionaire. It was as American Minister in Rome in the 1880s that Astor formed his collection, but in 1890 he inherited a vast fortune from his father and in 1893, having decided that 'America is not a fit place for a gentleman to live', left for England. In the same year he became one of the first Americans to acquire an English estate, the Duke of Westminster's Italianate Cliveden. In 1899 he became a naturalized British subject, and the restoration of the neglected baronial domain of Hever, famous as the home of Anne Boleyn, was a further step in his campaign to enter the peerage. Aided by his architect Frank Pearson, son of the

Gothic revivalist J.L. Pearson, he added Tudor-style panelling, carving and plasterwork to the interior but left the exterior of the semi-fortified house unaltered. Alongside he built a 'Tudor Village' for guests, and between the inner and outer moats he added a maze and an Anne Boleyn garden with topiary chessmen in golden yew, laid out by Joseph Cheal and Son of Crawley.

It was, however, in the so-called 'Italian Garden' that Astor was able to indulge his passion for the splendours of Rome. Begun in 1904 and laid out at a respectful distance from the castle, it is approached on either side of a semi-circular *bagnio* containing an antique Roman statue of Venus originally backed by porphyry columns against a tall yew hedge. Behind stretches a formal garden of gargantuan scale. Four acres in area, flanked by walls twelve feet high and by walks terminated at each corner by stone porticos and rotundas, it is divided by transverse corridors of yew into the square Loggia Lawn with box-edged rose beds, and a rectangular lawn with central sunk garden (originally containing a Roman bath). The main attraction ran along the northern side: the 'Pompeian Wall', over two hundred yards in length and divided by buttresses into bays to shelter Astor's enormous assemblage of Roman and Renaissance antiquities, including architectural fragments, statues, vases, fonts and sarcophagi. These treasures were not arranged artistically as at Iford, but strung out along the walk as in a monumental mason's yard, redeemed only by the planting of shrubs and climbers carried out by Cheal's from 1904–8,[89] which created a dreamlike vista of marble gods and goddesses festooned with *Clematis*, *Magnolia* and other delectable flowers and foliage, 'a fantasy in stone and shrub as dizzying, of its kind, as Piranesi's engraving of the Appian Way' (Plate 249).[90] Along the southern wall is a massive pergola, its stone piers supporting rustic *traversi* and *cordoni* covered with crab-apple and a rich variety of climbers. A low wall bordered with *Nepeta*, *Fuchsia* and peonies marks the outer edge, while inside are shady grottoes, (inspired by the Gallery of a Hundred Fountains at d'Este) where water trickles

249. Hever Castle, Edenbridge, Kent (Frank Pearson and Joseph Cheal, begun 1904): the Pompeian Wall. [From a watercolour by C. Essenhigh Corke, 1910]

over the carved buttresses to pools and moss-covered rocks harbouring moisture-loving plants: white and purple *Primula*, *Epimedium*, *Astilbe*, Welsh poppies, London's Pride, lilies of the valley, *Hosta* and ferns (Plate 250). At its eastern end the garden is enclosed by classical colonnades flanking a loggia from which staircases descend to a semi-circular piazza overlooking the thirty-five-acre lake which took some eight hundred men two years to complete. All this was a far cry from the picturesque medieval house of the Boleyns, which, according to Philip Tilden, was 'infinitely alluring as it sat as I first saw it in the nineties, with its grey skirts sweeping the waters of the moat, set around with the blue swords of the wild flag; but instead it has now become a miniature Metropolitan Museum of New York'.[91]

The rigid layout of Hever smacked more of the Beaux-Arts than the Italian garden. This French system of classical planning had

250. Hever Castle: the Grottoes. [Author 1984]

251. The Orchard, Southampton, Long Island, N.Y. (McKim, Mead and White, 1898): garden view to the south, c.1910. [From R.G. Wilson, *McKim, Mead and White*, 1983]

been established in America well before Platt entered the arena, and it, too, played a part in the formal-garden revival, an early example being Indian Harbor, Greenwich, Connecticut (1895) by Carrère and Hastings.[92] A purer and more evocative interpretation of the classical ideal appeared at The Orchard, Southampton, Long Island (1898), by the architects McKim, Mead and White, for James L. Breese, a New York financier.[93] Like Hastings, Charles McKim had studied at the Ecole des Beaux-Arts, his interest being directed mainly towards Roman and Italian models. For the garden at The Orchard he and White adopted a style of neo-classical severity, the axial layout of Roman proportions comprising Doric pergolas two hundred feet long flanking a grid of flower beds divided by brick paths and bordered with vases and herms (Plate 251).[94] When fully established the garden was almost submerged beneath luxuriant vegetation, but in its semi-pristine state *House and Garden* considered it 'more fitting for endless rows of cabbages'.[95] Stanford White was a close friend of Platt, some of whose turn-of-the-century garden layouts revealed classical as well as Renaissance influences, notably the enclosed garden laid out in the grounds of Glen Elsinore, Pomfret, Connecticut (1901) which, like The Orchard, was inspired by the villas of classical antiquity.[96] Such gardens helped determine the pattern of the formal-garden revival in America, which was firmly established by 1902 with the publication of Guy Lowell's *American Gardens*.

Back in Britain, this Roman brand of Beaux-Arts classicism was not to the taste of all the well-to-do. The Edwardian smart set hankered after something more opulent and luxurious, befitting the life-style of *La Belle Epoque*, and they found it in the flamboyant interiors and gardens of the *ancien régime*. The French garden with its elaborate fountains and *parterres de broderie* had been out of fashion since the 1850s, but interest was re-awakened by the Paris Exhibition of 1900, and after the *entente cordiale* of 1904, which gave everything French an official, and royal, seal of approval, it began to find favour again. In their search for appropriate styles many architects began to see that the Beaux-Arts had something to offer besides planning and composition.[97]

Blomfield was becoming increasingly Francophile and in 1905 included essays on French design in his *Studies in Architecture*.[98] In the same year even Detmar Blow, cradled in the Arts and Crafts Movement, took a French architect, the Beaux-Arts-trained Fernand Billerey, into partnership, an apparent abandonment of his principles enough to make Ruskin turn in his grave. Billerey's influence could be seen in stylish interiors such as 10 Carlton House Terrace for Viscount Ridley, and also Charles Hill Court, Tilford (1909) for Miss Lily Antrobus. This exotic intrusion into the Surrey vernacular scene took the form of a low-slung house in *dixhuitième* manner, complete with Mansard roof, dormers and French windows, and from whose loggia and terrace a grand succession of eponymous lily pools cascaded down the hillside.[99] In 1911 Blow was commissioned by Bendor, 2nd Duke of Westminster—whom he had known since his Wiltshire days—to remodel the East Garden at Eaton Hall, Chester, previously laid out in about 1851 by W.A. Nesfield. A central canal was added between topiary gardens consisting of formal beds within shaped compartments of clipped yew, a decidedly sober replacement for Nesfield's intricate and colourful parterre (Plate 252).[100]

The leading exponents of the new French manner were Mewès and Davis whose *chef d'oeuvre*, the Ritz Hotel, made its appearance on the London scene in 1906, its interiors striking the right note of luxury. Later Arthur Davis extended its elegance into the gardens by adding *treillage* to the terrace facing the park, as he did in the garden of the Royal Automobile Club (1908–11).[101] The *savoir faire* displayed at the Ritz had an immediate impact, an example being at Polesden Lacey, near Dorking, Surrey. This Regency villa had just been remodelled by Ambrose Poynter[102] for Sir Clinton Dawkins, but after he died it was snapped up in 1906 by Mrs Greville (created Dame Margaret Anderson in 1922) and her husband Captain Hon. Ronald Greville, eldest son of Lord Greville. A popular hostess of the 'Marlborough House Set', she lost no time in calling in Mewès and Davis to give the house the necessary glitter and *chic*, and in the following year Frank Murray of the gardening firm Durand, Murray and Seddon was commissioned to prepare grand schemes for the south front, one with a central *perron*

252. Eaton Hall, Chester (Blow and Billerey, 1913): east garden. [RCHME 1959]

and vast, semi–circular pergola flanked by parterres.[103] However, Captain Greville died suddenly in 1908 and the schemes were abandoned.

In 1903 Mewès and Davis had carried out a more complete French re-vamping of a country house for the diamond 'Randlord', Julius Wernher (created baronet in 1905), at Luton Hoo, Bedfordshire, an Adam house of 1766–74 standing in a spacious Capability Brown park. They also designed a pair of elegant, Ionic pavilions south of the house, but these marked the boundary of new formal gardens laid out in complementary style at the same time by the firm of Romaine-Walker and Besant, and consisting of a flower-bordered upper terrace from which semi-circular steps descend to the magnificent Rose Garden, enclosed by yew hedges, with box-edged beds and a central, circular fountain pool (Plate 253).[104]

W.H. Romaine-Walker (1854–1940) was one of those architects whose natural flair for stylish eclecticism and pastiche has caused his name to be erased from all historical accounts of the period. His successful practice ranged from the opulent interior of Her Majesty's Theatre (1895) to town houses like Sunderland House (designed in collaboration with Alphonse Duchêne) and to large country houses, many of which were set in extensive formal gardens.[105] The first of these, Rhinefield, in the New Forest, was an accomplished essay in the Elizabethan mode; and an equivalent panache was displayed by the gardens. It was built in 1888–91, on the site of a royal hunting lodge, for Mabel Zoë Walker, heiress to the Barber and Walker Nottinghamshire collieries, and her husband, Captain Lionel Munro. As though to compensate for the informal, picturesque house, Romaine-Walker laid out the grounds in grand, Louis-Quatorze style with bi-axial symmetry and long vistas carved through the forest. A canal was centred on the window of the Great Hall (Plate 254), and on either side were parterres and lawns enclosed by yew hedges. Broad, grass terraces

253. Luton Hoo, Bedford (Romaine-Walker and Besant, 1903): rose garden, c.1978. [Courtesy of Nicholas Phillips Esq.]

stepped down to the east, while to the west was a sunken topiary garden with intricately shaped enclosures, alleys and recesses for seats, urns and statuary.[106] This anticipated Lutyens's yew architecture at Ammerdown and resembled the nearby Italian-inspired garden of similar date laid out for E.J. Morant at Brockenhurst Park.[107]

Romaine-Walker's *magnum opus* was Danesfield (1899–1901), situated at Medmenham, Buckinghamshire, in a commanding position overlooking the Thames. It was built for Robert William Hudson, who inherited his fortune from his father, the Victorian soap magnate, Robert Spear Hudson. In 1895 he had bought Medmenham Abbey (venue of the notorious Hell-Fire Club) and restored it with the help of Romaine-Walker; and in 1897 he bought Danesfield, also part of the Medmenham estate. The new Danesfield, which replaced the old house, was Tudor in style faced

with rock chalk and of mammoth proportions, its imposing terraced gardens being laid out to the front facing the river (Plates 257, 258). The centre-piece was an elaborate parterre, notable for its examples of the topiarist's art, and the grounds contained also a cascade bordered by specimen trees.[108] In about 1910 Romaine-Walker built Moreton Paddox, Moreton Morrell, Warwickshire, which included expansive formal gardens laid out on the axis of the symmetrical garden front. The most prominent features were four, square *parterres de compartiment* enclosed by low, yew hedges and divided by a cross-walk and an axial canal leading to a sunk garden, all continuing the theme of Rhinefield but reflecting the current trend towards greater spaciousness (Plate 255).[109]

The grounds of Moreton Paddox were laid out in collaboration with the landscape gardener Edward White. Romaine-Walker's chief assistant, Gilbert H. Jenkins, was also closely involved in the

166

254. Rhinefield, near Brockenhurst, Hampshire (W.H. Romaine-Walker, 1888–91): the canal. [Author 1981]

design.[110] In 1911 Jenkins was taken into partnership by Romaine-Walker and was mainly responsible for their post-war garden work, including Great Fosters, Egham, Surrey (1918) for Gerald Samuel-Montagu, younger brother of the 2nd Lord Swaythling. This late-Elizabethan brick house had lain derelict for several years, and only a hedge-enclosed lawn remained of the original gardens. The task was 'to design such a garden as would re-create the old-world charm of the place and be interesting the year round'.[111] Immediately south of the house a parterre was laid out whose quadripartite form, centred on an old sundial, attempted to capture the spirit of a Tudor garden, each square compartment consisting of a pattern of box-edged beds filled with 'Old English' flowers and containing a ring of topiary (Plates 256, 259).[112]

Thomas H. Mawson

Tudor historicism or Beaux-Arts classicism may have appealed to some Edwardians, but when W.H. Lever—who like Hudson had made his fortune out of soap—embarked on the first of his spectacular gardens, he looked for more sober and practical guidance and found it in a garden designer who was to build up one of the largest international practices of his time, namely, the self-styled 'landscape architect', Thomas Hayton Mawson (1861–1933) (Plate 260).[113] Mawson took the first step on the ladder to professional fame when in 1884, together with his brothers, he set up Lakeland Nurseries in Windermere.[114] He was responsible for the landscape side of the firm and his first important commission came in 1889 when he was asked to lay out new gardens for Colonel T.M. Sandys, MP, at Graythwaite Hall, Sawrey, Windermere, an old house standing in landscaped grounds.[115] Graythwaite was a turning point in Mawson's career as it introduced him to a number of important clients, but his garden-design practice really began to prosper when in 1900 he brought out The Art and Craft of Garden

Making, with illustrations by C.E. Mallows—a timely move, as it met the growing need for technical guidance on garden layout. After some struggle with his conscience, Mawson decided to follow Kemp's *How to Lay Out a Garden* (1850), a work he much admired, and illustrate his book mainly with examples of his own work, including plans and details, with little reference to any other

255. Moreton Paddox, Moreton Morrell, Warwickshire (W.H. Romaine-Walker and Edward White, c.1910): aerial view. [Cambridge University Collection, 1952; Crown Copyright. Reproduced by permission of the Controller of Her Majesty's Stationery Office]

256. Great Fosters, Egham, Surrey (Romaine-Walker and Jenkins, 1918): aerial view. [RCHME 1930]

257 (left). Danesfield, Medmenham, Buckinghamshire (W.H. Romaine-Walker, 1899–1901): view of the parterre from the house. [Courtesy of Ian Meredith 1985]

258 (right). Danesfield: view of the south front. [Courtesy of Ian Meredith 1985]

259. Great Fosters: view of the parterre from the house. [Author 1986]

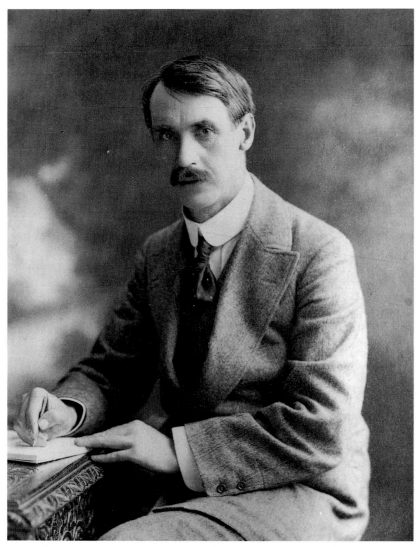

260. Thomas H. Mawson. [AWG Album c.1905]

gardener or garden architect. One of his aims was to bring together architecture and landscape gardening, a notion that naturally received short shrift from Robinson who wrote, 'Many, not satisfied with the good word "Landscape Gardener", used by Loudon, Repton and many other excellent men, call themselves "Landscape Architects"—a stupid term of French origin implying the union of two absolutely distinct studies.'[116] In spite of this, the book was a huge success, running into five editions, each time containing more illustrations of Mawson's work. In 1901 he opened a London office and commissions flowed in from country-house owners anxious to bring their gardens more into line with changes in both fashion and life-style.

A large proportion of Mawson's work was for existing houses whose owners wanted to give their gardens a new image. In the case of new houses he always preferred to be involved in the design with the architect from an early stage, an example being Voysey's Moor Crag, Lake Windermere (1898). An earlier instance was the terraced garden, striking in its day, at Wern, near Porthmadog, North Wales (1891–2), designed in collaboration with John Douglas of Chester, who remodelled and enlarged the house for Richard

Greaves, a slate-quarry-owner.[117] The ideal association was with Dan Gibson, who met Mawson when he was resident architect at Graythwaite and subsequently worked for George and Peto. The Flagstaff, Colwyn Bay, for the surgeon Walter Whitehead was designed during their partnership in 1898–9. Although the house was never built, the gardens were a skilful solution to a difficult hillside site and were praised by Muthesius.[118] Their work at a similar site, Wood, South Tawton, on the edge of Dartmoor (c.1904), for William Lethbridge, was more fruitful. The house was virtually rebuilt, and Mawson laid out two gardens on the steep hillside with vistas to west and south divided by a tree belt through which the approach drive was relocated (Plate 261). From the carriage court, steps ascend to a square tennis lawn, connected by a garden pavilion to the upper floor of the house and enclosed

261. Wood, South Tawton, Devon (T.H. Mawson and Dan Gibson, c.1904): layout plan [From *The Art and Craft of Garden Making*, 1912]

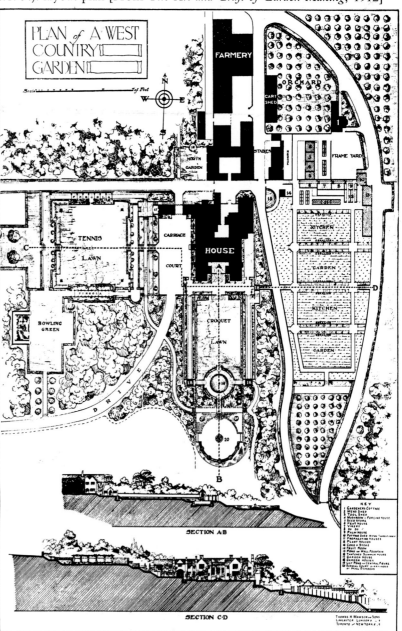

by yew hedges and pergolas. A raised viewing terrace was provided on the west side, the vista continuing along a grass glade between lines of cedars to a tea-house. The garden on the south front was designed to merge with the landscape, the foreground being formed by a croquet lawn with herbaceous borders, and the view across the valley framed by garden houses either side of a circular lily pool echoed by the sundial court below.

As with all his schemes, Mawson took care at Wood to relate the garden to the surrounding landscape. The layout also reflected the current vogue for axial planning; indeed Mawson was later to affirm his belief in the Beaux-Arts method of training, being

264. Foots Cray Place, Kent (T.H. Mawson and Dan Gibson, 1901–2): perspective by C.E. Mallows, 1901. [From *The Art and Craft of Garden Making*, 1912]

262. Shrublands, Windermere, Westmorland (T.H. Mawson, c.1907): the tennis court. [From a watercolour by E.A. Chadwick]

263. The Willows, Ashton-on-Ribble, Lancashire (T.H. Mawson, c.1899–1902): view of the arched wall and steps. [From a watercolour by E.A. Rowe, 1912]

influenced in his town-planning schemes by one of its American off-shoots, the City Beautiful movement, which made its first appearance at the Chicago Exposition of 1893.[119] Apart from a tendency towards monumentality, Mawson, like Mallows, did not develop an individual style but was open to a variety of modes, depending on the nature and location of the commission. At times he could display a sympathy for vernacular materials—at Wood, the rubble retaining walls of local, coarse-grained granite had their joints filled with rock plants—and some of his work had an Arts and Crafts flavour, for example, Shrublands, Windermere (c.1907), where he designed both house and garden for his brother, Robert, who was in charge of Lakeland Nurseries (Plate 262);[120] also The Willows, Ashton-on-Ribble, Lancashire (c.1899–1902), for W.W. Galloway of Preston, where the walls of the enclosed court suggest the attempt to reproduce at a stroke the mellow patina of age (Plate 263). Nevertheless, Mawson did not mention Gertrude Jekyll in his book—neither did she include his work in *Garden Ornament*—and he dismissed her in his autobiography with a cursory, 'There was Miss Jekyll writing about daffodils.'[121]

There must have been little doubt in Mawson's mind as to the kind of garden called for at Foots Cray Place, Kent (1901–2) for S.J. Waring (later Lord Waring) of the furniture firm of Waring and Gillow. This last and ill-fated English Villa Rotonda was built for Bourchier Cleeve in about 1756 and burnt down in 1949. Mawson's grandiose layout, designed in collaboration with Dan Gibson, was intended 'to accord with the Palladian style of the mansion',[122] although anything less likely to have done so than the succession of heavily balustraded terraces can hardly be imagined (Plate 264). However, here, as elsewhere, the gardens suited the taste of his Edwardian client admirably besides being eminently practical, and the photograph in his autobiography shows them coming into their own as a setting for one of Lord Waring's huge garden fêtes.

Mawson's wealthier clients were by no means only businessmen. In about 1899 he constructed waterfalls and walks at Mount Stuart for the 3rd Marquess of Bute; and in 1903, at Madresfield Court,

265. Hvidöre, near Copenhagen (T.H. Mawson, c.1908–10): trellis screen and rose arches. [From a watercolour by E.A. Rowe, c.1912]

Great Malvern, for the scholarly and artistic 7th Earl Beauchamp, he added formal gardens beyond the inner moat, consisting of terraces and a parterre divided by cross-walks with bays enclosed on three sides by low yew hedges.[123] One of his most delightful designs was the result of a recommendation by Waring: gardens at Hvidöre, Queen Alexandra's beloved summer retreat near Copenhagen, which she shared with her sister, the Empress Marie. In about 1908–10 Mawson added three long herbaceous borders, protected from sea winds by tall hedges and backed by rose-covered trellises and arches (Plate 265).

It was in 1905 that Mawson met the patron with whom he was to establish such a highly successful working partnership and who was to be a decisive influence on his future career. William Hesketh Lever (1851–1925), created baronet in 1911 and Lord Leverhulme in 1917 (Plate 266), entrepreneur and benevolent industrialist, was a larger-than-life product of Victorian self-help, best remembered as the founder in 1888 of the model village of Port Sunlight, which was laid out on picturesque lines with houses in a Cheshire version of 'Old English'. Although of simple tastes and not given to personal extravagance, he had a voracious appetite for building. As his

266. Lord Leverhulme, from a photograph by Cecil, post-1917.

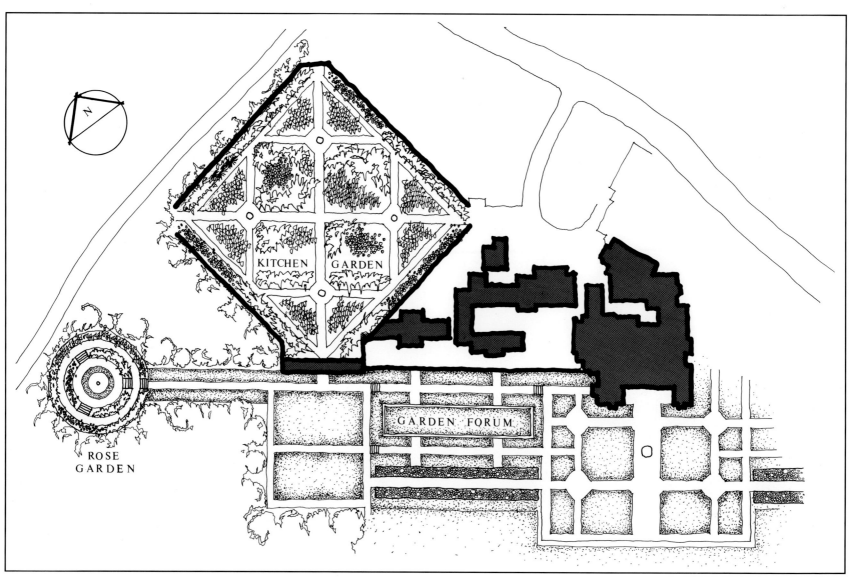

267. Thornton Manor, Thornton Hough, Cheshire (T.H. Mawson, from 1905): layout plan. [Miranda Ottewill]

son wrote, 'Altering the face of Nature was with him a passion. He was never happier than when seated in front of a plan with a drawing board, ruler and T-square ready to hand. Architecture was always an absorbing study for him.'[124] All his houses were generously planned, and the grounds, too, needed to accommodate summer garden parties for staff and business associates as well as annual events such as Sunday School picnics and works outings. In Mawson he had found the ideal person to aid him in his numerous landscaping campaigns. Possessed alike with inexhaustible energy, they shared a similar 'High Church Nonconformist', Lancashire background and, as an architect *manqué* with definite ideas of his own and the ability to transfer them to paper, Lever was likely to find someone of Mawson's down-to-earth approach, and horticultural rather than architectural background, more accommodating than any of the leading garden architects. Their association began after Mawson had written requesting a donation towards a screen he had designed for his church at Hest Bank on Morecambe Bay. Lever ended his reply:

Now that you have had the courage to ask me for a subscription, may I be so bold as to ask you to come and advise me upon the improvement of my garden at Thornton Manor? I have wanted to consult you for the last two years, but all my friends warned me that it would be useless, as you never worked for anyone holding less social rank than a Duke, whereas I am only a poor and indigent soap-maker. Let me know if you can come.[125]

After their initial meeting, Lever announced, 'I shall be out in the garden at a quarter-past six; I hope this is not too early for you. I can give you an hour and a quarter, and we breakfast at half-past seven.'[126]

Lever had bought Thornton Manor in 1891 mainly to house his growing art collection. Situated next to the village of Thornton Hough, it was, like all his houses, located to suit his business, being on the opposite side of the Wirral from Port Sunlight. As a result of successive additions and alterations, in which Lever used a variety of architects, it was growing from a modest Victorian

268. Thornton Manor: view of garden forum. [Author 1985]

west of his native Bolton in North Lancashire and rising some twelve hundred feet above sea level on the western, heather-clad slopes of Rivington Pike. Four hundred acres were converted into a park, accessible to the public, the topmost fifty being reserved as a garden for his private residence, Roynton Cottage, known as 'The Bungalow'.[130] From about 1906, working partly in collaboration with Lever's architect and life-long friend Jonathan Simpson (1850–1937) (J.Lomax-Simpson's father), Mawson laid out huge serpentine lawns one hundred feet below the house and landscaped the mountainside with steps and winding paths in keeping with the nature of the site (Plate 269), successfully establishing a wide variety of hardy, peat-loving shrubs and trees, including rhododendrons, azaleas, *Andromeda*, *Erica*, *Gaultheria*, together with pines, hollies, *Berberis* and *Cotoneaster*. There were bridges, loggias, garden houses, dovecotes, a look-out tower, grottoes and the inevitable Japanese garden. Next to the house was the square North Lawn, bordered by rockeries and shielded from the bracing winds by an arcaded pergola designed in rugged style using the

Gothic house to a full-blown Tudorbethan mansion.[127] Sometimes Lever's gardens outstripped their houses which then had to be increased to suit, but at Thornton in 1905 it was the turn of the gardens to expand. Lever had himself prepared a 'bundle of plans', including formal gardens of 'heroic proportions' which Mawson now helped him to put into effect. The backbone of the layout (Plate 267) consisted of a long path running westwards from the south terrace: as Lever wrote to Mawson, 'I am afraid I do not want a garden so much for rest as for promenades and walks. I have tried sitting down in the retreats and garden shelters, but I cannot rest in them two minutes, but on the contrary, I can walk about for a couple of hours at a time along the long stretch of walk I have made in the centre.'[128] South of the path was the 'Garden Forum', a lawn enclosed by rose pergolas supported by paired, pre-cast concrete, Tuscan pillars, while beyond was a pleached lime walk between holly hedges, with herringbone brick paving, reflected in a similar walk on the other side of the central axis of the house (Plate 268). The path continued to a circular, sunk rose garden, in descending tiers, while to the north stretched the huge, square kitchen garden laid out (as at Little Thakeham) at an angle to the house with diagonal cross-paths lined with fruit trees, and central rose arches. Lever 'looked upon his two-acre kitchen garden at Thornton as perhaps his best piece of planning and the circular rose garden near to it as one of his happiest conceptions'.[129] In 1912–14, when additions were in turn made to the garden front of the house by J. Lomax-Simpson, a tea-house, in the form of an arched loggia in the same red sandstone as the house, was added at the southern corner of the kitchen garden, with steps leading up to a roof terrace overlooking the tennis courts. In the grounds Mawson laid out a 250-yard canal through the woodland, later expanded into a twenty-acre lake. There was also a fernery, a rock border and, beyond the paddock to the south-west, ornamental pools and a thatched cricket pavilion.

Lever's most dramatic project was his mountain retreat at Rivington, an estate that he acquired in 1899, situated seven miles north-

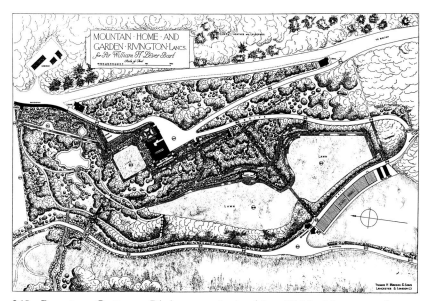

269. Roynton Cottage, Rivington, Lancashire (T.H. Mawson, from 1906): layout plan. [From *The Art and Craft of Garden Making*, 1912]

local grit stone, and with splendid views to the west (Plate 270). Mawson derived special satisfaction from this commission and wrote, 'of all the gardens which have administered to my professional enjoyment, none comes into competition with Roynton'.[131]

The third important garden designed by Mawson for Lever in 1905–6 was at his London home, The Hill, on the north-west slopes of Hampstead. The original house had been rebuilt in about 1895. Lever acquired it in 1904 and enlarged it with E.A. Ould as his architect, adding wings, subsequently linked by a loggia designed by Mawson. The gardens also needed to be remodelled to provide a suitable setting for garden parties and fêtes (which later became a regular feature at The Hill), but since they were overlooked by the public heath, the problem was to create a sense of

270. Roynton Cottage: pergola and rockery. [RCHME; W.J. Day c.1910]

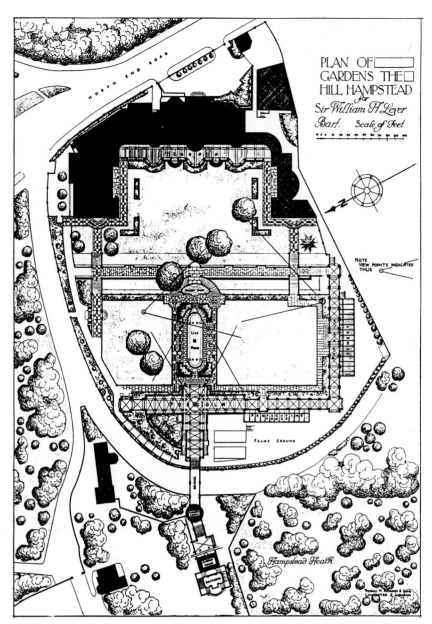

271. The Hill, Hampstead, London (T.H. Mawson, from 1905): layout plan. [From *The Art and Craft of Garden Making*, 1912]

enclosure without sacrificing the panoramic view west towards Harrow and Windsor. Mawson's solution was to provide a raised terrace and pergola walk above the west and south retaining walls of the new garden (Plate 271) (conveniently making use of excavated material from the Hampstead Underground as fill). The existing sloping lawns were terraced and divided by a paved walk and steep bank, but without disturbing the mature elms, chestnuts and copper beech. On the axis of the house a double curved stair was provided, sweeping down to a lily pool, with lead fountain by Derwent Wood,[132] from which steps ascended to a domed pergola temple (Plate 272). In 1911 Lever bought the grounds of the adjoining Heath Lodge and a bridge was constructed over the public lane to a circular garden house beyond which the pergola was continued westwards. An 'elaborate scheme in the manner of the great Italian gardens'[133] was also started but abandoned due to the War.

The pergola was the most striking feature of The Hill and was constructed of double rows of paired Tuscan columns in Portland stone, of noble proportions, supporting closely spaced beams with shaped projecting ends, similar to those at Thornton Manor. Just as the topiary hedge symbolized the Arts and Crafts garden, the rose-clad pergola evoked the Italian School, supported not by sturdy piers but by pillars recalling its country of origin. This free-standing example led to a belvedere with a distant view over the park to the west. It was also designed to secure instant privacy; Lever was too impatient to wait for planting to mature. The ranks of columns with their outer trellis-work looked austere at first, but soon all was entwined with climbing plants. Because of the strong architectural framework, the garden has retained some of its original appearance; it has even, like the old Italian gardens, acquired the quality of pleasing decay. The wanderer in this historic corner of Hampstead Heath, who happened by chance upon this pergola, might imagine himself in a magical secret garden where the shades of Leverhulme's guests still walk and talk amongst the overgrown roses, *Hydrangea petiolaris* and encircling *Wisteria* (Plate 273).[134]

Public gardens are more likely to survive both the passage of time and changes in fashion than private gardens, and apart from a few exceptions, such as Thornton Manor and the gardens he laid out in 1906 for Reginald Cory at Dyffryn, St Nicholas, near Cardiff,[135] Mawson's work is best preserved in his public parks which began with Hanley Park, Staffordshire (1892) and culminated in Stanley Park, Blackpool (1922) (see Chapter 8). Although not carried out, he considered his best scheme to be that prepared in 1903–4, in competition with Patrick Geddes, at Pittencrieff Park, for the Carnegie Dunfermline Trust. This was at about the same time that he made improvements to the gardens at Skibo Castle, Sutherland, for Andrew Carnegie. Municipal parks led to city

272. The Hill, pergola temple and lily pool. [From a Lumière autochrome c.1910; RCHME]

re-plan the town of Stornaway on the Isle of Lewis; but this abortive attempt to re-vitalize the community was not one of Lever's successes.

Mawson's output was prodigious and owed much to his business acumen, professional competence and the firm foundation of his experience with Lakeland Nurseries. An ingenious scheme like The Hill, for instance, depended for its realization on a high degree of technical knowledge in landscaping. While he could turn his hand to many styles, from the sympathetic use of natural materials of Wood to the elegance and charm of Hvidöre, most of his designs were monumental in character, Italianate in style, with a Beaux-Arts discipline in layout, befitting the life-style of his Edwardian clients. At times his work appears rather hard and mechanical, lacking the warmth, human scale and exuberant planting of the typical Lutyens and Jekyll garden. But more often than not this was the logical outcome of a different regional context, and to some extent it reflected Mawson's personal background. It is not difficult to see why he felt so much more at home with a kindred spirit like Lever and a rugged, windswept site like Rivington, than in the more protected and comfortable world of the 'Surrey School'.

273. The Hill: pergola. [Author 1982]

planning schemes notably in Canada, and in 1911 he published his *Civic Art*, handsomely illustrated by Robert Atkinson.[136] There was a logical progression in all this, the thread being a concern for architectural unity between buildings, gardens and public spaces, which, as Inigo Thomas wrote in his *Keystones of Building*, 'first found expression in the grounds of private houses, then in the garden cities, and from that it has developed into the town-planning movement of which we now hear so much'. Thomas was writing in 1912, the year of which, looking back on his career, Mawson could boast, 'I had now, metaphorically speaking, annexed America, and made this vast continent a part of my sphere of influence'.[137] In gaining America he almost lost the patronage of Lever, who had begun to feel that he was not getting the personal attention he had hitherto enjoyed. However, Lever continued to employ Mawson and in 1918 asked him and J. Lomax-Simpson to

His ambition and drive brought him professional recognition, his flourishing practice being furthered by his lecture tours,[138] and especially by his timely books. In 1923 he was President of the Town Planning Institute and a founder member of the Royal Fine Art Commission, and when the Institute of Landscape Architects was founded in 1929 he became its first President.

H. Inigo Triggs

Another familiar name in the architectural publishing world of the time was that of Harry Inigo Triggs (1876–1923), an architect with a substantial practice but whose most enduring memorial was his succession of weighty volumes of garden history. He studied under Banister Fletcher and at the Royal Academy Schools, gaining a Travelling Studentship in 1898. His first book, *Some architectural works of Inigo Jones* (1901), was written in collaboration with Henry Tanner, and it was while travelling around the country collecting material for it that he conceived the idea for his monumental *Formal Gardens in England and Scotland*, published in 1902. Sedding's and Blomfield's pioneering efforts had encouraged other works that aimed to satisfy the growing thirst for historical authenticity, but Triggs's folio volume was the first to include measured drawings as well as photographs. He followed it with *The Art of Garden Design in Italy* (1906), also superbly illustrated and based on visits to over eighty villas and palaces, including the Vatican Gardens. Although Triggs was steeped in the Italian tradition, his hero was Le Nôtre, and in 1913 he designed the architectural setting for the Monument Le Nôtre at the Tuileries, to mark the tercentenary of his birth.[139] Also in 1913, *Garden Craft in Europe* appeared, covering a wider field, including Spanish gardens whose influence can be seen at Ashford Chace, situated below the beautiful, wooded hangers at Steep, near Petersfield. Built in 1912 for the explorer and naturalist, Aubyn B.R. Trevor-Battye (d.1922), it was designed in collaboration with W.F. Unsworth (1850–1912) in whose office Triggs had worked earlier and with whom he was in partnership from 1908, laying out gardens for several houses in that part of Hampshire,[140] some of which were illustrated in *Gardens for Small Country Houses*. The inspiration they drew from their continental studies is evident in the symmetrical, stucco Ashford Chace, especially when glimpsed from the long, green vista between ornamental trees and shrubs which Triggs laid out alongside the Ashford stream, also in the sunken rose garden at the south-east corner of the house. This paved court is overlooked by an arcaded loggia and enclosed by vine-covered walls and a *Wisteria*-draped pergola. In his last summer, Unsworth prepared measured drawings of the Generalife,[141] and this is reflected in the lily tank which is fed from the terrace fountain through a Moorish 'water-maze', similar to that at the sixteenth-century Nilkanth pavilion at Mandu in India.[142]

The importance Triggs attached to water as a feature in garden design was apparent also at his own home, Little Boarhunt, Liphook, Hampshire, a remodelling of a seventeenth-century farmhouse carried out in 1910–11 (Plate 274). The farmyard to the south was excavated to form a sunken rose garden with saxifrages, pinks and *Veronica* growing in its rubble-stone retaining walls, and

274. Little Boarhunt, Liphook, Hampshire (H. Inigo Triggs, 1910–11): sunken garden. (From *Gardens for Small Country Houses*, 1912]

it was divided by a rill with central dipping pool from which rose a brick column supporting a *putto*, a copy of one at the Baptistery in Florence.[143] The two outer sides were enclosed by deep stone piers supporting beams and cross-pieces for climbing roses, possibly suggested by one of the Monks' Gardens at the Certosa di Pavia which he included in *Garden Craft in Europe*. Triggs was brought in by Frank Atkinson as landscaping consultant at Whiteley Model Village in Surrey (1914–21),[144] and he also laid out the Canadian Military Cemetery by the churchyard at Bramshott, Hampshire, which, with its heather bushes and sparingly planted flowering trees, is a model of calm dignity. His career was dogged by ill-health and, like those of Sedding and Mallows was cut short by his untimely death. Bramshott church contains his memorial tablet, but he was buried at Taormina, in a mortuary chapel near the Anglo-American Church of St George, both of which he had built.[145]

L. Rome Guthrie

For the illustrations of Scottish examples in *Formal Gardens in England and Scotland,* Triggs enlisted the able assistance of a promising young Scottish architect, Leonard Rome Guthrie (1880–1958). The plates for Triggs's book were prepared by Guthrie while he was serving articles with the Glasgow architect William Leiper and attending the Glasgow School of Art for which C.R. Mackintosh had just begun his remarkable new building; the influence of Mackintosh's style of drawing can be seen in Guthrie's perspective of Earlshall (see Plate 62). From 1901 he was head draughtsman to William Flockhart, becoming his partner in 1912 and carrying on his practice in 1913.[146] In 1907 he was busy with a number of important garden commissions, the first being at Chelwood Vetchery, Nutley, Sussex (1906–7) for Stuart Montagu Samuel, banker and Liberal MP for Whitechapel. To the south and east of Flockhart's red-brick, neo-Tudor house he laid out an impressive scheme of gardens including wide, terraced lawns descending to a long water garden with central well-head flanked by perfectly proportioned lily pools and canals (Plate 275). This lower

275. Chelwood Vetchery, Nutley, Sussex (L. Rome Guthrie, 1906–7): water garden. [Author 1984]

garden is also approached at its eastern end by dramatic flights of steps which descend beneath a group of mature limes, while it is separated from the main lawn by a bastioned, dry-stone, rubble retaining wall containing a rich variety of wall plants, including valerian, thrift, *Erigeron,* rock pinks, musk, *Lithospermum* and St John's wort. Guthrie's loving care for the details can be seen in the semi-octagonal fruit-room surrounded by a vine-wreathed pergola in a corner of the kitchen garden.[147]

Concurrently with Chelwood Vetchery, Guthrie laid out a river garden for Samuel's uncle, Sir Samuel Montagu Bt (1832–1911) (created 1st Baron Swaythling, 1907) at South Stoneham House, Southampton, originally of 1708 and attributed to Hawksmoor.[148] Lord Swaythling proved to be a valuable client, for in 1910 he acquired nearby Townhill Park and commissioned Guthrie to extend the house and provide new gardens. The original house of 1792 by Thomas Leverton[149] had grown since the 1840s but was now altered and enlarged further in an Italianate stucco manner, and the pastureland to the west of the house was laid out to include terraces, rose gardens and two tennis lawns, all enclosed by yew hedges (Plate 276). These were approached off a new north forecourt and were arranged asymmetrically to take account of the natural levels and some mature trees. After 1911, when the 2nd Lord Swaythling succeeded, an arboretum was developed to the south-west, including a woodland dell at Swan Copse containing hybrid rhododendrons, azaleas, and the celebrated species of *Lilium giganteum.*[150] From 1912 Guthrie extended the formal gardens on the central axis of the west front to include a bowling alley, a sunk garden and herb gardens all protected from the park by tree planting and ha-has (Plate 278). The sunken garden, measuring 140 by 120 feet, was surrounded by a raised pergola of generous width, constructed of paired, pre-cast concrete pillars standing on a rubble stone plinth and supporting shaped brackets and oak beams clothed with vines and *Wisteria* (Plate 279). The central area, an ornamental parterre of brick paving and marigold beds within borders of lavender, rosemary, hellebores and *Bergenia,* was planted by Miss Jekyll.[151] This pergola garden is one of the cardinal glories of Townhill Park. Set amidst the expanding suburbs of the South Hampshire conurbation, it has happily survived, a relic of a past age, and an oasis of green tranquillity (Plate 277).[152]

276. Townhill Park, Southampton, Hampshire (L. Rome Guthrie, 1910–22): layout plan. [Guthrie c.1920]

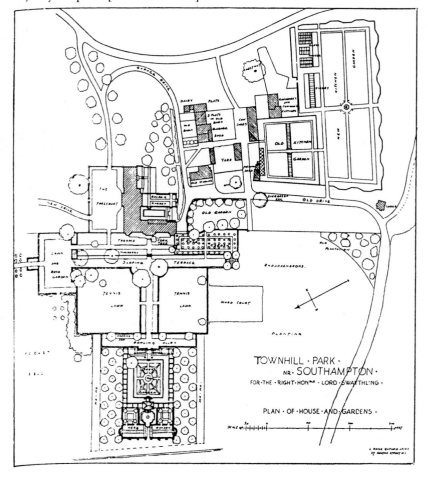

277. Townhill Park: sunken garden to the west. [N. Crighton 1984]

A classical pergola similar to that at Townhill Park formed the central feature at Moor Close, Binfield, Berkshire, designed for C. Birch Crisp just before the First World War by the young Oliver Hill (1887–1968); but it was only one element of a garden whose exuberance and decorative richness owed as much to the Baroque as to the sober formal revival. The link with Guthrie is understandable as Hill became a pupil in Flockhart's office in 1907, and the following year saw him busily sketching at Chelwood Vetchery.[153] By 1910, however, partly on the strength of the Moor Close commission, he set up on his own, rapidly developing an eclectic facility to match that of his master. An exact contemporary of Philip Tilden (see Chapter 8), he too attracted a wealthy clien-

278. Townhill Park: sunken garden to the east. [N. Crighton 1984]

279. Townhill Park: pergola. [Author 1984]

tele, aided no doubt by his readiness to turn his hand to any style of architecture.[154] Moor Close was a large, nondescript, red-brick house of 1881, and the main part of Hill's garden was laid out at a safe distance below to the south-east, reached from an upper terrace, across a bridge over a ravine, to where steps descended to a group of rectangular courts (Plate 280). The first of these had elaborate paving in stone, tile on edge and blue pebbles, and overlooked the central area from which a curving double staircase rose to the vine-clad pergola flanked by twin pavilions (Plate 281). The final enclosure comprised a lily pool bordered by flower beds and balustraded walls and with steps leading down into the water in the manner of Marsh Court.[155] Hill's friends in the 1920s included many well-known gardeners and garden architects including Harold Peto. He recalled later how his interest in gardens sprang from an early visit to the Venetian garden of Mrs Eden, who

introduced him to Miss Jekyll, 'at whose feet I sat for the rest of her life'.[156] Her influence could be seen in the planting of *Yucca, Hosta* and lilies around the pool at Moor Close, and she prepared plans for several of his post-War houses.

Clough Williams-Ellis

Most of the British examples described so far in this chapter derived their inspiration in one form or another from the Italian ideal, but as well as having to contend with a different climate, none had a setting approaching that of the original historic models. Probably the nearest one could hope to find was Snowdonia in North Wales, and it was in that austere and hilly terrain in 1908 that the young Clough Williams-Ellis began his dramatic garden at Plas Brondanw. This romantic but dilapidated Caroline house,

182

280. Moor Close, Binfield, Berkshire (Oliver Hill, 1910–14): layout plan. [BALDC 1913]

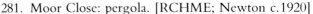
281. Moor Close: pergola. [RCHME; Newton c.1920]

situated two miles north of Penrhyndeudraeth in Merionethshire, had been inhabited by his forbears for four centuries and was given to him by his father as early as 1902. Gradually, its restoration and the creation of its garden became an absorbing interest in his life. As he wrote in his autobiography, 'it was for its sake that I worked and stinted, for its sake that I chiefly hoped to prosper. A cheque for ten pounds would come in and I would order yew hedging to that extent, a cheque for twenty and I would pave a further piece of terrace.'[157]

Dedicated custodian of the environment, self-styled 'Architect Errant', Sir Clough Williams-Ellis (1883–1978) is best known as the founder in 1926 of nearby Portmeirion, the sophisticated holiday village on which he lavished over fifty years of devoted attention. A *tour de force* of architectural make-believe, it transported some of the gaiety of the Italian Riviera townscape to a spectacular site on the Glaslyn estuary. Plas Brondanw struck another chord of his extraordinary and diverse character, its noble harmony of muted tones against a background of distant mountains contrasting with Portmeirion's fanfare of scenic effects. Its unity with the wild and timeless landscape owes much to the massive granite walls of the house, but these forms are reflected in the monumental yew of its garden layout.

He exploited the architectural potential of yew also at Little

Bognor House, near Petworth, Sussex, laid out in 1920 at about the same time as the main enclosures at Brondanw, for Sir Ivor Maxse (b.1862) who married Hon. Mary Wyndham, a daughter of the 2nd Baron Leconfield. To the south front of this late-nineteenth-century house he added a garden pavilion and a broad, flagged terrace with circular viewing platform at its eastern end, shaded by ilex and commanding a prospect towards the Downs. Through the grounds to the north and east ran a stream which descended in cascades in the lower greensand. This was transformed into an enchanting Valley Garden with south-facing terraces and naturalistic planting, becoming wilder where it merged into the woodland (see p. 3); while at the upper end, off the approach drive, a vista was created between massive yew hedges terminating in a bridge across a lily pool, fed from the stream, with steps up to a *Wiseria*-covered, five-arched loggia (Plate 282).[158]

282. Little Bognor, near Petworth, Sussex (Clough Williams-Ellis, 1920): loggia and lily pool. [Kemp 1987]

283. Plas Brondanw, Penrhyndeudraeth, Merionethshire (Clough Williams-Ellis, from 1908): general view from the north. [Author 1982]

At Plas Brondanw the vista was the dominant theme. The four-storey house was sheltered on the north-east by a wooded hillside and faced west across Traeth Mawr to the distant mountains (Plate 283). In the first phase, from 1908–14, he laid out the forecourt, and where gate-piers (now creeper-clad) mark steps descending to the terrace, set out the first of his many sight-lines (Plate 284), across the valley to Moel Hebog and up the hillside to where later he built the folly, 'Castel Brondanw'. Below the house an ancient ilex shades the sloping lawn, which is overlooked at its southern end by the orangery, built in 1914; while the northern corner contains a characteristic Clough conceit, a *clair-voyée* framing a view of Snowdon (Yr Wyddfa) itself (Plate 212). It was not until after the War, however, that he devised his most dramatic vistas. First, the flagged terrace that runs from the stables past the house was extended north-east to a circular belvedere enclosed by a low wall and commanding a panoramic view of the mountains round to the triple summit of Moelwyn. Then, to the south, he laid out a cluster of gardens enclosed by tall yew hedges. One of the cross-alleys begins at a retaining wall below the approach drive. The wall's arched recesses for statuary are reflected in yew at the western end, beyond which the view is again terminated by Moel Hebog. At right angles is a long walk, flanked by pillars of yew evoking ancient megaliths, and leading to the Apollo belvedere, a raised roundel overlooking the fields to the south. But it is on turning and looking back that one is confronted with the climax of Plas Brondanw. In most formal gardens it is the lines of the house that are projected outwards into the grounds. Here, it is the landscape that calls the tune and is itself brought into the very framework of the garden. As you ascend this alley up steps between tall, urn-capped piers to the gleaming fire-boy figure of the Fountain Lawn, there, towering above the yew, and framed by trees, rises the magnificent peak of Cnicht (Plate 285). When the mist rises on this vista, and, against the purple-tinted mountains, the viridescent yew and glinting stone catch the afternoon sun, the garden of Plas Brondanw, though imbued with Welsh imagery, comes closer possibly than any in Britain to echoing the spirit of those Elysian creations of sixteenth-century Italy.[159]

With the advent of war, work was suspended at Clough Williams-Ellis's beloved demesne, and 1915 found him occupied with the Welsh Guards and with his marriage to Amabel Strachey. But in that same summer, at Garsington Manor, a mellow Jacobean house on a hillside south-east of Oxford, overlooking the Thames Valley, Lady Ottoline Morrell (1873–1938) was seated beneath her ilex dreaming up one of the last Italian gardens of that vanishing era. In 1902 she had married the Liberal MP, Philip Morrell, their home in London becoming the centre of a bohemian circle of artists and writers; but in 1915 they moved to Garsington where both house and garden were to provide outlets for her highly individual and creative imagination. By 1 June she could write in her journal, 'It is already much more beautiful, we have made one terrace and a walk round the pond, and in the autumn we are arranging to plant yew hedges that will grow like a tall, dark wall round the water. It is more Italian than any other place in England that I have ever known.'[160] Later, when the yew hedges matured, the pond garden was furnished with Italian statues, past which peacocks trailed their proud, long tails. On the axis of the east door (where Philip Morrell later added the east terrace and loggia to designs by Philip Tilden), stretched the great, formal flower garden, a sloping, chequered carpet consisting of twenty-four, square, box-bordered beds (possibly inspired by Sir Frank Crisp's mediaeval gardens at nearby Friar Park; see Chapter 4), its paths lined with pillars of clipped Irish yew like miniature cypresses (Plate 286). Unlike Plas Brondanw, which had little place for them, Garsington was full of flowers: tulips in spring, lavender

284. Plas Brondanw: layout plan. Drawn by Clough Williams-Ellis 1954. [Courtesy of Euan Cooper-Willis]

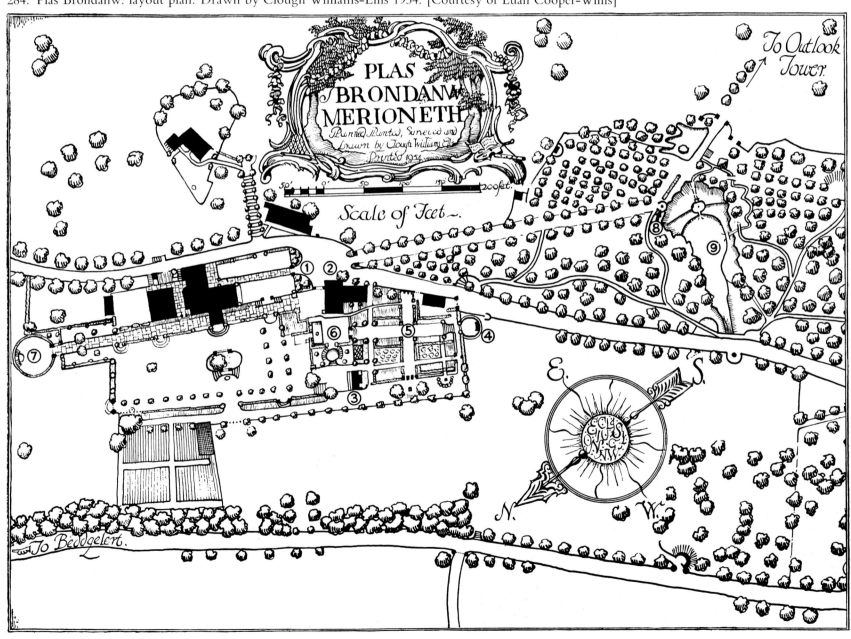

285. Plas Brondanw: vista towards Cnicht. [Author 1982]

286. Garsington Manor, near Oxford (Lady Ottoline Morrell, from 1915): formal flower garden. [Author 1985]

and rosemary, *Clematis* and *Wisteria,* roses, and a blaze of orange and red annuals in late summer.[161]

D.H. Lawrence likened Garsington to a villa in *The Decameron,* while to Lady Ottoline it was a place where one could feel 'isolated from the torrent of life', a beautiful theatre where, each weekend, her distinguished guests and protégés—Aldous Huxley, Bertrand Russell, the Murrys, Lytton Strachey, Carrington, Siegfried Sassoon—made their entrance to her intellectual salon. But as she herself became aware, in the midst of war it was no longer possible to 'stand aside and cultivate one's garden'.[162] The play was over.

287. Amport St Mary's, Andover, Hampshire (E. Lutyens and G. Jekyll, 1923): water terraces. [N. Crighton 1984]

8
Aftermath

Our England is a garden, and such gardens are not made
By singing:—'Oh, how beautiful!' and sitting in the shade,
While better men than we go out and start their working lives
At grubbing weeds from gravel-paths with broken dinner-knives.
Rudyard Kipling, 1911[1]

The First World War brought country-house building virtually to an end, and there was no longer an unlimited supply of labour to maintain large and elaborate gardens.[2] In previous years so immaculately cared for, they soon began to decline from lack of helping hands. Kitchen gardens were put into full production for the war effort, but were turned into paddocks and orchards after the war when many formal gardens were replaced by labour-saving plantations of rhododendrons and azaleas. As a result of increases in both population and the cost of land, there was a growing demand for guidance on smaller gardens, which had become more general in the 1900s and had resulted in Jekyll and Weaver's 'phenomenally successful' *Gardens for Small Country Houses*, published in 1912. Partly owing to books of that kind, Edwardian features such as the herbaceous border, rose trellis, pool or sundial, lived on in the gardens of the 1920s. Some even reached the suburban plots springing up on the fringe of every city. Influenced by the shortage of labour, gardening became more personal and many owners took advantage of the increasing range and supply of flowering trees and shrubs, arranging them in gardenesque manner around the inevitable lawn.

For the larger layout, patronage was shifting from private clients to the committees of civic or national corporations. Immediately after the war some of the leading architects of the Edwardian establishment were kept busy designing appropriate settings for the War Graves Cemeteries. In 1918 the Imperial War Graves Commission appointed Edwin Lutyens, Reginald Blomfield and Herbert Baker (joined by Charles Holden in 1920) as Principal Architects for France, with Robert Lorimer responsible for Italy and Macedonia.[3] All employed a monumental classicism, seen at its most abstract in Holden's Corbie Communal Cemetery Extension, Somme (1920s) (Plate 288), 'a stark, harsh and bare reminder of the tragedy of war'.[4] Miss Jekyll prepared plans for some of Lutyens's cemeteries, relieving their bleak monotony with familiar English shrubs and flowers, a mode of planting that became the general policy of the Commission.[5] She planted also Baker's South African War Memorial at Delville Wood, France (1925); while, closer to home, she devised borders primarily of roses and lilies for his War Memorial Cloister at Winchester College (1923), in

Kipling's opinion 'incomparably the best of all the War Memorials'.[6] The grand layout could also be employed to engender a feeling of civic pride, a notable post-war example being the Centre of Welwyn Garden City, Hertfordshire, laid out from 1920 on Beaux-Arts lines by Louis de Soissons, who had been a student in Pascal's *atelier* in 1910.[7] The main boulevard, Parkway, included formal gardens, a fountain, and double lines of trees *à la* Durand, all flanked by buildings in neo-Georgian style and influenced in its axiality by the *Town Planning Review* and the Liverpool School.

Public Parks

By the First World War most towns had their public parks and gardens, Loudon, who designed the Derby Arboretum in 1839,

288. Corbie Communal Cemetery Extension (Somme) (Charles Holden, 1920s). (Commonwealth War Graves Commission 1964]

having been one of their earliest advocates. Generally landscaped with serpentine walks in the style of Paxton's Birkenhead Park (1844), they often contained colourful bedding-out displays, a popular art form which, despite Robinson's censure, continued unabated. Towards the end of the nineteenth century, parks tended to incorporate more formal elements, producing a style that Mawson called 'composite', a term described by Edouard André (1840–1911), designer of Sefton Park, Liverpool (1867), in his *L'Art des Jardins* (1879). A late example—the last in the tradition of Loudon—was Mawson's Stanley Park, Blackpool (1922), where boating lake and golf course have naturalistic outlines, while areas for organized games radiate from a central, circular 'Italian' garden. A trend towards greater formality occurred also in Germany, for example at the Stadtpark, Hamburg, designed in 1909 by Fritz Schumacher, with zones for formal gardens and games enclosures disposed asymmetrically either side of a dominant east-west axis.[8] In 1910 Mawson prepared a monumental scheme for Queen's Park, Bolton; but the Beaux-Arts manner found favour more in North America, where his grandiose axial plan for Coal Harbour in Stanley Park, Vancouver, was accepted in 1912, although subsequently abandoned due to the war.[9]

In France there was a return to the formal garden in public parks towards the end of the nineteenth century. A similar revival came later to Spain; by the turn of the century its Moorish garden art had declined. Gardens retained their individuality according to location and climate but French influence predominated. The decorative art of mosaiculture was displayed in many public gardens, and the layout of parks usually consisted of uninspired versions of the *jardin inglés*, with little regard for the nature of the terrain.[10] It took a French architect, J.C.N. Forestier (1861–1930), to bring about a return to the traditional Spanish style. Forestier was Conservateur des Promenades de Paris and from 1905 laid out gardens at the Bagatelle, Bois de Boulogne, which had been acquired from the estate of Sir Richard Wallace.[11] His most important commissions, however, were in Spain. These included private gardens, several of which survive, such as the perfectly proportioned architectural garden for the Marqués de Castilleja de Guzmán on the outskirts of Seville, and the beautiful parterre at the Moratalla estate in Hornachelos (Córdoba) for the Marqués de Viana. But it is as an enthusiastic advocate of the urban park that Forestier is best remembered. In 1911 he re-designed the Maria-Luisa Park in Seville (Plate 289). Its avenues and vistas are in the French grand manner, but they enclose hedge-bordered water gardens recalling the ancient Moorish gardens that had made such a deep impression on him. His masterpiece, commissioned in 1915 and carried out up to 1929, was the Montjuich Park in Barcelona for the Ibero-americana exhibition, where a previously inaccessible hillside was transformed with terracing and hanging gardens. Both these parks were included in his *Jardins Mediterranéens: Carnet de Plans et Dessins* (1920), beautifully illustrated with garden plans and details.[12] On his return to Paris he was made director of the Bois de Boulogne and spent his last years in the house that from 1953 was the residence of the Duke and Duchess of Windsor.

Philip Tilden and Port Lympne

Owing to the difficulties of building after the war, some British country-house owners turned their attention to the gardens as a means of improving their properties. Mawson's garden practice had dwindled considerably, but he prepared several schemes, some revived from before the war, including an imposing layout in 1920 for W.G. Macbeth at Dunira, near Comrie, Perthshire.[13] However, nothing could compete with the splendour of the terraced gardens of Port Lympne, Kent (1918–21). In 1913 people had felt 'that *now* they must make the most of everything',[14] but even after the war some still had the panache, and the wealth, to defy both austerity and the prevailing 'good taste', and none more so than the connoisseur, statesman and multi-millionaire Sir Philip Sassoon. When he succeeded to a baronetcy in 1912 (also to his father Sir Edward Sassoon's constituency at Hythe), he had employed Herbert Baker to build a house on a magnificent virgin site facing south across Romney Marsh to the Channel. Originally named Belcaire, it was in a Kentish, Stuart-cum-Colonial style in red brick and tiles with curved colonnaded 'stoeps' enclosing the south terrace and Cape Dutch gables similar to those at Groote Schuur which Baker had designed in 1896 for Cecil Rhodes. By 1918, however, Sassoon's tastes had become more exotic, and he was full of flamboyant ideas which he was impatient to put into effect. Baker was fortunately occupied with New Delhi, so Sassoon commissioned Philip Tilden (1887–1956) to complete both house and garden.

This was a good choice for someone like Sassoon. Romantic, artistic, personable, and something of a dilettante himself, Tilden was to prove that he could turn his hand to almost anything from the repair of mediaeval houses to opulent interiors of the kind immortalized by Osbert Lancaster as 'Curzon Street baroque'. The son of Sir William Tilden, he was articled in 1908 to T.E. Collcutt, his drawing ability having been kindled as a child at Bedales School, which also fostered his interest and skill in both building and decorating crafts.[15] His subsequent career as a society architect

289. Maria-Luisa Park, Seville (J.C.N. Forestier, 1911): layout plan. [From J.C.N. Forestier, *Jardins Mediterranéens*, 1920]

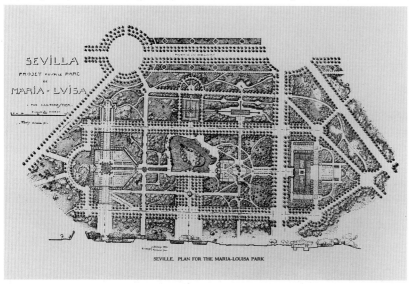

290. Port Lympne, Kent (Philip Tilden, 1918–21): *trompe l'oeil* map by Rex Whistler, 1930. [Courtesy of John Aspinall]

was to include a partial rebuilding of Easton Lodge for Lady Warwick (1919), Lloyd George's house at Churt (1922), the remodelling of Chartwell for Winston Churchill (1924), also drawings, prepared c.1917–22, for a mammoth castle (mercifully not realised) with elaborate formal gardens by Mawson at Hengistbury Head, opposite the Isle of Wight, for Gordon Selfridge. In 1913–14 Tilden restored and added wings and formal gardens to the seventeenth-century Kingston Russell House, Dorchester for George Gribble;[16] and in 1917–18 he helped Lady Conway to create a garden at Allington Castle, near Maidstone, which the explorer and art historian Sir Martin Conway had rescued from a ruin and gradually restored. Tilden felt strongly that nothing as colourful as flower beds should disturb the gaunt simplicity of an ancient building like Allington, and the garden was thus laid out in a field to the south of the castle. A long, central grass walk was made, flanked by yew hedges or borders of lavender, with rough-

291. Port Lympne: the stairway. [*CL* 1936]

stone piers at intervals supporting pergolas covered with roses and *Clematis*, and with enclosed gardens on either side devoted to the seasons, or to white, blue or purple flowers.[17] Tilden's friendship with the Conways was a turning-point in his career. At Allington he was introduced to Sir Louis Mallet who had restored and added formal gardens to a yeoman's house, Wardes, at Otham, nearby, in about 1912,[18] and it was through Mallet that he met Sassoon.

The design and layout of Port Lympne was dominated by its owner's exuberant and magical personality, but Tilden's skills were put to good use, first in the interior of the house. It was to be an aesthete's Elysium: 'no more of the modest week-end home, but rather the epitome of all things conducive to luxurious relaxation after the strenuousness of war. It was to be a challenge to the world, telling people that a new culture had risen up from the sickbed of the old.'[19] Within a courtyard off the staircase Tilden created a Moorish patio with white marble columns, almost devoid of vegetation, but paved in Swedish green marble with rills meeting in a central, well-head fountain; also an octagonal library where the Treaty of Paris was signed in 1921 (Sassoon was Private Secretary to Lloyd George, 1920–2). But most spectacular of all were the gardens, exquisitely portrayed in the *trompe l'oeil* tattered map entitled 'An inaccurate Plan of Port Lympne in the County of Kent' on the wall of Rex Whistler's Tent Room of 1930 (Plate 290).[20]

It was the Roman history of the site that fired Sassoon's imagination, for originally the sea had come up to the station of Lemanis at the foot of the wooded hillside. Partly in celebration of this, a stone stairway of Augustan dimensions was built at the side of the house. Mounting the hillside were 125 steps, with landings leading to gardens, each having a different colour as its theme. It resembled the tiered garden of Il Bozzolo, near Laveno,[21] except that in place of stone balustrades the terraces were enclosed by massive walls of *Cupressus macrocarpa* (Plate 291). Underneath, tunnels provided access for 'invisible' gardeners, while at the summit were twin

292. Port Lympne: the Fountain Pool. [*CL* 1923]

Roman loggias. It all smacked of a Hollywood film set, and Baker was so appalled by the loggias that he later convinced Sassoon that they should be removed, together with other over-elaborate stonework. Unlike Il Bozzolo the stairway led nowhere, the reward being the breathtaking vista down and across the marsh to the sea. At its foot was the West Garden on a cross-axis that formed another vista from the entrance forecourt through the long hall of the house to the Magnolia Avenue. This was carved out of the protective woodland to the west, planted with *Cyclamen* and autumn crocus and terminated by statuary. The *pièce de résistance* was the Great Fountain. Situated on the central axis of the house, it was approached from the south terrace with its sunken knot gardens. Steps descended against the retaining wall, first to a semi-circular platform with pool and quarter-spherical hood (bearing more than a passing resemblance to Hestercombe), and then by a segmental flight to the bathing pool, an important feature of life at Port Lympne. This was of imperial proportions with balustrades to each side incorporating date and monogram, and raised, quadrant seating platforms, seeming to float above the landscape like objects from outer space. The pool formed a link with the distant

sea, the single jet of the fountain contrasting with the wide horizon (Plate 292). Some of this architectural masonry including the side pools was later removed due to land subsidence, and, as trees and hedges matured, more attention was paid to the flower gardens.

These were planned to come into their own in August and the planting arranged accordingly throughout. Sassoon could then whirl his guests up in his airplane and dazzle them with his vivid display of summer flowers. The pool was flanked by alleys of pleached elm with, on one side, the striped Marigold Garden and, on the other, the Chess Board Garden with its squares of heliotrope and *Begonia*, all contained within shaped yew hedges. The terraced vineyard and figyard lay to the south, also morning and evening tennis courts. To the west, below the Bowling Alley, were Dahlia and Aster Terraces, while between, sloping towards the marvellous view, ran the gorgeous, double herbaceous border, 135 yards long, in broad masses and drifts producing a striking combination of harmonies such as blue, pink, red, and contrasts of purple with orange or yellow.

As photographed in 1923 for *Country Life*, the gardens of Port Lympne were undeniably the most sumptuous since the war, but in their pristine state, before the mellowing influence of mature hedges and other planting, they must have seemed verging on the vulgar to many, inviting comparison with Randolph Hearst's Neptune Pool at San Simeon.[22] To Chips Channon the place was 'a triumph of beautiful bad taste and Babylonian luxury';[23] and when Tipping compiled his *English Gardens* in 1925 he could not even bring himself to make a personal visit; 'the parts please, the whole jars', he wrote. It was the cacophony of irrelevant styles that upset him: Cape Dutch house, Spanish courtyard, Roman stairway and a bathing pool which evoked the spirit of Le Nôtre and the native land of Sassoon's mother, Aline de Rothschild. To Tilden, looking back from the 'fifties, it would have seemed at odds with his belief in a national architecture: 'Britain is not the home of the acanthus and cypress', he wrote, 'it is the home of the Gothic rose, the oak, the ash and the parasitic ivy.'[24]

His work at Sassoon's other estate, Trent Park in Middlesex, must have been more congenial if less exciting. The original Georgian house had been rebuilt at the end of the nineteenth century in 'mauve' and black brick, but after he acquired the freehold in 1923 Sassoon decided to remodel it 'in the pure English style'. Rebuilding began in 1926, the house being made as symmetrical as possible and re-faced with red bricks from William Kent's Devonshire House, Piccadilly, which had recently been demolished. The park included a lake, a water garden and a wild garden. Sassoon adorned it, not in imperial style, but with Renaissance statuary under ilex groves, an obelisk from Wrest in the lakeside wood, flowering trees and shrubs, and spectacular planting of daffodils. Tilden added an Italian, marble pergola, covered with vines and *Wisteria*, like the one he built at Chartwell, and in about 1935 Churchill, a frequent guest, painted it in the full glory of summer[25] with the same uninhibited *chiaroscuro* that he had painted the West Garden at Port Lympne in 1930. For Osbert Sitwell, staying there in the 1930s 'living in that state of luxury, imbued with the spirit of fun of which he [Sassoon] was the particular master', and walking in the gardens where 'innumerable flowers swooned in a perpetual hush of summer', it was also redolent with schoolday memories of the early 1900s.[26] Chips Channon considered it the loveliest of Sassoon's houses, 'a dream house, perfect, luxurious, distinguished with the exotic taste to be expected in any Sassoon Schloss'.[27]

Norah Lindsay

The summer borders of both Port Lympne and Trent were planted by Norah Lindsay (1873–1948) who, before and after the First World War, went from house to house, at home and abroad, dispensing her recipes for flower relationships. Artistic, and exotic in appearance, she had an instinctive grasp of the broad colour effect: 'She would trace out a whole garden with the tip of her umbrella.'[28] Born in County Galway, she married in 1895 Lieutenant-Colonel Harry Lindsay, a cousin of the Earl of Crawford. She rapidly absorbed the teachings of Miss Jekyll whose successor she might have been, in Tilden's view, had she too set down the fruits of her experience in books.[29] Her description of the borders which she re-planted at Trent provide a taste of her prose: 'There

must be...a cunning juxtaposition of contrasts; the sculptured leaves of funkia beside the flimsy fountain of gypsophila and the strong spears of poker and eremuri rising from the low bushes of santolina.' She also shows her debt to Miss Jekyll: 'The high water mark of this border is reached when the patches of alstroemeria bloom; their fiery orange can hardly be matched by any other flower, and it is like leaving liquid sunshine and plunging into the shade to go from the orange border to the cool deep blues and rich purples of the next pair of beds.'[30] At the Thames-side manor of Sutton Courtenay in Berkshire, her home from 1895, she created her famous garden, which had Lutyens enraptured when he spent a July night there with Christopher Hussey in 1931,[31] the same year that she described its unself-conscious charms in *Country Life*. Subdivided by mellow walls and yew hedges, it included a wild garden, the Hornbeam Alley, the Persian Garden and the Long Garden, 'set with high black yews and punctuated with heavy green humps of box'. Each walk ended in a pool or fountain, for as she observed,

> there is more than a memory of Italy in my garden...I would have been a much lesser gardener had I not worshipped at the crumbling shrines of the ancient garden gods of Florence and Rome. There I learned the magic of black sentinel cypresses, translated in our northern clime to Irish yew and juniper—a severe architectural note, but mollified by the invariable vicinity of water.[32]

The pillars of Irish yew recall nearby Garsington, but Sutton Courtenay had none of that garden's grandeur, rather 'an air of spontaneity in the planting', its beds filled through the seasons by a profusion of flowers common and uncommon. This floral paradise has by the nature of things passed into oblivion; nor has her work survived at Cliveden where she added herbaceous borders to the Italian Long Garden, and planted the triangular beds of the parterre with catmint.

Fortunately, however, Norah Lindsay's re-designing of the elaborate parterre at Blickling, Norfolk, a successful example of the informal planting of a formal layout, has been admirably preserved by the National Trust. The parterre had been added to the east front in 1872 by W.A. Nesfield for Constance, Marchioness of Lothian, for whom the architectural terracing had been prepared by Matthew Digby Wyatt. It was the Marchioness, however, who had had the last word on the planting, which included both climbing and herbaceous plants.[33] Viewed from the Long Gallery, with the vista beyond enclosed by the Woodland Garden and terminated by the Doric Temple, the effect was magnificent, but as Tipping observed, its dignity was 'singularly lessened by the restlessness and confusion of the innumerable, many-shaped and differently treated beds that pullulate on the lawn'.[34] In spite of Lady Lothian's artistic leanings, the parterre exhibited all the characteristics of Victorian *horror vacui*, something that, when he succeeded in 1930, suited neither the taste nor the purse of the 11th Marquess. A frequent visitor to Cliveden, he brought in Norah Lindsay to simplify the Blickling layout. The eighteenth-century stone urns and the blocks of yew shaped like grand pianos in the eastern sections were retained, also the central fountain and the

293. Blickling, Norfolk (Norah Lindsay, 1930): the parterre. [National Trust 1986]

four main beds with their corner yew topiary. The rest was turfed, but by contrast with the architectural severity of Blow and Billerey's remodelling of Nesfield's parterre at Eaton Hall (see Plate 252), the geometry was softened by her planting scheme. The beds were edged with her favourite *Nepeta X faassenii* mixed with polyantha roses, and filled with perennials graded in height towards the centre (Plate 293). The beds nearest the house contain mainly cool hues: *Veronica, Limonium latifolium, Lavatera*, lilies, globe thistle, *Phlox, Campanula, Delphinium;* while the further beds are yellow, orange and red: *Alchemilla mollis, Erigeron, Solidago* 'Goldenmosa', *Achillea*, irises, mullein, *Helenium*, perennial sunflower and *Rudbeckia*.[35]

Post-War Gardens of Lutyens and Jekyll

In the mid-1920s, while Norah Lindsay was exquisitely flowering Port Lympne and Trent, the octogenarian Miss Jekyll was still busily occupied with commissions from both owners and architects, including her last ones in collaboration with Lutyens: Amport and Gledstone. At all his main post-war gardens—the others were Tyringham and New Delhi—Lutyens revived the use of water as a major design element. Gledstone and Tyringham were grand versions of the canal motif first employed at Folly Farm (1912), but at Amport (1923) the theme of the planted rill, introduced at Deanery Garden, was developed into a large water terrace.

Amport St Mary's, near Andover, Hampshire, was built in 1857 in 'Tudorbethan' style, with yellow brick and stone dressings, for the 14th Marquess of Winchester by the Scottish architect William Burn. The entrance is as usual on the east, and to the west is an elaborate box parterre incorporating the Winchester crest and motto;[36] but it was to embellish the grounds to the south overlooked by the principal rooms that Lutyens was commissioned by Mrs Sofer-Whitburn. The garden was laid out symmetrically on two levels on the axis of the south front. The upper terrace contains an oval pool with fountain, surrounded by a rill which extends on either side to square pools with rose beds at each corner. Each rill then descends to the lower terrace where they are again turned at right angles, finishing to east and west at lily tanks bordered by flower beds and topiary. Amport consists essentially of terraced lawns finely channelled by the intricate, rectilinear pattern of the rills and pools with their simple, flush surrounds, its feeling of spaciousness heightened by the visual continuity with the field beyond whose boundary is marked only by a ha-ha (Plate 287). The design allowed Miss Jekyll to indulge in some of her favourite planting of irises, water lilies and roses, and for Lutyens it was an opportunity to try out some of the ideas he had planned for New Delhi.[37]

A foretaste of Delhi's monumentality was provided by Gledstone Hall, near Skipton (1922–5), considered by some to be

294. Gledstone Hall, Skipton, Yorkshire (E. Lutyens and G. Jekyll, 1922–5): layout plan. [Miranda Ottewill]

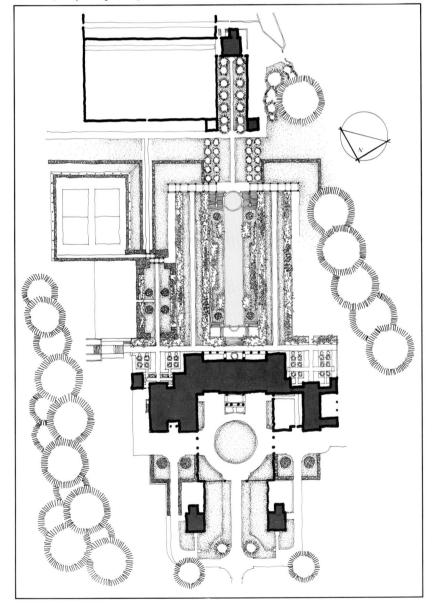

Lutyens's finest classical house, designed for a rich cotton merchant, Sir Amos Nelson.[38] It was the last major new garden of his partnership with Miss Jekyll.[39] Palladian, with a Louis-Seize accent, it was built of sandstone from the Salterworth quarry under an unbroken hipped roof of Cotswold stone slates, and its severity was in keeping with its setting in the bleak Yorkshire moors. The overall layout (Plate 294) continued the axial theme of Great Maytham, except that the garden now became the climax of an uninterrupted route from the forecourt through the hall to a superb central vista. The principal rooms face south towards the distant hills across a terrace extending at each side to a pergola but lowered in the centre to contain a sunken tank almost two hundred feet long (Plate 295). It was a bold, masterful treatment of the landscape, creating a total unity, the house reading as 'an introductory pavilion supporting the gardens'.[40] However, because of this subordination to the grand concept, the garden lacks the subtle fusion of art and nature of Lutyens's early houses. Their owners had been prepared to wait for the slow maturing of hedges and trees, but at Gledstone, house and landscape had to be created at once, both fashioned from the hard sandstone. Gone, too, is the complex configuration of Marsh Court, with its sequential layout, and its fresh, picturesque prospects opening up at each turn. Lutyens was now determined on grand axial planning, a course he had embarked upon in 1906 at nearby Heathcote, with the result that much of the interest and variety of his schemes was sacrificed, a point well illustrated by Gledstone. As with all gardens planned around an inaccessible central feature the visitor had to choose on which side of it to walk; there was no spring or summer garden to determine his direction. On emerging from the hall and descending the central flight of steps he was confronted with the usual dual stairway. After continuing to left or right he could meander between the beds bordering the canal and admire its differently coloured groups of water-lilies. This brought him to a

295. Gledstone Hall: sunk garden looking south. [CL 1935]

296. Gledstone Hall: sunk garden looking north. [*CL* 1935]

point where the vista continued below between Apple Houses and an avenue of apple trees closed by a gardener's cottage, but it was probably not enough to entice him down, across the axis, and up the steps on the other side of the circular pool. Instead he would have been drawn upwards to one of the pergolas (intended to be covered with *Laburnum*) from where there was only a straight walk back to the house along a flower-bordered upper path.

When, at the end of 1925, Miss Jekyll was called in to relieve this stark masonry, she reinforced its symmetry with a planting plan that was a mirror image about the central axis. The beds against the east and west retaining walls of the sunk garden contained symmetrical arrangements of suitably hardy plants from her own nursery at Munstead Wood. These included an edging of *Bergenia Megasea* alternating with London's Pride in front of *Artemisia lactiflora, Helenium pumilum* and yellow day lilies, backed by *Acanthus* and asters, with *Berberis* against the wall on either side (Plate 296).[41]

Tyringham, near Newport Pagnell, Buckinghamshire, continued this relentless symmetry, but allied to a more expansive classical theme made possible by its setting in the landscape park of the late eighteenth-century house by Sir John Soane. Lutyens's dramatic layout included a pool to rival Port Lympne's, a great sheet of water sixty feet wide extending five hundred feet from the garden front, the vista continuing in a long avenue of double rows of elms reaching out into the park. A pair of strategically placed, free-standing Tuscan columns and flanking, domed pavilions completed the *ensemble* (Plate 298). Such a palatial treatment of the modest but important house of 1793–7 would have been totally out of character had not the owners, the Silesian banker, Frederick Adolphus Konig and his musical, French wife, Gerda, already re-vamped the interior and drastically altered the exterior in c.1907–9 to designs by E. Von Ihne from Berlin. Only the famous gateway and bridge survived unscathed, and thus when

Lutyens was commissioned in 1926 he felt no need to bow down to his illustrious Georgian predecessor; as Hussey wrote in 1929, 'Since the house had lost its individual stamp through alterations, Sir Edwin Lutyens has been free to express his own personality unhampered.'[42] This was to forget the ornamental gardens added in about 1910 by Charles G.F. Rees and including a new forecourt, a rose garden on the south-west front (Plate 297) and a terrace garden to the north-west leading to a classical pergola with fishpond and fountain.[43] It was beyond this terrace, on the central axis of the house, that Lutyens laid out his grand canal (Plate 299). This was divided into two sections at a point two-thirds along its length by a cross axis punctuated by the columns on whose apex were poised lead leopards spouting into a circular basin. The longer pool was bordered by beds contained within box hedges resembling giant settees, while the pavilions served complementary functions, one ministering to the earthly ritual of bathing, the other dedicated to music, 'a shrine of the humanist faith'.[44]

Tyringham was the most spectacular example in this country of Lutyens's use of water in landscape design, but it was to reach its climax in the Viceregal gardens of New Delhi. Appointed architect of Viceroy's House in 1912, Lutyens submitted his first plan for its gardens at the beginning of 1917. These were specifically required to be of the Moghul type,[45] and he visited various historic sites, including the Taj Mahal, on which his verdict was, 'It is wonderful but it is not architecture'.[46] He was wearied by the endless reference to carpet patterns, so for the geometric basis of his layout he went back to the Persian paradise garden into which he meshed another potent symbol, the verdant English lawn, thus nicely juxtaposing the two cultures (Plate 300). The main parterre is 440 feet square with its principal axis aligned on the west front of the house, and a cross-axis between the North and South Forts. These

297. Tyringham, Newport Pagnell, Buckinghamshire (E. Lutyens, 1926): rose garden (by Charles Rees, c.1910) [RCHME 1912]

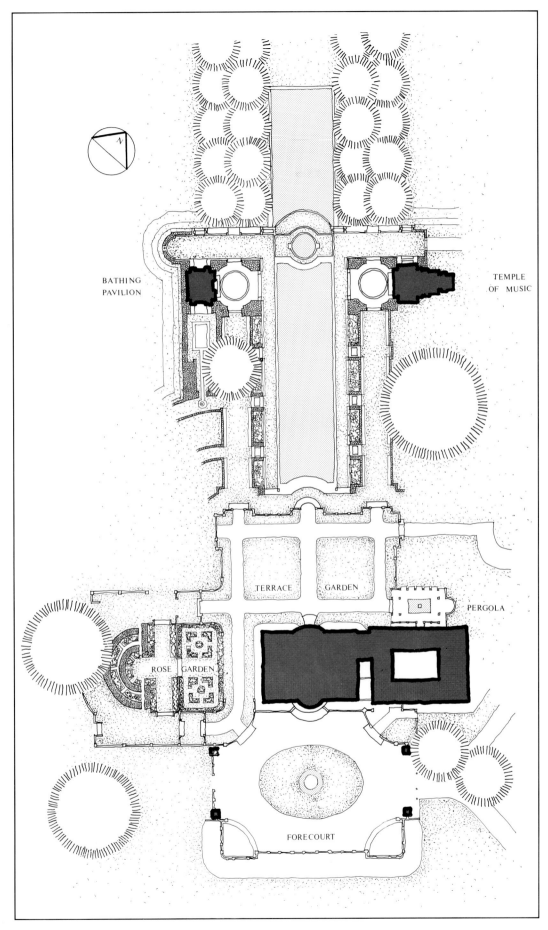

BATHING
PAVILION

TEMPLE
OF MUSIC

TERRACE   GARDEN

PERGOLA

ROSE   GARDEN

FORECOURT

298. Tyringham: layout
plan. [Miranda Ottewill]

299. Tyringham: view north-west from the house. [*AR* 1929]

forts have roof gardens which are linked to the house by terrace walks on top of the flanking bastion walls thus providing an alternative approach to the garden. The central lawn, where the Viceregal tent could be erected for garden parties, is surrounded by a system of eighteen-foot-wide canals which form crosses at each corner, 'rivers of life', with lotus-leaf fountains at their intersections.[47] Between the wings of the west front are large pools, also with fountains, from which water flows over semi-circular cascades into the main canals, whose outer arms are linked by rills which bisect beds filled mainly with roses. The central island is reached by bridges flanked by shrub-filled planting boxes and steps leading down into the channels, a reminder of that first water garden at Marsh Court. Though it lacks the overall repose of, for example, the Kashmir gardens of Shalamar Bagh and Achabal, the detailing is of the utmost simplicity throughout, water being the dominant element, while pleached Asoka trees, in groups of four, provide much-needed relief from scorching sun and the pink sandstone.[48]

Dividing the parterre from the tennis courts to the west are stone screens with circular openings (a characteristic Lutyens touch recalling the *clair-voyée* at Grey Walls); while, between the courts (Plate 301), further shade is provided under the vine-, rose- and jasmine-covered pergola with its extraordinary 'elephant trunk' counterweight pendants. This leads to the seclusion of the Round Pool Garden where, remote from the house, a sunken pool is encircled by a profusion of flowers in tiered beds with roses incarnadine spilling over the enclosing wall (Plate 302). It is the spirit of Heywood re-born but free from that garden's Italian loggia and elaborate fountain, only the ripples from the central bubble disturbing its tranquillity. The planting of the Viceregal garden was carried out from 1928 by the Director of Horticulture, W.R. Mustoe,[49] who breakfasted with Lutyens every morning during the latter's visit to Delhi in January 1929. Lutyens praised his achievement in a letter to Lady Emily on the seventeenth, and on the twenty-fourth he wrote, 'I am making a butterfly garden. The roses—wonderful, the mignonette perfumes the whole place.'[50]

The End of the Formal Revival

The opening of India's new capital took place in 1931, the garden of Viceroy's House serving as a majestic finale to the formal revival

300. Viceregal Garden, New Delhi (E. Lutyens, 1917–31): layout plan drawn by George Stewart, 1950. [Courtesy of R.W.M. and J.M. Monks]

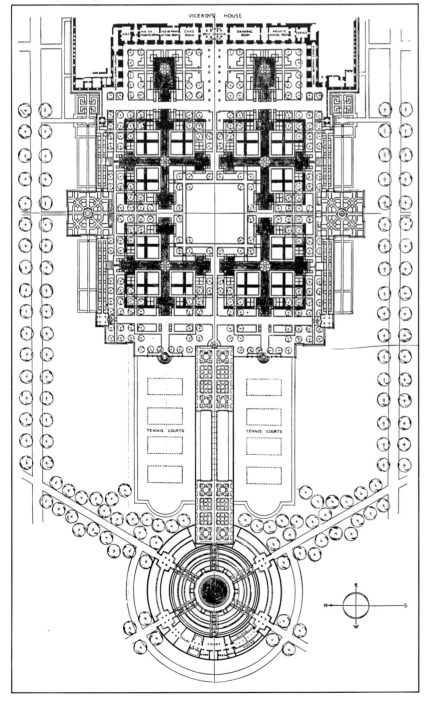

301. Viceregal Garden: pergola garden. [J. Sparkes 1976]

begun forty years earlier. Back in a Britain torn by financial crisis, the society that had fostered it was rapidly disappearing. A few architects still carried on the old, romantic traditions. In 1926, within a seventeenth-century walled enclosure at Lyegrove House, Old Sodbury, Gloucestershire, G.H. Kitchin created a fine, architectural framework for Lady Westmorland's garden.[51] His own house and garden, Compton End, south of Winchester, his home from 1897, had all the Arts and Crafts hallmarks and was fully illustrated in *Country Life* in 1919, its layout forming the endpapers of Tipping's *The Garden of Today* (1933).[52] In about 1925 the architect Walter Godfrey[53] added formal gardens at the eighteenth-century Kidbrooke Park, Forest Row, Sussex, for the banker, Olaf Hambro. These consisted of paved terraces with rose beds, and a pergola leading up to a monumental rotunda, which formed a link with a corner of the walled garden to the west in which a fan-

199

302. Viceregal Garden: round pool garden. [J. Sparkes 1976]

303. Ditchley Park, Charlbury, Oxfordshire (G.A. Jellicoe, 1933–6): Italian Garden (1936).

shaped herb garden was created.[54] Godfrey inherited his interest in garden design as a pupil of George Devey's partner, James Williams, and from 1905 carried on Devey's practice in partnership with Edmund Wratten. In 1914 he published *Gardens in the Making*, handsomely illustrated with pen-and-ink drawings; but the text did little more than reiterate what Sedding and Blomfield had said twenty-five years earlier. In 1931 he laid out gardens at Charleston Manor, Westdean, in the Sussex Downs, for the portrait painter Oswald Birley.[55] These consisted of a series of compartments embracing many of those qualities dear to Sedding which were to reach perfection in the outdoor rooms of Sissinghurst.[56]

French and Italian historical revivals made an impressive but final appearance at Blenheim and Ditchley. The two great water terraces at Blenheim (Plate 304) were laid out in the Le Nôtre manner in 1925–30 for the 9th Duke of Marlborough by Achille Duchêne, whose work had included the restoration of Courances just before the First World War.[57] After he succeeded in 1892, the Duke had created, also with the help of Duchêne, the East Parterre with its elaborate scroll-work and central Mermaid Fountain (1900s) by Ralph Waldo Story, the American sculptor, who lived in Rome and was responsible also for the Fountain of Venus at Ascott and the Fountain of Love (c.1895) at Cliveden.

The Italian Garden (1933–6) at nearby Ditchley Park, Oxfordshire, designed by Geoffrey Jellicoe for Ronald and Nancy Tree, was the last of its kind. Although Ronald Tree had an English upbringing, his parents were American and his wife a Virginian and niece of Nancy Astor. In 1933, the year he became MP for Market Harborough, he bought Ditchley which soon became a focus of Anglo-American admiration for eighteenth-century grandeur and elegance. The garden was a reinterpretation of one of the formal terraces proposed by Gibbs for the house of 1722. Approached from the south-west terrace with its flanking knot gardens in box, it consisted of a sunk parterre enclosed by rows of pleached limes backed by yew hedges, with a semi-circular pool

and fountain at the end, recalling the Villa Piccolomini at Frascati (Plate 303).[58] Ditchley came into its own at a house-warming ball in June 1937. There was a tent decorated by Oliver Messel, the fountain was floodlit, and while the orchestra played behind rose-covered *treillage*, the *beau monde* mingled elegantly with the incipient hedges and alleys, the Italian terracotta vases, and statues from Wrest.[59] Like Garsington and the Edwardian age, Ditchley also marked the end of an era whose values were in turn soon to be shattered by the Second World War. In the same year, a very different house and garden, expressing a new age, was taking shape in the Sussex Downs.

The Modern Movement Garden

Bentley, near Halland, East Sussex, was a seminal work of the Modern Movement. Designed for himself in 1935 by the Russian-born architect Serge Chermayeff, the house stood in a free-flowing landscape of grass and trees, based on the existing contours and woodland, and designed by the landscape gardener Christopher Tunnard as a foil to its severe rectangular grid (Plate 305). In essence it was a reversion to eighteenth-century landscape design, but, in addition, the interior of the house was conceived as part of the landscape, and the planting as part of the architecture. Glass walls slid back; paving slabs extended into the open plan living area; and the terrace was enclosed only by a wing wall and terminal screen which, like the house itself, provided the frame for a picturesque view of the landscape. What had begun in the 1890s as an attempt to reduce the barrier between inside and outside had reached its ultimate conclusion. The concept of 'garden' had, however, changed in the process; in fact, Tunnard questioned whether there should 'be a garden at all, in the conventional sense of the word'. At Bentley 'irregular "atmospheric" plantations of flowering trees and shrubs link the house to the landscape'. That the Jekyll garden could be considered the 'perfect adjunct' to the

304. Blenheim Palace, Oxfordshire (Achille Duchêne, 1925–30): water terraces. [Jeremy Whitaker 1976. Reproduced by permission of His Grace the Duke of Marlborough]

Lutyens house was to him 'a very good reason for its being unsuitable for a modern house.'[60]

What had precipitated this change of fashion? There was the underlying assumption that formal layouts were more costly to maintain, but other causes, both cultural and professional, can be identified. The turn of the century had been a fertile period for architecture and garden design, but as the Edwardian age gave way to the 1920s, gardeners increasingly focused their attenion on new varieties of plants and flowers, while architects, armed with an ever-growing supply of measured exemplars, fell back further on historical precedent. A pleasing and sometimes scholarly neo-Georgian was the most characteristic style, combined with a watered-down version of the pre-war formal garden. This bland good taste possessed none of the crusading vigour of the 1890s and had no appeal for the new generation of designers to whom the traditional garden represented both an outdated language and an obsolete economy. They looked for a new philosophy that would express the spirit of the times. What better therefore than to wipe the slate clean and raise once again the banner of nature with its call to a fresh start, a return to grass roots. In architecture this *tabula*

201

305. Bentley, Halland, Sussex (S. Chermayeff and C. Tunnard, 1936–7): south front. [*AR* 1939]

rasa opened the doors to the Modern Movement, ostensibly based on a natural approach to function, structure and materials but in fact derived from an aesthetic of Cubist forms set advantageously, like the Palladian Villa before it, in a natural landscape, its pristine whiteness contrasting with billowing sweeps of lawn and the accommodating tree.[61] A number of the leading exponents of this movement were architects who had temporarily taken refuge in England from Germany and Eastern Europe. Although 'functionalist' descendants of Muthesius, their designs paid little attention to that important element of *Das Englische Haus*, the garden. They were warmly welcomed by their English disciples whose work was illustrated in F.R.S. Yorke's *The Modern House in England* (1937). If one discounts the obligatory roof terraces, gardens were conspicuously thin on the ground in this and Yorke's earlier book, *The Modern House* (1934). To this band of reformers the individual garden seemed trivial and irrelevant by comparison with the English park which, paradoxically, evoked for them a vision of a new, healthy, communal society.[62]

Nevertheless, the few gardens that did accompany these pioneering houses were more appropriate as models for the smaller plots of the 1930s. Axes and vistas were replaced by asymmetrical compositions of grass and paving incorporating concrete planting boxes or geometrical beds, sometimes in chequerboard pattern, sometimes extending the plan of the house as at Amyas Connell's modern butterfly High and Over, Amersham, Buckinghamshire (1929).[63] The picturesque, or at least picturesqueness, had never been absent for long since the debate of the 1790s, and it now reappeared, as at Bentley, in the affection for framed pictures of the natural landscape. But this response to nature was an abstract one, and when a suitable vocabulary was sought, some turned for inspiration to the Japanese garden, albeit with an objectivity lacking in their Edwardian predecessors.[64] By the time of his death in 1935 much of what Robinson had fought for had gained acceptance. 'Modern landscape design has sprung from the Robinson period', enthused Geoffrey Jellicoe in 1954. 'He heralded a return-

to-nature movement and we cannot help feeling that he is, again, the basis of the modern way of thought in that regard...[Blomfield] has passed out of history, while Robinson is there to stay.'[65]

But questions of economy and style were not the only factors behind this shift to naturalism. In 1928 the British Association of Garden Architects was formed, soon changing its title, following American example, to the Institute of Landscape Architects, with Thomas Mawson, who had for some time practised under the style of landscape architect, agreeing to be its first President.[66] Leading members of the new Institute during the formative years included architects with a strong interest in garden design such as Romaine-Walker's partner Gilbert H. Jenkins, E. Prentice Mawson, Barry Parker of Letchworth Garden City fame, Oliver Hill, and the young Geoffrey A. Jellicoe, who became President in 1939.[67] Landscape design was represented by Edward White,[68] Madeline Agar[69] and her pupil Brenda Colvin, and Sylvia Crowe, who later worked in White's office. There were also significant links with the broader issues of town planning, Thomas Adams (President of the I.L.A. in 1937–9) having been the founder and first President in 1909 of the Town Planning Institute, followed by Thomas Mawson in 1923 and Parker in 1929.

In spring 1934 a new quarterly, *Landscape and Garden*, was launched, issued under the auspices of the Institute of Landscape Architects, and edited by the landscape gardener, Richard Sudell (1900–1968).[70] The first issue included an article on Gravetye by Maud Haworth Booth, who described the ninety-six-year-old Robinson as, 'the man who has re-made the entire English garden, turning it from the stereotyped lack lustre of the Early Victorians into a thing of nature beautified'. In its brief life up to the Second World War, the new journal contained a mixed bag of articles; historic gardens were mainly limited to examples abroad, the emphasis in this country being on new gardens, including Tunnard's Bentley. In format and content the journal reflected the modernist cause, a further instance of the increasing importance of taste and of the power of publishers to influence it. Whereas nineteenth-century periodicals in general, and horticultural journals in particular, gave a representative picture of what was actually being done at the time, *Landscape and Garden*, like the *Architectural Review*, adopted a more partisan approach, aiming to convert a sector of the public from historicism to modern design. More importantly, it set out to establish garden and landscape design as a profession in its own right, and to explore wider fields for the landscape architect. Yet another specialist path was thereby opened up.

Since the seventeenth century the pendulum of fashion had swung between the Renaissance garden, the Landscape School, the Victorian garden, the Robinsonian garden, the Blomfield formal revival and modern landscape design, each time favouring either garden architect or landscape gardener. Now it had come to rest at a new discipline, landscape architecture, which sought to encompass both roles; but this was at the expense of a growing separation not only from architecture, which had played a major part in its foundation, but also from the time-honoured occupation of gardening itself.

Notes

Where the names of authors are in capitals, see Bibliography for full details.

Introduction

1. Henry James, *The Portrait of a Lady*, 1881, beginning of Chapter 1.
2. M.E. Edes and D. Frasier (eds), *The Age of Extravagance*, Weidenfeld and Nicolson, 1955; see also S. Hynes, *The Edwardian Turn of Mind*, Princeton U.P., 1968.
3. I am grateful to Andrew Jacobs for guidance on the economics of the period.
4. In 1903 at Weston Park, Shropshire, the sixteen gardeners worked a fifty-one-hour week for wages ranging from 3s. 4d. to 2s. 4d. a day. See BINNEY and HILLS 1979, 29–30.
5. Edes and Frasier, *op.cit.*, 253.
6. *CL*, 12 November 1987, 170–71.
7. See Jan Marsh, *Back to the Land*, Quartet, 1982; Rosemary Treble, 'Victorian Painting' in G.E. Mingay (ed.), *The Victorian Countryside*, Routledge and Kegan Paul, 1981.
8. SEDDING 1895, 176.
9. N. Pevsner, *The Englishness of English Art*, Architectural Press, 1955, 163.
10. *CL*, 4 May 1901, 560–67; *GC*, 12 May 1956, 524–25. Sedgwick Park (1886 by George and Peto) was bought by Lord Rotherwick in 1947.
11. *CL*, 14 August 1909, 228.

1 The Formal Garden Revival

1. THOMAS 1896.
2. Reginald Blomfield was born in 1856, son of the Reverend G.J. Blomfield. He was a scholar of Exeter College, Oxford, then trained with his uncle, Sir Arthur Blomfield, a well-established ecclesiastical architect, before setting up practice in 1884; see FELLOWS 1985.
3. A charming early example of his Arts and Crafts phase is 20 Buckingham Gate, Westminster (1887) (see *The Builder*, 8 August 1896, 116) with its terracotta frieze by Henry Pegram (1862–1937). In 1895 Blomfield resigned in high dudgeon as Secretary of the AWG and ceased to be a member in 1903.
4. BLOMFIELD 1901. The subject was first explored by Blomfield in an article 'On Gardens', *Portfolio*, December 1889, 231–37.
5. H.E. Milner, *The Art and Practice of Landscape Gardening*, 1890, 2. Henry Ernest Milner (1845–1906) was the son of the Victorian gardener, Edward Milner. Nature was his 'great exemplar', although he included plans for formal parterres adjacent to the house.
6. *Ibid.*, 35.
7. BLOMFIELD 1901, 9.
8. *Ibid.*, 11–15. Goethe expressed the opposite view when he wrote, 'No one feels himself easy in a garden

which does not look like the open country', *Elective Affinities*, 1809, Book 2, Chapter 8.
9. BLOMFIELD 1901, 233. The turf had not always been 'close-shaven'. As Richard Bisgrove points out, 'The biggest stimulus to the development of the Edwardian lawn was the advance in lawn-mowers', *CL*, 15 and 22 May 1986.
10. BLOMFIELD 1901, 1.
11. *Ibid.*, 20.
12. Geoffrey Taylor, *Some Nineteenth-Century Gardeners*, Skeffington, 1951, 69. See Chapter 4 for a fuller discussion of Robinson.
13. SEDDING 1895, 157.
14. Taylor, *op. cit.*, 101.
15. ROBINSON 1892, ix.
16. *Ibid.*, x.
17. ROBINSON 1898, 20.
18. *Ibid.*, 31.
19. TIPPING 1925, 1xii.
20. See Brent Elliott, 'Mosaiculture', *GH*, Vol. 9, No. 1, 1981, 76–98.
21. William Morris, 'Making the Best of it', lecture given at Birmingham, published in *Hopes and Fears for Art*, Ellis and White, 1882.
22. Richard Gorer, 'The Victorian who said it all', *CL*, 13 March 1980, 750–51.
23. ELLIOTT 1985, 214–17.
24. The garden work was carried out by Paxton's assistant and protégé, Edward Milner (1819–84); see Alison Hodges, 'A Victorian Gardener: Edward Milner', *GH*, Vol. 5, No. 3, 1977.
25. ROBINSON 1883, iv.
26. Brent Elliott, 'Master of the Geometric Art', *G*, Vol. 106, December 1981, 488–91; ELLIOTT 1986, 140–43.
27. ROBINSON 1892, ix.
28. ROBINSON 1898, 14. For Witley Court see also ELLIOTT 1986, 144.
29. Alfred Barry, *The Life and Works of Sir Charles Barry*, John Murray, 1867, 113–19.
30. Trentham Hall was destroyed by fire in 1910 but the terraces are preserved as a public park. An earlier example of the nineteenth-century Italianate revival was the Italian Garden at Wilton. Laid out in the 1820s by Sir Richard Westmacott, it partly made up for the loss of Isaac de Caux's immense gardens of 1633 which were swept away in the 1730s. A plan by A.H. Cox is included in R.S. Nichols, *English Pleasure Gardens*, Macmillan, 1902, 234.
31. ROBINSON 1903, 78–86; see also ROBINSON 1898, 32, 51; ELLIOTT 1986, 77–78.
32. ROBINSON 1883, vi. Shrubland Hall is now a Health Clinic and the grounds are well maintained.
33. BLOMFIELD 1901, 16–17.
34. W. Kennet, *Antiquities of Ambrosden and Other Places*

in Oxfordshire and Buckinghamshire, 1695. The former manor house of c.1670 was rebuilt in about 1740 and demolished in 1768; see J. Sherwood and N. Pevsner, *The Buildings of England, Oxfordshire*, Penguin Books, 1974, 422.
35. ROBINSON 1903, 78.
36. *Ibid.*, 81.
37. ROBINSON 1892, 25.
38. ROBINSON 1903, 80.
39. William Lawson, *A New Orchard and Garden*, 1618.
40. See quote from James Dallaway in Peter Hunt (ed.), *The Shell Gardens Book*, Phoenix House, 1964, 44.
41. Edward Kemp, *How to Lay Out a Garden*, 1850, 39, 91–117. Kemp's book was re-issued in new editions in 1858 and 1864, and included plans of model gardens and advice on planting. (In 1874, Leslie Stephen wrote, 'Pope...was one of the first...to break through the old formal school of gardening', *Hours in a Library*, Vol. 1, 1892 edn, 120).
42. See Mrs Kegan Paul, 'Old-Fashioned Gardening', *The Nineteenth Century*, January 1880, 128–35.
43. BLOMFIELD 1901, 1.
44. ROBINSON 1892, 16.
45. *Ibid.*, xii. At Batsford, Robinson was probably interested mainly in the wild gardens taking shape under the direction of its owner, A.B. Freeman-Mitford (see Chapter 4 below).
46. ROBINSON 1898, 49–51. The terraces were probably constructed by the Dutch Earls of Rochford during the exile of the Powis family in 1690–1722, although possibly begun by William Winde in the 1680s. See *JRHS*, October 1962, 438–46.
47. ROBINSON 1898, 312 and plan; see also E.T. Cook and B. Parsons, *Gardens of England*, A. and C. Black, 1908, pl. 20. Golder's Hill was Anna Pavlova's home in the 1920s.
48. ROBINSON 1898, 24.
49. BLOMFIELD 1932, 61.
50. John Newman, *The Buildings of England, North East and East Kent*, Penguin Books, 1969, 488. See also *CL*, 24 and 31 July, 7 August 1969. After a fire in 1903 the mansion of 1762 was rebuilt incorporating the old portico. E.R. Barrow (1869–1948) was the architect. Most of the statues and urns date from the mid-nineteenth century. I am grateful to Mrs J. Loudon for help on Olantigh.
51. ASLET 1982, 134–40.
52. Manderston is one of the grandest and most elaborate Edwardian gardens surviving in Britain today; see *CL*, 29 May 1969, 1354–56.
53. See Chapter 7 for discussion of the influence of this movement on the revival of the Italian Renaissance garden.
54. For this 'golden age of architectural publishing' see

ASLET 1982, 129.

55. Tribute by Professor A.E. Richardson in *JRIBA*, January 1943, 65–67. Richardson singles out for praise Blomfield's scholarship rather than his buildings. Blomfield's essays published by the Arts and Crafts Exhibition Society included 'Public Spaces, Parks and Gardens', 1896, and 'The English Tradition', 1893, but his major writings were *A History of Renaissance Architecture in England* (1897), *The Mistress Art* (1908), *A History of French Architecture* (1911, 1920) and *Life of R. Norman Shaw* (1940).

56. BLOMFIELD 1901, 169.

57. C.H. Reilly, *Representative British Architects of the Present Day*, 1931, 58. For further discussion of the limitations of Blomfield's book see ELLIOTT 1986, 197–99, 226–27.

58. Pliny the Younger, *Letters*, translated by W. Melmoth, Harvard U.P., 1940, Vol. 1, 381–83.

59. L.B. Alberti, *De Re Aedificatoria*, 1452, first published in Florence in 1485, English translation by Leoni, 1726.

60. BLOMFIELD 1901, 45. Markham and Lawson were experienced gardeners and the first important garden writers, but, says Blomfield, 'they were evidently familiar with the accepted methods of garden design'. Unlike his nineteenth-century counterpart, the 'English gentlemen from the sixteenth to the eighteenth century did possess a general traditional knowledge of design and of the principles which govern it' (p. 52). For recent research into the identity of William Lawson (1553–1635), see John Harvey, 'William Lawson and his Orchard', *CL*, 28 October 1982.

61. For the romantic vision of the lost gardens of England up to the Civil War, see Roy Strong, *The Renaissance Garden in England*, Thames and Hudson, 1979, 11–13. For Hardwick, see GIROUARD 1977, 157; also *CL*, 27 November 1986, 1736–38. One of the few old formal gardens mentioned by Blomfield which had survived was Melbourne Hall, Derbyshire, where the gardens were remodelled by Henry Wise (1704–11), see *CL*, 23 September 1899, 368–73. Blomfield would probably have approved of recent restorations of seventeenth-century gardens by the National Trust, including the canal garden at Westbury Court, Gloucestershire, created between 1696 and 1705 by Maynard Colchester; also the formal gardens at Ham House dating from 1672; see *CL*, 9 October 1975, 902–3.

62. Blomfield's illustration of Badminton (c.1691) by De Caux, is similar to that prepared for Kip's *Britannia Illustrata*, 1709. Blomfield describes this book, together with Badeslade's *Views of Kent* (1720) and James Beeverell's *Les Délices de la Grande Bretagne* (1727) as 'almost the only sources of information available' on the great schemes of the late seventeenth century (p.62).

63. BLOMFIELD 1901, 82.

64. *Ibid.*, 85. Repton had implied a criticism of Blomfield's beloved Wren when he remarked in his *Landscape Gardening* (1803), 'The motley appearance of red bricks with white stone, by breaking the unity of effect, will often destroy the magnificence of the most splendid compositions'. He recommended covering bricks with plaster and stone colour.

65. H.H. Statham, 'Formal and Landscape Gardening', *Edinburgh Review*, Vol. 176, July 1892, 174–208, a review of Sedding, Blomfield and Milner. Henry Heathcote Statham (1839–1924) was editor of *The Builder* from 1883 to 1908, and a champion of the French school. He is remembered most for his *A Short Critical History of Architecture* (1912). See obituaries: *The Builder*, 6 June 1924; *JRIBA*, 28 June 1924.

66. Statham, *op. cit.*, 205–8, 185.

67. F. Inigo Thomas, 'Gardens', *JRIBA*, 12 June 1926, 431–39. In the 1850s and '60s W.B. Thomas's work was predominantly formal but in the early '70s he created lakes and rockwork in the natural manner, e.g., at Sandringham (see Chapter 4). See also ELLIOTT 1986, 147.

68. The Reverend Charles Edward Thomas (1823–1901) was the fifth son of Inigo Freeman Thomas (1767–1847) of Ratton, near Eastbourne, and Frances Ann Brodrick. Francis Inigo Thomas's mother, Georgiana (1828–1921) was a daughter of Col. Hon. Henry Hely-Hutchinson (see also Chapter 7, note 19). Thomas's eldest brother, William Henry Battie-Wrightson (1855–1903), married in 1884 Lady Isabella Cecil, eldest daughter of the 3rd Marquess of Exeter. Their aunt, Georgiana, daughter of Inigo Thomas of Ratton, married a Battie-Wrightson in the 1820s, and in 1891 William Henry inherited the entire Cusworth estates and assumed the name of Battie-Wrightson. For information on Thomas I am grateful to the following: Angus Macnaghten, whose great-grandfather, Revd Arthur Thomas (b.1816) was Thomas's uncle; Major Reginald Brodrick Freeman-Thomas, a nephew of Thomas; W.H. Gordon–Smith, Agent and Trustee (Cusworth Estate); Christopher Whittick, East Sussex Records Office, Lewes.

69. Ashbee included Thomas in his account of the 'curious lot' in Bodley's office in December 1886. See A. Crawford, *C.R. Ashbee*, Yale U.P., 1986, 23–24.

70. 'Notes on Bodley by J.N. Comper', c.1940–5, in the possession of Anthony Symondson, to whom, together with Peter Howell, I am indebted for help with Thomas. St Wilfrid, Hickleton, not far from Thomas's birthplace at Warmsworth, was restored by Bodley for the 2nd Viscount Halifax (1839–1934) (being rebuilt in 1987). It had beautiful furniture by both Bodley and Comper. Thomas laid out gardens for Lord Halifax in the early 1890s at the Georgian mansion, Hickleton Hall, but few records survive in the Halifax archive. The Halifax summer residence, Garrowby Hall (1892–3), was designed by Walter Tower, (see *CL*, 5 August 1949, 394–97). Thomas's gardens at Ufford Place, Suffolk, have disappeared along with the house which was demolished in the 1950s.

71. *CL*, 6 December 1902, 732–41; ELLIOTT 1986, 224. Hewell Grange was subsequently a Remand School and the gardens were much simplified; see BINNEY and HILLS 1979, 28–29.

72. Thomas Garner (1893–1906) was Bodley's partner from 1869 to 1898 and was mainly responsible for the domestic work. He laid out a terraced garden at Moreton, Prospect Place, Hampstead (1896). Bodley restored St Donat's Castle, Glamorgan, in 1901–7 and laid out an elaborate terraced garden.

73. Thomas was elected to the AWG in 1891 and served on the committee, 1902–4. In 1892–3 he was on the committee of Ashbee's School of Handicraft and several designs by him are in the 'Guild Workshop Record Book' at the Victoria and Albert Museum. I am grateful to Alan Crawford for pointing out entries on Thomas in Ashbee's journals. There is a chalk drawing by Thomas of his cousin, the composer Arthur Goring Thomas (1850–92), at the National Portrait Gallery (NPG 1316).

74. See entry in U. Thieme and F. Becker, *Allgemeines Lexicon der Bildenden Künstler von der Antike bis zur Gegenwart*, Wilhelm Engelmann, 1907, rev. 1951, 61. Thomas had a successful exhibition of his paintings in London in 1930, also shown at the Art Gallery and Museum, Doncaster.

75. He travelled by donkey from Rome to Frascati and fell in with brigands between Bagnaia and Caprarola. His book was abandoned but in his 1926 paper (see note 67 above) he praised Shepherd and Jellicoe's *Italian Gardens of the Renaissance* published the previous year.

76. THOMAS 1896.

77. Given on 4 November 1898. Talks followed by M. Macartney and J.A. Gotch; Alfred Parsons and E.S. Prior also spoke. From AWG Minutes provided by Desmond Mandeville.

78. Ashbee Journals, King's College, Cambridge, 8 April 1902.

79. Thomas's ashes were buried in the same grave as his brother and sister, George Pelham Thomas and Frederica Georgiana Frances Thomas, in Putney Cemetery. His house in Mulberry Walk was left to his nephew and the contents were sold including his portrait.

80. Ashbee Journals, 26 November 1914. In the catalogue of the exhibition of fifty-one of Thomas's paintings at Doncaster, 6 March–27 April 1930, entitled 'The Spell of England', the foreword states, 'During the second year of the Great War he was dispatched on a mission to Russia, and in the following year to Scandinavia, Holland and Spain. From then until 1928 he acted as liaison between the Federation of British Industries and Government Departments.' I am grateful to J. Barwick for providing a copy of this catelogue.

81. As note 67 above.

82. Edwin Lutyens to Lady Emily Lutyens, 26 July 1934, BALMC.

83. Ratton was sold in 1918 and a copy of the sales particulars are held at the East Sussex Record Office.

84. A. Cart de Lafontaine, F.S.A. (d.1944) was born in Hampstead and educated at Balliol. In 1918 he sold Athelhampton to George Cockrane, and in 1957 it was acquired by Robert V. Cooke, F.R.C.S., father of the recent owner, the late Sir Robert Cooke (1930–87), for whose help and enthusiasm regarding the garden I am especially grateful.

85. The house includes an excellent example of a late fifteenth-century hall with mid-sixteenth-century wing added at an angle to the west. It was illustrated in that influential but romantic evocation of the Middle Ages, Joseph Nash's *Mansions of England in the Olden Time*, 1849. In about 1910, Thomas Mawson prepared a scheme of alterations to the drive (unexecuted); see MAWSON 1912, fig. 86. For general descriptions of Athelhampton see *CL*, 2 September 1899, 272–78; 2 and 23 June 1906; 10, 17 and 24 May 1984.

86. THOMAS 1896, 105.

87. *Ibid.*, 135.

88. Perhaps Robinson had also got wind of the proposed yew pyramids, for he included a plate of Athelhampton Hall in his *Garden Design and Architects' Gardens*, p. 26, with the caption, 'Old English house with trees in their natural form'. There are similar pyramidal yews at Renishaw in which Thomas may have had a hand.

89. The original fifteenth-century, timber-framed house at Brickwall was enlarged in the late sixteenth or early seventeenth century. In 1666 it was bought by Stephen Frewen, and later in the century the back and sides were encased in brick by Sir Edward Frewen. In 1872 George Devey remodelled the garden front and rebuilt the east wing. Nathaniel Lloyd illustrated the 'Avenue of tetrahedrons at Brickwall' in his *Garden Craftsmanship in Yew and Box* (1925), pl. 31, estimating that they were planted 'about two hundred years ago'. A plan of the gardens is included in TRIGGS 1902. See also *CL*, 29 September 1900.

90. Both house and church were drastically restored in the 1880s.

91. See Rose Standish Nichols, *English Pleasure Gardens*, Macmillan, New York, 1902, 290–91; *CL*, 18 January 1902, 80–87. Barrow Court was leased to a College of Education until about 1974 when it was sold by the Gibbs family and divided into separate dwellings by the Barrow Court Residents Association who have maintained the grounds remarkably well.

92. *CL*, 14 August 1909, 228–36, partly reprinted in

TIPPING 1925, 315–18. An aerial view of Rotherfield was exhibited at the Royal Academy, London, in 1898, see *Academy Architecture*, 1898, Vol. 2, 20. The Sussex Historic Garden Restoration Society has a project for restoring part of the gardens.

93. The house was originally named Ffynnonau, meaning 'springs'. It remained in the Colby family until 1923. Haverfordwest Library holds a photograph album for Ffynnone produced in 1871 by Charles Smith Allen of Tredegar House, Tenby. I am grateful to the present owner for information on Ffynnone, also to Sally Moss, Assistant Curator, Carmarthen Museum; Peter Howell; and Wyn Jones, FRIBA, for notes on the history of the house (1977). See also P. Howell and E. Beazley, *Companion Guide to South Wales*, Collins, 1977, 87–88.

94. For a general article on Drakelow see *CL*, 16 March 1907, 378–84. Thomas's terrace is illustrated in HOLME 1908, pls 47–51. Thomas prepared additional schemes by the river (unexecuted), see *JRIBA*, 12 June 1926, 430. Blomfield also did work to the gardens, c.1906–12. The house was demolished before 1953.

95. In 1699 Chantmarle passed to the Oglander family who also succeeded to Parnham, near Beaminster, Dorset, in 1776. Parnham dates from 1554 and was bought from the Oglanders in 1896 by Vincent Robinson. In 1910 it was acquired by Dr Hans Sauer who landscaped the grounds and extended the formal gardens, adding the entrance forecourt, the south terrace with its corner rotundas (another reference to Montacute), and the lower terraces with their fifty clipped, conical yews and central water channel. This work bears the stamp of Inigo Thomas but has not been investigated by the author. The Oglander family seat was at Nunwell, near Brading, Isle of Wight; see *CL*, 19 and 26 February 1976, 402–5, 470–73. Parnham was bought by John Makepeace in 1976 and is now a School for Craftsmen in Wood. I am grateful to Mrs Makepeace for information on the garden.

96. The BALDC has measured drawings of Montacute by R. Shackleton Balfour, dated August 1894 and including a plan of the sunk garden.

97. See article by Arthur Oswald, *CL*, 30 June 1950, 1966–71, and 7 July 1950, 46–51. In 1919 Chantmarle was bought by C.H. St John Hornby who extended the gardens and made further alterations to the house with Edward Warren as his architect. Since 1951 Chantmarle has been a Police Training Centre and is immaculately maintained. I am grateful to Commandant G.S. Elliott for his assistance.

98. THOMAS 1896.

99. Thomas's plan is in the possession of the present owner, J. Mosesson, to whom I am grateful for information on Otley Hall. See also G. Moore, 'About the Garden at Otley Hall', privately printed, 1988. Otley Hall is open to the public on certain days of the year.

100. BLOMFIELD 1932, 60.

101. Blomfield's early gardens are illustrated in FELLOWS 1985. Caythorpe is now an Agricultural College. At Brocklesby part of the house has been demolished but most gardens remain.

102. *CL*, 20 and 27 March 1909, 414–23, 450–59; BINNEY and HILLS 1979, 20. Apethorpe was a school up to 1982.

103. BLOMFIELD 1901, 88.

104. There were no trees near the house, only parts of the shrubberies to the south-west planted by Driver who 'improved' the park at the end of the eighteenth century.

105. *CL*, 11 May 1907, 666–73; Tom Wright, *The Gardens of Britain: 4*, Batsford, 1978, 40–43. In 1916 Blomfield prepared designs for the Italian Garden next to the walled kitchen garden but this was modified in execution. It includes a central canal and delightful *Wisteria*-

clad Tuscan colonnade. I am grateful to the owner, Alan Wyndham Green, for information on Godinton.

106. *CL*, 12 March 1910, 378–85; Allen Paterson, *The Gardens of Britain: 2*, Batsford, 1978, 126–28. I am grateful to the owner, M.P. Andreae, for permission to visit this beautifully maintained garden.

107. BLOMFIELD 1932, 83.

108. BALDC. Illustrated in *The Builder*, 15 September 1911, 302 and plate; see also G. Stamp, *The Great Perspectivists*, RIBA Drawings Series, Trefoil, 1982. In 1912 Adrian Berrington produced an equally stunning perspective of the entrance forecourt of Blomfield's La Manoire de la Trinité, Jersey. Built in 1910–13 for Athelstan Riley, it includes a garden enclosed by pleached hornbeam leading to a canal; see article by Marcus Binney, *CL*, 7 August 1986, 420–25.

109. *CL*, 28 August 1958, 416–19; 4 September 1958, 476–79.

110. *Guidebook to Mellerstain*, Pilgrim Press, 1980, 13. I am grateful to the curator at Mellerstain for making available copies of old maps, including one dated 1765 showing the position of the canal.

111. BLOMFIELD 1901, 148–49.

112. Milner, *op. cit.*, 7.

113. Uvedale Price, *On the Decorations near the House*, 1794.

114. Quoted in Statham, *op. cit.*, 206–7.

2 Sedding and Garden-Craft

1. SEDDING 1895, vi.

2. Ibid., 127, 179, 167–69.

3. Edmund Sedding (1836–68) was also a musician and published carols and other music (see *DNB*). He was considered to be the more gifted of the two Sedding brothers but suffered from ill-health. In 1858 Philip Webb was chief assistant at Street's office but left the following year to build Red House for Morris. Webb was replaced by Norman Shaw.

4. According to W.R. Lethaby, 'Sedding soon developed views rather a reaction from than a direct result of the teaching, and devoted himself to a study of the later types of our Gothic, found in the village churches, the especial Englishness and home-wrought intimacy of which appealed to his regard.' See 'A Note on the Artistic Life and Work of John D. Sedding', *The Builder*, 10 October 1891, 270–71.

5. J. Paul Cooper, assisted by H. Wilson, 'The work of John D. Sedding', *AR*, Vol. 3, December 1897–May 1898, reprinted in Alastair Service, *Edwardian Architecture and its Origins*, Architectural Press, 1975. John Paul Cooper (1869–1933), architect, silversmith and jeweller, was articled to Sedding and then to Henry Wilson. He took up metalwork in 1897 and revived the use of shagreen.

6. Cooper, *loc. cit.*

7. SEDDING 1895, xxiii–xxiv. Sedding was sidesman (from 1878) then churchwarden (1883–9) at St Alban's, Holborn, a centre of Anglo-Catholicism. Sedding's death, of influenza on 7 April 1891 at Winsford Vicarage, Somerset, was followed a few days later by that of his wife, Rose. They were buried together in the churchyard of St John the Baptist, West Wickham. Among Rose Sedding's papers were found the seventeenth-century lines, 'Tis fit one flesh one house should have, one tomb, one epitaph, one grave'.

8. J. Ruskin, 'The Poetry of Architecture', first published in *The Architectural Magazine* (1837–8); see E.T. Cook and A. Wedderburn (eds), *The Works of Ruskin*, 1903, Vol. 1, 156–57.

9. E.F. Russell in SEDDING 1895, xi.

10. Lethaby, *op. cit.* Sedding contributed an essay on embroidery in *Essays by Members of the Arts and Crafts Exhibition Society*, 1893, 405–13.

11. W. Morris, *Works* (1910–14), Vol. 1, 151; first published in the *Oxford and Cambridge Magazine*, 1856; See also M. Batey, *Oxford Gardens*, Avebury, 1982, 174.

12. *Lilies* (1868) by Frederick Walker, was bought by William Graham, patron of the PRB. Lilies were also a favourite subject of J. Atkinson Grimshaw (1836–97); witness his *The Rector's Garden: Queen of the Lilies*, painted near Scarborough in 1877.

13. William Morris, 'Making the Best of it', in *Hopes and Fears for Art*, Ellis and White, 1882.

14. For Devey, see obituary in *The Builder*, 1886, 728; GIROUARD 1971, 103–7; A. Saint, *Richard Norman Shaw*, Yale U.P. 1976, 25–26; W.H. Godfrey in JRIBA, 29 September 1906, 501–25.

15. BLOMFIELD 1901, 229. According to Blomfield 'The garden of Penshurst was laid out by Lord Delisle personally—George Devey only designed the fountain at the end of the terrace' (p. 92). See also R.S. Nichols, *English Pleasure Gardens*, Macmillan, 1902, 99–100, plan opp. p. 96; T. Wright, *The Gardens of Britain: 4*, Batsford, 1978, 78–84.

16. For Rossetti on Northiam, see O. Doughty and J.R. Wahl (eds) *Letters of Dante Gabriel Rossetti*, Vol. 2, 1861–1870, Oxford, 1965, 609, 611. See also GIROUARD 1977, 152–59.

17. Thackeray built a house in a jejune version of the true Queen Anne style in Palace Green, Kensington (1861). See Elizabeth Aslin, *The Aesthetic Movement*, Elek, 1969.

18. For discussion of the 'Old-fashioned Garden' see GIROUARD 1977, 152–59; ELLIOTT 1986, 162–65; also Diana Baskervyle-Glegg, 'The Art of Beatrice Parsons (1870–1955)', *CL*, 19 March 1987, 68–70.

19. N. Pevsner, 'Kinmel Park', *AR*, March 1942; GIROUARD 1971, 137–40; *CL*, 16 and 23 March 1978. Kinmel was gutted by fire in 1975. For Bodrhyddan see *CL*, 20 and 27 July 1978. A letter from W.E. Nesfield to William Walker, dated 3 April 1876, regarding the grounds of Lea Wood, near Matlock, shows him working closely with his father. Information kindly provided by Andrew Saint.

20. I am grateful to the present owner, Sir Stephen Lycett Green, Bt, CBE, for pointing out that as Ken Hill was used only in the winter months extensive gardens were not required.

21. A bust of Sedding (at the AWG) by H.R. Pinker was completed in 1891. The AWG developed from the St George's Art Society (1883–86), which was founded by W.R. Lethaby (1857–1931), E.S. Prior (1852–1932), M. Macartney (1853–1932) and E. Newton (1856–1922), all assistants of Norman Shaw.

22. BLOMFIELD 1932, 60.

23. SEDDING 1895, 131.

24. Ibid., 129.

25. ROBINSON 1892, 67.

26. Ruskin, *op. cit.*, 155–56.

27. Alicia Amherst, *A History of Gardening in England*, Bernard Quaritch, 1895, 313. For a brief contemporary history of topiary in this country see, Charles H. Curtis and W. Gibson, *The Book of Topiary*, John Lane: The Bodley Head, 1904; see also ELLIOTT 1986, 118–21, 222–24.

28. HOLME 1908, pls 43 and 44. The topiary was removed in 1980.

29. SEDDING 1895, 180.

30. ROBINSON 1892, 73. Robinson pursued his attack on topiary in *The English Flower Garden*, 298–304.

31. The clipping of trees into representational forms had become one of Robinson's anathemas, although in his first book, *Gleanings from French Gardens* (1868), he had enthused over the beauty of the peach trees at Montreuil, grown to represent the owner's name, 'LEPERE' (pp. 188–90). In 1903 Lutyens waggishly

proposed to Blomfield that a statue of Robinson should be cut in yew 'as a monument to all he has done for gardening.' Letter to Lady Emily Lutyens, 24 August 1903, BALMC.

32. SEDDING 1895, 29–30.
33. Walter Butler, 'Garden Design in Relation to Architecture', Royal Victorian Institute of Architects, 30 June 1903, Melbourne, quoted in Marilyn McBriar, 'Formal or Natural Gardens for Australia? : An Edwardian Discussion', *Australian Garden History Society Newsletter*, No. 2, 1981. I am grateful to Peter Watts for bringing this article to my attention. See also Chapter 7 for reference to Walter Butler's work.
34. Written in the 1460s, first printed in Venice 1499, French translation 1554, published as a Gregg facsimile 1969. See Kenneth Woodbridge, *Princely Gardens*, Thames and Hudson, 1986, 23.
35. R. Blomfield, 'W.R. Lethaby: An Impression and a Tribute', *JRIBA*, 20 February 1932.
36. S. Backemeyer and T. Gronberg (eds), *W.R. Lethaby: Architecture, Design and Education*, Lund Humphries, 1984, 81. See also comments by May Morris in *JRIBA*, 20 February 1932, 303.
37. SEDDING 1895, 66–67; the quotation is from Lowell's 'Ode to Fielding'. These passages were quoted by C.R. Ashbee in *Reminiscences of Masters of the AWG, 1886–1934*, in AWG Library.
38. SEDDING 1895, 114, 118.
39. *Ibid.*, 135.
40. *Ibid.*, 134.
41. ROBINSON 1898, 26.
42. BLOMFIELD 1932, 91–94; see also L. Weaver, *Small Country Houses: Their Repair and Enlargement*, Country Life, 1914, 182–87.
43. Humphry Repton, *Designs for the Pavillion at Brighton*, 1808.
44. SEDDING 1895, 162–63, 180, 181–82.
45. The seventeenth-century Highnam Court, Churcham, near Gloucester, was the home from 1838 of the painter and philanthropist, Thomas Gambier Parry (1816–88), inventor of the 'spirit fresco' process and father of the composer, Sir Charles Hubert Hastings Parry (1848–1918) and the architect Sidney Gambier Parry. The gardens included a yew avenue, elaborate parterres, rock gardens with caves and grottoes, a winter garden and an early *pinetum*. The rockwork, dating from 1847, was by James Pulham; see *GH*, Vol. 12, No. 2, 1984 (see also Chapter 4 below). The gardens were illustrated in *CL*, 1 April 1899, 400–4; 7 November 1903, 644–46. See also *Garden History Society Newsletter*, No. 13, 1985, 12; *CL*, 8 October 1987, 102–3.
46. SEDDING 1895, 148–49.
47. Anna Pavord, *Observer Colour Supplement*, 13 April 1986, 39.
48. SEDDING 1895, 168–71.
49. *GC*, 9 April 1898, 217, 219. Sir John Gardner Wilkinson (1797–1875) was an Egyptologist. The full title of his book was, *On Colour and the Necessity for a General Diffusion of Taste among all Classes*; see ELLIOTT 1986, 126–27.
50. Cooper, *loc. cit.* The Downes is now a Home for Nursing Sisters, The Daughters of the Cross, within St Michael's Hospital. The parterre has been replaced by lawns. There is a fine church by Sedding at Hayle (1886). I am grateful to Graham Daw for help with The Downes.
51. MALINS and BOWE 1980, 153–55. See also *CL*, 23 May 1974, 1262–64. The house was gutted by fire in 1913 and the site redeveloped in 1956 but photographs made in the 1890s by the firm of W. Lawrence are preserved at the National Library of Ireland.
52. Russell, *loc. cit.*, xvii.
53. *Ibid.*, xviii.
54. JEKYLL 1896, 178–79.
55. *Ibid.*, 184.
56. They probably met through their common interest in Byzantine work, although Rowand Anderson was rebuilding Mount Stuart for Lord Bute when Schultz was in his office. For a more detailed study of Schultz see, David Ottewill, 'Robert Weir Schultz (1860–1951): An Arts and Crafts Architect', *Architectural History*, Vol. 22, 1979; also, Gavin Stamp, *Robert Weir Schultz, Architect, and his work for the Marquesses of Bute*, Mount Stuart, 1981.
57. J. Mordaunt Crook, 'Villas of Regent's Park', *CL*, 4 and 11 July 1968; see also the same author's 'Patron Extraordinary: John, 3rd Marquess of Bute', *Victorian South Wales—Architecture, Industry and Society*, Victorian Society, 1969.
58. See Fiona Pearson, *Goscombe John at the National Museum of Wales*, exhibition catalogue, Cardiff, 1979, 12. A bronze cast of the statue is at the Cardiff National Museum but the original was removed to a site as yet unknown.
59. The garden furniture was probably made in Bute's Cardiff workshops.
60. F.W.H. Myers (1843–1901), Founder of the Society for Psychical Research: obituary notice, *Journal of the Society for Psychical Research*, November 1900. In 1916, when the lease expired, the Dowager Lady Bute moved to Mansfield Street, St Marylebone. Later the house was occupied by the Institute of Archaeology, and the chapel and extra library were destroyed. From 1969 to 1982 it housed the classics and history departments of Bedford College. In 1930 the land reverted to the Crown and the gardens were subsequently altered as part of the public park. The statue of St John the Baptist was replaced by a bronze group, 'Hylas', by Henry Pegram, R.A. (1862–1937), presented by the Royal Academy of Arts through the Leighton Fund, 1933. A bronze figure by C.E. Hartwell was placed on the north side of the fountain garden. Buildings have been erected on the site of the old rose garden.
61. Quoted in David Hunter Blair, *John Patrick, Third Marquess of Bute*, John Murray, 1921, 171.
62. SEDDING 1895, 163.

3   The Scottish Pleasaunce

1. SCOTT 1828, 307.
2. For a general survey of the history of garden design in Scotland see BROGDEN 1981.
3. SCOTT 1828, 309.
4. Sir Walter Scott, introduction to *Quentin Durward*, 1823, xxxix–xl. In this novel, set in fifteenth-century France, 'Scott rises to new and hitherto unexplored heights of horror'; see Christina Keith, *The Author of Waverley*, Robert Hale, 1964, 53. Scott's own efforts at garden design and, especially, architecture were influential though 'antiquarian rather than artistic' (ELLIOTT 1986, 67). To Ruskin, Abbotsford was the 'incongruous pile', and Dean Stanley described it as 'a place to be visited once and never again'; Hunter Blair, *A New Medley of Memories*, 1922, 53.
5. SCOTT 1828, 310.
6. The garden has grass cross-walks enclosed on the north-south axis by yew hedges and to east and west of a central fountain by a pergola of iron hoops. It was laid out by Lord and Lady Haddington in conjunction with their head gardener Robert Pace Brotherston (1848–1923), best known for his *The Book of Cut Flowers* (1906). See T. Hinde, *Stately Gardens of Britain*, Ebury, 1983; *CL*, 22 October 1987, 80–83. The gardens of both Mellerstain and Tyninghame were embellished from the 1950s with additional planting, especially of old roses, by Lady Haddington.
7. W. Douglas-Simpson, *Edzell Castle*, H.M.S.O., 1952.
8. J.E. Robson, 'Gardens of the National Trust for Scotland, Part 2', *JRHS*, October 1961, 452–53.
9. B. Elliott, 'Victorian Garden Design', *The Garden*, exhibition catalogue, Victoria and Albert Museum, 1979, 57, 59.
10. *GC*, 8 May 1880.
11. John James Joass was born at Dingwall and articled to Sir John Burnet in Glasgow. On winning the Pugin Studentship in 1892 he travelled in Italy, moved to London in 1895 and became a partner of John Belcher in 1905. He was described as a 'brilliant draughtsman and a marvellous rapid designer'. See Alastair Service, *Edwardian Architecture and its Origins*, Architectural Press, 1975, 317; obituary in *JRIBA*, 1952, 386.
12. J.J. Joass, *The Studio*, Vol. 2, 1897, 165–76. Joass's drawings are at the BALDC.
13. Joass designed the Mappin Terraces at the Zoo. On 6 February 1913 C.E. Mallows wrote to his seven-year-old son, 'My Dear Wilfrid, What do you think I heard today? They are going to make a new zoo! There will be real mountains and hills with paths up and down them on which you will see lions and tigers walking about! They won't be in cages as they are now but quite free! How do you think they will be stopped from getting in the streets? That is the puzzle you must see if you and Dorothy can guess before I come home tomorrow about 7.30! Tell Mummie Mr Joass is designing the new zoo'; from a letter in the possession of Professor Wilfrid Mallows.
14. In 1948 Kellie was bought by the Lorimer family, and in 1971 taken over by the National Trust for Scotland. See article by Christopher Hussey, *CL*, 20 and 27 August 1964. For a full description of the gardens see Peter and Patricia Cox, 'Boxed-in Victoriana Preserved', *CL*, 7 August 1980. Lorimer's second eldest brother was the painter John Henry Lorimer (1856–1936), who, after 1900, specialized in genre scenes of middle-class family life.
15. For a full account of Lorimer's life and work see SAVAGE 1980, also Christopher Hussey, *The Work of Sir Robert Lorimer*, 1931. For Lorimer's gardens see also articles by P. Savage in *GH*, Vol. 5, No. 2, 1977, 30–40, and *G*, Vol. 104, August 1979, 319–24.
16. Quoted in MAXWELL 1908, 107–8.
17. Illustrated in *The Builder*, 13 July 1895. John Begg was joint editor of the *Architectural Association Sketch Book Series*.
18. Triggs and Guthrie are discussed in Chapter 7.
19. Nathaniel Lloyd, *Garden Craftsmanship in Yew and Box*, Ernest Benn, 1925, pls 48 and 52.
20. R.S. Lorimer, 'On Scottish Gardens', *AR*, November 1899, 195–205.
21. Lorimer's quotation was from 'A Chat about Gardens' by the novelist Marie Louise de la Ramée (1839–1908), alias Ouida, a member from 1871 of the Anglo-Italian community in Florence; see *CL*, 21 May 1987, 140.
22. *CL*, 12 and 19 August 1982.
23. Hill of Tarvit is now owned by the National Trust for Scotland. The house has retained its serenity but the gardens have suffered change: 'The hedges have encroached on the architectural stonework in a way that cannot have been intended and where the sunken garden was open to the south a tall hedge completely encloses it. The evergreens around the east rose garden have gone, leaving the clutter of fire escapes behind in full view, and in the walled garden behind, the rectangular plots, formerly busy with fruit, flowers and vegetables, are now empty and grassed over to reduce the costs of maintenance, leaving but a ghost of its former self'; SAVAGE 1980, 103. In about 1899 Lorimer added Italianate terraces and a statue walk at Torosay Castle, Isle of Mull; see G.A. Little (ed.), *Scotland's Gardens*, 1981, 237–38.
24. *CL*, 12 November 1910.
25. *CL*, 14 August 1986, 490–94. The house and park are

now being restored and opened to the public by the Formakin Trust.

26. *CL*, 21 March 1931.

27. J. Cooper (ed.), *Mackintosh Architecture*, Academy Editions, 1980, 40–41; R. Macleod, *Charles Rennie Mackintosh*, Country Life, 1968, 23, 151.

28. T. Raffles Davison (ed.), *The Arts Connected with Building*, Batsford, 1909, 13.

29. D. Hunter Blair, *A Medley of Memories*, Edward Arnold, 1919, 126.

30. *CL*, 3 August 1912, 162–67.

31. SAVAGE 1980, 104. Lorimer's work did not, however, develop the intricate geometrical classicism of Lutyens. They remained friends and worked together in 1918 as principal architects to the Imperial War Graves Commission.

32. Lorimer, *loc. cit.*, 204.

33. *Ibid.*, 25. Letter to R.S. Dods, 10 October 1897, quoted in SAVAGE 1980. Miss Jekyll prepared a planting layout for Whinfold (now greatly altered), and Lorimer consulted her in 1901 over High Barn, nearby, for Hon. Stuart Pleydell-Bouverie, and again for Barton Hartshorn, near Buckingham, where in 1908 she helped to lay out flower gardens and terraces; see L. Weaver, *Small Country Houses, Their Repair and Enlargement*, Country Life, 1914, 121–25.

34. BROGDEN 1981, 19–22.

35. According to E.H.M. Cox, 'the landscape garden only became a danger in Scotland when its popularity was on the wane in England, which probably accounted for the influx of itinerant garden designers of the utmost mediocrity who wandered through South Scotland trying to persuade landowners to employ them'; *A History of Gardening in Scotland*, Chatto and Windus, 1935, 87. E.H.M. Cox (1893–1977) accompanied Reginald Farrer on his last plant-collecting expedition in 1919–20. His woodland and wild garden at Glendoick, Glencarse, Perthshire has been continued by his son, Peter Cox, and is occasionally open to the public.

36. TAIT 1979, 173–80; see also the same author's 'Wild Landscape into Gardens', *CL*, 9 August 1979, 394–96; and *The Landscape Garden in Scotland*, Edinburgh U.P., 1980.

37. Sir Herbert Eustace Maxwell, Bt, F.R.S. (1845–1937), was President of the Society of Antiquaries of Scotland. He was a prolific writer on a wide range of subjects including biography, history, archaeology, topography and horticulture. Sir John Maxwell Stirling-Maxwell, Bt (1866–1956) was sometime Chairman of the Forestry Commisson, the Royal Fine Art Commission for Scotland, and the Ancient Monuments Board (Scotland), and author of *Shrines and Homes of Scotland* (1937). In 1901 he married Ann Christian, daughter of Sir Herbert Maxwell. He also laid out the gardens at his home, Pollok House, Glasgow. From 1910 Sir John planted an unusual collection of rhododendrons at Corrour, see G, Vol. 109, June 1984, 221–24. The National Monuments Record of Scotland have copies of Falconer's plans for the house and gardens with notes by Sir John.

38. Sir Herbert Maxwell, *Scottish Gardens*, Edward Arnold, 1908, 87–88.

4 The Naturalistic Garden

1. 'The Growing Individuality of the American Garden', in Gustav Stickley's *The Craftsman* (U.S.A.), April–September 1911, 54; quoted in BALMORI 1983, 21.

2. No authoritative study of Robinson exists at present. Mea Allan, *William Robinson, 1838–1935*, Faber and Faber, 1982, is a useful general account but should be read with caution; see review by E. Charles Nelson, 'An Irish Bachelor as Father of the English Flower Garden', *Moorea*, Vol. 2, 1983, 54–56. See also Geoffrey

Taylor, *Some Nineteenth-Century Gardeners*, Skeffington, 1951; Ruth Duthie, 'Some Notes on William Robinson', *GH*, Vol. 2, No. 3, 1974.

3. ELLIOTT 1986, 168; see also *DNB*, Vol. 12, 1077–78.

4. ROBINSON 1898, vii–viii.

5. In the 1898 edition of *The English Flower Garden*, ninety contributors were listed, but their initials were omitted from Part 2, and by the 1933 edition all reference to them had vanished; see also ELLIOTT 1985, 214–17.

6. Described in William Robinson, *Gravetye Manor: or Twenty Years' Work round an old Manor House*, John Murray, 1911. It includes selections from his diaries of 1884–1904.

7. Robinson wrote a description of the West Garden in *CL*, 28 September 1912, 409–11.

8. Gravetye suffered neglect after Robinson's death in 1935 but in 1957 it became a country hotel and is now well maintained. The pergolas have long since gone and, regrettably, so have the celebrated beds in the paved garden. The woodland suffered devastation in the great storm of October 1987 which destroyed most of the planting carried out by Robinson from 1884, but an appeal has been launched and restoration work is proceeding; see *CL*, 19 November 1987.

9. ROBINSON 1903, 80.

10. ROBINSON 1894, xxx.

11. ROBINSON 1898, 4.

12. Millais painted the background to *Ophelia* on the Hogsmill river near Ewell in Surrey. He added some flowers of his own: poppies, meadow-sweet, pheasant's eye, fritillaries and forget-me-nots. See *The Pre-Raphaelites*, Tate Gallery, 1984, 96–98.

13. Maurice Maeterlinck, *Old-Fashioned Flowers and other Open-Air Essays*, George Allen, 1906, 13.

14. ROBINSON 1894, 211.

15. *CL*, 13 March 1980, 750–51.

16. See D. Nevins, introduction to 1985 Hamlyn edition of *The English Flower Garden*, xx.

17. See ELLIOTT 1985.

18. Quoted in Miles Hadfield (ed.), *British Gardeners*, A. Zwemmer, 1980, 120.

19. Mrs C.W. Earle, *Pot-Pourri from a Surrey Garden*, Smith, Elder and Co., 1897, 180, 239.

20. Maighréad Henley, 'Fota', *Moorea*, Vol. 4, 1985, 13–15.

21. These and other 'Robinsonian' gardens are fully described in Chapter 5 of MALINS and BOWE 1980, 108–17.

22. Another Garinish Island, nearby in Bantry Bay, now officially named Ilnacullin, was made into a paradise garden from 1910; see Chapter 7.

23. R. Bisgrove, 'From Grotto to Mountain Peak', *CL*, 2 December 1982, 1821–24.

24. R. Negus in JEKYLL and WEAVER 1912, Chapter 21.

25. Sally Festing, 'Pulham has done his work well', *GH* Vol. 12, No. 2, 1984, 138–58; Brent Elliott, 'We must have the Noble Cliff,' *CL*, 5 January 1984, 30–31.

26. In 1881 Queen Victoria wrote about Thomas's plan for a belt of trees along the Grosvenor Place wall, 'Mr Thomas always wants to alter and change— as he did at Sandringham. The Queen is very fond of the garden. It is beautifully laid out and extremely well kept. The only wants trees planted where they are dead, and the new ones planted near those that are dying off...she wants NO CHANGES'; Royal Archives, Windsor, 1/40; see P. Coats, *The Gardens of Buckingham Palace*, Michael Joseph, 1978. For a brief list of Thomas's work see ELLIOTT 1986, 261 n.188; see also *CL*, 19 July 1979, 163.

27. James Pulham, *Picturesque Ferneries and Rock-Garden Scenery*, c.1877. I am grateful to Dr Brent Elliott of the Lindley Library for bringing this to my notice. Above the rockery is a summer-house known as 'The Nest', presented to Queen Alexandra in 1913.

28. Official Guide. See also *Journal of Horticulture*, Vol. 22, 1872, 59–62, 103–6; *JRHS*, 1932, 165–74.

29. FORSYTH 1983, pls 96, 97.

30. White married the daugther of H.E. Milner and practised from 1903 as Milner, Son & White; see *GC*, 1 April 1922, 146.

31. FORSYTH 1983, pl. 100.

32. See, Mea Allan, *E.A. Bowles and His Garden*, Faber and Faber, 1973; also Frances Perry, 'Church's Loss, Garden's Gain', *CL*, 9 May 1985, 1256–57.

33. E.A. Bowles, *My Garden in Spring*, T.C. and E.C. Jack, 1914, vii.

34. *Guidebook to Friar Park*, 1914, copy housed at RHS Lindley Library; ASLET 1982, 297–98; FORSYTH 1983, pls 69, 98; *CL*, 5 August 1905, 162–66. In 1924, Crisp's two volumes of *Mediaeval Gardens* were published posthumously by his daughter.

35. R. Gathorne-Hardy, *Ottoline: The Early Memoirs of Lady Ottoline Morrell*, Faber and Faber, 1963, 128.

36. For a note on the Japanese garden at Compton Acres see letter in *CL*, 27 October 1966, 1096.

37. A.B. Freeman-Mitford, *Memories*, 1915; see also J. and C. Guinness, *The House of Mitford*, Hutchinson, 1984, 93–94; obituary, *The Times*, 18 August 1916, 11.

38. *CL*, 4 July 1903; John Sales, *West Country Gardens*, Alan Sutton, 1981, 37–39. The Batsford Park Arboretum is open to the public.

39. Quoted in Hugh Cortazzi (ed.), *Mitford's Japan: Memoirs & Recollections, 1866–1906*, Athlone, 1985, 238–45.

40. Preface to the first edition published in Tokyo by Kelly and Walsh. A revised edition was published in 1912 and re-issued in 1964 by Dover Publications, New York. Harriet Osgood Taylour, whose *Japanese Gardens* was published in 1912, also lived in Japan, but she wisely preferred to view her subject as 'the outcome of the Japanese spirit' and beyond literal description.

41. *CL*, 27 February 1915; 29 November 1984.

42. *CL*, 1 May 1909, 639–41; HOLME 1908, pls LVI, LVII.

43. G, 6 August 1921, 388–89.

44. R. Bisgrove, *Gardens of Britain*, Vol. 3, Batsford, 1978, 74–75. The neo-Tudor rebuilding of the Queen Anne house was by W. Wood Bethel and was illustrated in *AR*, Vol. 18, 1905, 269–77; it is now the Building Societies' Association Staff College.

45. J. Colleran and E. McCracken, 'The Japanese Garden, Tully, Kildare', *GH*, Vol. 5, No. 1, 1977, 30–41; J. Colleran, *Japanese Gardens*, 1981; *CL*, 13 July 1978, 86–87.

46. L. Fleming and A. Gore, *The English Garden*, Michael Joseph, 1979, 210, pl. 131. A convincing Japanese garden was laid out by Japanese workmen in 1910 at Tatton Park, Knutsford, Cheshire; see THOMAS 1979, 225.

47. MALINS and BOWE 1980, 94.

48. *CL*, 27 February 1915, 277.

49. An important example of a Japanese-influenced wild garden was created at Gunnersbury Park for Leopold de Rothschild by James Hudson around 1900; see *JRHS*, 1907, 1–10; for Hudson's writings see ELLIOTT 1986, 201, 265 n.72.

50. ROBINSON 1894, 101.

51. ROBINSON 1898, 256. B. Latour-Marliac (c.1832–1911) was the leading (and first) hybridist of water-lilies; obituary, *GC*, 29 April 1911.

52. For a full description of Bodnant see the National Trust Guide; see also THOMAS 1979, 107–9; E. Hyams, *The English Garden*, Thames and Hudson, 1964, 207–11; *CL*, 17 July 1920, 84–90; 26 September 1931, 330–36; *JRHS*, 1950, 261–69. I am grateful to Charles Puddle for information on Bodnant.

53. *Irish Times*, 27 May 1978.

54. Stephen Gwynn, *Claude Monet and his Garden*, Country Life, 1934, 57.

55. Claire Joyes, *Monet at Giverny*, Matthews Miller Dun-

bar, London, 1975, 37. This is the best description of Giverny. Amended portions were included in the same author's *Claude Monet: Life at Giverny*, Thames and Hudson, 1985.

56. *Ibid.*, 38. Monet's home is now a museum open to the public. The garden has been restored but the original planting has not been maintained.

57. For detailed accounts of Gertrude Jekyll's life and work see JEKYLL 1934; BROWN 1982; TOOLEY 1984.

58. Joan Edwards, *Gertrude Jekyll: Embroiderer, Gardener and Craftswoman*, Bayford Books, 1981.

59. Gertrude Jekyll, 'Some Early Reminiscences', *Gardening Illustrated*, 27 August 1927; included also in F. Jekyll and G.C. Taylor (eds), *A Gardener's Testament*, Country Life, 1937.

60. Decimus Burton assisted Birket Foster in the design of his house, The Hill (demolished), and Burne-Jones, Rossetti, Holman Hunt and Morris helped to decorate it; see Marcus B. Huish, *Birket Foster: His Life and Work*, special Christmas number of the *Art Journal*, 1890.

61. Illustrated in, Marcus B. Huish, *Happy England: Helen Allingham*, Adam and Charles Black, 1903. Helen Allingham (née Paterson) entered the Royal Academy Schools, London, in 1867, married the poet William Allingham in 1874 and lived in Chelsea until she moved to Sandhills in 1881. Her first exhibition was held at the Fine Art Society in 1886. See also Christopher Neve, 'Mrs. Allingham's Cottage Gardens', *CL*, 21 March 1974, 632–33.

62. See R. Treble, 'The Victorian Picture of the Country', in G.E. Mingay (ed.), *The Victorian Countryside*, Routledge and Kegan Paul, 1981.

63. For a layout plan see TOOLEY 1984, 66. The mixed border at Munstead House was described by W. Goldring in *G*, Vol. 22, No. 562, 1882, 191–93.

64. Jekyll, 'Some Early Reminiscences', 1927.

65. See B. Seaton, 'The Garden Writing of Henry Arthur Bright', *GH*, Vol. 10, No. 1, 1982.

66. *CL*, 6 May 1899, 561–65; Vol. 105, 1949, 1374–77, 1438–41. Eleanor Boyle was also an illustrator of children's books; obituary *The Times*, 18 August 1916. Huntercombe Manor is now a Remand Home.

67. 'E.V.B.', *Days and Hours in a Garden*, Elliot Stock, 1884, 125.

68. Followed by *More Pot-Pourri* (1898), *A Third Pot-Pourri* (1903), and *Memoirs and Memories* (1911). See LUTYENS 1980, 64; MASSINGHAM 1982, 74–87; T. Clark, 'Mrs C.W. Earle: A Reappraisal of her Work', *GH*, Vol. 8, No. 2, 1980, 75–83.

69. *Elizabeth and her German Garden*, Macmillan, 1898, 46, 40, 83. The 1906 edition had suitably idyllic illustrations by Simon Harmon Vedder. Mary Annette Beauchamp, a successful novelist, was born in Sydney and married Count Henning August Von Arnim. He died in 1910, and in 1916 she married the 2nd Earl Russell, brother of Bertrand Russell. See K. Usborne, 'Elizabeth', Bodley Head, 1986.

70. A general description is included in JEKYLL and WEAVER 1912, Chapter 5.

71. Recorded in watercolour in 1901 by George S. Elgood, illustrated in JEKYLL and ELGOOD 1904, 122.

72. *G*, Vol. 22, No. 562, 1882, 177, with further comments in No. 572, 470.

73. ELLIOTT 1986, 205–9.

74. J.W. Goethe was both botanist and enthusiastic gardener and his *Theory of Colours*, translated by Charles Eastlake in 1840, was based on a close, scientific observation of nature. The theories of the chemist, Michel Chevreul, were more abstract. His treatise, originally published in 1839, was translated into English in 1854 and published in London as *The Principles of Harmony and Contrast of Colours and their Application to the Arts*, see BROWN 1982, 41–44; TOOLEY 1984, 20, 29.

75. See ELLIOTT 1986, 123–28.

76. J. Ruskin, 'The Poetry of Architecture', first published in *The Architectural Magazine* (1837–8); see E.T. Cook and A. Wedderburn (eds), *The Works of Ruskin*, 1903, Vol. 1, 157.

77. JEKYLL 1908, 61.

78. *Ibid.*, 52.

79. *Ibid.*, 90.

80. Gertrude Jekyll, 'Colour in Garden Planning', *JRHS*, 1929, 283.

81. JEKYLL 1908, 49.

82. JEKYLL 1899, 212. For a detailed description of the Munstead border, see BROWN 1982, 44–46; P. Hobhouse, *Gertrude Jekyll on Gardening*, National Trust, 1982, 257–98.

83. ROBINSON 1898, 289.

84. JEKYLL and WEAVER 1912, 43–44.

85. Jekyll 1899, 270. A similar point was made in 1888 by Charles Sargent in *Garden and Forest*; see BALMORI 1983, 19. Charles Sprague Sargent's *Garden and Forest* (1888–97) was an important forum of ideas for the American landscape profession.

86. JEKYLL 1899, 156–57.

87. M. Girouard, *Life in the English Country House*, Yale U. P., 1978, 314.

88. Kay N. Sanecki, 'Hard Work in High Society', *Hortus*, No. 2, 1987, 64–74; (for Lady Warwick see also Chapter 7 below).

89. Viscountess Wolseley, *Gardens, Their Form and Design*, Edward Arnold, 1919, introduction. Frances Wolseley's interest in gardening dates from about 1888 when she made her first visit to Gravetye. Her book on garden design demonstrated her admiration for both Robinson and Le Nôtre, sometimes with unfortunate results. See also article by Sally Festing, *G*, Vol. 106, October 1981, 404–6; MASSINGHAM 1982, 159–76.

90. *CL*, 12 November 1910, 689–91. Warley Place had its rock garden, and Miss Willmott designed the one at Newby Hall, N. Yorkshire. She also had an exotic wild garden at Villa Boccanegra, Ventimiglia; see W.T. Stearn, 'Ellen Willmott', *G*, Vol. 104, June 1979. See also P. Hobhouse and C. Wood, *Painted Gardens*, Pavilion, 1988, 192–201, including a layout plan (1904) of Warley Place.

91. Susan E. Schnare and Rudy J. Favretti, 'Gertrude Jekyll's American Gardens', *GH*, Vol. 10, No. 2, 1982, 147–67.

92. See MASSINGHAM 1982, 139–49.

93. Beatrix Farrand began practice in New York in 1896, her campus work dating from 1912. In 1899 she was the sole woman founder of the American Society of Landscape Architects. Her only commission abroad was at Dartington Hall, Totnes, Devon (1933–8) for Leonard and Dorothy Elmhirst; see Laurence J. Fricker in *Beatrix Jones Farrand: Fifty Years of American Landscape Architecture*, Dumbarton Oaks, 1982; Michael Young, *The Elmhirsts of Dartington*, 1982. In 1948 she purchased Gertrude Jekyll's garden plans which she housed at her library at Reef Point, Maine until she donated them to the University of California, Berkeley in 1955; see TOOLEY 1982, v; also *Garden History Society Newsletter*, No. 13, 1985, 11–12. Microfilm copies of the plans are held at the National Monuments Record in London.

94. BALMORI 1985, 65–74.

5 *The Lutyens and Jekyll Garden*

1. SEDDING 1895, 180.

2. For general accounts of the life and work of Lutyens see HUSSEY 1950, also PERCY and RIDLEY 1985.

3. Osbert Sitwell, *The Scarlet Tree*, Macmillan, 1946, 224.

4. See Alice Coats, 'The Mangles Family', *GH*, Vol. 1, No. 3, 1973.

5. E. Lutyens, in foreword to JEKYLL 1934.

6. From a letter to Betty Massingham quoted in MASSINGHAM 1966, 93. Harold Falkner helped to preserve and reinforce the Geogian image of Farnham from 1910 with Ernest Borelli. He visited Miss Jekyll regularly every month for the last twenty years of her life.

7. In *Pepita* (1937), Vita Sackville-West called Lutyens 'That most delightful, good-natured, irresponsible, imaginative jester of genius'.

8. Letter to Lady Emily Lutyens, 11 April 1897; all letters to Lady Emily refer to the collection of Lutyens Family Papers, BALMC.

9. See RICHARDSON 1983, 37, 61–62. Miss Jekyll included a photograph of The Hut in *Old West Surrey*, 1904, 270; also in *Colour in the Flower Garden*, 1908, Chapter 5, describing the June Garden.

10. JEKYLL and WEAVER 1912, 36.

11. JEKYLL 1908, 17.

12. Lady Emily Lutyens, *A Blessed Girl*, Rupert Hart-Davis, 1953, 297.

13. BROWN 1982, 54.

14. JEKYLL 1934, 160–61. Sir William Chance (1853–1935), 2nd Bt from 1902, was the son of the head of Chance Brothers, glass manufacturers. His sculptress wife, Julia, was the daughter of Col. Henry Strachey and sister of St Loe Strachey, one-time owner of the *Spectator* and father of Amabel Williams-Ellis. The unfortunate ousted architect was Halsey Ricardo (1854–1928).

15. For a description of the planting at Orchards, see *CL*, 31 August 1901, 272–79, a rare article by Miss Jekyll on one of the partnership's gardens, but not including the 'Dutch' garden.

16. There is a sketch drawing of the 'Dutch' garden in the BALDC.

17. M.L. Gothein, *A History of Garden Art*, Vol. 2 (originally published in 1913), English edition edited by Walter P. Wright, J.M. Dent, 1928, 403–5. Cyril Flower (1843–1907) married Constance, daughter of Sir Anthony de Rothschild, in 1879. In 1892 he was created Lord Battersea, his motto being, ironically, *Flores curat Deus*. The 'Italian' Garden was only a small formal element of the extensive naturalistic gardens. The Pleasaunce is now a Christian Endeavour Holiday Home but little remains of the original gardens.

18. BUTLER 1950, Vol. 2, 11.

19. SEDDING 1895, 157.

20. JEKYLL 1901, 54.

21. HUSSEY 1950, 174.

22. Notes on garden design attached to letter to Lady Emily Lutyens, 8 April 1908.

23. G.F. Chadwick, *The Park and the Town*, Architectural Press, 1966, 247; BROWN 1982, 25.

24. BROWN 1982, 170.

25. F. Jekyll and G.C. Taylor (eds), *A Gardener's Testament*, Country Life, 1937, 44–45.

26. JEKYLL AND WEAVER 1912, 2.

27. Tintinhull (c.1600) was remodelled in 1720, its formal gardens being laid out after 1898 by the botanist Dr S.J.M. Price. See description by Graham Thomas in the National Trust Guide, 1977; also, Sylvia Crowe, *Garden Design*, Country Life, 1958, 181–84.

28. MASSINGHAM 1966, 101.

29. For a detailed description of the planting at Millmead see BROWN 1982, 111–20.

30. Thomas Newcomen Archibald Grove (d.1920) was a businessman, Liberal MP and founder of the *New Review*. He had previously commissioned terraced houses in Hans Road, London, designed by C.F.A. Voysey in 1891–2. Lutyens was working on the initial designs for Berry Down at the time of his betrothal to

Lady Emily Lytton at the beginning of 1897. A firm bond of friendship was created between the young couple and the Groves. It was at Berry Down in 1899 that the Lutyenses first met J.M. Barrie who became a life-long friend, Lutyens designing the scenery for *Quality Street* in 1902, and later the sets for *Peter Pan*.

31. Hon. Alfred Lyttleton (1857–1913) was the youngest son of Lord Lyttleton of Hagley Hall and married first, Laura, daughter of Sir Charles Tennant, Bt, and second, Edith Balfour. He was probably instrumental in getting Lutyens appointed as consultant architect at Hampstead Garden Suburb in 1908. At this time Lutyens was altering Wittersham House, near Rye, for Lyttleton, who had sold Grey Walls to Willie James of West Dean Park in 1906.
32. LUTYENS 1980, 65.
33. See TOOLEY 1982, 10–15. Lindisfarne now belongs to the National Trust.
34. JEKYLL 1901, Chapter 12, 'Tanks in garden design', 138–39. For description of the Generalife see Marquesa de Casa Valdes, *Jardines de Espana*, Aguilar, 1973; Oleg Grabar, *The Alhambra*, Allen Lane, 1978; also Fred Whitsey, 'Islamic Paradise in Europe', *CL*, 11 January 1979, 96–97. Although Miss Jekyll must have known these gardens, it was not until 1915 that Lutyens made his first visit to Spain in connection with the project for a palace at El Guadalperal, near Toledo for the Duke of Penaranda.
35. LUTYENS 1980, 119–22.
36. See Mea Allan, *William Robinson*, Faber and Faber, 1982, 187; *CL*, 21 and 28 May 1981; *CL*, 14 July 1983. Le Bois des Moutiers has fortunately remained in the Mallet family. In spite of an unfriendly climate and limited resources, they have maintained it in superb condition. Now named 'Parc Floral des Moutiers', it is associated with the Fondation des Parcs de France and is open to the public from March to November.
37. SHEPHERD and JELLICOE 1927, 227.
38. Letter to Lady Emily Lutyens, 24 July 1904. For a detailed description of the garden at Little Thakeham see article by H. Avray Tipping, *CL*, 28 August 1909.
39. JEKYLL 1901, 145–47. Originally, four hippocampi, modelled in lead by Lady Chance, added a note of gaiety to this court, see JEKYLL and WEAVER 1912, 161, figs 208, 209, 221. Marsh Court is now a school. I am grateful to the headmaster, E.G. Broadbent, for his help.
40. HUSSEY 1950, 117.
41. Letter to Lady Emily, 19 March 1910. Lambay was illustrated in *CL*, 20 and 27 July 1929; see also P. Inskip, *Edwin Lutyens*, Architectural Monographs 6, Academy Editions, 1979.
42. For details of the planting see BROWN 1982, 70, 100–1.
43. MALINS and BOWE 1980, 157; *GC*, 8 April 1911, 211.
44. HUSSEY 1950, 115–17.
45. Sir W. Hutcheson Poë, Bt (1848–1934) was severely wounded in the Sudan in 1884–5. According to Hussey, Lutyens was recommended to Poë in 1906 by Sir Henry Macmahon (1862–1949), Secretary to the Government of India, Foreign Dept, 1911–14.
46. Letter to Lady Emily Lutyens, 31 March 1911. Lutyens's sketch designs for the fountain (1907) are in the BALDC.
47. Charles Nelson, 'Three Centuries of Gardening at Heywood', *Moorea*, Vol. 4, 1985, 45–52. This volume of *Moorea* also contains an article by M.J. Tooley on Gertrude Jekyll's gardens at Mount Stewart (1920) for the Marchioness of Londonderry.
48. *CL*, 4 and 11 January 1919, 22.
49. Since 1941 Heywood has belonged to the Salesian Order, who are attempting to recreate some of its former glory, with the assistance of ANCO, a State Youth Training Programme, and under the guidance of Graham Stuart Thomas, and Charles Nelson of the

National Botanic Gardens, Dublin, and with the help of the Irish Garden Plant Society. A full pictorial record of the garden in its heyday is included in BUTLER 1950. As well as Lambay and Heywood, Lutyens laid out a formal parterre at Howth Castle in 1910 for Gaisford St Lawrence, see MALINS and BOWE 1980, 157–58. One of his finest works was the Irish National War Memorial garden, Islandbridge, Dublin (1930–40), currently being restored.

50. Ian C. Laurie, 'Landscape Gardens at Eaton Park, Chester, Part 2', *GH*, Vol. 13, No. 2, 1985; *CL*, 20 April 1901, 496–503. Lutyens's sketch schemes for the garden, gate, sundial, etc. are in the BALDC.
51. JEKYLL 1934, 100.
52. JEKYLL 1896, 164–65.
53. Letter to Lady Emily Lutyens, 22 October 1909.
54. Lord Hylton was a Fellow of the Society of Antiquaries and wrote a history of the local parish of Kilmersdon. For a note on Lady Hylton see BROWN 1982, 199, note 17. An aerial view of Ammerdown is included in BINNEY and HILLS 1979, 19.
55. SHEPHERD and JELLICOE 1925, pl. 88.
56. JEKYLL and WEAVER 1912, 60–65.
57. HUSSEY 1950, 569–70. Sir Saxton Noble (1863–1942) succeeded as 3rd Baronet in 1937. Hussey described Ammerdown in *CL*, 2 March 1929, 292–98. This was about the time he took Lutyens on a weekend tour to Somerset. They called at Sutton Courtenay on the way to discuss the planting of the 'green mansion' with Norah Lindsay, then went on to Hestercombe, also Mells, so presumably Lutyens was able to see Ammerdown in its maturity.
58. These had not fully taken shape when the garden was illustrated in HOLME 1907 and were not to reach their spectacular maturity until the 1920s.
59. Such 'garden theatres' grew out of the Renaissance love of drama, the finest example being the amphitheatre at the Villa Rizzardi, near Verona, laid out from 1796; see G. Masson, *Italian Gardens*, 1966 edn, 242–46.
60. Lutyens's preliminary sketch design for the Abbotswood garden is in the BALDC, illustrated in BROWN 1982, 102. Abbotswood was also notable for its rock and water gardens and plantations of shrubs behind the house; see P. Coats, *Great Gardens of Britain*, Weidenfeld and Nicolson, 1967.
61. ROBINSON 1898, 20.
62. JEKYLL 1901, 176.
63. H. Avray Tipping, *CL*, 17 October 1908, 522–30; see also *CL*, Vol. 61, 1927, 598–605, 638–45; L. Weaver, *Houses and Gardens by E.L. Lutyens*, Country Life, 1913. In 1953 Hestercombe was leased to Somerset County Council as the headquarters of the County's Fire Service, and the garden was restored by the Council in 1974–9. For a good account of the gardens before restoration see L.J. Fricker, 'Gardens at Hestercombe House', *Journal of the Institute of Landscape Architects*, February 1963, 8–11; and for the restoration itself see W.E. Mount, 'Hestercombe Renascent', in TOOLEY 1984.
64. In a letter to Herbert Baker of 15 February 1903 Lutyens wrote, 'In architecture, Palladio's the game!', but Heathcote, for which Lutyens used the Doric Order of Sanmicheli, belongs more to the Edwardian Baroque.
65. Harold John Tennant (1865–1925) was a son of Sir Charles Tennant, Bt—who doubled his inherited fortune in the chemical industry—and brother of Edward Tennant of Wilsford Manor, and F.J. Tennant of Lympne Castle. He was also brother of the emancipated Tennant sisters: Laura, who married Alfred Lyttleton, later of Grey Walls, in 1885, but died a year later in childbirth, and Margot, who married in 1894 Rt Hon. H.H. Asquith, the future Liberal Prime Min-

ister (see Anita Leslie, *Edwardians in Love*, Hutchinson, 1972, Chapter 21). The Tennants lived at Great Maytham in grand style until 1936. After the war the house fell into disrepair and its gardens became overgrown. Its rescue was due to the efforts of the landscape architect, Anthony du Gard Pasley, and in 1961 the house was bought by the Mutual Households Association Ltd who have maintained it and its gardens in excellent condition. See also their booklet *Great Maytham Hall* by John Faviell. Great Maytham was illustrated in *CL*, 30 November 1912; also SHEPHERD and JELLICOE 1927.

66. ELLIOTT 1986, 241.
67. Illustrated in F. Whitsey, 'Where Three Styles Meet', *CL*, 5 July 1979.
68. See A.G.L. Hellyer, 'The Seven Gardens of Folly Farm', *CL*, 6 July 1961.
69. LUTYENS 1980, 146–50.
70. JEKYLL 1901, quoted in MASSINGHAM 1982, 119.
71. See Mavis Batey, 'Gertrude Jekyll and the Arts and Crafts Movement', In TOOLEY 1984, 17–22.

6 The Arts and Crafts Garden

1. E.S. Prior, 'Garden-Making', *The Studio*, Vol. 21, 1901, 28–36, 86–95, 176–90.
2. C.F.A. Voysey, 'Ideas in Things', in T. Raffles Davison (ed.), *The Arts Connected with Building*, Batsford, 1909, 111.
3. Morris's first wallpaper 'Trellis' (1864) derived from the rose trellises of Red House garden; the birds were drawn by Philip Webb.
4. Mavis Batey, *Oxford Gardens*, Avebury, 1982, 174.
5. J.W. Mackail, *The Life of William Morris*, Oxford U.P., 1899.
6. Quoted in Jessie Macgregor, *Gardens of Celebrities and Celebrated Gardens in and around London*, Hutchinson, 1919, 295.
7. John Brandon-Jones writes, 'Webb was a keen naturalist, interested in animals, birds and plants...his drawings were used whenever birds or animals appeared in designs for tapestries, textiles or wallpapers', 'The Importance of Philip Webb', *William Morris and Kelmscott*, The Design Council, 1981, 87–92.
8. ROBINSON 1892, xii.
9. W.R. Lethaby, *Philip Webb and His Work*, Oxford U.P., 1936, 96–104.
10. GIROUARD 1971, 51–52.
11. The eldest sister, Mary Wyndham (1862–1937) married Lord Elcho of Stanway; and the youngest, Pamela (1871–1928), married Edward Tennant (later Lord Glenconner) for whom Detmar Blow built Wilsford Manor; see Angela Lambert, *Unquiet Souls*, Macmillan, 1984.
12. John Brandon-Jones, 'The Work of Philip Webb and Norman Shaw', *Architectural Association Journal*, June and July 1955.
13. *CL*, 19 November 1904, 738–48. See also Edith Oliver, *Four Victorian Ladies of Wiltshire*, Faber and Faber, 1945.
14. The house was later altered almost beyond recognition.
15. Arthur Grogan, *Standen National Trust Guidebook*, 1977; *CL*, 28 April 1983, 1100–2.
16. *CL*, 21 January 1905; JEKYLL and ELGOOD 1904, 8–10 and plate; 'The Gardens of Great Tangley Manor', *AR*, October 1910, 157–60. Wickham Flower was a patron of the Morris circle. Norman Shaw designed Swan House, Chelsea for him in 1875, and Mrs Flower became a great friend to Webb, visiting him at Worth, Sussex, after he retired.
17. Lethaby was chief assistant to Norman Shaw from 1879 to 1891 and was the central figure of the group of Shaw's and Sedding's assistants which included

Newton, Macartney, Prior, Schultz, the Barnsley brothers, Gimson and Alfred Powell. Lethaby laid out a charming garden for his influential suburban house, The Hurst, Four Oaks, near Birmingham (1893). This has been demolished but was illustrated in WEAVER 1910. Lethaby was buried in the same grave as his wife Edith (1850–1927), in the churchyard of St Mary's, Hartley Wintney.

18. *CL*, 11 March 1911, 7★–11★ (supplement), included in part in JEKYLL and WEAVER 1912, 13–16.

19. *JRIBA*, 20 February 1932, 303.

20. ASLET 1982, 218–24; *CL*, 13 August 1981, 566–69. Melsetter is lovingly cared for by the present owner. The parterre, which was carried out in an amended version of that indicated on the sketch plan, has been replaced by a lawn.

21. Introduction to W.G. Newton, *The Work of Ernest Newton, R.A.*, Architectural Press, 1925.

22. SEDDING 1895, 164. For Redcourt see R. Gradidge, *Dream Houses, The Edwardian Ideal*, Constable, 1980.

23. Mea Allan, *William Robinson*, Faber and Faber, 1982, 174.

24. WEAVER 1910, 97; *The Builders' Journal*, 23 March 1904, 136–37. A good example of a Macartney house with formal garden to match is Bussock Wood, Winterbourne, Berkshire (1906–7).

25. Edward Schroder Prior was, like Blomfield and Macartney, both scholar and architect. Educated at Harrow and Caius College, Cambridge, he wrote several books on mediaeval art and architecture. In 1912 he became Slade Professor of Fine Art at Cambridge and established its School of Architecture. Prior's Graystones, Highcliffe, Hampshire (1911–12) is now hedged in by an old people's home and bereft of its extensive formal gardens. I am grateful to Dr Lynne Walker for help on Prior (unpublished Ph.D. thesis, University of London, 1978).

26. G. Hoare and G. Pyne, *Prior's Barn and Gimson's Coxen*, Budleigh Salterton, 1978.

27. ELLIOTT 1986, 236–37.

28. Jill Franklin, 'Edwardian Butterfly Houses', *AR*, April 1975.

29. *The Studio*, Vol. 21, 1901, 88.

30. *G*, 27 November 1920, 587.

31. Lawrence Weaver, *CL*, 6 November 1909, 634–42. Home Place was bought in 1929 by Leicester Corporation as a convalescent home together with Lutyens's Overstrand Hall, near Cromer, of 1899. Home Place was sold in 1985.

32. P. Davey, *Arts and Crafts Architecture*, Architectural Press, 1980, 74.

33. A mediaeval spirit lingers in the walled garden of one of Voysey's later houses, Brooke End, Henley-in-Arden, Warwickshire (1909), illustrated in J. Brandon-Jones *et al.*, *C.F.A. Voysey: Architect and Designer*, Lund Humphries, 1978, 64; see also p. 49 for an unexecuted design at Streatham Park (1899), for R.W. Essex, with flower beds in the much-loved heart shapes and the client's name spelt out phonetically: 'SX'. Voysey's symmetrical layout at Prior's Garth, Compton, Surrey (1900) was illustrated in MUTHESIUS 1979, pl. 180.

34. C.F.A. Voysey, *loc. cit.*, 116.

35. New Place was illustrated in MUTHESIUS 1979; see also W. Duggan, 'The Gardens at New Place, Haslemere', *G*, 6 August 1921; J. Brown, 'The Garden of New Place', *G*, Vol. 108, June 1983. A.M. Stedman (1856–1924) founded the publishing firm of Methuens in 1889 and became Sir Algernon Methuen, 1st Bt, in 1916.

36. RICHARDSON 1983, 134–35; G. Stamp, *The Great Perspectivists*, RIBA Drawings Series, Trefoil, 1982, 77.

37. Obituary by Alfred W.S. Cross, *JRIBA*, 26 June 1915,

417–18.

38. C.E. Mallows, 'Architectural Gardening', *The Studio*, Vol. 45, August 1908, 184.

39. This was exhibited at the Royal Academy, London, in 1908, presumed unexecuted.

40. JEKYLL and WEAVER 1912; this also included a converted homestead by Mallows at Happisburgh (1909), with sheltered gardens, and a scheme of planting suitable for that part of the Norfolk coast devised by H.A. Tipping. In the same year Mallows designed a seaside golfing village at Happisburgh (unexecuted), illustrated in *The Builder*, 16 April 1910, a commission which may have come through Detmar Blow and the Cator family. For the golfing village, Mallows collaborated with the landscape gardener Edward White (1873–1952), and, also in 1909, he drew the perspective (exhibited at the Royal Academy) for White's formal garden at Ardross Castle for C.W. Dyson-Perrins.

41. Stamp, *op. cit.*, 77; also illustrated in *CL* supplement, 'Country House of Tomorrow', c.1910. These supplements were not normally included in bound volumes of *CL*.

42. The best testimony to Mallows's Arts and Crafts faith is Nettlebed Village Hall, Oxfordshire, built in 1911–12 for the Fleming family.

43. Article by H. Avray Tipping, *CL*, 29 January 1910, xxxvi–xl, a supplement in the series 'The Lesser Country Houses of Today'.

44. Algernon Winter Rose (1885–1918) was articled in Bedford and spent much of his time with Mallows's pupils; see *The Builder*, 29 November 1912, 647–50. The garden he designed for Arthur Dacres Rendall at Eastwood Cottage, Walberswick, Suffolk, was illustrated in *Gardens for Small Country Houses* (pp. 69–71), and later became Mea Allan's garden, West Wood; see A. Lees-Milne and R. Verey, *The Englishwoman's Garden*, 1980, 15–19. I am indebted to Grace Woodbridge for information on West Wood.

45. A design for a pond garden at Three Gables, beautifully drawn by Griggs, was exhibited at the Royal Academy, London, in 1903 but not executed. The collection of Mallows's work at the BALDC includes this drawing, also one in coloured crayons for Brackenston, Pembury, Kent (1904), built for his mother-in-law's cousin, the Reverend R.F.W. Molesworth. The house is now one of the offices of Tonbridge District Council: see RICHARDSON 1983, 87, 135–36. From 1902 Griggs illustrated thirteen volumes in the *Highways and Byways* series and in 1904 he moved to Chipping Campden; see *CL*, 17 April 1986, 1070–72.

46. Illustrated in *Building News*, 27 December 1901; See also MAWSON 1927, 83–84; *The Studio*, August 1908, 181–82. Dalham Hall was illustrated in *CL*, Vol. 54, 1923, 280–85.

47. 19 August 1912, from diary in possession of Professor E.W.N. Mallows. The Kendal Record Office has two planting plans by Mawson for Tirley Garth. R.H. Prestwich died in 1940 and in 1949 his daughter, Irene, bought Tirley from I.C.I. and made it available to Moral Re-Armament as a conference and training centre, continuing to live there until her death in 1974. See Irene Prestwich, *Irene Prestwich of Tirley Garth: A Personal Memoir*, The Irene Prestwich Trust, 1971; also article by Clive Aslet, *CL*, 18 March 1982, 702–5. The gardens have been maintained by the Tirley Garth Trust in remarkably good condition. For information on Tirley I acknowledge the generous help of the late James Silver.

48. *The Studio*, Vol. 60, 1913, 215–21; *Building News*, 19 September 1913, 400–1; *Academy Architecture*, 1913. Craig-y-Parc is now a residential school run by The Spastics Society.

49. C.E. Mallows, 'Architectural Gardening', *The Studio*,

October 1908, 34.

50. TIPPING 1925, 82. See also *CL*, 28 October 1916, 518–26; *Academy Architecture*, vol. 1, 1911, 27. Arthur Du Cros was a friend of Lady Warwick and paid her debts in 1914. Canons Park was subsequently taken over by the North London Collegiate School.

51. Osbert Sitwell, *Great Morning*, Macmillan, 1948, 280. See also extract from Estate Correspondence: 'March 20, 1913. We have C.E. Mallows, the architect, on with Barber's garden'; quoted in Osbert Sitwell, *Laughter in the Next Room*, Macmillan, 1949, 264. After Mallows's death in June 1915, it appears that Sir George called in Lutyens to prepare a drawing for the completion of the garden. This drawing, dated April 1916, is in the archives at the Renishaw Estate Office. (I am grateful to Sir Reresby Sitwell for this information.).

52. Cross, *loc. cit.* I am indebted to Professor Wilfrid Mallows for generously providing information on his father's life and work.

53. M.L. Gothein, *A History of Garden Art*, Vol. 2, 1928 edn, J.M. Dent, 358–60. See also Willy Lange, *Die Gartengestaltung der Neuzeit*, Leipzig, 1907, which contains a chapter on 'Der Architekturgarten' by Otto Stahn including illustrations of English gardens.

54. *Hausgarten, Skizzen und Entwurfe aus dem Wettebewerb der Woche*, August Scherl, Berlin, 1908.

55. G.F. Chadwick, *The Park and the Town*, Architectural Press, 1966, 251–54.

56. P. Vergo, *Vienna 1900*, H.M.S.O., 1983, pl. 6.

57. W. Schweiger, *Wiener Werkstätte, Design in Vienna, 1903–32*, Thames and Hudson, 1984, 64–68, 177.

58. For instance, Gamble House, Pasadena (1908) by Greene and Greene; see *CL*, 4 April 1985, 882–87.

59. The landscape designer Wilhelm Miller collaborated with Frank Lloyd Wright on some of his early houses and was the author of *The Charm of English Gardens*, re-published in 1911 as *What the English can teach us about Gardening*; see introduction by Deborah Nevins to the 1985 Hamlyn edition of William Robinson's *The English Flower Garden*, xxi.

60. Grace Tabor, 'Pergolas in American Gardens', *The Craftsman*, April–September 1911, 33.

61. Gertrude Jekyll, 'The Pergola in English Gardens, its Making and Planting', *JRHS*, 1902, 93–97.

62. At Cecil Brewer's Acremead, Crockham Hill, Kent (1906), the pergola was designed to step down the steeply sloping site. Illustrated in WEAVER 1910, 155–59; JEKYLL and WEAVER 1912, 188, 191. Cecil Claude Brewer (1871–1918), was the talented designer of the firm Smith and Brewer. He worked in Schultz's office in 1897 and married Irene Macdonald, sister-in-law of Francis Troup's eldest brother, Edward. Formal gardens were also a feature of his Ditton Place, Balcombe, East Sussex (1904); see JEKYLL and WEAVER 1912, 229.

63. Later Authur Rackham drew a similar panel for 'The Lesser Country Houses of Today' supplements to *CL*.

64. SHEPHERD and JELLICOE 1927, 49. At one time such a comment would have roused Robinson, but in 1927 he was almost a nonagenarian and past taking up the cudgels.

65. Angela Thirkell, *Three Houses*, Oxford U.P., 1931, 77–82. Kipling's mother, Alice, was one of the Macdonald sisters who included Georgiana, wife of Sir Edward Burne-Jones, Agnes, wife of Sir Edward Poynter, and Louisa, wife of Alfred Baldwin.

66. Rudyard Kipling, *Something of Myself*, Macmillan, 1937, 178.

67. This was published first in a periodical and then included in Kipling's *A School History of England*, 1911.

68. Kipling's watercolour plan of this garden hangs in his study at Bateman's and is reproduced in THOMAS

1979, 101.

69. Sir Edward Poynter, 1st Bt (1836–1919), was the first Slade Professor of Fine Art at University College (1871–5), and President of the Royal Academy (1896–1918). His son, the architect Sir Ambrose Poynter, Bt (1867–1923), designed Polesden Lacey, Surrey, in 1905 (see also Chapter 7).

70. Bateman's National Trust Guidebook, 1976, 25.

71. See Richard Haslam, 'The Houses of H. Avray Tipping', *CL,* 6 and 13 December 1979; see also Tipping's own articles on his houses in *CL*: Mathern, 19 November 1910, 718–25; Mounton, 28 July 1917, 84–91; High Glanau, 8 and 15 June 1929, 822–29, 854–60.

72. From the poem 'When Earth's Last Picture is Painted' (1892), quoted by Lady Congreve, 'The Late H. Avray Tipping: A Personal Recollection', *CL,* 25 November 1933, 566–68; also includes an appreciation by Christopher Hussey. Obituary, *The Times,* 18 November 1933, 7. Tipping's upbringing benefited from the individualism of his parents, both of whom were descended from Quakers, his mother's father being an inventor and his father, William Tipping, MP, Squire of Brasted Place, Kent, being active in archeology, sketching and horticulture. See H.G. Singleton, 'H. Avray Tipping in Monmouthshire', *Severn and Wye Review,* Vol. 2, 1970–1, 43–47.

73. Singleton, *loc. cit.,* 45.

74. TIPPING 1925, 225.

75. *Ibid.,* 226.

76. A description and plan of this pergola garden was included in Tipping's last book, *The Garden of Today,* Martin Hopkinson, 1933.

77. FELLOWS 1985, 50–54.

78. *CL,* 20 October 1917, 372–79.

79. SITWELL 1909, 38.

80. Christopher Hussey described the gardens at Harefield House as Tipping's greatest *tour de force*; see *CL,* 25 November 1933.

81. H. Avray Tipping, 'The Garden of Pleasure in England from Plantagenet to Victorian Times', *JRHS,* 1929, 271. In 1925, at Dartington Hall, Devon, Tipping assisted Beatrix Farrand with the gardens near the house.

82. L. Weaver, *Small Country Houses of Today,* Second Series, Country Life, 1919, 22–27. St Mary's is now a country club, but only vestiges of the garden remain.

83. From a letter in the possession of John Brandon-Jones quoted by Rory Spence, 'Theory and Practice in the Early Work of the S.P.A.B.', *A School of Rational Builders,* Society for the Protection of Ancient Buildings, 1982, 9. The S.P.A.B. also recommended Blow for the repair of Lake House, Woodford in 1897 for John Lovibond.

84. *CL,* 29 September 1906, 450–57. The garden was transformed by Stephen Tennant into a dreamlike wilderness of tropical plants and decaying statues of animals and birds. See Simon Blow, 'A Tennant like a flutter'd bird', *Tatler,* September 1983, 114–21. For Blow's Wiltshire houses see *CL,* 3 July 1986, 18–23.

85. *CL,* Vol. 45, 1919, 526–27.

86. *CL,* vol. 32, 1912, 566–74. Blow and Billerey also built 9 Halkin Street, off Belgrave Square, for Hugh Morrison, one of London's finest Edwardian houses.

87. R.B. Cunninghame Graham, 'With the North-West Wind', *Saturday Review,* 10 October 1896. For Hilles see ASLET 1982, 244–50.

88. *CL,* 8 October 1981, 1186; 6 November 1986, 1418–19. The Lodge (re-named Cranmer House) is now part of Felixstowe College, but little remains of Schultz's garden. I am grateful to the headmistress, Miss E.D. Guinness, for her help, also to Michael Talbot. Schultz also laid out the Hamilton Terrace Cliff Gardens for the town of Felixstowe in 1904.

89. Herbert W. Palliser (1883–1963) studied at the Central

School of Arts and Crafts, and at the Slade. He was Professor of Sculpture at the Royal College of Art.

90. For a detailed history of Cottesbrooke see articles by Arthur Oswald *CL,* 15 and 22 February 1936. The gardens have been altered since Captain Brassey sold the property in 1937. The main entrance was relocated on the north front and a lawn with statues and yew topiary provided on the south. After the Second World War, Schultz's parterre was replaced by a modern pool garden and denuded of its Arts and Crafts features, including the sundial which was banished to one of the kitchen gardens. Some of Schultz's work was illustrated in *CL,* 17 March 1955, 736–39, but his name was not mentioned. The kitchen gardens are described in Susan Campbell, *Cottesbrooke, An English Kitchen Garden,* Century Hutchinson, 1987.

91. Dr Playfair's son, Sir Nigel Playfair, ran the Lyric Theatre, Hammersmith, 1918–32. West Green House was given to the National Trust in 1957 by Sir Victor Sassoon. Much of Schultz's work has been altered, and since 1973 a number of interesting but inappropriately grand additions have been made to the garden, designed by Quinlan Terry.

92. Schultz planted over a mile of hedges at The Barn but wished later he had built walls. He wrote to A.B. Waters, his last assistant, on 24 August 1940: 'As to hedges they all draw substance from the ground—privet is particularly hungry. I have all sorts of hedges here and wish I had never planted half of them. The best boundary hedge is a mixture of thorn (quick) and beech planted double. The beeches generally hold their leaves through the winter which gives some screen and the thorn gives protection against animals getting through' (Keith Collection). Schultz was buried in the churchyard of St Mary's, Hartley Wintney, not far from his old friend Lethaby.

93. Neil Jackson, *F.W. Troup,* The Building Centre Trust, 1985, catalogue of an exhibition held at the RIBA Heinz Gallery. I am grateful to Dr Jackson for his help, also to Troup's niece, Mrs Freda Levson. Troup also laid out the garden at Thistlegate, the house he designed in 1911 for Mrs A. Capper Pass at Charmouth, Dorset.

94. Troup's mother was a cousin of the Scottish poet and novelist, George Macdonald (1824–1905) whose sister-in-law was the mother of Joseph King Jr (1860–1943), MP for North Somerset (1910–18). King's wife, Maud Egerton Hine, started the Haslemere Weaving Industry in 1894. From 1925 until his death, King was curator of the peasant Art Collections; see E.W. Swanton, *A Country Museum,* 1947, Chapter 11. See also R.E.D. Sketchley, 'Haslemere Arts and Crafts', *The Art Journal,* 1906, 337–42; T.D.L. Thomas, 'Rustic Renaissance', *CL,* 15 April 1982.

95. *The British Architect,* 28 May 1909; *CL,* 27 August 1910, 296–302. Sandhouse, now re-named Kingswood, has been converted into four dwellings.

96. JEKYLL and WEAVER 1912, 185, 188.

97. *Ibid.,* figs 259 and 267.

98. For a more detailed description of Tylney see Andrew Saint and David Ottewill, 'Arts and Crafts in Berks and Hants', Victorian Society Notes, 1978. See also *Academy Architecture,* 1904, Vol. 1, 49; *GC,* 29 April 1905, 257–59. In the early 1920s Tylney was bought by the shipping magnate, Herbert Cayzer, MP (1881–1958), created Baron Rotherwick in 1939. It now belongs to Tylney Hall Hotel Ltd who, guided by the Hampshire Gardens Trust, are restoring the gardens under the direction of Land Use Consultants who have prepared a master plan of the grounds.

99. In 1910 Lutyens was asked to design an Art Gallery in Johannesburg founded by Florence Phillips; see LUTYENS 1980, 91–92.

100. RPG Collection; illustrated together with Miss Jekyll's

plan in Jane Brown (ed.), *Miss Gertrude Jekyll, Gardener,* catalogue of an exhibition at the Architectural Association, 1981, 20.

101. A similar layout had been proposed by her in 1898 for a water garden at West Dean Park, Sussex, for Mrs Willie James; also in the beautiful leaflike 'Plan of the Rock Garden' in *Wall and Water Gardens*; and these sweeping curves were to be repeated for the pond garden at Combend Manor, Gloucestershire (1925), and the quarry garden at Blagdon, Northumberland, for Viscount Ridley, one of her last works.

102. *CL,* 27 May 1976, 1394–95. L. Weaver, *Small Country Houses: Their Repair and Enlargement,* Country Life, 1914, 36–41.

103. Illustrated in TOOLEY 1982, 6–9 and 44–46. Gardens for two other Brierley houses in Yorkshire, Northcliffe, Filey (1891), and The Close, Northallerton, were illustrated in MUTHESIUS 1979, 112–22; see also *CL,* 23 and 30 September 1982. In her own commissions for formal gardens Miss Jekyll was sometimes required to design the layout as well as the planting, an important example being the terraced garden (now demolished) for Sandbourne, near Bewdley, Worcestershire (1911–13), although the plan reveals some awkward junctions that an architect could have avoided; see TOOLEY 1984, 70–76.

104. BLOMFIELD 1901, 4.

105. THOMAS 1979, 100–1, pl. XXI. Miss Jekyll's plans are in the RPG Collection, which includes another scheme for Forbes and Tate, the magnificently gradated flower borders for Brambletye, East Grinstead (1919) for Mrs Guy Nevill.

106. JEKYLL 1934, 144. King Edward VII began by sponsoring an essay competition which was won by Dr Arthur Latham and the architect William West. The design of the Sanatorium was based on their plan. For a detailed study of Holden see D. Anstis, 'Charles Holden: The Enigma', RIBA Essay Prize, 1963–4. Sir Ernest Cassel later commissioned a Lutyens and Jekyll garden at Putteridge Park, Luton (1911), now Luton College of Education.

107. For a detailed description of the wall gardening see *CL,* 20 November 1909, 701–5. See also S.E. Large, *King Edward VII Hospital, Midhurst 1901–86,* Phillimore, 1986, 26. I am grateful to W.H. Mitchell, Administrative Secretary, for his assistance.

108. *Gardening Illustrated,* 14 June 1924 and 10 October 1925.

109. Thackeray Turner was a son of the Rector of Wroughton, Wiltshire. His brothers included the landscape painter Hawes Turner (1851–1939), Keeper of the National Gallery, and the carver Laurence Turner, (1864–1957); see article by Jane Wight, *Spectator,* 21 August 1976. Thackeray married the daughter of R.W. Powell of Piccards Rough (1877), a Norman Shaw house. In 1891 he went into partnership with Eustace Balfour, brother of the future Prime Minister, and together they acted as architects to the Grosvenor Estate in London.

110. See also article by her in *CL,* 24 July 1915, 119–21.

111. 2 May 1913 at Queen Square with Edward Warren, Master, in the chair. Other speakers were Inigo Thomas, Halsey Ricardo, Schultz, Francis Newbolt and Henry M. Fletcher.

112. *CL,* 31 May 1930, 782–89; *G,* Vol. 111, Feburary 1986, 55–61; *Hortus,* Vol. 1, No. 2, 1987, 84–88. The planting was mainly the work of D'Oyly Carte's wife, Lady Dorothy. Coleton Fishacre now belongs to the National Trust.

113. William Morris, *News from Nowhere,* 1890, Chapter 31.

114. In September 1876 Morris visited Cormell Price at Broadway and later described the cottage he had seen there with Philip Webb; see 'The Prospects of Archi-

tecture in Civilisation' (1881), published in *Hopes and Fears for Art,* Ellis and White, 1882, 180–83.

115. Alan Crawford, *C.R. Ashbee: Architect, Designer and Romantic Socialist,* Yale U. P., 1985.

116. The painting is in the Tate Gallery; see also Evan Charteris, *John Sargent,* Heinemann, 1927, 72–76; this biography includes an 'In Memoriam' by Vernon Lee.

117. Henry James, 'Our Artists in Europe', *Harper's Magazine,* Vol. 79, No. 469, 1889, 50–66.

118. Wightwick (1887–93) was timber-framed by Edward Ould, with Arts and Crafts decorations by C.E. Kempe and others; GIROUARD 1971, 165–67; THOMAS 1979, 255. The gardens by Parsons at Wightwick were 'improved' by Mawson in about 1910.

119. Batey, *op.cit.,* 190. Parsons was a cousin of Dr Daniel's wife, Emily Olive. For Parsons and other garden painters of the period see P. Hobhouse and C. Wood, *Painted Gardens,* Pavilion, 1988.

120. MAWSON 1927, 138–39.

121. See Roy Brooks, 'Thomas H. Mawson and the Garden at Hartpury House', *NCCPG Newsletter,* No. 2(1), 1987, 25–26. I am grateful to Mike Hill of the Gloucestershire Survey of Historic Buildings for help with Hartpury and other Cotswold gardens.

122. The gateway is illustrated in MAWSON 1927, 139, and a view of the lower lawn is included in the fifth edition of *The Art and Craft of Garden Making,* 1926, 126. See also *The Gardener's Magazine,* 15 February 1913. Hartpury House is now the Gloucestershire College of Agriculture.

123. For Nether Swell Manor see *CL,* Vol. 28, 1910, 754–60. Professor Reilly wrote of Dawber, 'Here was a man who could be trusted to build in any village or park without spoiling the surroundings. Indeed, in a year or two his work would be hardly distinguishable from the old'; *Representative British Architects of the Present Day,* 1931, 86; see also obituary, *JRIBA,* 9 May 1938, 666–69.

124. See Alan Crawford, 'New Life for an Artist's Village', *CL,* 24 and 31 January 1980. Mary Anderson was a hit on the London stage in the 1880s; see Madame de Navarro, *A Few Memories,* and *A Few More Memories* (1936). For the garden at Lamb House, Rye, see *Hortus,* Vol. 1, No. 3, 1987, 117–21.

125. For a good description of Hidcote see V. Sackville-West in *JRHS,* Vol. 74, November 1949, reprinted in the Guidebook of the National Trust which acquired Hidcote in 1948. See also Alvilde Lees-Milne, 'Lawrence Johnston, Creator of Hidcote Garden', *Hortus,* Vol. 1, No. 2, 1987, 75–83. Norah Lindsay was a close friend of Johnston: see Chapter 8, note 35 below.

126. WEAVER 1910, 1–7.

127. Rosemary Verey, 'The Garden at Rodmarton Manor', *G,* Vol. 107, 1982, 263–68; see also *CL,* Vol. 69, 1931, 422–27; 16 December 1976, 1844–46; 19 October 1978, 1178–81.

128. I am grateful to the late Edward Barnsley of the Edward Barnsley Educational Trust, Petersfield, for this information concerning his uncle.

129. SEDDING 1895, 164.

130. Lutyens designed a similar, long, grass plat with hebaceous borders terminated by a garden house with conical roof at Wittersham House, Kent, 1906–9, for Alfred Lyttelton.

131. N. Jewson, *By Chance I did Rove* (1952), republished 1986 by Gryffon Publications, Barnsley, Gloucestershire. One of the jobs he finished for Sidney Barnsley was Cotswold Farm, near Duntisbourne Abbots, a seventeenth-century farmhouse altered and enlarged for Lady Birchall from 1926 and including terraced formal parterres. Favourite of his own works was Garden House (1939), built in the old nursery garden of Westonbirt Arboretum. I am grateful to Nancy Jewson for information on her father's work.

132. Owlpen Manor was rescued by Jewson from a dilapidated condition in 1926; the garden is illustrated in JEKYLL and WEAVER 1912, xx–xxii.

133. From the National Trust booklet of Wade's *Haphazard Notes* (1945), edited by Aidan de la Mare, 1979.

134. *Ibid.* Like his friend, Sir Albert Richardson, Wade refused electric light and was also an inveterate collector of antiques, handicrafts, curios and *objets d'art* with which he filled Snowshill Manor. In 1951 he gave the property to the National Trust and went to live in the West Indies where he owned sugar estates inherited from his father. He died in 1956 on a return visit to the Cotswolds. Richardson contributed an article on Snowshill in *CL,* 1 October 1927, 470–75.

135. *GC,* 8 May 1880, quoted in Chapter 3.

136. M.H. Baillie Scott, *Houses and Gardens,* George Newnes, 1906, 150, 152.

137. The subject had been discussed in a paper at the RHS: H.P.G. Maule, 'Design in the Suburban Garden', *JRHS,* Vol. 29, 1904/5, 68–76.

138. J.D. Kornwolf, *M.H. Baillie Scott and the Arts and Crafts Movement,* Johns Hopkins Press, 1972, 284. In 1907 Miss Jekyll prepared a planting plan for one of Scott's houses in Sunningdale, Berkshire, probably Greenways (1906) for the Earl of Lindsay.

139. For Snowshill's gardens see articles by Tony Venison, *CL,* 18 May 1978 and 17 April 1980.

140. Wade was responsible for Asmuns Place, Hampstead Garden Suburb (from 1907), a scheme of cottages around central gardens. He also illustrated Raymond Unwin's, *Town Planning in Practie,* 1909; also Mary Stratton's *Bruges,* Batsford, 1914.

141. G. Darley, 'Cottage and Suburban Gardens', in *The Garden,* exhibition catalogue, Victoria and Albert Museum, 1979.

142. BALMORI 1983, 26.

143. RICHARDSON 1983, 129.

7 The Italian School

1. WHARTON 1904, 7.

2. In 1809 Percier and Fontaine had published *Choix des plus célèbres Maisons de Plaisance de Rome et de ses Environs,* but although it included plans it was confined to the area of Rome and gave no impression of the appearance of these gardens.

3. Barry visited Italy during his Grand Tour of 1817–20, but his attention was almost exclusively directed towards buildings; see Alfred Barry, *Life and Works of Charles Barry,* 1867, 48–63.

4. SEDDING 1895, 65–66.

5. BLOMFIELD 1901, 17.

6. See Reresby Sitwell, 'The Gardens of Renishaw' in Sacheverell Sitwell *et al., Hortus Sitwellianus,* Russell, 1984. Sir Reresby Sitwell, 7th Baronet, son of the late Sir Sacheverell Sitwell of Weston Hall, Northamptonshire, took over Renishaw in 1965. See also article by Lanning Roper, *CL,* 1 September 1977, 522–25; P. Hobhouse, *Private Gardens of England,* Weidenfeld and Nicolson, 1986, 175–79. One of Sir George's first projects was the construction of a seventeen-acre lake, and in 1890, assisted by the landscape architect, William Milner, he planted trees to screen signs of encroaching industry, including the colliery and the ironworks to which he owed his wealth.

7. SITWELL 1909, viii.

8. *Ibid.,* 69–70.

9. *Ibid.,* 11.

10. JEKYLL 1896, 165.

11. SITWELL 1909, 14–15.

12. Illustrated in H. Inigo Triggs, *The Art of Garden Design in Italy,* Longmans Green, 1906, pl. 24. The natural beauty of these cypresses was noted by Robinson; see ROBINSON 1903, 79.

13. SITWELL 1909, 16–17.

14. *CL,* 26 May 1906, 738–46. Sir Geoffrey Jellicoe considered Gamberaia 'the greatest composition of its kind', *GH,* Vol. 10, No. 1, 1982, 83. Before the First World War Gamberaia belonged to the mysterious artist, Princess Ghika. For plans of these historic Italian gardens see SHEPHERD and JELLICOE 1925.

15. Osbert Sitwell, *Left Hand, Right Hand,* Macmillan, 1945, 3. In 1965, Sir Osbert decided to follow in his father's footsteps and live permanently in Italy, handing over his estates at Renishaw to his nephew, Reresby Sitwell.

16. *CL,* 5 October 1901, 423. The obelisks, dating from 1793, belonged to the original garden. They are now situated flanking the steps at the eastern end of the Flag Walk.

17. Sitwell, *op. cit.,* 4.

18. Christopher Hussey in *CL,* 7 May 1938, 480.

19. Inigo Thomas's mother, Georgiana (1828–1921), was the third sister of Louisa Hely Hutchinson, co-heir of Weston Hall, Northamptonshire, and wife of Sir Reresby Sitwell, 3rd Bt. Georgiana Thomas, as widow of Revd Charles Thomas, lived at Weston Hall from 1911–21; see *CL,* 22 and 29 January 1976. Lutyens was invited to Renishaw in September 1908 and wrote from there, 'They want me to do the Garden, the Ball Room, Billiard Room, Great Drawing Room, Dining Room, etc.... Sir George wants to build a little water palace (one room) on the lake, which would be a delightful thing to do, and to build a house in Sicily which would be fun, he is going to take me to Italy!'; letter to Lady Emily Lutyens, 17 September 1908, BALMC. He did re-decorate the ballroom, but the only garden work to materialize was at The Green, Eckington, which he took over from Mallows in 1916.

20. *CL,* 3 November 1900, 560–67. This article on Renishaw also shows the obelisks which were later replaced by statuary.

21. Osbert Sitwell, introduction to 1949 edition of *On the Making of Gardens,* reprinted in Sacheverell Sitwell *et al., op. cit.*

22. Osbert Sitwell, *Great Morning,* Macmillan, 1948, 59; the book also describes the encounters between Lutyens and the erratic and authoritarian Sir George.

23. TOOLEY 1982, 16–19.

24. Sitwell, *op. cit.,* 60.

25. *CL,* 11 February 1928, 184–91; *La Mortola Garden,* Oxford U. P., 1938; *G,* Vol. 105, May 1980, 181–86. In 1960, Sir Cecil Hanbury's widow, Mrs Dodo Hanbury-Forbes, handed over La Mortola to the Italian State. The gardens are open every day of the year. Ellen Willmott's garden at Boccanegra was nearby.

26. The original house was built in 1717–20, and the grounds were landscaped from 1774 which included forming the lake. Hanbury's formal gardens were laid out to the west so as not to disturb this setting. The house was depicted by Thomas Hardy, who lived nearby, as Knapwater House in *Desperate Remedies* (1870). Bought by Dorset County Council after 1947, it is now the Dorset College of Agriculture.

27. TOOLEY 1984, 113–14.

28. F. Eden, *A Garden in Venice,* Country Life, 1903, 24.

29. *CL,* 21 July 1900, 72–76. Its enchantment was reflected in the lily walk designed by Lady Downe for Dingley Park, Northamptonshire, illustrated in E.T. Cook and Beatrice Parsons, *Gardens of England,* A. and C. Black, 1908, 162; *CL,* 14 February 1903, 208.

30. In the late 1890s the Edens bought the Villa Salce, sixty miles north of Venice, high up overlooking the valley of the Piave, to which they went in the hot summer months; see *CL,* 26 January 1901, 101–3.

31. Published by Harper and Brothers and based on a series of articles, 'Formal Gardening in Italy', which

32. For an account of Platt's garden designs, see MORGAN 1985, Chapter 2; see also Alan Emmet, 'Faulkner Farm: An Italian garden in Massachusetts', *Journal of Garden History*, Vol. 6, No. 2, 1986, 162–78.

33. MORGAN 1985, 49–52. These lodges in turn derived from Brunelleschi's Pazzi Chapel (1429–46).

34. *Ibid.*, 53.

35. GIROUARD 1971, 188. Sir Morton Peto married, first, Mary Grissell, who died in 1842, leaving a son and three daughters; and second, Sarah Ainsworth Kelsall, by whom he had six sons and four daughters. He was created baronet in 1855. See also *CL*, 3 June 1982, 1668–72.

36. In 1905–7 Peto was responsbile for the interior decoration of the first-class accommodation of the Cunard *Mauretania*; see Alastair Forsyth, 'The Grand Hotel Afloat', *CL*, 26 December 1985, 2034–36.

37. *CL*, 3 December 1910, 824–25. I am grateful to Graeme Moore for help with Peto; also to Dr Hilary Grainger (Ph.D. thesis, 'The Architecture of Sir Ernest George and his Partners, c.1860–1922', University of Leeds, 1985).

38. Quoted by H.A. Tipping, *CL*, 2 September 1922, 272.

39. ELLIOTT 1986, 57, pl. 21.

40. Iford Manor Guidebook, ed. Elizabeth Cartwright, 1975, 3.

41. George designed this north wing rather than Peto because the latter was prevented from practising in the U.K. up to 1907 under the terms of his agreement with the firm.

42. For a full description of the planting see Patrick M. Synge, 'The Gardens at Wayford Manor', *JRHS*, 1956, 528–34; see also John Sales, *West Country Gardens*, Alan Sutton, 1980, 184–86; *CL*, 7 March 1985, 560–63. In 1910, for another of his sisters, Sarah Crossley, Peto added formal gardens to Burton Pynsent, near Langport, Somerset, whose park had been improved by Brown in 1765; see *CL*, 6 October 1930, 360–66.

43. Anita Leslie, *Edwardians in Love*, Hutchinson, 1972, 154. See also *DNB*.

44. After a further fire, Philip Tilden prepared a scheme of rebuilding in 1919; see TILDEN 1954, 106–9. Lady Warwick left Easton Lodge to the T.U.C. on her death. Later it was demolished and the gardens have now virtually disappeared.

45. HOLME 1908, pl. CVII.

46. JEKYLL and ELGOOD 1904, 90–92. The plant labels were made to order by the Castle Hedingham Potteries but destroyed by vandals in the Second World War. I am grateful to Mrs Felice Spurrier for this information.

47. Countess of Warwick, *An Old English Garden*, Arthur L. Humphreys, 1898. For a small garden Ruskin recommended that 'we must read Shelley to learn how to use flowers, and Shakespeare to learn to love them', 'The Poetry of Architecture' (1837–8), 157–58. Suggestions for making a Shakespeare Garden, with plan, were included in Eleanour Sinclair Rohde, *Shakespeare's Wild Flowers*, The Medici Society, 1935.

48. I am grateful to Graeme Moore for bringing this to my attention. An example of a garden supposed to have been based on Bacon's model was the Countess of Bedford's terraced garden at Moor Park, Hertfordshire, see HOLME 1907, vi–vii.

49. *CL*, 23 November 1907, 738–48; 1 May 1909, 639–41. In about 1903 Lady Warwick commissioned Peto to prepare a scheme for an Orangery Garden at Warwick Castle (unexecuted). Peto also used *treillage* in 1907 for the rose garden at Crichel, near Wimborne, Dorset, for Lord Alington, where he also laid out a new parterre with strategically placed garden temple

for which he erected a full-scale timber mock-up to ensure its correct size and placing. See *CL*, 18 January 1908, 90–96. This parterre was criticized, with some justification, for its surfeit of topiary uprights, in Jekyll and Hussey, *Garden Ornament*, 1927 edn, 190. Both the rose garden and the parterre have been removed.

50. *CL*, 29 November 1984, 1682–86; P. Hobhouse, *Private Gardens of England*, Weidenfeld and Nicolson, 1986, 84–89. Peto designed additional formal gardens in 1911 but these no longer exist.

51. *CL*, 17 January 1985, 114–15.

52. *CL*, 21 October 1916, 490–96; 18 May 1940, 502–7. The section between the bridge and the lake was completed in 1911.

53. An illustration of the Garden Room was included in ROBINSON 1898, 365.

54. TIPPING 1925, 33–40; *CL*, 24 October 1908, 558–66. House and garden no longer exist. Peto would have known of Faulkner Farm from American publications including *Country Life in America*, April 1902, and Guy Lowell, *American Gardens*, 1902.

55. This garden no longer exists but was beautifully recorded in *CL*, 7 August 1909.

56. *CL*, 8 October 1910; JEKYLL and WEAVER 1912, pl. 350.

57. For example, *Expectations* (1885), *Silver Favourites* (1903), *The Voice of Spring* (1910).

58. See paper on Sandringham by T.H. Cox, *JRHS*, 1932, 165–74.

59. See *Victorian High Renaissance*, catalogue of the exhibition organised by the Minneapolis Institute of Art, 1978; for a general account see W. Gaunt, *Victorian Olympus*, Jonathan Cape, 1952. Frederic Leighton was awarded the RIBA Gold Medal in 1894 and Alma-Tadema in 1906.

60. See MALINS and BOWE 1980, 95–100; also *JRHS*, 1959, 463–67, and 1966, 16–18. The island was bequeathed to the State in 1953 and is now in the care of the National Parks and Monuments Service of the Office of Public Works. Its official name is now Ilnacullin; see illustrated guide by Cormac Foley, 1982. There is another Garinish (which means 'near island') nearby along the coast of County Kerry at Parknasilla.

61. M. Pearce, 'West Dean Estate', Dissertation, Portsmouth Polytechnic, 1981. The pergola was built for Willie James who married in 1889, Evelyn, daughter of Sir Charles Forbes, Bt. A renowned society beauty, she was an intimate of the King, and her son, Edward James (1907–84), was his godson. Harold Peto was at Harrow with Willie James.

62. The pergola at High Wall was built against the boundary wall of a house of 1910–11 by Walter Cave (1863–1939); See CANE 1927, 26–28; *CL* (supplements), 10 and 17 November 1917.

63. These villas were illustrated in JEKYLL 1918, also in *CL*: Villa Sylvia, 16 July 1910, 90–97; Villa Maryland, 3 and 10 December 1910, 816–25, 862–70; Villa Rosemary, 30 March 1912, 468–74 and 14 January 1928, 48–54.

64. Julia Cartwright (Mrs Ady, d.1924) was a granddaughter of Lord Cottesloe and in 1880 married Revd W.H. Ady, Rector of Ockham, Surrey. Her many works of art history included *The Painters of Florence* (1901) and *Isabella d'Este, A Study of the Renaissance* (1903). Her previously published essays on gardens were issued as *Italian Gardens of the Renaissance* in 1914.

65. P. Gunn, *Vernon Lee, Violet Paget*, Oxford U. P., 1964; see also *DNB* entry by Cecelia M. Ady.

66. Vernon Lee, *Limbo and Other Essays*, first English edn, Grant Richards, 1897.

67. Percy Lubbock, *Portrait of Edith Wharton*, Jonathan Cape, 1947, 112–13.

68. Vernon Lee took her to many villas around Florence

and on one occasion they were joined by Lady Sybil Cutting whose description of it is included in Lubbock, *op. cit.*, 108–10. Lady Sybil married Percy Lubbock (1879–1965) in 1927, and in 1931–2 Cecil Pinsent designed a villa and flower garden (now dilapidated) for her at Gli Scafari, Lerici, where she spent the last years of her life. In her autobiography, *A Backward Glance* (1933), Edith Wharton wrote, 'I never enjoyed any work more than the preparing of that book' (1972 edn, Constable, 136).

69. WHARTON 1904, 11–12.

70. *Garden and Forest*, No. 6, 2 August 1893, 322.

71. JEKYLL 1934, 169–70.

72. Victoria Padilla, *Southern Californian Gardens*, University of California Press, 1961.

73. Butler was articled in Barnstaple in 1880–85; see entry in *Australian Dictionary of Biography, 1891–1939*, Vol. 7, Melbourne U. P., 1979; also Marilyn McBriar, 'Formal or Natural Gardens for Australia?: An Edwardian Discussion', *Australian Garden History Society Newsletter*, No. 2, 1981; also the same author's thesis, 'Gardens of Federation and other Edwardian Houses in Melbourne, c.1890–1914', Royal Melbourne Institute of Technology, 1980. Butler's paper was entitled 'Garden Design in Relation to Architecture' and was published in the *Royal Victorian Institute of Architects Journal*, Vol. 1, July 1903, 78–98.

74. C. Bogue Luffman, 'Garden Design in Accord with Local Needs', *R.V.I.A. Journal*, Vol. 2, May 1904, 39–50. Luffman was Principal of the Burnley School of Horticulture.

75. H. Tanner, *The Great Gardens of Australia*, Macmillan, 1976, 44, 130–32; P. Watts, *Historic Gardens of Victoria*, Oxford U. P., Melbourne, 1983, 52–53, 202.

76. P. Watts, *The Gardens of Edna Walling* (Australia), National Trust, 1981, 64–72.

77. 'The Garden in Relation to the House', *Garden and Forest*, 7 April 1897, 132–33, quoted in BALMORI 1985, 23–24.

78. R.W.B. Lewis, *Edith Wharton: A Biography*, Harper and Row, New York, 1975, 421, 489.

79. For Villa Noailles see *G*, Vol. 102, September 1977, 361–66; obituary notice, *Garden History Society Newsletter*, No. 4, 1982; for La Serre de la Madone see *CL*, 10 July 1986, 80–81; also note by Alastair Finlinson in *GHS Newletter*, No. 13, 1985.

80. See Sylvia Sprigge, *Berenson*, Houghton Mifflin, New York, 1960; Meryle Secrest, *Being Bernard Berenson*, Weidenfeld and Nicolson. 1980; Ernest Samuels, *Bernard Berenson: The Making of a Legend*, Harvard U. P., 1987.

81. Morris Carter, *Isabella Stewart Gardner and Fenway Court*, Houghton Mifflin, New York, 1925, 200. See also Joseph J. Thorndike, *The Magnificent Buiders*, American Heritage, 1978, 193–98. From 1885 Isabella Gardner remodelled the grounds of the Green Hill estate, Brookline, Mass. in various eclectic styles, including a Japanese and an Italian garden. Peto met Isabella Gardner in 1887 and in about 1894 supplied some sculpture for her collection.

82. See foreword by David Watkin to the 1980 edition published by the Architectural Press, ix–xxix. Scott was a nephew of C.P. Scott, editor of the *Manchester Guardian* from 1872 to 1929. He won the Newdigate Prize at Oxford in 1906. In 1917 he married Lady Sybil Cutting, had a hopeless affair with Vita Sackville-West in 1923, was divorced in 1927 and died in New York in 1929 at the age of forty-six; see Nigel Nicolson, *Portrait of a Marriage*, Weidenfeld and Nicolson, 1973, 194–98. The RIBA has a portrait of Scott.

83. Geoffrey Scott, *The Architecture of Humanism*, 1980 edn, 77–78. Blomfield later attacked Scott's book as 'wilfully perverse' in his *Modernismus*, 1934, 16–17.

84. Sprigge, *op. cit.*, 202.

85. B. Berenson, *Sketch for a Self-Portrait*, Constable, 1949, 133. See also *CL*, 29 March 1979, 906–7. Pinsent's work included the exquisite vaulted library. Berenson bequeathed I Tatti to Harvard University. It is now the Centre for Italian Renaissance Studies.

86. See *AR*, Vol. 71, January 1932, 6–7, including plan. Villa Le Balze subsequently belonged to the sister of Margaret Strong (a Rockefeller), married to the Marchese de Cuevas, and was later bequeathed to the Charles A. Strong Centre of Georgetown University. For help with Le Balze I am grateful to the Provost, J. Donald Freeze, S.J.

87. According to Marchesa Origo, the garden at Villa Ombrellino was sometimes marred after its completion by Mrs Keppel's nostalgia for England and the Royal Gardens. She also recalls seeing her prodding her old gardener with her umbrella and saying, 'Bisogna begonia!' (in a letter of 23 January 1988 to the author.)

88. Iris Origo, *Images and Shadows*, John Murray, 1970, 253. I am especially grateful to the late Marchesa Origo (obituary, *The Times*, 1 July 1988) for information on Pinsent's gardens. For a general description of his work see Erika Neubauer, 'The Garden Architecture of Cecil Pinsent', *Journal of Garden History*, Vol. 3, No. 1, 1983, 35–48; see also P. Hobhouse, 'The Gardens of the Villa La Foce', *Hortus*, Vol. 1, No. 3, 1987, 73–81. He died on 5 December 1963 at Hilterfingen am Thunersee, Switzerland. His nomination papers for Fellowship of the RIBA contain a detailed list of his work up to 1933.

89. Joseph Cheal gave a paper on 'The Old Gardens of Italy' at the RHS, see *JRHS*, 1908–9, 446–51.

90. ASLET 1982, 302; see also 190–98.

91. TILDEN 1954, 114.

92. MORGAN 1985, 52–53.

93. The architectural firm of C.F. McKim (1847–1909), W.R. Mead (1848–1928) and Stanford White (1856–1906) was for almost thirty years the largest in the world, their most celebrated buildings being the Pennsylvania Railroad Station (1906–10), and the Boston Public Library (1887–93) which included decorations by Sargent. Peto met McKim and Stanford White on his visit to America in 1887.

94. Illustrated in L. Shelton, *Beautiful Gardens in America*, Scribners, New York, 1915; R.G. Wilson *McKim, Mead and White*, Rizzoli, New York, 1983, 198–201.

95. John A. Grade, 'Long Island Country Places', *House and Garden* (U.S.A.), March 1903, 117.

96. MORGAN 1985, 58–60.

97. The Beaux-Arts form of training differed from the British pupillage system in being based on a tradition of systematic instruction through the *atelier*. Its impact on Britain was centred on the architectural schools: first through R. Phené Spiers, Master at the R.A. Schools (1870–1916); then Charles Reilly at Liverpool (1904–34); and finally A.E. Richardson at the Bartlett from 1914.

98. Followed in 1911 and 1921 by the four volumes of *A History of French Architecture*.

99. *CL*, 23 January 1958, 164–65. H.S. Goodhart-Rendel described Billerey as 'a very, very good architect', Alastair Service, *Edwardian Architecture and its Origins*, Architectural Press, 1975, 479. Blow's work with Billerey included the Playhouse Theatre, London (1906), and formal gardens at Breccles Hall, Norfolk (c.1910), for Charles Bateman-Hanbury, *CL*, Vol. 83, 1938, 194–99; also at Horwood House, Little Horwood, Bucks (1912), for Frederick A. Denny, *CL*, 10 November 1923, 645–51.

100. Ian C. Laurie, 'Landscape Gardeners at Eaton Park, Chester', *GH*, Vol. 13, No. 2, 1985; *CL*, 29 May 1920, 724–31. Blow was private secretary to the 2nd Duke of Westminster and exercised much influence on the running of the Grosvenor estates after the First World War up to 1930.

101. Arthur J. Davis (1878–1951) trained first at the Ecole des Beaux-Arts and then in the *atelier* of Jean-Louis Pascal (1837–1920). In 1900 he became the London partner in the international practice of the French architect, Charles Mewés (1860–1914) see *JRIBA*, October 1947, 603–4. The idea for small decorative urns on the trellis-work of the descent to the lower hanging terrace at Bodnant apparently came from decorative stonework at the Ritz Hotel. I am grateful to Charles Puddle for this information.

102. Son of the painter, Sir Edward Poynter, Bt, his work included the Franco-British Pavilion at Shepherd's Bush, also the marble balustrade outside the Athenaeum, Pall Mall, London, designed with Alma-Tadema.

103. The National Trust at Polesden Lacey have the original drawing of this scheme; see also National Trust Guidebook; *CL*, 12 and 19 February 1981, 378–81, 442–45.

104. Julius Wernher was principal of Wernher Beit and Co. of which Lionel Phillips (of Tylney) was General Manager; ASLET 1982, 33, 322; P. Coats, *Beautiful Gardens of the World*, 1985, 200. I am grateful for information to the present owner, Nicholas Phillips, great-grandson of Sir Julius Wernher. Luton Hoo is open to the public during the summer.

105. Obituary, *The Builder*, 17 May and 21 June 1940. Romaine-Walker went into partnership with Francis Besant in 1900.

106. *CL*, Vol. 162, 1977, 640; CANE 1927. The gardens are being restored by the present owners with the help of the Hampshire Gardens Trust, see their newsletter No. 4, spring 1986, which includes some contemporary photographs and a master plan prepared by Land Use Consultants.

107. Designer unknown; *CL*, Vol. 10, 1901, 656–61, 688–93; HOLME 1907, pls 27–30; A. Paterson, *The Gardens of Britain*, Vol. 2, 1978, 61–62; FORSYTH 1983, pl. 77.

108. *AR*, 1924, 189, pl. 6; N. Pevsner, *The Buildings of England: Buckinghamshire*, Penguin Books, 1960, 204–5; BINNEY and HILLS 1979, 41; Plaisted, *The Manor and Parish Registers of Medmenham*, 1925. In 1897 R.W. Hudson established Medmenham Ware which manufactured art pottery up to 1907 and produced the bathroom tiles for Danesfield House. I am grateful to Miss S.M. Purser and Ian Meredith for information on Danesfield.

109. *GC*, 1915 (i), 323; 1916 (ii), 132–33, 137; BINNEY and HILLS 1979, 16; ELLIOTT 1986, 241.

110. See RIBA Biographical Record, also obituaries, *The Times*, 25 May 1957; *Journal of the I.L.A.*, July 1957. Articles by Jenkins include, 'Formal Gardens', *AR*, 1924, 186–91; 'Garden Design', *JRHS*, 1929, 284–90.

111. *Landscape and Garden*, Vol. 1, No. 4, 1934, 14–16.

112. *CL*, 11 November 1922, 610–16; FORSYTH 1983, pl. 76. Great Fosters is now an hotel. Romaine-Walker also laid out gardens at Chatsworth; Exbury House, Hampshire; Knowsley Hall, Lancashire; Holme Lacy, near Hereford.

113. For detailed accounts of Mawson's career see Geoffrey Beard, *Thomas H. Mawson: A Northern Landscape Architect*, University of Lancaster, 1976; David Mawson, 'T.H. Mawson (1861–1933) Landscape Architect and Town Planner', *Journal of the Royal Society of Arts*, February 1984, 184–99; also Mawson's autobiography, *The Life and Work of an English Landscape Architect*, Batsford, 1927. The latter includes, as a frontispiece, the portrait of Mawson of 1913 painted by Sir Hubert von Herkomer, R.A. (1849–1914), painted in lieu of fees for the rose garden Mawson designed at Herkomer's house, Lululaund, Bushey, Hertfordshire. This house, built in 1886–94, included the only European example of the work of H.H. Richardson, but, except for the

114. When Lakeland Nurseries closed, the Mawson archive was offered to the University of Lancaster who turned it down. It is now housed at the Cumbria Record Office, Kendal.

115. *CL*, 23 December 1982, 2016–18. Mawson dedicated the first edition of *The Art and Craft of Garden Making* to Colonel Sandys.

116. ROBINSON 1903, 81.

117. The structure survives of the garden at Wern, now a nursing home; I am grateful to Bronwyn Williams-Ellis for information.

118. Muthesius drew heavily on Mawson's book for his section on gardens. After the death of Dr Whitehead in 1913 substantial changes were made to Mawson's work at The Flagstaff by subsequent owners. It is now the Welsh Mountain Zoo.

119. MAWSON 1927, 138–39, 142. Mawson sent his son, Edward Prentice Mawson, to the Ecole des Beaux-Arts. He prepared some of the illustrations to later editions of his father's book. See also Walter L. Creese, *The Search for Environment*, Yale U. P., 1966, 135–39.

120. HOLME 1911, xxxii-iii, pl. CXVII.

121. MAWSON 1927, 17.

122. *Ibid.*, 81. Nothing remains of Mawson's garden scheme.

123. MAWSON 1912, 111–12; BINNEY and HILLS 1979, 20; FORSYTH 1983, pl. 84; *Cl*, 5 July 1984, 6–7.

124. 2nd Viscount Leverhulme, *Viscount Leverhulme*, Allen and Unwin, 1927, 86.

125. MAWSON 1927, 116.

126. *Ibid.*, 117.

127. *CL*, 1 and 8 July 1982, 18–21, 110–13. For a full description of the grounds see *CL*, 5 September 1985, 602–5.

128. Leverhulme, *op. cit.*, 291.

129. *Ibid.*, 290.

130. The timber house erected in 1900–1 was burnt by suffragettes, rebuilt in 1913, and demolished in 1948; see article by Michael Shippobottom, *CL*, 13 September 1984, 678–80.

131. MAWSON 1927, 128. The Rivington Estate is now a public park and is being restored.

132. Francis Derwent Wood (1871–1926), studied at the R.A. Schools (1894), was elected to the AWG (1901), and was Professor of Sculpture, Royal College of Art (1918–23). His work included busts of C. Harrison Townsend (c.1904, at AWG Hall); Henry James (1913, at the Tate), and the Machine Gun Corps Memorial Hyde Park Corner (1925).

133. Leverhulme, *op. cit.*, 294.

134. *CL*, 23 February 1918, 186–93; FORSYTH 1983, pl. 88. The Hill has recently been sold by the Manor House Hospital. The pergola was administered by the Greater London Council Parks Department until handed over to the local council. Its future remains uncertain. Another fine pergola by Mawson with summer-house and circular rose garden was designed for Newton Green Hall, Leeds (1910) for Sir Wilfred Hepton; see MAWSON 1912, 106, 115, 118; HOLME 1911, pls 99 and 100.

135. The Italianate mansion at Dyffryn had been built by Cory's father, Sir John Cory, in 1891, and its ninety acres of gardens were begun in 1893. Mawson's work included a large lawn with axial canal and lily pond, surrounded by an eclectic range of formal and informal gardens. See T. Mawson, *The Art and Craft of Garden Making*, 5th edn, 1926, 386–89; see also *GC*,

1914 (ii), 379–81, 387; 1920 (ii), 5–8; Beard, *op. cit.*, 16–17; *G*, Vol. 111, April 1986, 151–57; *CL*, 30 October 1986, 1368–69. Reginald Cory was an amateur horticulturist and a Vice-President of the RHS. He left half his collection of horticultural books to the Lindley Library. In about 1905 Mawson travelled to Italy with him visiting gardens and art galleries. Dyffryn is now a conference centre and the garden is administered by the Mid and South Glamorgan County Councils and is open to the public during the summer. It contains one of the most important plant collections in Wales.

136. Robert Atkinson (1883–1953) worked for Mallows in about 1904, and in 1909 designed the tower at Rivington. In 1913 he laid out a sunken rose garden at The Road Farm, Churt, Surrey; see L. Weaver, *Small Country Houses, Their Repair and Enlargement,* Country Life, 1914, 161–67.

137. Mawson 1927, 187.

138. Mawson gave several lecture tours in America and his 1908 lectures at the RHS were printed in *JRHS*, 1908–9, 361–93. He was a visiting lecturer at the Department of Civic Design, University of Liverpool, founded by Lever in 1909.

139. I am grateful to Margaret G. Triggs, O.B.E., for this and other information concerning her father. Triggs's admiration for Le Nôtre was shared with Frances Wolseley and they both contributed talks at a meeting at Steep on 12 July 1910 on 'Women in Horticulture'.

140. Described in David Ottewill, 'Arts and Crafts in the Petersfield and Steep Area', Victorian Society, October 1980. One of their best houses was Broad Dene, Haslemere (1909) for the portrait artist, Walter Tyndale (1855–1943).

141. Illustrated in *CL*, 16 December 1916, 738.

142. Illustrated in S. Crowe, *Gardens of Mughal India,* 1972, 43. This symbol also appears in the courtyard of Djennan-el-Mufti, Algiers, see Jekyll and Hussey, *Garden Ornament,* 2nd edn, 1927, 415. For Ashford Chace see *CL*, 18 December 1920, 814–20; *Garden Design,* No. 24, 1935, 109–15; A. Paterson, *Gardens of Britain,* Vol. 2, 1978, 50–51.

143. *CL*, 13 July 1912, 7★–11★ (supplement); Jekyll and Weaver 1912, 55–59.

144. Gillian Darley, 'Informality in a Formal Layout', *CL*, 18 November 1976, 1484–85.

145. Obituary by Mrs Winifred de L'Hôpital, *JRIBA*, 12 May 1923, 431–32.

146. Guthrie married Flockhart's daughter in 1910. In 1927 he joined Wimperis and Simpson, one of their London buildings being Grosvenor House, Park Lane, with Lutyens as consultant. Guthrie's father, John Guthrie, carried out stained glass and decorative work for C.R. Mackintosh. I am grateful to Christine Loeb for information about her father.

147. Jekyll and Weaver 1912, fig. 266. The BALDC have a good set of drawings of Chelwood Vetchery gardens including Guthrie's fruit-tree planting lists. In 1927 it was sold to GKN and in 1955 acquired by B.A.T. Industries who have maintained the grounds in excellent condition.

148. *Journal of Horticulture and Cottage Gardener,* Vol. 49, 17 November 1904, 438–39; *The Builder,* 18 December 1909, 670 and plate. Plans and perspectives at BALDC (51/J/3). The house and most of the estate were purchased from the 2nd Lord Swaythling after the First World War by the University College of Southampton and most of the gardens were destroyed. It is now a Hall of Residence of the University of Southampton.

149. Howard Colvin, *Dictionary of British Architects, 1600–1840,* John Murray, 1978, 516–17.

150. *CL*, 14 October 1933; Lady Rockley, *Historic Gardens of England,* Country Life, 1938, pl. 94.

151. RPG plans, 1912; Gertrude Jekyll prepared another planting plan for Guthrie, at Caen Wood Towers,

Highgate (1920) for Lady Waley Cohen.

152. For general description of Townhill Park see *CL*, 14 and 21 April 1923, 502–9, 536–41. The work was interrupted by the First World War, resumed in 1920 and completed in 1922. Townhill Park is now a hostel of the Southampton College of Higher Education. The Hampshire Gardens Trust, in collaboration with the Hampshire County Council, is hoping to restore the gardens.

153. These sketches are amongst the magnificent collection of Hill's drawings at the BALDC; see *Catalogue of the Drawings Collection of the Royal Institute of British Architects (G–K),* 1973. For a brief account of Hill's colourful career see Richardson 1983, 137–39; *CL*, 1 October 1987, 158–61; obituary, *JRIBA,* June 1968, 277. Some of his gardens were illustrated in Cane 1927.

154. In spite of settling in the 1950s at a house redolent of the Arts and Crafts, Daneway House, Sapperton, in the Cotswolds, Hill apparently had no compunction about replacing Philip Webb's seminal Joldwynds, Holmbury St Mary, Surrey (1873) with his modern monster of 1930–2.

155. *CL*, 31 May 1924, 875–76; *Academy Architecture,* Vol. 53, 1921; Forsyth 1983, v, pls 75, 91–93. Moor Close now belongs to Newbold College.

156. *CL*, 12 January 1967, 70–72.

157. Clough Williams-Ellis, *The Architect,* Geoffrey Bles, 1929, 109. See also obituary, *The Times,* 10 April 1978; *CL*, 21 July 1983, 130–32; A. Saint, *The Image of the Architect,* Yale U. P., 1983, 105–13.

158. *CL*, 30 November 1929, 767–70; Shepherd and Jellicoe 1927, 52.

159. *CL*, 31 January 1931, 130–36; 5 and 12 September 1957, 434–37, 488–91. Clough Williams-Ellis was responsible for installing the Pin Mill at Bodnant. Other formal gardens by him in Wales included Llangoed, near Llyswen (1913–19) for Archibald Christy, his first major work (now much dilapidated); see *CL*, 22 October 1987, 108; also Plas-Yn-Rhiw, Porth Neigwl (1939), now owned by the National Trust.

160. Robert Gathorne-Hardy, *Ottoline at Garsington,* Faber and Faber, 1974, 34. Garsington was Lady Ottoline's home up to 1926.

161. *Ibid.*, 185.

162. *Ibid.*, 35. For the gardens of Garsington see also *CL*, 18 March 1982, 690–92.

8 Aftermath

1. Rudyard Kipling, 'The Glory of the Garden', *A School History of England,* 1911.

2. A. Le Lievre, 'When Surpluses were Sought After', *CL*, 23 January 1986, 180–81.

3. Gavin Stamp, *Silent Cities,* RIBA exhibition catalogue, 1977.

4. David Anstis, 'Charles Holden: The Enigma', RIBA Essay Prize, 1964.

5. Brown 1982, 137–38.

6. Herbert Baker, *Architecture and Personalities,* Country Life, 1944, 96–97. The planting plan is included in Jane Brown, *Miss Gertrude Jekyll, Gardener,* Architectural Association exhibition catalogue, 1981, 44.

7. Obituary, *The Times,* 24 September 1962.

8. For layouts of Blackpool and Hamburg see G.F. Chadwick, *The Park and the Town,* Architectural Press, 1966, 235, 261; for the nineteenth-century public park in Germany see also review of E. Schmidt, *Abwechslung im Geschmack, Raumbildung und Pflanzenverwendung beim Stadtparkentwurf; Deutschland 19. Jahrhundert* (1984) in *GH*, Vol. 13, No. 2, 1985, 169–70.

9. David Mawson, 'Thomas H. Mawson', *Landscape Design,* August 1979, 30–33.

10. Marquesa de Casa Valdés, *Jardines de España,* Aguilar, 1973, 245–54, (English translation, Antique Collector's Club, 1987). I am grateful to Teresa Briales and Roma Gelder for information on the gardens of Spain.

11. Bagatelle (1777) was by Joseph Bélanger, the grounds being an early example of the *jardin anglais*. The house was a typical model for the Edwardian revival of French classicism after the *entente cordiale*. The most famous of its modern gardens is the Rose Garden laid out in 1906 by Quentin Bauchart. The gardens are open daily.

12. Translated in 1924 by Helen Morgenthau Fox as *Gardens: A Notebook of Plans and Sketches,* Scribners, New York. Forestier founded the School of Gardening at Montjuich where he taught botany.

13. See *The Art and Craft of Garden Making,* 5th edn, 1926, 398–403; *CL*, Vol. 69, 1931, 379–82. The original house of 1798 by Henry Holland, which stood in a landscape park, was rebuilt in 1851 in Scottish Baronial style to designs by William Burn with later additions by David Bryce. It was demolished in 1963 except for one small wing. Information kindly provided by Miss C.H. Cruft, RCAHMS.

14. J.B. Priestley, *The Edwardians,* Heinemann, 1970, 254.

15. Tilden acknowledged a debt to Malcolm Powell, furniture-maker, who was one of the remarkable Arts and Crafts family that included Oswald Byrom Powell (1867–1967), second master at Bedales from its foundation in 1893; the bookbinder Edgar Powell; and the architect Alfred H. Powell (1865–c.1960): see David Ottewill, 'Arts and Crafts in the Petersfield and Steep Area', Victorian Society, October 1980. For general accounts of Tilden's life and work see his autobiography *True Remembrances,* 1954; also James Bettley, *Lush and Luxurious,* RIBA, 1987.

16. *CL*, 16 November 1951, 1628–31.

17. Tilden 1954, 20–23, 35; *CL*, 31 March 1928, 438–44.

18. *CL*, 30 August 1919, 270–79. Sir Louis Mallet was Ambassador in Constantinople in 1914. The Varengeville Mallets were a separate branch of the family.

19. Tilden 1954, 42.

20. Oliver Hill, 'Mr Rex Whistler at Port Lympne', *CL*, 4 February 1933, 116–17.

21. Georgina Masson, *Italian Gardens,* Thames and Hudson, 1966 edn, 261–62.

22. Joseph J. Thorndike, *The Magnificent Builders,* American Heritage Publishing Co. Inc., New York, 1978, 328–36.

23. R.R. James (ed.), *Chips: The Diaries of Sir Henry Channon,* Weidenfeld and Nicolson, 1967, 7.

24. Tilden 1954, 172. For Port Lympne see *CL*, 19 May 1923, 678–84; 19 October 1929, 513–17; 14 March 1936, 276–82; *Landscape Design,* June 1983, 31–33. The house and gardens are open to the public as part of the Zoo Park, and the present owner, John Aspinall, has attempted to restore them to some of their former glory; see Guidebook.

25. Aslet 1982, pl. xxxvi.

26. Osbert Sitwell, *The Scarlet Tree,* Macmillan, 1949, 132–34.

27. James, *op. cit.*, entry for 18 March 1935. The flower borders at Trent were described by Norah Lindsay in *CL*, 20 July 1929, 78–80; see also *CL*, 21 February 1903, 240–46; 10 January 1931, 40–47; 21 February 1931, 237–39; S.G. Doree, 'Trent Park, A Short History to 1939', Trent Park College of Education, 1974. In 1947 Trent Park became a Teacher Training College and is now part of Middlesex Polytechnic. I am grateful to S. Cross for information.

28. Russell Page, 'English Gardens from 1910 to the Present Day', in *The Garden,* Victoria and Albert Museum exhibition catalogue, 1979, 74. Obituary, *The Times,* 22 June 1948. Norah Lindsay was one of Lawrence Johnston's closest friends, and after her

death, her daughter, the botanist, Nancy Lindsay (d.1973), who lived at Manor Cottage, Sutton Courtenay, helped advise on the management of Hidcote. He left his garden at La Serre de la Madone to her.

29. TILDEN 1954, 33–34.
30. *CL*, 20 July 1929, 78–80. Norah Lindsay designed some similar borders at Godmersham Park, Kent.
31. HUSSEY 1950, 570.
32. *CL*, 16 May 1931, 610–16.
33. Brent Elliott, 'Master of the Geometric Art', *G*, December 1981, 488–91.
34. TIPPING 1925, lxii; see also *CL*, 5 and 29 February 1898; 7 June 1930, 814–21.
35. Fully described in Blickling National Trust Guidebook. See also *Shell Gardens Book*, 1964, col. pl. 1. The Knot Garden at Mottisfont Abbey (1938) by Norah Lindsay has also been preserved by the National Trust.
36. *CL*, 13 February 1909, 251.
37. For a full description of the planting at Amport see BROWN 1982, 141–45. Amport is now the Royal Air Force Chaplains School and the gardens are well maintained.
38. Amos Nelson (1860–1947) bought the estate in 1919. It included the old Hall, probably by Carr of York, which he commissioned a local architect, Richard Jaques, to enlarge. Subsequently it was decided that another architect be brought in as collaborator and Jaques suggested Lutyens who prepared a scheme in December 1920 on board the SS *Caledonia* bound for India with Nelson. This was abandoned and plans for a new house on a site nearby were begun in 1921–2. The old hall was pulled down soon after the new house was built.
39. Their swan-song was in 1928 at the moated manor of Plumpton Place, Sussex, for Edward Hudson.
40. P. Inskip, *Edwin Lutyens*, Academy Editions, 1979, 24.
41. For details of the planting at Gledstone see TOOLEY 1982, 20–27; *CL*, 13 and 20 April 1935, 374–79, 400–5; 31 December 1981, 2292–94. Gledstone Hall is now a home for the elderly.
42. *CL*, 25 May 1929, 743.
43. The pergola is illustrated in M. Hadfield (ed.), *British Gardeners*, Zwemmer, 1980, 194, incorrectly ascribed to Lutyens. The avenue was a victim of Dutch elm disease and has not been replaced. Rees also added an upper storey to Soane's service wing on the northeast. For information on Rees's and Von Ihne's work at Tyringham I am indebted to Barry Clayton of ABC Design. Tyringham is now a clinic.
44. HUSSEY 1950, 473. See also *CL*, 25 May and 1 June 1929, 740–46, 780–86; BROWN 1982, 140–41.
45. PERCY and RIDLEY 1985, 256. Lady Hardinge, Vicereine (1910–16), had written enthusiastically to Lutyens as early as 1912 about Persian and Moghul gardens.
46. *Ibid.*, 16 February 1913; see also 17 February 1916.
47. The fountains are usually described as being derived from the leaves of the *Victoria regia* water-lily of Paxton fame. This was the horticultural symbol of the Crystal Palace, the building which Lutyens suggested should be put into a glass case!
48. Viceroy's House was built mainly of buff sandstone but the lowest section of the walls was pink which was continued as the predominant colour of the garden stonework.

49. William Robertson Mustoe was from Kew, worked in the Punjab, and was seconded to New Delhi in 1919 where he remained until 1931; see entries by Gavin Stamp in *The Work of the English Architect Sir Edwin Lutyens*, Arts Council exhibition catalogue, 1981, 174.
50. PERCY and RIDLEY 1985, 416. Lutyens designed a 'butterfly garden' in 1918 at 184 Ebury Street for Lady Sackville; see LUTYENS 1980, 236–37. The Viceregal Garden is fully illustrated in BUTLER 1950; see also *CL*, 27 June 1931; R.G. Irving, *Indian Summer*, Yale U.P., 1981, 215–26.
51. John Sales, *West Country Gardens*, Alan Sutton, 1981, 87–90; *CL*, 14 December 1929, 864–70.
52. *CL*, 23 August 1919, 240–48. Compton End is also illustrated in TIPPING 1925; the garden still exists. George Herbert Kitchin (c.1871–1951) was a son of Dean Kitchin (1827–1912), Dean of Durham from 1894. The Hampshire Record Office has a collection of his topographical sketches, and the BALDC has a sketch by him of Munstead Wood, dated 1901; see RICHARDSON 1983, 63.
53. Walter H. Godfrey (1881–1961) was also a scholar and antiquarian and in 1941 was first Director of the National Buildings Record. Obituary, *The Times*, 18 September 1961; entry in *DNB* by John Summerson.
54. Eric Byford, *Forest Row: Historical Aspects and Recollections*, Vol. 1, Part 4, 1984, 9; see also CANE 1927; *CL*, Vol. 79, 1936, 404–9. Repton worked at Kidbrooke Park in about 1803. From 1874 to 1909 Kidbrooke belonged to the Freshfield family. The mountaineer and explorer Douglas W. Freshfield built the nearby Wych Cross Place (1900–03) designed by Edmund Fisher and with extensive terraced gardens laid out by Mawson; see *CL*, 7 April 1988, 178. I am grateful to Eric Byford for information on Kidbrooke Park which is now the Steiner School, Michael Hall.
55. *CL*, 31 May 1962, 1286–88; 5 August 1976, 350–53. (Charleston Manor is not to be confused with the nearby Charleston, West Firle, of Bloomsbury Group fame.) From 1922 Oswald Birley (1880–1952) lived in a house in St John's Wood designed by Clough Williams-Ellis whose portrait he painted; see C. Reilly, *Representative British Architects of the Present Day*, 1931, 89.
56. Designed in the 1930s by Harold Nicolson and Vita Sackville-West (1892–1962); see Jane Brown, *Vita's Other World*, Viking, 1985.
57. Alphonse Duchêne and his son, Achille, restored many château gardens in the late nineteenth and early twentieth centuries. A. Duchêne and M. Fouquier, *Des Divers Styles des Jardins* was published in Paris in 1914. See K. Woodbridge, *Princely Gardens*, Thames and Hudson, 1986, 279–83.
58. Sir Geoffrey Jellicoe, 'Ronald Tree and the Gardens of Ditchley Park', *GH*, Vol. 10, No. 1, 1982, 80–91; *CL*, 24 October 1985, 1173–77. After Tree left Ditchley in 1947, Jellicoe designed Heron Bay in Barbados for him, based on Palladio's Villa Maser and completed in 1949; see *CL*, 5 November 1959. Since 1958 Ditchley has belonged to the Anglo American Ditchley Foundation. The parterre has been replaced by a lawn but the structure of the garden remains. I am grateful to Sir Reginald Hibbert for information on Ditchley.
59. Ronald Tree, *When the Moon was High*, Macmillan, 1975, 68. In 1937 Sir George Sitwell told Geoffrey

Jellicoe, 'all the sculpture at Ditchley was too small in scale, an error common to most English design'; Jellicoe, *loc. cit.*, 87.
60. C. Tunnard, *Gardens in the Modern Landscape*, Architectural Press, 1938, 59, 76; see also *Landscape and Garden*, spring 1939, 25. The book was based on articles published in the *AR*. Tunnard trained briefly at the RHS Wisley and in 1939 emigrated to the U.S.A., as did many continental pioneers of modern design. He became an important influence on garden design after the Second World War.
61. The dissemination of this architectural style in Britain owed much to Frederick Etchell's translation in 1927 of Le Corbusier's cathartic *Vers Une Architecture*. Lutyens reviewed its horrific vision of 'mass-made cages suitable for machine-made men' in 'The Robotism of Architecture', *The Observer*, 29 January 1928, included in LUTYENS 1980, 285–87. Also in 1927, Shepherd and Jellicoe's *Gardens and Design* appeared, introducing wider aesthetic concepts but still based on a traditional language of form and space which was to be supplanted by the modern movement.
62. Maxwell Fry, 'Garden Design in Relation to Modern Architecture', *Landscape and Garden*, spring 1939, 37–39. 66 Frognal, Hampstead (1936–8), was a *cause célèbre* of modern architecture. Its architects, Connell, Ward and Lucas, had to contend with fierce opposition from neighbours, including Reginald Blomfield. See Jeremy Gould, *Modern Houses in Britain, 1919–1939*, Society of Architectural Historians, 1977.
63. See Jane Brown, *The English Garden in Our Time*, Antique Collectors' Club, 1986, 122.
64. R. Bisgrove, 'A Gardener Ahead of her Time', in TOOLEY 1984, 57.
65. G.A. Jellicoe, 'Consider your Forbears', *Journal of the Institute of Landscape Architects*, November 1954, 2–11.
66. The American Society of Landscape Architects was formed in 1899. For an account of the early years of the Institute of Landscape Architects see L.J. Fricker, 'Forty Years A-Growing', *Landscape Design*, May 1969.
67. Early Presidents of the I.L.A. were Edward White (1931–3), E.P. Mawson (1933–5), and Gilbert Jenkins (1935–7).
68. Obituary, *Journal of the I.L.A.*, March 1952. White's 1913 lectures on 'Garden Design' to the RHS were published in *JRHS*, 1913–14, 559–80.
69. Madeline Agar trained in America, taught at Swanley Horticultural College, and was elected a Fellow of the I.L.A. in 1931. Her publications included *Garden Design in Theory and Practice* (1911), and in 1936–7 she contributed five articles on Repton to *Landscape and Garden*. A brief account of her work is given by Brenda Colvin (1897–1981) in *Landscape Design*, February 1979, 8. (Colvin's article on Sutton Courtenay Manor surprisingly does not mention Norah Lindsay, stating merely 'it is difficult now to unravel the history of house and garden', *Journal of the I.L.A.*, November 1953, 5–8.)
70. *Landscape and Garden* continued up to summer 1939, then in 1941 the *Wartime Journal of the Institute of Landscape Architects* made a modest appearance. For a detailed account of the early years of *Landscape and Garden* see S. Hervey and S. Rettig (eds), *Fifty Years of Landscape Design*, The Landscape Press, 1985.

Bibliography of Principal Sources

Contemporary Books and Articles

BLOMFIELD 1901: Reginald Blomfield and F. Inigo Thomas, *The Formal Garden in England*, Macmillan (1st edn, 1892); all references are to the 3rd edn, 1901.

BLOMFIELD 1932: R. Blomfield, *Memoirs of an Architect*, London.

HOLME 1907: Charles Holme (ed.), *The Gardens of England in the Southern and Western Counties*, special no. of *The Studio*, 1907–8.

HOLME 1908: C. Holme (ed.), *The Gardens of England in the Midland and Eastern Counties*, special no. of *The Studio*, 1908–9.

HOLME 1911: C. Holme (ed.) *The Gardens of England in the Northern Counties*, special no. of *The Studio*.

JEKYLL 1896: Gertrude Jekyll, 'Gardens and Garden-Craft', *Edinburgh Review*, July 1896.

JEKYLL 1899: G. Jekyll, *Wood and Garden*, Longmans, Green and Co.

JEKYLL 1900: G. Jekyll, *Home and Garden*, Longmans, Green and Co.

JEKYLL 1901: G. Jekyll, *Wall and Water Gardens*, Country Life.

JEKYLL and ELGOOD 1904: G. Jekyll and G.S. Elgood, *Some English Gardens*, Longmans, Green and Co.

JEKYLL 1908: G. Jekyll, *Colour in the Flower Garden*, Country Life.

JEKYLL and WEAVER 1912: G. Jekyll and L. Weaver, *Gardens for Small Country Houses*, Country Life.

JEKYLL 1918: G. Jekyll, *Garden Ornament*, Country Life.

MAWSON 1912: Thomas H. Mawson, *The Art and Craft of Garden Making*, Batsford (1st edn, 1900); unless otherwise noted, references are to the 4th edn, 1912.

MAWSON 1927: T.H. Mawson, *The Life and Work of an English Landscape Architect*, Batsford.

MAXWELL 1908: Sir Herbert Maxwell, *Scottish Gardens*, Edward Arnold.

MUTHESIUS 1979: Hermann Muthesius, *Das Eng-lische Haus* (first published in Berlin, 1904); all references are to the 1979 translation, *The English House* (ed. D. Sharp), Crosby Lockwood Staples, based on the 1908 edition.

ROBINSON 1883: William Robinson, *The English Flower Garden*, John Murray, 1st edn.

ROBINSON 1892: W. Robinson, *Garden Design and Architects' Gardens*, John Murray.

ROBINSON 1894: W. Robinson, *The Wild Garden*, John Murray (1st edn, 1870); all references are to the 1894 edition.

ROBINSON 1898: W. Robinson, *The English Flower Garden*, John Murray, 6th edn.

ROBINSON 1903: W. Robinson, 'Garden Design and Recent Writings upon it', *Flora and Sylva*, May 1903.

SCOTT 1828: Sir Walter Scott, 'On Ornamental Plantations and Landscape Gardening', *Quarterly Review*, Vol. 37.

SEDDING 1895: J.D. Sedding, *Garden-Craft Old and New*, Kegan Paul (1st edn, 1891); all references are to the 1895 edition.

SITWELL 1909: Sir George Sitwell, *On the Making of Gardens*, John Murray. (An illustrated edition was published in 1949 with an introduction by Osbert Sitwell).

THOMAS 1896: F. Inigo Thomas, 'The Garden in Relation to the House', *The Gardeners' Magazine*, 15, 22 and 29 February 1896.

TIPPING 1925: H. Avray Tipping, *English Gardens*, Country Life.

TRIGGS 1902: H. Inigo Triggs, *Formal Gardens in England and Scotland*, Batsford.

WEAVER 1910: Lawrence Weaver, *Small Country Houses of Today*, Country Life, 1st edn.

WHARTON 1904: Edith Wharton, *Italian Villas and Their Gardens*, John Lane: The Bodley Head (1st edn, 1903); all references are to the 1904 edition.

Modern Books and Articles

ASLET 1982: Clive Aslet, *The Last Country Houses*, Yale University Press.

BALMORI 1983: Diana Balmori, 'The Arts and Crafts Garden', *Tiller* (U.S.A), Vol. 1, No. 6, 1983.

BALMORI 1985: D. Balmori, D.K. McGuire, E.M. McPeck, *Beatrix Farrand's American Landscapes*, Sagapress, New York.

BINNEY and HILLS 1979: Marcus Binney and Anne Hills, *Elysian Gardens*, SAVE.

BROGDEN 1981: W. Brogden, 'The History of Garden Design in Scotland', in G.A. Little (ed.), *Scotland's Gardens*, Spurbooks.

BROWN 1982: Jane Brown, *Gardens of a Golden Afternoon*. Allen Lane.

BUTLER 1950: A.S.G. Butler, *The Architecture of Sir Edwin Lutyens*, Country Life.

CANE 1927: Percy Cane, *Modern Gardens*, Studio.

ELLIOTT 1985: Brent Elliott, 'Some Sceptical Thoughts about William Robinson', *The Garden*, Vol. 110, May 1985.

ELLIOTT 1986: Brent Elliott, *Victorian Gardens*, Batsford.

FELLOWS 1985: Richard A. Fellows, *Sir Reginald Blomfield: An Edwardian Architect*, Zwemmer.

FORSYTH 1983: Alastair Forsyth, *Yesterday's Gardens*, HMSO.

GIROUARD 1971: Mark Girouard, *The Victorian Country House*, Yale University Press.

GIROUARD 1977: M. Girouard, *Sweetness and Light*, Yale University Press.

HUSSEY 1950: Christopher Hussey, *The Life of Sir Edwin Lutyens*, Country Life.

JEKYLL, 1934: F. Jekyll, *Gertrude Jekyll: A Memoir*, Jonathan Cape.

LUTYENS 1980: Mary Lutyens, *Edwin Lutyens*, John Murray.

MALINS and BOWE 1980: E. Malins and P. Bowe, *Irish Gardens and Demesnes since 1830*, Barrie and Jenkins.

MASSINGHAM 1966: Betty Massingham, *Miss Jekyll*, David and Charles.

MASSINGHAM 1982: B. Massingham. *A Century of Gardeners*, Faber and Faber.

MORGAN 1985: Keith Morgan, *Charles A. Platt*, M.I.T. Press.

PERCY and RIDLEY 1985: C. Percy and J. Ridley, *The Letters of Edwin Lutyens*, Collins.

RICHARDSON 1983: Margaret Richardson, *Architects of the Arts and Crafts Movement*, RIBA Drawings Series, Trefoil.

SAVAGE 1980: P. Savage, *Lorimer and the Edinburgh Craft Designers*, Paul Harris.

SHEPHERD and JELLICOE 1925: J.C. Shepherd and G.A. Jellicoe, *Italian Gardens of the Renaissance*, Ernest Benn.

SHEPHERD AND JELLICOE 1927: J.C. Shepherd and G.A. Jellicoe, *Gardens and Design*, Ernest Benn.

TAIT 1979: A.A. Tait, 'Scottish Gardens', in *The Garden*, exhibition catalogue, Victoria and Albert Museum.

THOMAS 1979: G.S. Thomas, *Gardens of the National Trust*, National Trust.

TILDEN 1954: Philip Tilden, *True Remembrances*, Country Life.

TOOLEY 1982: M.J. and R. Tooley, *The Gardens of Gertrude Jekyll in Northern England*, Michaelmas Books.

TOOLEY 1984: M.J. Tooley (ed.), *Gertrude Jekyll: Artist, Gardener, Craftswoman*, Michaelmas Books.

Gazetteer

The following is a representative selection of gardens in Britain and Ireland of the period covered by this book and arranged alphabetically by county. It consists mainly of country-house gardens and does not include municipal or botanical gardens. It must be emphasized that most of these gardens are private and not open to the public. Some are open at specified times for which reference should be made to the following annual publications: *Gardens of England and Wales*, The National Gardens Scheme (Yellow Book); *Historic Houses Castles and Gardens Open to the Public*, British Leisure Publications; *The National Trust Handbook* (England, Wales and N. Ireland); *Scotland's Gardens*, Scotland's Gardens Scheme (including gardens of the National Trust for Scotland); *Historic Houses Castles and Gardens* (Ireland), Historic Irish Tourist Houses and Gardens Association. See also E. Drury and H. Bridgeman, *Guide to the Gardens of Britain and Europe*, Granada, 1979. Further details of many of the gardens in this gazetteer are given in the *Register of Parks and Gardens of Special Historic Interest in England*, 1988, published by English Heritage. For fuller lists of Lutyens and Jekyll gardens see BROWN 1982, and TOOLEY 1982.

The gazetteer lists gardens that are substantially intact, except as otherwise noted. A few important examples are included even though they no longer exist. The condition of those that have been well maintained is indicated by (g), good; (vg), very good. NT denotes a property of the National Trust. Many of the gardens in the South-East suffered extensive damage in the great storm of October 1987.

England

AVON

Barrow Court, Barrow Gurney
F. Inigo Thomas for Martin Gibbs, 1892–6
Formal garden with architectural enclosures, added to existing terrace of Jacobean house. Now belongs to Barrow Court Residents Association. (g)

BEDFORDSHIRE

Luton Hoo, nr Luton
W.H. Romaine-Walker and F. Besant for Julius Wernher, 1903
Formal terraces including rose garden. Added to an Adam house in a Capability Brown park. (vg)

BERKSHIRE

Bussock Wood, Winterbourne, nr Newbury
M. Macartney, 1906–7
Characteristic Macartney house and formal garden. (g)

Deanery Garden, Sonning
E. Lutyens and G. Jekyll for Edward Hudson, 1899–1901
One of the partnership's most important layouts. (vg)

Folly Farm, Sulhamstead, nr Reading
E. Lutyens and G. Jekyll for H. Cochrane, 1906, and Z. Merton, 1912
Superb compartmental layout including canal garden and sunk rose garden linked by vistas. Planting simplified. (g)

Moor Close, Binfield
Oliver Hill for C. Birch Crisp, 1910–14
Series of courts including classical pergola added to grounds of house of 1881. Now Newbold College.

Sutton Courtenay Manor, nr Abingdon
Norah Lindsay from 1895
Norah Lindsay's own garden, famous in its time for a profusion of cottage garden flowers. No longer existing.

BUCKINGHAMSHIRE

Danesfield, Medmenham, nr Marlow
W.H. Romaine-Walker for Robert William Hudson, 1899–1901
Splendid terraced gardens overlooking the Thames including elaborate parterre with topiary. (g)

Tyringham, Newport Pagnell
E. Lutyens for F.A. Konig, 1926
Dramatic composition of canal, Tuscan columns and flanking pavilions. Added to formal gardens by Charles F. Rees (1909) and house by Soane. Now a clinic. (g)

Woodside (now Chenies Place), Chenies
E. Lutyens and G. Jekyll for Adeline, Duchess of Bedford, 1893
The partnership's formal-garden *début*, added to an existing house.
The most important elements remain. (vg)

CHESHIRE

Eaton Hall, Chester
E. Lutyens for 1st Duke of Westminster, 1897–8
Italian Garden, with statuary, pool and 'Dragon Fountain'.

Eaton Hall, Chester
Detmar Blow and F. Billerey for 2nd Duke of Westminster, 1913
East Garden. Remodelling of Nesfield's garden of c.1851. Formal compartments enclosed by clipped yew with central canal.

Tatton Park, Knutsford
Japanese Garden for Lord Egerton, 1910
Good example, laid out by Japanese workmen within extensive grounds including work by Repton and Paxton. NT

Tirley Garth, Tarporley
C.E.Mallows for R.H. Prestwich, 1906–12
Terraced gardens with vistas and fan-shaped rose garden descending to a wild garden in the dell. Immaculately maintained by the Tirley Garth Trust. (vg)

CUMBRIA

Brockhole, Windermere, Westmorland
T.H. Mawson and D. Gibson for W. Gaddum, from 1899
Formal garden, shrubberies and woodland. Now the Lake District National Park Centre. (vg)

Graythwaite Hall, Ulverstone, Windermere, Westmorland

T.H. Mawson for Col. T.M. Sandys MP, 1889
One of Mawson's first major gardens. Planted mainly with flowering shrubs. (g)

Shrublands, Windermere, Westmorland
T.H. Mawson for R. Mawson, c.1907
Now a social centre. Little remains of the garden.

DERBYSHIRE

Drakelow, nr Burton-on-Trent
F. Inigo Thomas for Sir Robert Gresley, 1902
Riverside garden. House demolished.

Ednaston Manor, Brailsford
E. Lutyens for W.G. Player, 1912–13
Enclosed parterre to the south, stepped terraces to the east. Jekyll-style planting. (g)

Renishaw Hall, Eckington
Sir George Sitwell, from 1890
Important early example of the Italian revival with terraces, yew-hedged enclosures, pools, statuary and vistas, added to house of 1625. (vg)

DEVON

Wood, South Tawton, nr Okehampton
T.H. Mawson and D. Gibson for W. Lethbridge, c.1904
Hillside formal terraces with vistas. Now a country-house hotel. (g)

DORSET

Athelhampton, nr Dorchester
F. Inigo Thomas for A. Cart de Lafontaine, 1891–3
Important early example of the formal revival, added to a sixteenth-century house. Series of enclosures with topiary, fountains and cross-vistas. (vg)

Chantmarle, Frome St Quintin
F. Inigo Thomas for F.E. Savile, 1910
Major work by Thomas, influenced by Montacute. Dramatic cross-vistas and boundary canal. Added to house of 1612–23. Now a Police Training Centre. (vg)

Compton Acres, Poole
For T.W. Simpson, from 1919
Ten individual gardens added to a neo-Tudor villa, including rock, water, Japanese and Italian gardens. (vg)

Kingston Maurward, Stinsford, nr Dorchester
Cecil and Dorothy Hanbury, 1918–20
Yew-hedged enclosures added to west of Georgian house in landscape park. Now the Dorset College of Agriculture.

Kingston Russell House, Long Bredy, Dorchester
P. Tilden for George Gribble, 1913–14
Formal yew-hedged enclosures added to eighteenth-century house.

Parnham, Beaminster
For Dr Hans Sauer, from 1910

South Terrace with corner pavilions. Lower terrace with yew cones and water channel. Probably by Inigo Thomas. Added to sixteenth-century house. Now the John Makepeace School for Craftsmen in Wood. (vg)

ESSEX

Easton Lodge, Little Easton, nr Great Dunmow
H.A. Peto for Countess of Warwick, 1902
Situated north of the house it included lawns, arched pergolas and a sunken water garden. Now completely overgrown.

Warley Place, Great Warley, nr Brentwood
Ellen Willmott from 1880s
Famous gardener and horticulturist's garden. House largely demolished. Parts of garden survive. Maintained as a country park.

GLOUCESTERSHIRE

Abbotswood, Swell, nr Stow-on-the-Wold
E. Lutyens for Mark Fenwick, 1902
Large parterre, also water, rock and woodland gardens. Well maintained in simplified form. (g)

Batsford Park, Moreton-in-Marsh
George and Peto for A.B. Freeman-Mitford (later Lord Redesdale), 1888–93
Originally famous for its bamboos. Now an arboretum. (vg)

Burdocks, nr Fairford
E. Guy Dawber for J. Read, 1911
Charming Queen-Anne-style Cotswold house with yew-hedged formal garden to match.

Combend Manor, Elkstone
Sidney Barnsley and G. Jekyll for Asa Lingard, 1921–5
Terraced, walled enclosures and water garden. Some of the Jekyll planting being restored.

Hartpury House, nr Gloucester
T.H. Mawson for Mrs Gordon Canning, 1907
Formal terraces added to Georgian house remodelled by Guy Dawber in 1895. Original planting by Alfred Parsons. Now the Gloucestershire College of Agriculture. (g)

Hidcote Manor, Hidcote Bartrim
Lawrence Johnston, from 1907
Famous Edwardian garden with varied enclosures off a central vista. Profusion of luxuriant planting. NT

Lyegrove House, Old Sodbury
G.H. Kitchin for Lady Westmorland, 1926
Formal garden within seventeenth-century walled enclosure. (vg)

Rodmarton Manor, nr Cirencester
E. Barnsley for Claud Biddulph, 1909–29
Series of garden compartments including Long Garden with herbaceous borders. Topiary, vistas. Outstanding Arts and Crafts Cotswold house. (vg)

Snowshill Manor, nr Broadway
Charles Wade, 1919–23

Arts and Crafts architect's own hillside garden with walled enclosures and restrained old-fashioned planting. Manor house dating from c.1500. NT

Upper Dorvel House, Sapperton
E. Barnsley from 1901
Architect's own garden with box-edged beds and abundant topiary. (vg)

HAMPSHIRE

Amport St Mary's, nr Andover
E. Lutyens and G. Jekyll for Mrs Sofer-Whitburn, 1923
Large water terrace with fountain, pools and rills and characteristic Jekyll planting. Added to house of 1857 by William Burn. Now the Royal Air Force Chaplains' School. (vg)

Ashford Chace, Steep, nr Petersfield
H. Inigo Triggs and W.F. Unsworth for A.B.R. Trevor-Battye, 1912
Spanish-inspired fountain court and sunk garden. Long vista through trees and shrubs alongside stream. (g)

The Barn, Phoenix Green, Hartley Wintney
Robert Weir Schultz from 1900
Arts and Crafts architect's own garden of hedge-bordered enclosures with topiary. Parts near the house survive. (g)

Compton End, Winchester
G.H. Kitchin from 1897
Architect's own garden. Arts and Crafts cottage garden with yew and box hedges and topiary. (vg)

Little Boarhunt, Liphook
H. Inigo Triggs, 1910–11
Architect's own garden. Old farmhouse remodelled with sunken rose garden divided by a canal and dipping pool.

Marsh Court, Stockbridge
E. Lutyens and G. Jekyll for Herbert Johnson, 1901–4.
Good example of Lutyens's romantic phase. Neo-Tudor house of chalk surrounded by formal terraces, pergola and sunken pool. Now a school. (g)

Moundsmere, Preston Candover
R. Blomfield for Wilfred Buckley, 1908
Characteristic Blomfield house and garden. Sunken terrace with canal, rose beds and yew cones. (vg)

Rhinefield, nr Brockenhurst
W.H. Romaine-Walker for Captain and Mrs Walker-Munro, 1888–91
Grand layout with canal, vistas and topiary garden. Neo-Elizabethan house. Now a country-house hotel. Being restored.

Rosebank, (now Macartneys), Silchester Common
M. Macartney, 1895
Architect's own house and garden. Compartments off a long vista. (g)

Townhill Park, Southampton
L. Rome Guthrie for Lord Swaythling, 1910–22
Formal gardens added to Italianate house. Sunk garden enclosed by a pergola and planted by G. Jekyll. Arboretum and woodland dell. Now a hostel of Southampton College of Higher Education. (g)

Tylney Hall, Rotherwick
R. Weir Schultz for Lionel Phillips, 1901–5
Extensive gardens added to house of 1897 by R. Selden Wornum. Included herbaceous borders between thatched loggias, and wild garden designed by G. Jekyll. Now a country-house hotel. Gardens being restored.

HEREFORD AND WORCESTER

Hergest Croft, Kington
William H. Banks, from 1896
Naturalistic garden of about fifty acres influenced by William Robinson. Fine collection of flowering shrubs and trees. Old kitchen garden. (vg)

Madresfield Court, nr Great Malvern
T.H. Mawson for 7th Earl Beauchamp, 1903
Addition of formal parterre beyond the inner moat, set within extensive parkland. (vg)

Spetchley Park, Worcester
Rose Berkeley and Ellen Willmott, c.1900
Wide range of gardens including the Fountain Garden. (vg)

HERTFORDSHIRE

Cottered, nr Buntingford
Seyemon Kusumoto for Herbert Goode, 1905–23
Impressive Japanese garden arranged along a 'path of life'. (g)

Fanhams Hall, Ware
Professor Suzuki for Lieutenant (Ret'd) R.B. Croft, 1900–1
Japanese garden with genuine tea-house. Rare trees and shrubs. Now the training centre for J. Sainsbury plc.

Trent Park, Barnet
P. Tilden and Norah Lindsay for Sir Philip Sassoon, from 1926
Italian pergola by Tilden. Herbaceous borders by N. Lindsay. Now a College of Education of Middlesex Polytechnic.

KENT

Acremead, Crockham Hill
Cecil Brewer for Dr Philpot, 1906
Terraced garden with stepped pergola. (g)

Godinton, nr Ashford
R. Blomfield for G.A. Dodd, 1902–6
Formal gardens enclosed by large yew hedge. Added to eighteenth-century park and gardens. (vg)

Great Maytham, Rolvenden
E. Lutyens for H.J. Tennant, 1909

Walled garden and terraced lawns. Now owned by Country Houses Association Ltd. (vg)

Hever Castle, Edenbridge
Frank Pearson and Joseph Cheal for W.W. Astor (later Viscount Astor), from 1904
Four-acre 'Italian Garden' enclosed by pergola, grottoes based on the Villa d'Este, 'Pompeian' wall, and loggia overlooking lake. (vg)

Lympne Castle, Lympne
R. Lorimer for F.J. Tennant, 1907–12
Terraces overlooking Romney Marsh. Formal rose garden. (g)

Olantigh, nr Wye
Burnett Brown and Barrow for J. Sawbridge-Erle-Drax, 1906–11
Edwardian remodelling of Georgian house and Victorian garden. Includes shrubbery, water and rock gardens. (vg)

Port Lympne, Lympne
P. Tilden for Sir Philip Sassoon, 1918–21
Spectacular terraced gardens including Roman Stairway, Great Fountain and herbaceous borders planted by Norah Lindsay. Now a zoo park. (vg)

The Salutation, Sandwich
E. Lutyens for G. and H. Farrar, 1911
Formal layout on axes of south and east fronts of 'Wrenaissance' house. (g)

Swaylands, Penshurst
G. Drummond from 1886
Good example of strata system of rock garden construction. Now a school.

LANCASHIRE

Roynton Cottage, Rivington, nr Chorley
T.H. Mawson for W.H. Lever (later Lord Leverhulme), from 1906
Rockeries and pergola above vast landscaped hillside. Now a public park run by the North Western Water Authority. Being maintained in 'picturesque decay'

The Willows, Ashton-on-Ribble, Preston
T.H. Mawson for W.W. Galloway, c. 1899–1902
Includes a court enclosed by arcaded rubble stone walls. Now a school. (g)

LINCOLNSHIRE

Brocklesby Park, nr Grimsby
R. Blomfield for Lord Yarborough, 1899
Axial drive with ornamental pools and topiary. House partly demolished, gardens mostly remain. In Grade I park with work by Brown and Repton.

Caythorpe Court, nr Grantham
R. Blomfield for Edgar Lubbock, 1899–1901
Blomfield's first new house and garden. Terraced lawns with buttressed walls and stairways. Now an agricultural college.

Gunby Hall, Burgh-le-Marsh, nr Skegness
S. and M. Massingberd from 1900

Formal gardens added to house and grounds of 1700. Walled kitchen garden. NT

GREATER LONDON

Canons Park, Edgware
C.E. Mallows for Arthur Du Cros, 1910–12
Elaborate gardens to north and south fronts of Georgian house on site of Duke of Chandos's garden. Now the North London Collegiate School. Only the terraces and walls remain.

The Hill, Hampstead
T.H. Mawson for W.H. Lever (later Lord Leverhulme), from 1905
Lily pool and pergola temple leading to Italian pergola walk and belvedere. Enchanting garden partly within public park run by local council. In need of restoration.

Myddelton House, Bulls Cross, Enfield
E.A. Bowles, from 1890s
Famous, naturalistic plantsman's garden. Owned by the Lee Valley Regional Park Authority, being restored and now open to the public.

St John's Lodge, Regent's Park
R. Weir Schultz for the 3rd Marquess of Bute, from 1891
Important early example of formal revival, added to Regency villa. Now administered by the Department of the Environment as a Royal Park. Very well maintained in simplified form. (g)

MERSEYSIDE

Thornton Manor, Thornton Hough, Bebington
T.H. Mawson for W.H. Lever (later Lord Leverhulme), from 1905
Extensive layout including circular rose garden, 'Garden Forum', Fernery and Lake. (vg)

WEST MIDLANDS

Wightwick Manor, nr Wolverhampton
Alfred Parsons for Theodore Mander, c.1890
Formal gardens with yew hedges and topiary for house of 1887–93 by Edward Ould. Additional gardens by Mawson of c.1910. NT

NORFOLK

Blickling, Aylsham
Norah Lindsay for the 11th Marquess of Lothian, 1930
Remodelling and replanting of the parterre. NT

Home Place, Holt
E.S. Prior for Revd Percy R. Lloyd, 1903–5
Geometrically laid out sunk garden to Arts and Crafts 'butterfly' plan house. The bones survive.

The Pleasaunce, Overstrand, nr Cromer
E.L. Lutyens for Lord Battersea, 1897–9
'Italian' garden and extensive naturalistic gardens planted by the Batterseas. Now one of the Christian Endeavour Holiday Homes. Only the framework of the formal gardens remains.

NORTHAMPTONSHIRE

Cottesbrook Hall, nr Northampton
R. Weir Schultz for Captain R.B. Brassey,
1911–14
Garden enclosures ingeniously added to Georgian
house in a landscape park. Well maintained but
altered and denuded of its Arts and Crafts
ornament. (g)

NORTHUMBERLAND

Lindisfarne Castle, Holy Island
E. Lutyens and G. Jekyll for Edward Hudson,
1911
Small walled garden laid out on two vanishing
points. NT

OXFORDSHIRE

Blenheim Palace, Woodstock
Achille Duchêne for the 9th Duke of Marlborough, 1925–30
Parterre and water terraces in the French grand
manner. (vg)

Buscot Park, nr Faringdon
H.A. Peto for Alexander Henderson (later Lord
Faringdon), 1904, 1911
Water garden with vista connecting house with
lake. NT

Ditchley Park, Spelsbury
G.A. Jellicoe for Ronald and Nancy Tree,
1933–6
Italian garden. Sunk parterre enclosed by
pleached limes with semi-circular pool. Now the
Anglo-American Ditchley Foundation. Parterre
replaced by lawn. (vg)

Friar Park, Henley-on-Thames
Frank Crisp, from 1896
Wide range of eclectic compartments including
mediaeval gardens and fantastic rock garden
with model of the Matterhorn.

Garsington Manor, nr Oxford
Lady Ottoline Morrell, from 1915
Italian pond garden and formal box-bordered
flower garden with Irish yew pillars. (vg)

High Wall, Headington, Oxford
H.A. Peto for Miss Katherine Feilden, c.1912
Rose garden, summer house and pergola. House
of 1910–11 by Walter Cave.

SOMERSET

Ammerdown, Kilmersdon, nr Radstock
E. Lutyens for the 3rd Baron Hylton, 1902
Ingenious geometrical layout in yew linking
Georgian house and orangery by James Wyatt.
(vg)

Barrington Court, nr Ilminster
Forbes and Tate for Col. A.A. Lyle, from 1917
Series of walled compartments added to Tudor
house. Planting scheme by G. Jekyll. NT

Hestercombe, Cheddon Fitzpaine, nr Taunton
E. Lutyens and G. Jekyll for E.W.B. Portman,
1904–9

The partnership's masterpiece. Terraces descending to square parterre with pergola. Orangery
and Dutch garden. Now the headquarters of the
Somerset Fire Brigade. (vg)

Tintinhull House, nr Yeovil
Dr S.J.M. Price from 1898
Delightful compartmental garden added to
Georgian house. Re-planted from 1933 by Mrs
Reiss. NT

Wayford Manor, nr Crewkerne
H.A. Peto for Helen Baker, 1902
Terraced hillside garden skilfully added to Elizabethan house, with central vista leading to wild
garden. (vg)

SUFFOLK

The Lodge, (now Cranmer House), Felixstowe
R. Weir Schultz for Felix T. Cobbold, 1902
Clifftop Arts and Crafts garden with fine per-
gola overlooking sunken garden. Now part of
Felixstowe College. Little remains.

SURREY

Charles Hill Court, Tilford
D. Blow and F. Billerey for Miss Lily Antrobus,
1909
Hillside garden with succession of lily pools.
French-style house.

Great Fosters, Egham
Romaine-Walker and Jenkins for G. Samuel-
Montagu, 1918
Tudor-inspired parterre enclosed by yew hedges
with box-edged beds and topiary. Japanese bridge
and sunk rose garden. Added to Elizabethan
house. Now a country-house hotel. (vg)

Great Tangley Manor, Wonersh Common, nr
Guildford
Philip Webb for Wickham Flower, 1885
Walled garden within moat. Rustic pergola lead-
ing to rock garden and dell. (g)

Millmead, Snowdenham Lane, Bramley
E. Lutyens and G. Jekyll for G. Jekyll, 1904–6
Important small, terraced garden and 'Wrenais-
sance'-style house. Main structure survives.

Munstead Wood, nr Godalming
E. Lutyens and G. Jekyll, from 1883
Miss Jekyll's famous garden, now altered.

New Place, Farnham Lane, Haslemere
C.F.A. Voysey for A.M. Stedman, 1897–1901
Important Arts and Crafts house and garden.
Succession of terraces falling to rock, water and
Japanese gardens. Being restored.

Orchards, Busbridge, nr Godalming
E. Lutyens and G. Jekyll for William and Julia
Chance, 1897–1902
The partnership's most important early work,
notably the 'Dutch' garden. Now sub-divided
but restored. (vg)

Phillips Memorial, Godalming
Thackeray Turner for Godalming Council, 1913

Arts and Crafts memorial garden with planting
by G. Jekyll

Redcourt, Haslemere
E. Newton for Louis Wigram, 1894
Series of yew-hedged enclosures around Arts-
and-Crafts-cum-Georgian revival house.

Royal Horticultural Society, Wisley, nr Ripley
G.F. Wilson and others, from 1878
Includes notable Wild Garden, also Rock Garden
by E. White and Pulham and Sons, 1911. (vg)

Sandhouse, (now Kingswood), Sandhills, nr
Witley
F.W. Troup for Joseph King, 1902
Elaborate formal garden with vistas. Arts and
Crafts house. Now sub-divided.

Vann, Hambledon
W.D. Caröe, 1907–11
Architect's own garden. Enclosures around old
house and barn. Water garden planted by G.
Jekyll. (vg)

Westbrook, Godalming
Thackeray Turner, 1899
Arts and Crafts architect's own house. Compartmented garden including circular, sunk flower
garden. Jekyll-style planting. Main structure
intact.

EAST SUSSEX

Bateman's, Burwash
Rudyard Kipling, from 1902
Formal garden with additions by Kipling includ-
ing Pond Garden (1906). NT

Charleston Manor, Westdean
W.H. Godfrey for Oswald Birley, 1931
Formal enclosures added to house dating from
c.1200. (vg)

Chelwood Vetchery, Nutley
L. Rome Guthrie for Stuart Montagu Samuel,
1906–7
Impressive formal layout including pool garden.
House by W. Flockhart. Now a Group Manage-
ment Centre. (vg)

Gravetye Manor, West Hoathly
William Robinson, from 1884
Robinson's home (1884–1935). Paved flower
garden, Alpine Meadow, large estate including
woodland. Elizabethan house. Now a country-
house hotel. (vg)

Great Dixter, Northiam
E. Lutyens for Nathaniel Lloyd, 1910
Formal garden with topiary around fifteenth-
century timber-framed house restored by Lut-
yens. Outstanding planting. Now Christopher
Lloyd's garden. (vg)

The Hoo, Willingdon, nr Eastbourne
E. Lutyens for Alexander Wedderburn, 1902
Upper terrace with *patte d'oie* of circular steps,
large lawn, flanking gazebos and stairways descending to fish pool and terrace walk. (vg)

Kidbrook Park, Forest Row
W.H Godfrey for Olaf Hambro, c.1925
Formal garden with pergola and rotunda added to eighteenth-century house and park. (g)

Rotherfield Hall, Crowborough
F. Inigo Thomas for L. Lindsay-Hogg, 1897
Axial layout of woodland vista, forecourt and parterre flanked by garden houses. Remodelled house of 1666. Gardens in need of restoration.

Wych Cross Place, Forest Row
T.H. Mawson for Douglas W. Freshfield, 1900–3
Extensive terraced gardens. House by Edmund Fisher. (vg)

WEST SUSSEX

King Edward VII Sanatorium, Midhurst
Charles Holden and G. Jekyll, 1902–6
Series of garden enclosures and terraced lawns with planted, dry-stone retaining walls. (vg)

Little Bognor House, nr Petworth
C. Williams-Ellis for Sir Ivor Maxse, 1920
Naturalistic valley garden alongside stream. Lily pool and loggia. (g)

Little Thakeham, nr Storrington
E. Lutyens for Ernest Blackburn, 1902
One of Lutyens's finest houses set within a ring of formal enclosures. Central axis extended to raised pergola. Now a country-house hotel. (vg)

Sedgwick Park, Nuthurst, nr Horsham
George and Peto for Mrs Emma Henderson, 1886
Grand axial layout with large canal enclosed by yew hedges, added to 'Old English'-style house. The basic layout survives.

WARWICKSHIRE

Moreton Paddox, Moreton Morrell
W.H. Romaine-Walker and Edward White, c.1910
Large formal parterre with central canal and sunk garden. House (c.1906) by Romaine-Walker (demolished)

WILTSHIRE

Hartham Park, nr Corsham
H.A. Peto for Sir John Dickson-Poynder, c.1903
Walled garden with canal and loggia (now much altered), also raised South Terrace extending into park.

Hatch House, nr Tisbury
Detmar Blow for Lt-Col. Bennett Stanford Fane, 1908
Restoration and additions to sixteenth-century house and garden including terraces and walled garden with loggia.

Heale House, Woodford, nr Salisbury
H.A. Peto for Louis Greville, 1906, 1911
Formal gardens around seventeenth-century house enlarged by Detmar Blow. Grounds include Japanese garden (c.1901). (vg)

Iford Manor, Westwood, nr Bradford-on-Avon
H.A. Peto, from 1899
Peto's own garden on a steep hillside. Main terrace with antique fragments, colonnade, casita. (vg)

NORTH YORKSHIRE

Gledstone Hall, West Marton, nr Skipton
E. Lutyens and G. Jekyll for Sir Amos Nelson, 1922–5
Lutyens's finest classical house. Axial garden layout with central vista and sunken canal. Planting by G. Jekyll. Now a home for the elderly. (g)

Newby Hall, Skelton, nr Ripon.
Ellen Willmott, c.1900
Rock garden. Also important series of garden compartments laid out from 1923 by Major Compton, including outstanding double herbaceous borders. Adam house. (vg)

St Nicholas, Richmond
Robert James, from 1905
Topiary work, rock garden. Trees, shrubs and shrub roses of considerable horticultural interest. (g)

Wales

CLWYD

The Flagstaff, Colwyn Bay, Denbighshire
T.H. Mawson and D. Gibson for Walter Whitehead, 1898–9
Large hillside layout. Now the Welsh Mountain Zoo. Very little remains.

DYFED

Ffynnone, Boncath, Pembrokeshire
F. Inigo Thomas for John Colby, 1904
Nash house remodelled. Terrace with grotto. Being restored.

GLAMORGAN

Craig-y-Parc, Pentyrch, nr Cardiff
C.E. Mallows for Thomas Evans, 1913–15
Terraced hillside garden falling to water and woodland gardens. Tudor-vernacular-style house. Now a school run by The Spastics Society. (g)

Dyffryn, St Nicholas, nr Cardiff
T.H. Mawson for Reginald Cory, 1906
Additions to gardens begun in 1893 by Sir John Cory. Wide range of types. One of the most important plant collections in Wales. Administered by Mid and South Glamorgan County Councils. (vg)

GWENT

High Glanau, Lydart, nr Monmouth
H.A. Tipping, from 1923
Tipping's last home in Monmouthshire. Terraced hillside descending to wild and woodland gardens. House by E.C. Francis. (vg)

Mathern Palace, nr Chepstow
H.A. Tipping, from 1894
Tipping's first garden in Monmouthshire. Formal enclosures with topiary around restored fifteenth-century house. Now owned by British Steel Corporation. Basic structure intact.

Mounton House, nr Chepstow
H.A. Tipping, from 1911
Tipping's most important house and garden in Monmouthshire. Extensive formal and naturalistic gardens including fine pergola garden. House by E.C. Francis. Now a school. Only the bare structure survives.

GWYNEDD

Bodnant, Tal-y-Cafn, Colwyn Bay (originally in Denbighshire)
Laura and Henry McLaren (later 2nd Lord Aberconway), from c.1900
Magnificent garden. Fine collection of trees and shrubs in The Dell (begun 1875). Formal terraces (1904–14). NT

Plas Brondanw, Tremadoc, nr Penrhyndeudraeth, Merionethshire
C. Williams-Ellis, from 1908
Architect's own house and garden. Outstanding layout with topiary and vistas of surrounding mountains. (vg)

Wern, nr Porthmadog, Merionethshire
T.H. Mawson for Richard Greaves, 1891–2
House by J. Douglas. Terraced garden. Structure survives. Now a nursing home.

POWYS

Llangoed, nr Llyswen, Breconshire
C. Williams-Ellis for Archibald Christy, 1913–19
The architect's first major work. Large formal and naturalistic gardens. Now dilapidated.

Scotland

ARGYLL

Torosay Castle, Craignure, Isle of Mull
R.S. Lorimer, c.1899
Italianate terraces and statue walk added to Scottish Baronial house of 1858 by David Bryce. (g)

BERWICKSHIRE

Manderston, Duns
John Kinross for Sir James Miller, 1901–5
One of the best-preserved examples of an Edwardian house and garden. Grand formal terraces, Japanese and woodland gardens. (vg)

Mellerstain, nr Gordon
R. Blomfield for Lord Binning, 1909
Grand layout of parterre and lawns falling to lake. Added to an Adam house. (vg)

FIFE

Earlshall, Leuchars
R.S. Lorimer for R.W. Mackenzie, begun 1892
Important compartmented garden with topiary laid out within large walled enclosure of sixteenth-century tower house. (vg)

Hill of Tarvit, nr Cupar
R.S. Lorimer for Frederick Sharp, 1906–7
Remodelling of house of 1696 with addition of terraced gardens. National Trust for Scotland

INVERNESS-SHIRE

Corrour, Loch Ossian
Sir John Stirling-Maxwell, 1894–1904
Remarkable alpine gardens laid out between shooting lodge (by L. and J. Falconer) and the loch. Also notable collection of rhododendrons from 1910.

EAST LOTHIAN

Grey Walls, Gullane
E. Lutyens for Alfred Lyttleton, 1901
New house and walled gardens. Now a country-house hotel. (vg)

Tyninghame, nr Linton
Lord and Lady Haddington and R.P. Brotherston, 1890s
Flower garden within large, eighteenth-century walled enclosure detached from Baronial house of 1829 by William Burn. (vg)

ORKNEY

Melsetter, Island of Hoy
W.R. Lethaby for Thomas Middlemore, 1898
Formal walled enclosures around Arts and Crafts house. Parterre replaced by lawn.

PERTHSHIRE

Balmanno, Dron, nr Bridge of Earn
R.S. Lorimer for W.A. Miller, 1916–21

Lorimer's finest restored tower house and garden. Rose and sundial gardens and large walled garden. (vg)

Dunira, nr Comrie
T.H. Mawson for W.G. Macbeth, 1920
Imposing layout added to Baronial house of 1851 by W. Burn. House mostly demolished, bones of the garden survive.

RENFREWSHIRE

Formakin, nr Bishopton
R.S. Lorimer for J.A. Holmes, 1908–10
New house with walled gardens. Being restored by the Formakin Trust.

WIGTOWNSHIRE

Old Place of Mochrum, nr Port William
R. Weir Schultz for 4th Marquess of Bute, 1903
New walled parterre with diagonal paths. Added to restored tower house.

Republic of Ireland

COUNTY CORK

Annes Grove, Castletownroche
R. Grove Annesley, begun 1905
Woodland garden and enchanting naturalistic water garden in gorge below eighteenth-century house. (vg)

Ilnacullin, (formerly Garinish Island), Glengarriff
H.A. Peto for J. Annan Bryce, begun 1910
Succession of gardens along a circulatory route culminating in a sunken lily pool with pavilion. Australasian genera prosper. (vg)

COUNTY DUBLIN

Irish National War Memorial, Islandbridge, Dublin

E. Lutyens, 1930–40
Rose garden with accompanying buildings. Being restored.

Lambay, Rush
E. Lutyens and G. Jekyll for Cecil Baring (later Lord Revelstoke), 1905
Walled courts around a restored and enlarged fortress within a circular rampart on a desolate island.

COUNTY KILDARE

Tully, Kildare
Tasa Eida for Col. W. Hall Walker (later Lord Wavertree), 1906–10
Japanese garden with layout symbolizing the life of man. Authentic Japanese tea-house. (vg)

COUNTY LAOIS

Heywood. Ballinakill
E. Lutyens and G. Jekyll for Sir. W. Hutcheson Poë, 1909–12
Formal gardens added to eighteenth-century house in landscape park. Terrace, pergola walk, Yew Garden and Fountain Garden. Now belongs to the Salesian Order. House demolished but gardens being restored. (vg)

Northern Ireland

COUNTY DOWN

Mount Stewart, Newtownards
Marchioness of Londonderry, begun 1921
Outstanding range of eclectic gardens added to grounds of Georgian house including Sunk Garden based on a design by Gertrude Jekyll. NT

Index

225